U0120196

·英·汉·对·照·

MODERN ENGLISH PROSE

英国散文精选

范存忠 柳无忌·编注

范家宁 王 英·译

译林出版社

扫码收听英文有声书

· 序言 ·

1982 年初春，我考入南京大学外文系英国文学专业，有幸成为范存忠先生的硕士研究生，深得范先生教诲之恩。1984 年秋，我获得硕士学位后留校任教，同时也继续充任先生的"编外"学生。1987 年 8 月，我告别范先生赴美求学，不料竟成永诀：先生竟于年末仙逝！然而先生严谨的治学态度和严格的教学风格，三十年来我未敢须臾忘怀并一直奉为楷模。记忆犹深的是，在我硕士生的第一年里，先生对我的一项要求是"一周两文"：每个星期写一篇英文文章，题目自定；同时每个星期熟读一篇先生选定的英文范文。先生耳提面命，叮嘱这些范文务必"读懂、读熟、读透"。每次去先生家上课，先生都花不少时间评点范文和我的英文习作的优劣高下之别，虽常常令我如坐针毡自惭形秽，却让我在提高自己的英文写作能力上获益良多。

范文的效益确实是无穷的。孔夫子曰："不学《诗》，无以言。"意思就是说，只有熟读《诗经》中的篇章，才能使自己具备优雅的言辞表达能力。我国民间更熟悉的说法是："熟读唐诗三百首，不会作诗也会吟。"说的虽然都是中国的古代诗歌，但是同样的道理也完全适用于英文散文。真正读懂、读熟、读透几十篇优秀的英文散文，自己英文写作能力的提高就一定是水到渠成的事情。

我后来才知道，范先生让我熟读的英文范文，其中不少篇目来自他 1940 年与同在当时的国立中央大学任教的柳无忌先生合编的《近代英国散文选》一书。最初这本书是作为英文专业的学生阅读材料问世的，出版后为多所大学采用，深受学子欢迎，多次重印，一时洛阳纸贵。几年后，两位先生又推出增订版，扩充篇目并增加注释，使《近代英国散文选》更得读者青睐。1986 年，鉴于当时英语教学的需求，该书曾由江苏教育出版社再版。此次译林出版社出版的这本《英国散文精选》在原有版本的基础上采用英汉双语形式，实乃广大学英文的青年朋友的福音。书中的汉译者是范先生公子范家宁先生暨夫人王英女士。家宁、王英伉俪国内英文科班出身，20 世纪 80 年代赴美深造，之后长期侨居芝加哥，中英文均造诣深厚。二位的汉译，译义准确，行文流畅，且在风格上尽力与英文原文保持一致，对读者在不同的层面理解各篇英国散文一定大有裨益。

需要强调的是，这本《英国散文精选》绝不只是一本帮助读者英文写作的范文集。书中收集的散文作品都出自 18 和 19 世纪英国名家之手，有很高的文学欣赏价值。大体上说，18 世纪的英国文学艺术处于新古典主义时期，同时也是浪漫主义时期。这个时期的文学作品大多崇尚理性、公正、平等，注重古典传统的秩序，追求协调、统一、和谐与典雅的艺术风格。华兹华斯和柯勒律治于 1798 年共同发表的《抒情歌谣集》一般被认为是英国浪漫主义的宣言，为浪漫主义思潮在其后的大约半个世纪的英国文学中的主流地位奠定了基础。浪漫主义文学思潮崇尚激情和大自然，弘扬创造力和想象力，对工业革命的负面后果持批判态度，并且在法国大革命的激励下竭力鼓吹人类自由。诚然，在品鉴近代英国散文时，我们切不可简单地把新古典主义和浪漫主义当作标签来使用，但是这两股文学思潮确实为本书中的各篇散文提供了可供参照的宏观背景。譬如，约瑟夫·艾迪生（Joseph Addison）的平实而优雅的时评，乔纳森·斯威夫特（Jonathan Swift）对社会不公现象尖刻的鞭挞，切斯特菲尔德勋爵（Lord Chesterfield）充满世俗智慧的家书，以及塞缪尔·约翰逊（Samuel Johnson）博士在耗时七年的词典大功告成之日对嗟来之食的断然拒绝，莫不与启蒙主义的时代精神有某种关联。另一方面，孑然一身的查尔斯·兰姆（Charles Lamb）对儿女绕膝的家庭生活充满温情的想象，威廉·赫兹里特（William Hazlitt）与湖畔诗人（Lake Poets）的亲密交往和对法国大革命的强烈认同，显然都表现出他们的某些浪漫主义情愫。

中文的"散文"一词，内涵不易界定。广义的"散文"大体上对应英文 prose 一词，泛指诗歌以外的所有非韵体文，自然也涵盖小说。而相对狭义的"散文"更接近英文的 essay 或者 familiar essay，在中文中指的基本上就是我们常提到的"小品文""随笔""随感""杂文"等，在篇幅、内容和风格上与小说都有一定的距离。本书书名中的"散文"一词大体对应 familiar essay 一类，但是中文"散文"在词义上的含混在这里倒恰恰成了一个"必要的纰漏"(necessary evil)。18 和 19 世纪分别是英国小说的兴起期和全盛期，在本书所选的一些散文篇目中我们可以看到它们与小说之间"剪不断理还乱"的联系。理查德·斯梯尔(Richard Steele)的《旁观者俱乐部》(*The Spectator Club*)即为一例。作者虚构一个俱乐部，以当时的伦敦各社会名流为原型，逐一介绍并刻画俱乐部各位成员，其手法和风格与小说极为相似。奥利弗·哥尔德斯密斯(Oliver Goldsmith)的《世界公民》(*The Citizen of the World*)借一位旅英中国学者之口发表作者对英国社会文化的评说，与英国 18 世纪一度盛行的书信体小说颇为神似。甚至托马斯·德·昆西(Thomas De Quincey)以自传标榜的《一个英国鸦片吸食者的自白》(*Confessions of an English Opium Eater*)中的主人翁也未必百分之百就是作者本人，而更可能掺糅了一些小说的成分。还有一点不容忽视：18 和 19 世纪，英国的出版业相当发达，文学杂志盛行，在伦敦尤其如此。本书中收集的散文，不少最初都是以分期连载形式发表于不同的文学杂志上的。本书所选，一般仅为发表于单期的片段。若就整体连载篇幅而论，则与通常所见的中国杂文、小品文大相径庭。

　　然而，优秀的英国散文虽然跟优秀的中国散文风格各异，但是都能给读者极大的美感享受。如品佳茗，虽有龙井毛峰之别，但都令人余香满口，回味无穷。熟悉中国散文的读者朋友，不妨来读读本书中的英国散文，就好比喝惯了西湖龙井的茶客大有必要尝尝黄山毛峰的别样风味。

葛良彦

美国圣母大学

2022 年 12 月

· 前言 ·

　　我们的父亲范存忠先生离开我们已经三十多年了……这本《英国散文精选》是他留给我们的又一部文学遗产。

　　抗日战争爆发后，国立中央大学搬迁到了重庆沙坪坝，那时叫敌后方。在那个年代，没有正规的教科书，尤其是英国文学，很难有一本正规完整的课本，都是由教授自己撰写而成。为了满足学生的求知欲，提高学生的英语专业水平，父亲范存忠先生和柳无忌先生对英国文学散文做了选编，由此产生了这本书的原稿，于1940年编印成书。该选编本被定为国立中央大学英国文学本科生的教材。在父亲的自序中可以看到，这本书一直在增订，不仅仅是国立中央大学本校在用，而且其他的高校英语专业都在选用。一直到"文革"前，还有很多高校都在沿用这本书。"文革"结束恢复高考后，父亲的学生，几乎都是全国高等院校英文专业的教授和学者。由于当时缺少英国文学阅读教材，他们又想起了父亲在国立中央大学沙坪坝出版的《近代英国散文选》，希望父亲能够再版，于是有了江苏教育出版社1986年10月的再版，只是英文版本。

　　此次出版的这本《英国散文精选》在原书的基础上增加了中文译本。这本书收集了二十五篇短篇散文，以18和19世纪英国文学鼎盛时期广泛流传的名家名篇为主，其中有乔纳森·斯威夫特（Jonathan Swift）、詹姆斯·鲍斯威尔（James Boswell）、托马斯·卡莱尔（Thomas Carlyle）、罗伯特·路易斯·斯蒂文森（Robert Louis Stevenson）等。精选散文以记叙文、说明文、议论文、应用文四大写作体裁呈现，涉及了哲理、政治、经济、社会、宗教、文化、艺术、玄学等各个方面，面广量大。每一位作者的语言、用词、文笔都有所不同，都有他们自己的文学艺术特点和风格——语言生动而富有情感，幽默而不失风趣，笔锋严谨，用词巧妙，论点鲜明，阐述清晰。这个选本对每一位作者的生平，每一篇作品的疑难词句、作品特色等，都有详细注释，让读者容易领悟，从而不失阅读的趣味性。

在译林出版社的大力支持下，我们整理了父亲的全集，于 2016 年出版了"范存忠文集"。在文集出版之后，我们想到了这本书。我们知道，我们的翻译水平有限，秉承父亲"治学严谨、态度认真"的谆谆教诲，我们尽自己的力量将这本书翻译成中文，成双语版呈现给读者，让更多的人能欣赏到这本书的文学价值。也谨以此书献给我们的父亲，以及老一辈辛勤耕耘的教育工作者，让父亲曾经在中西文化教书育人方面做出的努力和贡献，以及留下的文化遗产得以传承；让更多的人了解中西文化的差异，汲取精华剔除糟粕，适应社会的变迁，更好地为社会服务，为社会做出自己应有的贡献。

我们有幸请到葛良彦先生为此书审稿并作序。葛良彦先生是美国圣母大学终身教授，曾任美国圣母大学东亚语言文学院院长，美国华裔汉学家，全美大学教科书《中文版说读写》编委。葛良彦先生 20 世纪 80 年代初期曾是南京大学外文系硕士研究生，师从先父范存忠先生。当时他的研究方向即为 18 世纪英国文学。葛良彦先生于 80 年代后期赴美深造，90 年代中期获得美国印第安纳大学比较文学博士学位后，一直在圣母大学执教，并在中西文学文化研究的多个领域中建树颇丰。在此，我们对葛良彦先生在百忙之中给予我们的支持和帮助表示最诚挚的感谢！

范家宁　王英

写于 2022 年 12 月 22 日

PREFACE

This volume of *Modern English Prose* grows out of materials we have used for classroom readings in the last few years. It was first published two years ago to meet an urgent demand for textbooks in our colleges and universities. Since then we have received much encouragement by its warm reception and a number of valuable suggestions for its improvement from various quarters. Now that there is a call for a second edition, we have taken the chance to enlarge it and make whatever modifications and corrections that are necessary.

In undertaking the selection of these essays, we have kept constantly in view two aims: First, they are to serve as model essays for classroom perusal and imitation. Within the page limits we have endeavoured to present the best, and nothing but the best, of the prose masters of the two great centuries. Second, it is hoped that a study of these specimens will stimulate a deeper interest on the part of the readers in a field which is by far the most fertile of English prose.

In a sense this volume is unique. Instead of making it representative of all types of English prose writings, we have included in it only one type of prose, the Informal Essay, which attained the perfectness of form in the hands of Steele and Addison, reached the culmination of its splendour in Lamb and Hazlitt, and retained much of its exuberance in the inimitable writings of Stevenson and Ruskin who closed the past century. On this account we are forced to make many omissions and exclusions. It is regrettable that some great names, especially of the nineteenth century, have to be left out from this collection.

In preparing this revised edition, we have introduced some new essays and authors and verified the texts, making them reasonably accurate. We have also added many new entries in the Notes, which have now grown to a considerable size. But there is hardly any scholarly pretense. We have drawn freely on the learning of our predecessors who by their arduous and noble labour have added copiously to an understanding and appreciation of these essays. What little contributions we have been able to make are therefore quite insignificant in view of the great mass of borrowings, which are too many to be enumerated.

Our thanks are due to our colleagues and others who have helped us in the making of these selections. We are also grateful to Mr. John Blofeld, Cultural Attache of the British Embassy in Chungking, who has kindly made the arrangement for a generous grant from the British Council in London, without which the publication of this new edition would be practically impossible.

Tsen-Chung Fan
Wu-Chi Liu
National Central University,
Chungking.
June 6, 1944.

CONTENTS

目 录

SIR RICHARD STEELE (1672—1729)

AND

JOSEPH ADDISON (1672—1719)

    Richard Steele (1672—1729), the son of an Irish attorney, and Joseph Addison (1672—1719), the son of an English clergyman, were born in the same year and were acquainted with each other from childhood. They were schoolmates at the Charterhouse and continued their association at Oxford. Steele, being too impatient to submit to the routine of academic life, left the university for the army. Addison, the more scholarly of the two, stayed on for his degree and obtained a fellowship at Magdalen. Steele was the author of four plays, M.P., Gazetteer, and Commissioner on Forfeited Estates in Scotland. Addison was the author of *The Campaign* (poem), *Cato* (tragedy), and *Drummer* (comedy), and for a time served as

Secretary of State. But their real fame rests on their essays. In 1709, Steele started the *Tatler*, a periodical published three times a week—Tuesday, Thursday, and Saturday. Addison was one of the chief contributors. In 1711, when the *Tatler* was discontinued, they collaborated in a new paper known as *Spectator*, which was published daily until December, 1712. These papers, remarkable for wit and gentle raillery, were the literary instruments by which Steele and Addison tried to reform the society of Queen Anne.

Steele and Addison differed in temperament and character. One was lively and sentimental, and the other sedate and somewhat unimpassioned. One was perhaps a more delightful companion, and the other a better teacher. And they differed characteristically in their prose styles. Steele wrote hurriedly; he lacked the patience to polish and refine his expression. His style is less 'correct' and was therefore rated much lower than that of Addison. Dr. Johnson advised all ambitious writers to give their nights and days to Addison, for he had attained a perfect medium between the vulgar and the learned. 'But,' says Austin Dobson, with equal truth, 'for words which the heart finds when the head is seeking; for phrases glowing with the white heat of a generous emotion; for sentences which throb and tingle with manly pity or courageous indignation—we must turn to the essays of Steele.'

【作者简介】

理查德·斯梯尔（1672—1729）是爱尔兰一位律师的儿子，约瑟夫·艾迪生（1672—1719）是一位英国牧师的儿子；他们出生于同一年，从小就相识。他们是卡尔特公学的同学，后来一同上了牛津大学，仍然继续来往。斯梯尔性情急躁，无法适应平静的学生生活，于是离开大学去参了军。艾迪生则比较有学者风度，继续留在牛津大学攻读学位并在莫德林学院获得了奖学金。斯梯尔写过四部戏剧，当过议员、公报记者和苏格兰没收房地产的专员。艾迪生是《战役》（诗）、《卡托》（悲剧）和《鼓手》（喜剧）的作者，曾担任过国务大臣，然而真正使他们成名的是他们的小品文。1709年，斯梯尔创办了《闲话报》，这是每周出版三期的刊物——周二、周四和周六。艾迪生是主要撰稿人之一。1711年，《闲话报》停刊，斯梯尔与艾迪生联合创办了《旁观者》，这是日报。《旁观者》持续发行到1712年12月。《旁观者》上的文章以机智与温和的讽刺而著称，是斯梯尔和艾迪生试图改革安妮女王社会的文学工具。

斯梯尔与艾迪生的气质和性格各有不同。斯梯尔充满激情，却容易多愁善感；艾迪生沉着稳重，似乎对一切都无动于衷。斯梯尔也许是一位令人愉快的同伴，而艾迪生则也许是一位更好的老师。他们的文风也有各自不同的特点。斯梯尔性情急躁，行文粗枝大叶，缺乏耐心去推敲文字以完善他的语言表达。人们认为他的文风不够"正确"，因此对他的评价也比艾迪生要低得多。约翰逊博士建议所有雄心勃勃的作家要以艾迪生为楷模，刻苦研究他的文体，因为艾迪生在通俗和高雅之间找到了两全齐美之道。"然而，"诗人奥斯汀·多布森却说，"字词是深思熟虑的心声，短语要闪烁着丰富的情感，句子则应是带有强烈同情心或英勇愤怒的呐喊；我们应当效仿斯梯尔的散文。"他的话也不无道理。

Recollections of Childhood

Richard Steele

Dies, ni fallor, adest, quem semper acerbum,
Semper honoratum, sic dii voluistis, habebo.

There are those among mankind who can enjoy no relish of their being, except the world is made acquainted with all that relates to them, and think everything lost that passes unobserved; but others find a solid delight in stealing by the crowd and modelling their life after such a manner, as is as much above the approbation as the practice of the vulgar. Life being too short to give instances great enough of true friendship or goodwill, some sages have thought it pious to preserve a certain reverence for the **manes**[1] of their deceased friends, and have withdrawn themselves from the rest of the world at certain seasons, to commemorate in their own thoughts such of their acquaintance who have gone before them out of this life; and indeed, when we are advanced in years, there is not a more pleasing entertainment than to recollect in a gloomy moment the many we have parted with, that have

---

1　本书中加粗单词或句子在文末有参考注解。——编注

been dear and agreeable to us, and to cast a melancholy thought or two after those with whom, perhaps, we have indulged ourselves in whole nights of mirth and jollity. With such inclinations in my heart, I went to my closet yesterday in the evening, and resolved to be sorrowful; upon which occasion I could not but look with disdain upon myself, that, though all the reasons which I had to lament the loss of many of my friends are now as forcible as at the moment of their departure, yet did not my heart swell with the same sorrow which I felt at that time; but I could, without tears, reflect upon many pleasing adventures I have had with some who have long been blended with common earth. Though it is by the benefit of nature that length of time thus blots out the violence of afflictions, yet with tempers too much given to pleasure it is almost necessary to revive the old places of grief in our memory, and ponder step by step on past life, to lead the mind into that sobriety of thought which **poises the heart** and makes it beat with due time, without being quickened with desire, or retarded with despair, from its proper and equal motion. When we wind up a clock that is out of order to make it go well for the future, we do not immediately set the hand to the present instant, but we make it strike the round of all its hours before it can recover the regularity of its time. 'Such,' thought I, 'shall be my method this evening; and since it is that day of the year which I dedicate to the memory of such in another life as I much delighted in when living, an hour or two shall be sacred to sorrow and their memory, while I run over all the melancholy circumstances of this kind which have occurred to me in my whole life.'

The first sense of sorrow I ever knew was upon the death of my father, at which time I was not quite five years of age; but was rather amazed at what all the house meant than possessed with a real understanding why nobody was willing to play with me. I remember I went into the room where his body lay, and my mother sat weeping alone by it. I had my battledore in my hand, and fell a-beating the coffin, and calling 'Papa'; for I know not how I had some slight idea that he was locked up there. My mother caught me in her arms, and, transported **beyond all patience of** the silent grief she was before in, she almost smothered me in her embrace, and told me, in a flood of tears, Papa could not hear me, and would play with me no more, for they were going to put him under ground, whence he could never come to us again. She was a very beautiful woman, of a noble spirit, and there was a dignity in her grief amidst all the wildness of her transport, which, methought, struck me with an instinct of sorrow which, before I was sensible of what it was to grieve, seized my very soul, and has made pity the weakness of my heart ever since. The mind in infancy is, methinks, like **the body in embryo**, and receives impressions so forcible that they are as hard to be removed by reason, as any mark with which a child is born is to be taken away by any future application. Hence it is that good-nature in me is no merit; but having been so frequently overwhelmed with her tears before I knew the cause of any affliction, or could **draw defences from my own judgment**, I imbibed commiseration, remorse, and an unmanly gentleness of mind, which has since ensnared me into ten thousand calamities, and from whence I can reap no advantage, except it be that in such a humour as I am now in, I can the better indulge myself in the softnesses of humanity, and enjoy that sweet anxiety which arises from the memory of past afflictions.

We, that are very old, are better able to remember things which befell us in our distant youth than the passages of later days. For this reason it is that the companions of my strong and vigorous years present themselves more immediately to me in **this office of sorrow**. Untimely or unhappy deaths are what we are most apt to lament, so little are we able to make it indifferent when a thing happens, though we know it must happen. Thus we groan under life, and bewail those who are relieved from it. Every object that returns to our imagination raises different passions according to the circumstance of their departure. Who can have lived in an army, and in a serious hour reflect upon the many gay and agreeable men that might long have flourished in the arts of peace, and not join with the imprecations of the fatherless and widow on the tyrant to whose ambition they fell sacrifices? But gallant men who are cut off by the sword move rather our veneration than our pity; and we gather relief enough from their own contempt of death, to make it no evil, which was approached with so much cheerfulness and attended with so much honour. But when we turn our thoughts from the great parts of life on such occasions, and instead of lamenting those who stood ready to give death to those from whom they had the fortune to receive it,—I say, when we let our thoughts wander from such noble objects, and consider the havoc which is made among the tender and the innocent, pity enters with an unmixed softness, and possesses all our souls at once.

Here (were there words to express such sentiments with proper tenderness) I should record the beauty, innocence, and untimely death of the first object my eyes ever beheld with love. The beauteous virgin! **How ignorantly did she charm**, how carelessly excel! Oh death! Thou hast right to the bold, to the ambitious, to the high, and to the haughty; but why this cruelty to the humble, to the meek, to the undiscerning, to the thoughtless? Nor age, nor business, nor distress can erase the dear image from my imagination. In the same week, I saw her dressed for a ball and in a shroud. How ill did the **habit of death** become the pretty trifler! I still behold the smiling earth —

A large train of disasters were coming on to my memory, when my servant knocked at my closet door and interrupted me with a letter, attended with a hamper of wine, of the same sort with that which is to be put to sale on Thursday next at **Garraway's Coffee-house**. Upon the receipt of it, I sent for three of my friends. We are so intimate that we can be company in whatever state of mind we meet, and can entertain each other without expecting always to rejoice. The wine we found to be generous and warming, but with such a heat as moved us rather to be cheerful than frolicsome. It revived the spirits without firing the blood. We commended it till two of the clock this morning; and, having to-day met a little before dinner, we found that, though we drank two bottles a man, we had much more reason to recollect than forget what had passed the night before.

Notes

This essay, from the *Tatler*, No. 181 (June 6, 1710), reveals Steele's tender Irish heart. An incorrigible sentimentalist, Steele delighted in depicting misery and producing tears, and he was candid enough to admit that he enjoyed melancholy for its own sake. The passage about the death of his father is autobiographical; Steele lost his father when he was 'not quite five years of age.'

Motto, from Virgil, *The Aeneid*, V, 49: 'The day has come, if I mistake not, which I shall hold always bitter, always memorable, if ye gods will it.' Compare Dryden's verse translation:

'And now the rising day renews the year;
A day for ever sad, for ever dear.'

manes, spirits.

poises the heart, gives the heart its true balance.

beyond all patience of, beyond all power of enduring.

the body in embryo, the body before it is born.

draw defences from my own judgment, apply my reason to check my emotions.

this office of sorrow, this sorrowful duty.

How ignorantly did she charm, etc. How little she knew her own power of attracting, how little trouble she took to outshine others.

habit of death. Here 'habit' means dress or garment (archaic).

Garraway's Coffee-house, a rendezvous of commercial people. The 'hamper of wine' here mentioned is an allusion to an advertisement, which appeared in the same number of the *Tatler*, of the sale of 'forty-six hogsheads and one half of extraordinary French claret.'

【作品简介】

本文选自《闲话报》181 期（1710 年 6 月 6 日），揭示了斯梯尔那一颗温柔的爱尔兰之心。斯梯尔是一个不可救药的情感主义者，喜欢描写苦难和催人泪下的情景；他坦率地承认自己很享受这种悲壮的感觉。他的自传里记载了他父亲去世的一段往事；斯梯尔在他"不满五岁"时，便失去了父亲。

篇首格言出自维吉尔的《埃涅阿斯纪》第五卷："这一天已经到来，如果我没有弄错，如果上帝愿意的话，那么我将永远怀揣着苦涩。"而用德莱顿诗歌形式翻译则是："一年到头 / 每一天都带着悲伤，也带着亲情和爱。"

【作品解析】

manes：这里指死者的灵魂。

poises the heart：让心灵得到真正的平静。

beyond all patience of：无法忍受。

the body in embryo：尚在胚胎中的人体。

draw defences from my own judgment：用理性控制感情。

this office of sorrow：这悲痛的职责。

How ignorantly did she charm, etc.：她对自己的魅力毫无察觉，几乎不费什么力气就可以超越别人。

habit of death：这里"habit"是指衣着（古义）。

Garraway's Coffee-house：商人聚会场所。这里的"hamper of wine"（一篮子的葡萄酒）指的是当时刊登在同期《闲话报》上的一则销售广告，内容是出售"四十六桶半法国优质红葡萄酒"。

【参考译文】

童年的回忆

斯梯尔

一年到头，

每一天都带着悲伤，也带着亲情和爱。

有些人，只会注重当时与自己相关的人和事，而不知道如何去欣赏人生；他们认为往事如烟，无人再会问津了。有些人，则会悄悄地无声无息地藏在人群中，以超凡脱俗的方式，大大超出了人们的想象，塑造自己的生活方式，并以此为乐。人的生命实在是太短暂了，甚至无法有足够的时间在生前去表达自己对诚恳、真挚、友善和美好的意愿。于是乎，圣贤们认为：我们应当虔诚地保留对已故朋友英灵的敬仰和尊敬，并在某段时间，闭门谢客，用自己的方式与他们交流，借以纪念往日的情谊。在我们步入老年的时候，在一个令人沮丧的时刻，追忆与我们永别的亲朋好友，并让自己沉溺于曾经同他们一起整夜嬉闹的欢乐之中，然后再释怀一些悲痛；没有什么比这更加愉悦的了。这正是我的心愿。于是，在昨天晚上，我上了阁楼，把自己锁在了悲痛之中。当时，我不得不用鄙视的眼光看待自己。尽管我哀悼他们的心情，就像当时与他们永别一样，但在我的心里，却没有那么悲痛，甚至没有流泪。我脑海里，闪现出来的都是和这些已故亲朋好友在一起的种种奇遇和经历，尽管他们早已化作了尘土。这个世界的好处之一，就是随着时间的推移，可以减轻悲伤带来的剧痛。然而，由于过度沉浸在欢乐的记忆中，我们往往需要重新激活埋藏在记忆深处的伤感与悲痛，勾起我们对过去生活中每一个细节的沉思，并使我们的神志逐渐变得清晰，逐渐理性化。这样可以使我们的心灵平静下来，使心率变得自然平稳，间隙均匀，不会因某种欲望而加速，也不会因某种绝望而减速。当我们给一个停摆的钟表上发条时，并非立刻把时针拨放在正确的时间上，而是需要让它逐一敲过钟点，然后再恢复到正常的运转。"这就是我今天晚上用的方法，"我在心里默默地说，"从今天开始，我将会每天用上一两个小时，让自己沉浸在悲痛和回忆之中；用这种方式来纪念曾经在我生活中出现，让我愉悦但早已化作尘埃的每一个生命，以寄托我对他们的哀思。"

有生以来，我第一次感到悲痛是在我父亲去世的时候，那时我还不满五岁。当时，我只是感到惊讶，整栋楼房里，居然没一个人愿意和我玩。而我，却不知是何原因。记得我走进停放父亲遗体的房间，看到母亲独自一人坐在那里哭泣。我拿着手中的板羽球拍敲打着棺材，嚷着要和爸爸玩，根本不知道他怎么就躺在了里面。在寂静中，母亲把我抱在了怀里，她再也无法忍受之前那种默默的悲伤，紧紧地抱着我，几乎使我透不过气来。她泪流满面，哽咽着告诉我，爸爸再也听不到我的声音了，再也不能和我玩了，因为他们就要把他安葬了，他再也回不到我们的身边了。母亲很美，也很高雅，在极度的悲痛之中，仍然保持着尊严。母亲深深地打动了我，激起了我悲痛的本能。在我还没有意识到什么是悲痛之前，悲痛的本能就早已占据了我的全部心灵，从此怜悯便成了我内心的弱点。幼儿的心灵，就像胚胎中的身体那样，在受到强烈的刺激之后，总会留下印记，很难抹去，如同胎记一样。这种善良的品德并非是什么优点。我常常无法面对母亲的眼泪，因为我并不知道她为何而哭泣，也无法用理性来控制自己的情感。这往往使我沉浸于同情和悔恨之中，并表现出一种非男子气的温柔。同时，这也给我带来了无穷无尽的烦恼。这种性格并没有给我带来什么好处，除了我此时处于这样一种心情之外，我更愿意沉溺于人类的温情之中，尽情地享受着回忆过去的痛苦而给我带来的那种既甜蜜而又焦躁不安的感觉。

　　迈入老年以后，我常常回忆往事，更加容易回忆起那遥远的青年时代。因此，在我沉浸于悲痛时，首先跳进我脑海中的是那些陪伴着我度过青春年华的朋友。最让我悲伤的是不幸的死亡。当它们发生的时候，我们几乎没有任何能力去挽回，只能眼睁睁地看着。因此，我们只能在生活中呻吟，为那些在挣扎中丧失生命的人而悲哀。出现在我记忆中的每一位魂灵，由于场景不同，都会激起我的一段情怀。那些曾经生活在军营里的人，在危难时刻，想着那些本可以在和平年代快快乐乐大有作为的人，哪一个不会同孤儿寡母一起诅咒那些因利令智昏的野心使他们沦为牺牲品的暴君呢？而那些慷慨就义的勇士，把我们的同情化作了崇拜与敬仰。于是，我们从他们对死亡的蔑视中得到了足够的宽慰，认识到死亡并非邪恶，因为当死亡来临时，他们竟然如此兴奋，并感到如此荣耀。但是在这种场合，如果我们不去这样想，不去考虑人生伟大的一面，不去哀悼那些挺身而出，把生命献给他人的勇士，而是想到那些有幸接受死亡的人，我是说，我们的思想就会在这些高贵的魂灵中徘徊，同时去考虑那些给弱者和无辜者带来的灾难，怜悯和纯粹的温柔就会一并进入我们的心灵，占据我们的整个灵魂并沉迷其中。

如果有文字可以表达这种带有温柔的伤感，我应该记下美丽和纯真。这也正是我亲眼所见第一位深爱的亲友过早离世的感受。她是多么美丽无瑕的处女啊！她对自己的魅力居然毫无察觉，然而她的美丽却又是那样毫不费力地超凡脱俗！死神啊……你有权利对付那些胆大妄为、雄心勃勃、权高位重、高傲自大的人；可是你，为何要对那么谦卑、那么顺从、那么老实、那么温柔随和的人，如此残忍冷酷呢？岁月的流逝，生活中的繁杂事务和悲痛，都不能抹去我心中的她，她是那样可爱。就在同一周，我先是看见她为舞会而打扮，而后又看到她丧衣裹身。如此令人沮丧的丧衣此时已变得微不足道了！我依然看见她的遗体面带着微笑——

一连串的不幸闪现在我的回忆之中。这时我的仆人敲门进来了，打断了我的回忆。她带来了一封信和一大篮子葡萄酒，这是下周四嘉利伟咖啡馆将要减价出售的法国优质红葡萄酒。收到之后，我便立即邀请我的三位好友。我们的友谊至深。当我们相聚时，都会亲密无间畅怀痛饮，无论各自的心境怎样，我们都可以相互陪伴在一起，可以互相招待，而并非奢望总是开心。这种酒比较温和，它的热量使我们感受到了愉悦，而不会让我们酒后乱了性情。这些葡萄酒并没有使我们的血管膨胀，而是帮助我们恢复神志，清醒了许多。我们一直待到凌晨两点。晚餐前，我们又见面了，发现昨天晚上虽然我们每个人都喝了两瓶酒，但对昨晚发生的一切，我们有更多的理由牢牢地记住而不是忘却。

The Spectator Introduces Himself

Joseph Addison

Non fumum ex fulgore, sed ex fumo dare lucem
Cogitat, ut speciosa dehinc miracula promat.

I have observed that a reader seldom peruses a book with pleasure till he knows whether the writer of it be **a black or a fair man**, of a mild or choleric disposition, married or a bachelor, with other particulars of the like nature, that conduce very much to the right understanding of an author. To gratify this curiosity, which is so natural to a reader, I design this paper and my next as prefatory discourses to my following writings, and shall give some account in them of the several persons that are engaged in this work. As the chief trouble of compiling, digesting, and correcting will fall to my share, I must do myself the justice to open the work with my own history.

I was born to a small hereditary estate, which, according to the tradition of the village where it lies, was bounded by the same hedges and ditches in **William the Conqueror**'s time that it is at present, and has been delivered down from father to son whole and entire, without the loss or acquisition of a single field or meadow, during the space of six hundred years. There runs a story in the family, that when my mother was gone with child of me about three months, she dreamt that she was brought to bed of a judge. Whether this might proceed from a lawsuit which was then depending in the family, or my father's being a justice of the peace, I cannot determine; for I am not so vain as to think it presaged any dignity that I should arrive at in my future life, though that was the interpretation which the neighbourhood put upon it. The gravity of my behaviour at my very first appearance in the world, and all the time that I sucked, seemed to favour my mother's dream; for, as she had often told me, I threw away my rattle before I was two months old, and would not make use of my **coral** till they had taken away the bells from it.

As for the rest of my infancy, there being nothing in it remarkable, I shall pass it over in silence. I find that, during my nonage, I had the reputation of a very sullen youth, but was always a favourite of my schoolmaster, who used to say that my parts were solid and would wear well. I had not been long at the university before I distinguished myself by a most profound silence; for during the space of eight years, excepting in the public exercises of the college, I scarce uttered the quantity of a hundred words; and indeed do not remember that I ever spoke three sentences together in my whole life. Whilst I was in this learned body, I applied myself with so much diligence to my studies that there are very few celebrated books, either in the learned or the modern tongues, which I am not acquainted with.

Upon the death of my father, I was resolved to travel into foreign countries, and therefore left the university, with the character of an odd, unaccountable fellow, that had a great deal of learning, if I would but show it. An insatiable thirst after knowledge carried me into all the countries of Europe, in which there was anything new or strange to be seen; nay, to such a degree was my curiosity raised, that having read the **controversies of some great men** concerning the antiquities of Egypt, I made a voyage to **Grand Cairo** on purpose to take the measure of a pyramid; and as soon as I had set myself right in that particular, returned to my native country with great satisfaction.

I have passed my latter years in this city, where I am frequently seen in most public places, though there are not above half a dozen of my select friends that know me; of whom my next paper shall give a more particular account. There is no place of general resort wherein I do not often make my appearance; sometimes I am seen thrusting my head into a round of politicians at **Will's** and listening with great attention to the narratives that are made in those little circular audiences. Sometimes I smoke a pipe at Child's; and while I seem attentive to nothing but the *Postman*, overhear the conversation of every table in the room. I appear on Sunday nights at St. James's Coffee-house, and sometimes join the little committee of **politics** in the inner room, as one who comes there to hear and improve. My face is likewise very well known at the Grecian, the Cocoa Tree, and in the theatres both of **Drury Lane** and the **Haymarket**. I have been taken for a merchant upon **the Exchange** for above these ten years, and sometimes pass for a Jew in the assembly of stock-jobbers at **Jonathan's**. In short, wherever I see a cluster of people, I always mix with them, though **I never open my lips** but in my own club.

Thus I live in the world rather as a spectator of mankind than as one of the species; by which means I have made myself a speculative statesman, soldier, merchant, and artisan, without ever meddling with any practical part in life. I am very well versed in the theory of a husband, or a father, and can discern the errors in the economy, business, and diversion of others better than those who are engaged in them; as standers-by discover **blots**, which are apt to escape those who are in the game. I never espoused any party with violence, and am resolved to observe an exact neutrality between the **Whigs and Tories**, unless I shall be forced to declare myself by the hostilities of either side. In short, I have acted in all the parts of my life as a looker-on, which is the character I intend to preserve in this paper.

I have given the reader just so much of my history and character as to let him see I am not altogether unqualified for the business I have undertaken. As for other particulars in my life and adventures, I shall insert them in following papers, as I shall see occasion. In the meantime, when I consider how much I have seen, read, and heard, I begin to blame my own taciturnity; and since I have neither time nor inclination to communicate the fullness of my heart in speech, I am resolved to do it in writing, and to print myself out, if possible, before I die. I have been often told by my friends that it is pity so many useful discoveries which I have made should be in the possession of a silent man. For this reason, therefore, I shall publish a sheetful of thoughts every morning for the benefit of my contemporaries; and if I can any way contribute to the diversion or improvement of the country in which I live, I shall leave it, when I am summoned out of it, with the secret satisfaction of thinking that I have not lived in vain.

There are three very material points which I have not spoken to in this paper, and which, for several important reasons, I must keep to myself, at least for some time: I mean, an account of my name, my age, and my lodgings. I must confess I would gratify my reader in anything that is reasonable; but as for these three particulars, though I am sensible they might tend very much to the embellishment of my paper, I cannot yet come to a resolution of communicating them to the public. They would indeed draw me out of that obscurity which I have enjoyed for many years, and expose me in public places to several salutes and civilities, which have been always very disagreeable to me; for the greatest pain I can suffer is the being talked to and being stared at. It is for this reason likewise that I keep my complexion and dress as very great secrets; though it is not impossible but I may make discoveries of both in the progress of the work I have undertaken.

After having been thus particular upon myself, I shall in tomorrow's paper give an account of those gentlemen who are concerned with me in this work, for, as I have before intimated, a plan of it is laid and concerted (as all other matters of importance are) in a club. However, as my friends have engaged me to stand in the front, those who have a mind to correspond with me may direct their **letters to the** *Spectator*, at **Mr. Buckley's** in **Little Britain**. For I must further acquaint the reader that though our club meets only on Tuesdays and Thursdays, we have appointed a committee to sit every night for the inspection of all such papers as may contribute to the advancement of the public weal.

Notes

This essay, being the opening paper of the *Spectator* (March 1, 1711), is Addison's humourous portrait of himself.

Motto, from Horace, *Ars Poetica*, 143—144:

'One with a flash begins, and ends in smoke;
Another out of smoke brings glorious light,
And (without raising expectation high)
Surprises us with dazzling miracles.' —Roscommon.

a black or a fair man, a man of dark or fair complexion.

William the Conqueror, William I, of Normandy, King of England, 1066—1087.

coral, a kind of teething ring, made of coral or similar material and fitted with bells.

controversies of some great men, an allusion to *Pyramidographia, or a Discourse of the Pyramids of Egypt* (1646), by the Persian scholar John Greaves (1602—1652), who visited Egypt and measured the pyramids with mathematical instruments.

Grand Cairo, the capital of modern Egypt, on the right bank of the Nile.

Will's etc. The first coffee-house in London is said to have opened in 1652. By 1708 it is estimated in a pamphlet that the number was then 3000, each catering more or less to particular professions and classes of patrons. There were a score or more, especially well-known as rendezvous of the more influential of various classes: Will's and Button for the literary men; Jonathan, Lloyd's, and Garraway's for commercial people; the Chocolate (or Cocoa Tree) and St. James for the Tories and Whigs respectively; Child's for ecclesiastics and other professional men;

the Grecian for lawyers and soldiers; and Giles's and the Rainbow for the exiled French Protestants.

Postman, a favourite newspaper, published three times a week, it had some reputation for its foreign news and correspondence.

politics, politicians (archaic).

Drury Lane, one of the popular theatres of the day. It was established in the reign of James I, and was rebuilt several times in the 17th century. In 1715 Steele was appointed its supervisor.

Haymarket, so called from the Hay Market there. Her Majesty's Theatre, Haymarket (called also Opera House), was the first opera house in London.

the Exchange. The Royal Exchange, London, was founded by Sir T. Gresham in 1566 and opened by Queen Elizabeth. It was destroyed in the Great Fire of 1666. Its successor, the second Royal Exchange, to which Addison here referred, was likewise burnt in 1838.

Jonathan's. The London Stock, for the sale and purchase of securities, was originally conducted at Jonathan's Coffee-house.

I Never open my lips, a humourous exaggeration. Addison could shine in a small circle of friends, but (says Pope) 'with any mixture of strangers, and sometimes only with one, he seemed to preserve his dignity much, with a stiff sort of silence.'

blots, exposed cards in backgammon.

Whigs and Tories, two great political parties in England that became prominent after 1689. In the years of the *Tatler* and the *Spectator,* the two parties, 'loud, restless, and violent, each with plausible declarations, and each perhaps without any distinct termination of its views, were agitating the nation.' (Johnson)

There are three very material points which I have not spoken to. In parliamentary language, one *speaks to* a question, resolution, or subject under discussion.

letters to the Spectator. The letters of correspondents became a feature of the *Spectator*. They were collected and published, together with letters which had appeared in the *Tatler*, in two volumes in 1725.

Mr. Buckley's. At the end of the original sheets of the *Spectator*, one reads: 'London; Printed for Sam. Buckley, at the Dolphin, in Little Britain.'

Little Britain, a short street in the centre of London, a favourite mart for booksellers. It was so called because it was formerly the residence of the Duke of Brittany. Washington Irving gives an interesting account of it in his *Sketch Book*.

【作品简介】

本文是《旁观者》的开篇首卷（1711 年 3 月 1 日），是艾迪生幽默的自我写照。

篇首格言出自贺拉斯的《诗艺》，罗斯康芒伯爵将其译成英文，参见第 19 页注解，中文大意为：这不是从闪光中产生的烟雾，而是从烟雾中放射出来的光芒，由此便产生了耀眼的奇迹。

【作品解析】

a black or a fair man：一个肤色黝黑或白皙的人。

William the Conqueror：征服者威廉一世，诺曼王朝的英国国王（1066—1087 年在位）。

coral：一种磨牙环，由珊瑚或类似材料制成，并配有铃铛。

controversies of some great men：这里是指英国波斯学者约翰·格里夫斯（1602—1652）于 1646 年发表的《金字塔学，埃及的金字塔论考》，他曾访问埃及并用数学仪器测量了金字塔。

Grand Cairo：现代埃及首都，坐落在尼罗河右岸。

Will's etc.：据说伦敦第一家咖啡馆于 1652 年开张。据一本小册子估计，到了 1708 年，咖啡馆已达 3000 家，每个咖啡馆都有其服务范围，为某些特定的职业和特定阶层的顾客服务。其中有二三十家咖啡馆作为各个阶层中较有影响力的人士出入的聚会场所而特别出名：为文人服务的是威尔斯和巴顿咖啡馆，为商业人士服务的是乔纳森、劳埃德和嘉利伟咖啡馆，为托利党和辉格党人士服务的是巧克力（或称可可树）和圣詹姆斯咖啡馆，为教会和其他专业人士服务的是查尔德斯咖啡馆，为律师和士兵服务的是希腊人俱乐部，为流亡法国的新教徒服务的是贾尔斯和彩虹咖啡馆。

Postman：《邮差报》是一份受欢迎的报纸，每周出版三次，它在国外新闻和通讯方面享有一定的声誉。

politics：政客（古义）。

Drury Lane：德鲁里街剧院，英国伦敦皇家歌剧院，是当时最受欢迎的剧院之一。建立于詹姆士一世治理时期，17 世纪几经重建。1715 年，斯梯尔出任该剧院经理。

Haymarket：海马基特剧院，以那里的干草市场命名。也称女王陛下剧院，是伦敦第一家歌剧院。

the Exchange：伦敦皇家交易所由托马斯·格雷欣爵士始建于 1566 年，由伊丽莎白女王开办。交易所在 1666 年的大火中被摧毁。艾迪生在这里提到的是交易所的后继者，第二个皇家交易所，也于 1838 年被烧毁。

Jonathan's：伦敦证券交易所，出售和购买证券的地方。伦敦证券交易最初是在乔纳森咖啡馆里进行的。

I Never open my lips：这是一种幽默的夸张。艾迪生可以在一小群朋友圈中大放光彩，然而诗人蒲柏则说"一旦他发现人群中有陌生人，有时哪怕只有一个，他似乎就会用一种沉默来保持他的尊严"。

blots：十五子棋中暴露的棋子。

Whigs and Tories：辉格党和托利党，英国两大政党，在 1689 年后迅速壮大。在《闲话报》和《旁观者》的年代里，这两党"互相争吵，没有休止，甚至动用暴力；每个政党都有自己似是而非的声明，用以鼓动这个国家，然而每个政党却都没有明确的最终目的"(约翰逊)。

There are three very material points which I have not spoken to：议会用语中，人们对提议中的疑问、解决方法和主题进行阐述。

letters to the *Spectator*：信件来往是《旁观者》的一大特色。这些信件后来收集整理成册，并与《闲话报》的信件一起于 1725 年出版，共两大卷。

Mr. Buckley's：《旁观者》原稿结尾时写着："伦敦，小不列颠街，海豚印刷厂山姆·巴克利先生。"

Little Britain：伦敦市中心的一条短街，是书商最喜爱的集市。之所以称为小不列颠，是因为以前是布列塔尼公爵的住所。在《素描》中，华盛顿·欧文对这条街做了有趣的叙述。

【参考译文】

旁观者自述

艾迪生

> 这不是从闪光中产生的烟雾，而是从烟雾中放射出来的光芒，
> 由此便产生了耀眼的奇迹。

我发现，读者很少会高兴地阅读一本书，只有在他们了解到作者的肤色是黑是白，个性特征是温和还是暴躁，婚姻状况是已婚还是单身，以及有关其他这一类细节之后，才能在某种程度上真正地理解作者。为了满足读者这种自然的好奇心，我将把这一篇和下一篇文章作为序言，并且我也会介绍在该报工作的几位同仁。由于编纂、设计和校对工作都是由我自己负责，就让我用这开卷首篇，谈谈我自己吧！

　　我出生在一个世袭的小地主家庭。按照当地的习俗，我们家族的地产仍沿用征服者威廉时期的篱笆墙和小渠沟围拢着。这块地产世代相传，面积既没有扩大也没有缩小，至今已有六百多年了。据说，母亲在怀我三个月的时候，居然梦见自己生下了一位法官。这种传说是源于当时家里正在忙于法律诉讼，还是因为父亲是民政官，我无法考证，也无法判定。我也没有那么虚荣，认定托梦这件事会给我的前途带来什么显贵的好兆头。然而，我的邻居们却都是这么想的。我一生下来表情就很严肃，而且一直保持着严肃，这似乎是应验了母亲的梦；母亲还常常告诉我，我生下来不满两个月就扔掉了我的拨浪鼓了，嘴里不咬任何带有响声的磨牙环，除非把磨牙环上的铃铛摘掉。

　　除了严肃，我的婴儿时期并没有什么值得注意的，也没有什么值得好写的。在我未成年的时候，我就有着沉闷少年的名声，然而校长却很喜欢我，他经常说我的知识很扎实，以后会大有作为。上了大学以后，我很快就以沉默寡言而著称。在大学的八年里，除了学院的公开演讲外，我说过的话加起来还不到一百个字。我甚至不记得我曾经连续说过三句话。在大学里，我学习非常刻苦努力，研读过几乎所有的古典和当代名著。

　　父亲去世后，我便离开了大学，下决心到国外游历。当时的我，性情古怪、难以捉摸；学识渊博，却又深藏不露。对知识的渴望，使我走遍了欧洲大陆，观察和体验到了各种新生事物。在读到某些学术巨人有关埃及古迹的争论之后，我的好奇心又驱使我远航大开罗，丈量金字塔。直到弄清情况后，我才心满意足地打道回府。

　　之后，我就一直待在这座城市里，经常出没于公共场所。然而，我真正的知己不过五六位。我将在下一篇中，对他们一一做介绍。这个城市里的每一处消遣胜地，无不留下鄙人的足迹。有时，我会去威尔斯咖啡馆，探头探脑聚精会神地倾听政治家在他们小圈子里的演讲。有时，我也会在查尔德斯咖啡馆，抽上几斗烟，似乎是在专注阅读《邮差报》；然而我却在留意房间里每一张桌子上的谈话。有时星期天晚上，我会去圣詹姆斯咖啡馆的包厢，加入政治家小组的讨论，以此丰富自己的知识。我也是希腊人俱乐部、可可树咖啡馆、德鲁里街皇家歌剧院和海马基特歌剧院的常客。在过去的十年里，我常被当作股票交易所的经纪人，却有时在乔纳森证券交易所被误认为是犹太人。总而言之，只要有人的地方，我就和他们混在一起，然而我却从不开口说话，只有在自己的俱乐部里，才会发表评论。

因此，在这个世界里，我不过是人类生活的旁观者，并非是一个有真实身份的人；我的意思是，我只不过一个自己臆想中的政治家、士兵、商人和工匠，但从未有过他们的真实生活。我非常精通怎样做丈夫、怎样做父亲的道理；并比专业人士更能发现他们在经济、商业上所存在的问题以及偏颇之处；就像一位旁观者，具有敏锐的观察力，比当事人更能发现弊端所在。我从不过激地偏袒任何政党，力求在辉格党和托利党之间保持中立；除非逼不得已，只好表明自己的立场。简而言之，在生活中，我只是一个旁观者，这也正是我想要在本报中继续扮演的角色。

我向读者介绍了我的人生经历和性格，就是想让他们知道，作为本报的编辑，我还是合格的。至于我的其他经历，我将会在合适的场合，在今后的文章中，向读者描述。同时，每当我想起看到的、读到的和听到的经历时，不禁有些对自己沉默寡言的行为感到不满。既然我没有时间也不愿意在公开场合演讲，向公众敞开自己的心扉，我只能在我离世之前，以书面的形式来表达自己。朋友们经常为我惋惜；我有许多有价值的发现，却是个不善于言表的人。因此，为了同龄人，我计划每天早上发表一些文章，阐述我个人的观点。如果我能以这种方式促进国家社会的改良，在上帝召唤时，我将会毫无愧疚地去面对，因为我没有白白地浪费人生。

有三点，在这里我没有向读者介绍，那就是我的姓名、年龄和住址，这样做有几个重要的原因，至少现在我得保密。我必须承认，我应当满足读者的合理要求，虽然我知道这三点细节可以更好地点缀我的文章，但我还是不能在这里公之于众。这三点细节会把我从多年所习惯的默默无闻的生活中拽出来；于是我就不得不在公共场所中，与各种人物进行社交。这对于我来说，并非是件愉快的事情，我最大的痛苦就是被别人谈论和关注。也正是由于这个原因，我把自己的肤色和衣着也作为秘密隐藏了起来；说出来也并非不可能，也许在我今后的办报工作中，会向人们透露点这两方面的事情。

这就是我的自我介绍。明天我将在《旁观者》上介绍与该报有关的诸位先生。我们的计划，正如我之前所暗示的那样，就像所有其他重要的事情一样，都是在俱乐部里制订的，并将它们协调一致加以完善。然而，我只不过是被朋友们推到了前面而已。因此，想和我们联系的绅士、淑女们，请把信件直接寄到：小不列颠街，巴克利先生转《旁观者》收。另外我还得告诉读者，虽然俱乐部成员只是在星期二和星期四聚会，但我们有一个委员会，每晚负责查收信件，看看信件里是否会有促进公共福利的建议。

The Spectator Club

Richard Steele

Ast alii sex

Et plures uno conclamant ore.

The first of our society is a gentleman of Worcestershire, of ancient descent, a baronet, his name Sir Roger de Coverley. His great-grandfather was inventor of **that famous country-dance** which is called after him. All who know that shire are very well acquainted with the parts and merits of Sir Roger. He is a gentleman that is very singular in his behaviour, but his singularities proceed from his good sense, and are contradictions to the manners of the world, only as he thinks the world is in the wrong. However, this humour creates him no enemies, for he does nothing with sourness or obstinacy; and his being unconfined to modes and forms makes him but the readier and more capable to please and oblige all who know him. When he is in town, he lives in **Soho Square**. It is said he keeps himself a bachelor by reason he was crossed in love by a perverse beautiful widow of the next county to him. Before this disappointment, Sir Roger was what you call a fine gentleman, had often supped with my **Lord Rochester**

and Sir George Etherege, fought a duel upon his first coming to town, and kicked **Bully Dawson** in a public coffee-house for calling him youngster. But being ill-used by the above-mentioned widow, he was very serious for a year and a half; and though, his temper being naturally jovial, he at last got over it, he grew careless of himself, and never dressed afterwards. He continues to wear a coat and **doublet** of the same cut that were in fashion at the time of his repulse, which, in his merry humours, he tells us, has been in and out twelve times since he first wore it. It is said Sir Roger grew humble in his desires after he had forgot this cruel beauty, insomuch that it is reported he has frequently offended in point of chastity with beggars and gypsies; but this is looked upon by his friends rather as matter of raillery than truth. He is now in his fifty-sixth year, cheerful, gay, and hearty, keeps a good house both in town and country; a great lover of mankind; but there is such a mirthful cast in his behaviour, that he is rather beloved than esteemed. His tenants grow rich, his servants look satisfied, all the young women profess love to him, and the young men are glad of his company. When he comes into a house, he calls the servants by their names, and talks all the way upstairs to a visit. I must not omit that Sir Roger is a **Justice of the Quorum**; that he fills the chair at a quarter-session with great abilities, and three months ago gained universal applause by explaining a passage in the **Game Act**.

The gentleman next in esteem and authority among us is another bachelor, who is a member of the **Inner Temple**; a man of great probity, wit, and understanding; but he has chosen his place of residence rather to obey the direction of an old humoursome father, than in pursuit of his own inclinations. He was placed there to study the laws of the land, and is the most learned of any of the house in those of the stage. **Aristotle** and **Longinus** are much better understood by him than **Littleton or Coke**. The father sends up every post questions relating to marriage-articles, leases, and tenures, in the neighbourhood; all which questions he agrees with an attorney to answer and take care of in the lump. He is studying the passions themselves, when he should be inquiring into the debates among men which arise from them. He knows the argument of each of the orations of **Demosthenes** and **Tully**, but not one case in the reports of our own courts. No one ever took him for a fool; but none, except his intimate friends, know he has a great deal of wit. This turn makes him at once both disinterested and agreeable. As few of his thoughts are drawn from business, they are most of them fit for conversation. His taste of books is a little too just for the age he lives in; he has read all, but approves of very few. His familiarity with the customs, manners, actions, and writings of the ancients, makes him a very delicate observer of what occurs to him in the present world. He is an excellent critic, and **the time of the play** is his hour of business; exactly at five he passes through **New Inn**, crosses through Russell Court, and takes a turn at Will's till the play begins; he has his shoes rubbed and his periwig powdered at the barber's as you go into **the Rose**. It is for the good of the audience when he is at the play, for the actors have an ambition to please him.

The person of next consideration is Sir Andrew Freeport, a merchant of great eminence in the City of London—a person of indefatigable industry, strong reason, and great experience. His notions of trade are noble and generous, and (as every rich man has usually some sly way of jesting, which would make no great figure were he not a rich man) he calls the sea the **British Common**. He is acquainted with commerce in all its parts, and will tell you that it is a stupid and barbarous way to extend dominion by arms; for true power is to be got by arts and industry. He will often argue that if this part of our trade were well cultivated, we should gain from one nation; and if another, from another. I have heard him prove that diligence makes more lasting acquisitions than valour, and that sloth has ruined more nations than the sword. He abounds in several frugal maxims, among which the greatest favourite is, 'A penny saved is a penny got.' A general trader of good sense is pleasanter company than a general scholar; and Sir Andrew having a natural unaffected eloquence, the perspicuity of his discourse gives the same pleasure that wit would in another man. He has made his fortunes himself; and says that England may be richer than other kingdoms by as plain methods as he himself is richer than other men; though at the same time I can say this of him, that there is not a point in the compass but blows home a ship in which he is an owner.

Next to Sir Andrew in the club-room sits Captain Sentry, a gentleman of great courage, good understanding, but invincible modesty. He is one of those that deserve very well, but are very awkward at putting their talents within the observation of such as should take notice of them. He was some years a captain, and behaved himself with great gallantry in several engagements and at several sieges; but having a small estate of his own, and being next heir to Sir Roger, he has quitted a way of life in which no man can rise suitably to his merit, who is not something of a courtier as well as a soldier. I have heard him often lament that in a profession where merit is placed in so conspicuous a view, impudence should get the better of modesty. When he has talked to this purpose, I never heard him make a sour expression, but frankly confess that he left the world because he was not fit for it. A strict honesty and an even regular behaviour are in themselves obstacles to him that must press through crowds, who endeavour at the same end with himself, the favour of a commander. He will, however, in his way of talk excuse generals for not disposing according to men's desert, or inquiring into it. 'For,' says he, 'that great man who has a mind to help me has as many to break through to come at me as I have to come at him.' Therefore, he will conclude that the man who would make a figure, especially in a military way, must get over all false modesty, and assist his patron against the importunity of other pretenders, by a proper assurance in his own vindication. He says it is a civil cowardice to be backward in asserting what you ought to expect, as it is a military fear to be slow in attacking when it is your duty. With this candour does the gentleman speak of himself and others. The same frankness runs through all his conversation. The military part of his life has furnished him with many adventures, in the relation of which he is very agreeable to the company; for he is never overbearing, though accustomed to command men in the utmost degree below him; nor ever too obsequious, from a habit of obeying men highly above him.

But that our society may not appear a set of **humourists**, unacquainted with the gallantries and pleasures of the age, we have among us the gallant Will Honeycomb, a gentleman who, according to his years, should be in the decline of his life, but having ever been very careful of his person, and always had a very easy fortune, time has made but very little impression, either by wrinkles on his forehead, or traces in his brain. His person is well turned, and of a good height. He is very ready at that sort of discourse with which men usually entertain women. He has all his life dressed very well, and remembers habits as others do men. He can smile when one speaks to him, and laughs easily. He knows the history of every mode, and can inform you from which of the French king's wenches our wives and daughters had this manner of curling their hair, that way of placing their hoods; whose frailty was covered by such a sort of petticoat, and whose vanity to show her foot made that part of the dress so short in such a year. In a word, all his conversation and knowledge has been in the female world. As other men of his age will take notice to you what such a minister said upon such and such an occasion, he will tell you when the **Duke of Monmouth** danced at court such a woman was then smitten, another was taken with him at the head of his troop in the park. In all these important relations, he has ever about the same time received a kind glance or a blow of a fan from some celebrated beauty, mother of the present Lord Such-a-one. If you speak of a young commoner that said a lively thing in the House, he starts up, 'He has good blood in his veins, **Tom Mirabell** begot him, the rogue cheated me in that affair; that young fellow's mother used me more like a dog than any woman I ever made advances to.' This way of talking of his very much enlivens the conversation among us of a more sedate turn; and I find there is not one of the company but myself, who rarely speak at all, but speaks of him as of that sort of man who is usually called a well-bred fine gentleman. To conclude his character, where women are not concerned, he is an honest, worthy man.

I cannot tell whether I am to account him whom I am next to speak of as one of our company, for he visits us but seldom; but when he does, it adds to every man else a new enjoyment of himself. He is a clergyman, a very philosophic man, of general learning, great sanctity of life, and the most exact good breeding. He has the misfortune to be of a very weak constitution, and consequently cannot accept of such cares and business as preferments in his function would oblige him to; he is therefore among divines what a chamber-counsellor is among lawyers. The probity of his mind and the integrity of his life create him followers, as being eloquent or loud advances others. He seldom introduces the subject he speaks upon; but we are so far gone in years that he observes, when he is among us, an earnestness to have him fall on some divine topic, which he always treats with much authority, as one who has no interests in this world, as one who is hastening to the object of all his wishes, and conceives hope from his decays and infirmities. These are my ordinary companions.

Notes

From the *Spectator*, No. 2 (March 2, 1711). Here we have the original design of an imaginary club, consisting of several types of character grouped round the central figure of the *Spectator*. This paper was written by Steele—probably with the corroboration of Addison.

Dr. Johnson was of the opinion that the personages of the *Spectator* were not 'merely ideal,' but 'known and conspicuous in various stations.' Attempts have been made to identify them. It is said that Sir Roger's original was Sir John Pakington (1671—1727), a Tory squire of Worcestershire, and that Captain Sentry and Will Honeycomb are portraits of Colonels Kempenfelt and Cleland. Even the 'perverse beautiful widow' has been discovered! It was Mrs. Catherine Boevey, 'one of those dark and lasting beauties that strike with reverence and yet delight.' But some ingenious editors have fixed on Lady Warwick, whom Addison was to marry in 1716.

Motto, from Juvenal, *Satires*, VII, 167: 'Six more, at least, join their consenting voice.'

that famous country-dance. There existed, in the late 17th century, a tune called *Roger of Caulverley*. It was later associated with the country dance, known since the days of the *Spectator* by that name.

Soho Square, originally King's Square built in 1681. In Steele's time it was still the most fashionable part of London.

Lord Rochester and Sir George Etherege, 'wits' and courtiers of the Restoration period. John Wilmot, Earl of Rochester (1647—1680), was a poet, and Etherege (1634 ? —1691?) a dramatist.

Bully Dawson, a contemporary of Rochester and Etherege, notorious as a gamester and swaggerer.

doublet, a close-fitting body garment, with or without sleeves.

Justice of the Quorum, justice of the peace, who, with other justices, constituted the county court, which met four times a year.

Game Act, act of Parliament for the protection of game. Under the Act, for instance, only the possessor of specified property qualifications might take or kill deer, hares, pheasants, partridges and rabbits. In the current phrase, such were 'within the Game Act.'

Inner Temple, one of the four sets of buildings in London inhabited by students and practitioners of laws.

Aristotle (4th century B.C.), the great Greek philosopher, author of *Poetics, Rhetoric, Politics*. His *Poetics* was accepted as the highest authority in criticism from the Renaissance to the 18th century.

Longinus (3rd century A.D.), the supposed author of the celebrated treatise *On the Sublime*, which was regarded, especially in the 18th century, as an authority on the artistic qualities of style.

Littleton or Coke. Sir Thomas Littleton (1422—1481) and Sir Edward Coke (1552—1634) were English legal authorities, best known in the phrase 'Coke on Littleton,' being the commentary of Coke on the legal treaties by Littleton.

Demosthenes (4th century B.C.), Greek orator.

Tully, Marcus Tullius Cicero (1st century B.C.), Roman orator, philosopher, and statesman.

the time of the play. It was several hours earlier than at present.

New Inn, an attachment of the Middle Temple, one of the Inns of Court.

the Rose, a tavern near Drury Lane Theatre, a resort of playgoers.

British Common. Here 'Common' is a legal term, meaning 'the profit which a man has in the land or waters of another' (O.E.D.).

humourists, in the old sense of the word, whimsical or capricious characters.

Duke of Monmouth, the illegitimate son of Charles II, famous for his fine manners.

Tom Mirabell. There had been several Mirabels or Mirabells in English plays (see for instance Congreve's *The Way of the World*). Steele uses this name which has a flavour of the fop and the rake about it.

【作品简介】

本文选自《旁观者》第2期（1711年3月2日）。在这里，我们可以看到一个想象中的俱乐部的原始设计，其中包括围绕着《旁观者》的不同类型的人物。本文由斯梯尔撰写，可能在写作中得到过艾迪生的帮助。

约翰逊博士认为，《旁观者》中的人物并非"仅仅是理想化的"，而是"在各个方面都为人熟知和引人注目的人物"。人们曾经试图寻找《旁观者》中的人物。据说，罗杰爵士的原型是约翰·帕金顿爵士（1671—1727），他是伍斯特郡的托利党乡绅。森特里上尉和威尔·霍尼康姆则是肯彭费尔特和克莱兰上校的化身。就连那位"美丽无比的寡妇"也有其原型，那就是凯瑟琳·贝维太太，她是"一位令人尊敬而又给人们带来快乐的肤色黝黑的美丽的女人"。然而，一些精明的编辑却认定是沃里克女士，艾迪生是于1716年与她结婚的。

篇首格言出自尤维纳利斯的《讽刺诗》第七首："至少有六个，加入了他们的同盟。"

【作品解析】

that famous country-dance：17世纪后期，流传着一首名为《科弗利的罗杰》的乡间小曲。后来这首曲子便与乡村舞蹈联系在了一起，从《旁观者》问世后，就以这个名字为人所知。

Soho Square：苏豪广场，原来的国王广场，建于1681年。在斯梯尔时期仍是伦敦最时尚的地方。

Lord Rochester and Sir George Etherege：罗切斯特勋爵和乔治·埃瑟里奇爵士，复辟时期的"智者"和朝臣。约翰·威尔莫特，即罗切斯特勋爵（1647—1680），也是诗人；埃瑟里奇爵士（约1634—约1691），也是戏剧家。

Bully Dawson：布利·道森，他与罗切斯特和埃瑟里奇是同时代的人，却是臭名昭著的赌徒和骗子。

doublet：紧身上衣，有时带袖子，有时不带袖子。

Justice of the Quorum：治安法官也译为地方法官，与其他法官一起组成县

（地方）法庭，每年开庭四次。

Game Act：狩猎法案，议会保护贵族狩猎的法令。例如，该法案规定，只有拥有特定财产资格的人才可以射杀鹿、野兔、野鸡、山鹑和兔子。这在当时都属于"狩猎法案"之内的行为。

Inner Temple：英国内殿律师学院，伦敦四所律师学院之一，是学生及法律从业人员居住并被授予执业资格认可的地方。

Aristotle：亚里士多德（公元前 4 世纪），伟大的古希腊哲学家，著有《诗学》《修辞学》《政治学》。从文艺复兴时期到 18 世纪，《诗学》被公认为是文学评论的最高学术权威著作。

Longinus：朗吉努斯（公元 3 世纪），据说是著名文论《论崇高》的作者；特别是在 18 世纪，《论崇高》是论艺术风格特点的权威之作。

Littleton or Coke：托马斯·利特尔顿爵士（1422—1481）和爱德华·科克爵士（1552—1634）是英国法律界权威，因《科克论利特尔顿》而出名，这是科克爵士对利特尔顿《论土地保有权》法律条文的评注。

Demosthenes：德摩斯梯尼（公元前 4 世纪），古希腊演说家。

Tully：即马库斯·图留斯·西塞罗（公元前 1 世纪），古罗马演说家、哲学家和政治家。

the time of the play：比演出提前了几个小时。

New Inn：新客栈，隶属中殿律师学院。

the Rose：玫瑰酒馆，德鲁里街剧院附近的小酒馆，戏剧爱好者的胜地。

British Common：这里的"Common"是一个法律术语，意思是"一个人在其他人的土地或水域中所得的利益"（参见《牛津英语词典》）。

humourists：指异想天开或反复无常的人物（古义）。

Duke of Monmouth：蒙茅斯公爵，查理二世的私生子，以其优雅的举止而闻名。

Tom Mirabell：汤姆·米拉贝尔，在英语剧本里有许多米拉贝尔，例如康格里夫的《如此世道》。斯梯尔使用这个名字，具有嘲笑纨绔子弟的意味。

【参考译文】

旁观者俱乐部

斯梯尔

至少有六个，加入了他们的同盟。

  我要介绍的旁观者俱乐部的第一位成员是伍斯特郡的一位绅士——罗杰·德·科弗利爵士。他的家族历史悠久，血统高贵。他的曾祖父是著名乡村舞蹈的原创者，而那个舞蹈就是以他曾祖父的名字命名的。那个郡所有的人都非常熟悉罗杰爵士的人品和美德。他的行为非常独特怪异。这种独特的行为出自他对事物的判断；只有在他认为不合常规的时候，他的举止才会有悖常理。然而，这并没有使他处处树敌，因为他从未做过任何动机不纯和偏执的事情。而他的不拘世俗，使他更加愿意去帮助他所熟知的人，并想尽办法让他们愉悦。进城时，他住在苏豪广场。他一直单身，据说是因为被邻县一位美丽寡妇的爱情之箭不幸射中了，结果失望而归。在这之前，罗杰爵士堪称绅士的典范。他经常与罗切斯特勋爵和乔治·埃瑟里奇爵士一起品酒，并在第一次进城时，就与人决斗。他还在一家公共咖啡馆教训了一个叫布利·道森的人，这家伙竟敢当众对他不敬，斥责他年少无知。由于受到上面提到的寡妇的虐待，尽管他天性开朗，却变得非常严肃，这样持续了一年半。后来，他终于渡过了这一关，然而却变得不拘小节，从未穿过正式的礼服，依旧穿着他在遭受虐待时期还算时髦的那种外套和西装背心。他颇为幽默地告诉我们，自从他第一次穿上这套服装以来，这一款式已经来来回回流行了十二次。据说，罗杰爵士在忘却了那位冷酷的美人之后，在表达自己意愿时变得越来越谦卑；小道消息说，他经常在有关贞操的问题上得罪乞丐和吉卜赛人；然而，他的朋友们却认为这不过是个玩笑而已，并非事实。他今年五十六岁，性格开朗，热心而阳光，在城镇和乡村都有不错的房子。他与人为善，受人尊敬，但更受人爱戴。他的举止中有一种令人愉悦的气质。他的佃户比较富有，仆人们也很心满意足。年轻的女性对他公开示爱，年轻的男子也喜欢与他一起共事。他每次来访时，总是对仆人以姓名相称，并与他们攀谈，直到上楼走进自己的卧室。值得一提的是，罗杰爵士是少数几位钦定的治安法官；他以自己出色的能力填补了当地季审法庭主席的职位。三个月前，他解释狩猎法案中的一项条款，获得了公众的赞扬。

我们中间另一位备受尊敬的绅士也是个单身汉，他是伦敦内殿律师学院的成员；一位廉洁奉公、聪明睿智、善解人意的人。但是，他在选择自己的居住地时，并没有追求自己的喜好，而是顺从脾气暴躁的老父亲的旨意。他在那里学习当地的土地法，是当时所有学院里最有学问的。他对亚里士多德和朗吉努斯的研究，比对利特尔顿爵士和科克爵士更加深入。他父亲经常给他邮寄一些邻里之间有关婚姻条款、租赁契约和土地使用权的问题，他对这些问题的解答都与律师相同并能一次性处理完毕。他本应当去调查人们由激动的情绪而产生的争论，而他却研究各种激情本身。他熟知德摩斯梯尼和西塞罗演说中的每一个论点，然而却不知我们自己法庭中所报道过的任何一桩案例。没有人会把他当傻瓜；但，除了他的亲密朋友之外，也没有人知道他的雄才大略。他既廉洁奉公又和蔼可亲。他的想法很少来自商业事务，因此大部分只适合于与人交流和谈心。他对书的品味在当时的年代，有点过于认真；他阅书万卷，但很少赞同。他熟知古人的风俗习惯、行为举止和著作，这使他成为一位非常精确的观察家，能把四周的世界观察得细致入微。他是一位出色的文学评论家，看戏的时间就是他工作的时间；在戏剧开演之前，五点整，他走过新客栈，穿过拉塞尔小巷，然后在威尔斯咖啡馆转一圈；当你还在玫瑰小酒馆的时候，他已经让人擦亮了皮鞋，并在理发店里把假发梳了一下。他在剧院看戏，对观众来说是件好事；许多演员都会迫不及待地想要讨好他，演出特别卖力。

下一位我要介绍的是安德鲁·弗里波特爵士，他是伦敦一位地位显赫的商人，一位孜孜不倦、极有理性和经验丰富的商人。他对贸易的观念既高尚又慷慨，他把海洋称为英联邦的领地（每一个有钱人通常都会说些俏皮话，如果没有钱，那么他的俏皮话也就不会有什么影响了）。他熟知商业的各个方面，并会告诉你，用武器和武力扩张统治是一种愚蠢和野蛮的方式；真正的力量来自艺术和工业。他经常与人争辩，说如果我们把这一部分贸易做好，我们将会从这个国家获得利益；如果我们把另一部分贸易做好，我们将会从另一个国家获得利益。我听过他的论证：勤奋比勇敢更能持久地获得财富，懒惰比刀剑更能摧毁国家。他有许多节俭的格言，其中最受欢迎的就是"节省一分钱就等于赚了一分钱"。与一个普通但机智的商人交往，往往比与一个普通学者打交道更加愉快。而安德鲁爵士具有天生的口才，从不受别人的影响，他能言善辩，条理清晰，使人愉悦。他自己发了财，并说大英帝国如果采用了他发财致富的方法，可能现在会比其他国家更加富有。我可以这样说，指南针指向的任何一点，都会有他名下的船只在往回行驶。

在俱乐部的房间里，安德鲁爵士旁边坐着的是森特里上尉，他是一位勇敢、善解人意而又无比谦逊的绅士。他本应得到关注，然而他却不知怎样展示自己的才华去引人注目。他当了几年上尉，在交战和围攻中表现得非常英勇。他拥有一小块房地产，又是罗杰爵士的下一任继承人。于是他放弃了军旅生活，因为在这种生活方式中，没有一个人可以获得与其才华相匹配的职位，除非他既是一名士兵，又擅长吹牛拍马，阿谀奉承。我经常听他哀叹，在这个功勋显赫的职业中，厚颜无耻的骄横要比谦虚更吃得开。每当他谈到这里时，我从来没有听到他的语气中有任何的讥讽，只是坦率地承认，他之所以离开军队，是因为他不适合这种氛围。诚实和循规蹈矩的举止，对他来说都是在排挤同僚、升官晋爵时必须逾越的障碍；而他的同僚也与他一样，竭力想得到指挥官的青睐。然而，他却能谅解军官们不论功行赏和不深查细究的做法。"因为，"他说，"那位想要帮助我的伟人，要费很大的劲才能找到我，就像我要费很大的劲才能找到他一样。"因此，他得出这样一个结论：凡是能成为名人的军人，必须克服一切虚情假意的谦卑，要会为自己辩护来证明自己的清白，并帮助长官排除他人的恶意诽谤。他说，在正当辩护时的退却和让步，如同临阵逃脱或者是进攻缓慢，是一种怯懦。他在谈论自己和谈论别人时都是如此地率真。这种率真贯穿他所有的谈话。他一生中的军旅生涯使他经历了许多冒险，每当谈起这些时，同伴们都很爱听；因为尽管他习惯以最大限度去指挥下级，但从不盛气凌人；尽管他有服从上司的习惯，但从不盲从。

在我们这个俱乐部里，似乎没有异想天开、反复无常的滑稽人物，甚至对时代的英勇气概、风尚和乐趣也不甚了解；然而，在我们中间却有一位风流倜傥的绅士——威尔·霍尼康姆。这位绅士年事已高，他举止非常检点，保养得很好，而且常常走好运。时间对他并没有多大的影响，既没有在他的额头上留下多少皱纹，也没有在他脑海中留下任何痕迹。他身材很好，个头高大。对男人们讨好女人的各种甜言蜜语，他都在行，记得滚瓜烂熟。他一生穿着讲究，并能记住其他人的穿着。与他说话时，他面带笑容，并常常发出爽朗的笑声。他熟知各种时尚，可以告诉你，英国太太、小姐们烫的鬈发和所戴兜帽的式样是从哪一位法国国王的情妇那里学来的；他还可以告诉你，哪位女士为了遮羞而设计了内裙，哪位女士哪年为了展示她的美脚而设计了短裙。总之，他所有的谈话和知识都离不开女性。与他同龄的男子，常常会关注政府首脑们在各种场合的演讲，而他所关注的则是蒙茅斯公爵在宫廷跳舞时，某位女子为之倾心；蒙茅斯公爵与他的随从在海德公园露面时，与某位女子一见钟情。在所有这些重要的关系中，他可以同时接受名流美女亲切的一瞥或一扇清风的吹拂；当时，某某爵士的母亲就是其中的一位。如果你提到某个年轻的下议员在议会里精彩的演讲，他就会说："他是个好种，是汤姆·米拉贝尔的后裔，那个流氓把我给坑苦了。他的母亲比其他女人更加厉害，把我折磨得连狗都不如！"他这样的说话方式，就像剧情急剧大转弯，使我们的谈话变得有声有色。我发现在这种场合除了我一人很少说话，没有人不认为他是那种通常所称的有教养的绅士。至于他的性格，只要不谈女人，他还是一位诚实的、很有气质的绅士。

我不知道下一位我将要介绍的是否能算得上我们俱乐部的一员，因为他很少光顾我们的俱乐部。然而，每当他光顾时，都为我们每个人增添了新的快乐。他是一位牧师，具有哲学家的风范，学识渊博，心地纯洁，教养极好。不幸的是，他的身体太虚弱了，无法承受升职后所要承担的繁重事务；因此他在神职人员中的地位就像律师职业中律师协会的高级顾问一样。有人靠口才扬名于世，而他，却只有清廉和正直，但他依然成为人们效仿的对象。他很少向别人介绍他演讲的主题。多年以来，他发现每当和我们在一起的时候，我们都会诚心诚意地希望他能讲解一些宗教上的问题，在这方面他很有权威，谈起来头头是道；他对这个世界早已无牵无挂，一心只想尽快地完成他的使命，从他衰老和虚弱的身体里得到永生。这些，就是我的工作伙伴。

Sir Roger de Coverley at Home

Joseph Addison

Hinc tibi copia

Manabit ad plenum benigno

Ruris honorum opulenta cornu.

Having often received an invitation from my friend Sir Roger de Coverley to pass away a month with him in the country, I last week accompanied him thither, and am settled with him for some time at his country-house, where I intend to form several of my ensuing speculations. Sir Roger, who is very well acquainted with my **humour**, lets me rise and go to bed when I please, dine at his own table or in my chamber as I think fit, sit still and say nothing without bidding me be merry. When the gentlemen of the country come to see him, he only shows me at a distance. As I have been walking in his fields, I have observed them stealing a sight of me over a hedge, and have heard the knight desiring them not to let me see them, for that I hated to be stared at.

I am the more at ease in Sir Roger's family because it consists of sober and staid persons; for as the knight is the best master in the world, he seldom changes his servants; and as he is beloved by all about him, his servants never care for leaving him. By this means his domestics are all in years, and grown old with their master. You would take his **valet de chambre** for his brother, his butler is gray-headed, his groom is one of the gravest men that I have ever seen, and his coachman has the looks of a privy-counsellor. You see the goodness of the master even in the old house-dog, and in a gray pad that is kept in the stable with great care and tenderness out of regard to his past services, though he has been useless for several years.

I could not but observe with a great deal of pleasure the joy that appeared in the countenances of these ancient domestics upon my friend's arrival at his country-seat. Some of them could not refrain from tears at the sight of their old master; every one of them pressed forward to do something for him, and seemed discouraged if they were not employed. At the same time the good old knight, with a mixture of the father and the master of the family, tempered the inquiries after his own affairs with several kind questions relating to themselves. This humanity and good nature engages everybody to him, so that when he is **pleasant** upon any of them, all his family are in good humour, and none so much as the person whom he diverts himself with. On the contrary, if he coughs, or betrays any infirmity of old age, it is easy for a stander-by to observe a secret concern in the looks of all his servants.

My worthy friend has put me under the particular care of his butler, who is a very prudent man, and, as well as the rest of his fellow-servants, wonderfully desirous of pleasing me, because they have often heard their master talk of me as of his particular friend.

My chief companion, when Sir Roger is diverting himself in the woods or the fields, is a very venerable man who is ever with Sir Roger, and has lived at his house **in the nature of a chaplain** above thirty years. This gentleman is a person of good sense and some learning, of a very regular life and obliging conversation. He heartily loves Sir Roger, and knows that he is very much in the old knight's esteem, so that he lives in the family rather as a relation than a dependant.

I have observed in several of my papers that my friend Sir Roger, amidst all his good qualities, is something of a humourist, and that his virtues, as well as imperfections, are as it were tinged by a certain extravagance, which makes them particularly his and distinguishes them from those of other men. This cast of mind, as it is generally very innocent in itself, so it renders his conversation highly agreeable, and more delightful than the same degree of sense and virtue would appear in their common and ordinary colours. As I was walking with him last night, he asked me how I liked the good man whom I have just now mentioned, and without staying for my answer, told me that he was afraid of being insulted with Latin and Greek at his own table; for which reason, he desired a particular friend of his at the university to find him out a clergyman rather of plain sense than much learning, of a good aspect, a clear voice, a sociable temper, and if possible, a man that understood a little of **backgammon**. 'My friend,' says Sir Roger, 'found me out this gentleman, who, besides the endowments required of him, is, they tell me, a good scholar, though he does not show it. I have given him the parsonage of the parish; and, because I know his value, have

settled upon him a good annuity for life. If he outlives me, he shall
find that he was higher in my esteem than perhaps he thinks he is.
He has now been with me thirty years; and, though he does not know
I have taken notice of it, has never in all that time asked anything of
me for himself, though he is every day soliciting me for something
in behalf of one or other of my tenants his parishioners. There has
not been a lawsuit in the parish since he has lived among them. If
any dispute arises, they apply themselves to him for the decision; if
they do not acquiesce in his judgment, which I think never happened
above once, or twice at most, they appeal to me. At his first settling
with me, I made him a present of all the good sermons which have
been printed in English, and only begged of him that every Sunday
he would pronounce one of them in the pulpit. Accordingly, he
has digested them into such a series that they follow one another
naturally, and make a continued system of practical divinity.'

As Sir Roger was going on in his story, the gentleman we were
talking of came up to us; and upon the knight's asking him who
preached to-morrow (for it was Saturday night) told us the **Bishop
of St. Asaph** in the morning and Dr. South in the afternoon. He then
showed us his list of preachers for the whole year, where I saw with a
great deal of pleasure Archbishop Tillotson, Bishop Saunderson, Dr.
Barrow, Dr. Calamy, with several living authors who have published
discourses of practical divinity. I no sooner saw this venerable man in
the pulpit but I very much approved of my friend's insisting upon the
qualifications of a good aspect and a clear voice; for I was so charmed
with the gracefulness of his figure and delivery, as well as with the
discourses he pronounced, that I think I never passed any time more

to my satisfaction. A sermon repeated after this manner is like the composition of a poet in the mouth of a graceful actor.

I could heartily wish that more of our country clergy would follow this example, and, instead of wasting their spirits in laborious compositions of their own, would endeavour after a **handsome** elocution and all those other **talents** that are proper to enforce what has been penned by greater masters. This would not only be more easy to themselves, but more edifying to the people.

Notes

From the *Spectator*, No. 106 (July 2, 1711).
Motto from Horace, *Odes*, I, xvii, 14:
    'Here Plenty's liberal horn shall pour
    Of fruits for thee a copious show'r,
    Rich honours of the quiet plain.'

humour, in the old sense of the word, temperament.
valet de chambre (French), a personal attendant.
pleasant, in a humourous or joking mood.
in the nature of a chaplain. Bishop Hurd remarks: 'The word "nature" is used here a little licentiously. He should have said "in the office" of a chaplain.' In modern usage we should rather say, 'in the *character* or *capacity* of a chaplain.'
backgammon, a favourite card game of the 18th century.
Bishop of St. Asaph, etc. The Bishop of St. Asaph may mean Beveridge, whose sermons were published in 1708; or Dr. William Fleetwood (1656—

1723), Beveridge's successor. Dr. Bobert South (1634—1716) was a high Churchman and a Tory, famous for wit and eloquence. Dr. John Tillotson (1630—1694) was the 'great and good' Archbishop of Canterbury. His sermons, which have been heavy reading, were greatly admired. Dr. Robert Saunderson (1587—1663) was Bishop of Lincoln at the Restoration. Dr. Isaac Barrow (1630—1677) attained his eminence at Cambridge both as a mathematician and theologian. For five years before his death he was Proctor of Trinity College. Dr. Edmund Calamy was one of the leading Presbyterian ministers under the Commonwealth.

handsome, suitable.

talents, acquired abilities.

【作品简介】

本文选自《旁观者》第 106 期（1711 年 7 月 2 日）。

篇首格言出自贺拉斯的《歌集》第一卷：“这里有充裕的自由号角／为你带来了丰硕的果实／为这宁静的朴实无华，带来了丰富的荣耀。”

【作品解析】

humour：气质、禀性（古义）。

valet de chambre（法语）：家庭雇佣。

pleasant：愉快、幽默或者开玩笑的状态。

in the nature of a chaplain：赫德主教评论说：“‘本性’（nature）一词用在这里有点放肆。他应该说‘在职的’牧师。现代用法通常说‘以牧师的身份’。”

backgammon：西洋双陆棋，18 世纪最受欢迎的纸牌游戏。

Bishop of St. Asaph, etc.：此段中，圣·阿萨夫主教或许是指贝弗里奇，他的布道文发表于 1708 年；或许是指威廉·弗利特伍德博士（1656—1723），贝弗里奇的继任者。罗伯特·索斯博士（1634—1716）是一位权高位重的教会牧师和托利党人，以机智和雄辩的口才著称。约翰·蒂洛森博士（1630—1694）是坎特伯雷"伟大而善良"的大主教。他的布道广受好评，深受人们的赞赏。罗伯特·桑德森博士（1587—1663）是复辟时期林肯郡的主教。伊萨克·巴罗博士（1630—1677）在剑桥大学获得了他杰出数学家和神学家的声望。他去世前的五年里，曾任三一学院的院长。埃德蒙·卡拉米博士是英联邦领导下的长老会主要牧师之一。

handsome：恰到好处。

talents：后天能力。

【参考译文】

<h1 style="text-align:center">家中的罗杰爵士</h1>

艾迪生

这里有充裕的自由号角，

为你带来了丰硕的果实，

为这宁静的朴实无华，带来了丰富的荣耀。

我经常接到朋友罗杰爵士的邀请，让我去他乡下家里住上一个月。我上周动身，下榻在他的乡间别墅。我打算在他乡下的别墅里和他住上一段时间，好在那里对即将发生的事情做一番揣测。罗杰爵士深知我的秉性，让我起居随意，只要我喜欢，就可以随自己的意愿选择同他一起用餐，或在自己的房间里用餐。我可以整天坐在那里不用做任何事情，也不用说任何话。他以祝愿我玩得高兴。当乡间的绅士来拜访他时，他只是远远地把我介绍给他们。在庄园里散步时，我注意到有人远远地透过树篱，偷偷地窥视我，并听到爵士提醒他们不要让我发现，因为我不喜欢被旁人盯着瞧。

住在罗杰爵士家里，我很舒服。那里的人都很讲道理，而且做事也很稳重。罗杰爵士是世界上最好的主人，很少解雇仆人；因此，他深受人们的爱戴，他的仆人也从未想过要离开他。这意味着他家所有的仆人都已雇用多年，并且和他们的主人一起在变老。你会以为他的贴身男仆是他的兄弟，他的管家头发已灰白，他的马夫是我见到过最严肃的人，他的车夫看上去一副英国枢密院官员的模样。即便是在老家犬的身上，你也能看到主人的善良，尽管这条犬已经有好几年没能看家护院了，顾及它以往的服务，主人仍然把它豢养在马厩里并为它安置了一块灰色的垫子，非常小心和精心地照料着。

令我高兴的是，我发现在我的朋友回到乡间别墅时，这些老仆人对他表达出了极大的喜悦，有的甚至流下了激动的泪水。每个人都争先恐后想为主人做点什么，而那些没有被叫到的仆人似乎有点失望。与此同时，善良的罗杰爵士以主人和父亲的口吻，向仆人询问了一些有关商务和家务方面的事情。这种善良的性格扣住了每个人的心弦。因此，只要他高兴，整个庄园都会为之而高兴；没有人会因此而有什么其他的想法。同样，如果他咳嗽了，或者是由于年老体弱而感到不适，一个旁观者很容易从在场每一个仆人的表情中，清楚地看到他们内心流露出的一丝不安和担忧。

我这位德高望重的朋友把我托付给了男管家，要他特别地照顾我。男管家是一个事事谨慎的人。他与其他仆人一样，处处讨我欢喜，因为他们经常听到主人说，我是他的贵客。

当罗杰爵士在树林或乡间散步时，主要陪伴着我的是一位尊敬的长者。他以牧师的身份一直与罗杰爵士住在一起，大约已有三十多年了。这位先生性格很好，而且学有所长。他生活得很有规律，而且和蔼可亲，善于交谈。他打心眼里喜欢罗杰爵士，也知道这位老爵士对自己很尊重。罗杰爵士把这位牧师当作家庭中的一员，而不仅仅是来串串门的亲朋好友。

我曾经在多篇文章里提到，我的朋友罗杰爵士除了具有上述各种优点外，还带有一点幽默的气质，他的这些美德以及他的不完美之处，似乎沾染了某种奢侈气质，将他与其他人区分开来。他的这种美德非常纯洁，因此与他交谈的过程非常愉快；即便具有他这种美德的人也未必会有如此令人愉悦的效果。昨晚我和罗杰爵士一起散步时，他问我是否喜欢我刚刚提到的那位好人。还没等我回答，罗杰爵士就告诉我，他害怕在自己的饭桌上出拉丁文和希腊文的洋相。于是，他就拜托了一位关系特别好的朋友在大学里物色一位牧师，不要求他有多少学问，但要相貌端正，声音清晰，善于交际，最好还懂一点双陆棋。"我的朋友，"罗杰爵士说，"帮我找到了这位绅士。他们告诉我，除了满足上述的要求之外，他还是一位很好的学者，尽管他并不显露自己的学问。我把教区的牧师职位给了他；因为我知道他的能力，并给了他相当不错的终身年俸。如果他的寿命比我长，他就会发现，我比他想象的更加尊重他。我们在一起已经三十年了；这些年来，他每天都在为教区的居民奔走，代表教区的居民向我提出各种诉求，但从未为自己提出过任何要求。他以为我不知道，其实我已经注意到了这一点。自从他来了以后，教区从未有过任何法律方面的诉讼案件。如果发生争议，他们首先向他申诉；如果对他的裁决有异议，再向我申诉，这种情况最多发生过两次。在他第一次和我确定做教区牧师时，我就把所有英文版的优秀布道文献作为礼物赠送给了他，要求他每个星期天从中选一篇，在教堂讲台上布道。按照我的要求，他将我送给他的所有的布道文献融会贯通，并把每篇布道文有机地联系在了一起，制定了一个适合于本教区的神学体系。"

正当罗杰爵士和我闲聊时，我们谈到的那位先生向我们走了过来。罗杰爵士问他这个星期天谁来布道，他告诉我们早上是圣·阿萨夫主教，下午是索斯博士。他又向我们展示了全年布道牧师的名单，我非常高兴地看到其中有：蒂洛森主教、桑德森主教、巴罗博士、卡拉米博士以及几位发表过神学论文的当代作者。我刚在讲坛上见到这位令人尊敬的先生，现在我非常理解我的朋友为什么要坚持相貌端正和声音清晰这两条标准；因为我被他完美的身材、温文尔雅的举止和交谈时的语音语调迷住了。似乎我还从来没有对任何人这样满意过，他以这种方式布道就像优雅的演员在颂诗。

我衷心地希望所有的神职人员也都能像他这样，不要把精力浪费在他们自己苦思冥想的创作上，而是要在恰到好处的演说和演讲技巧以及其他习得的能力上下功夫，以此来传播和发扬光大伟大人物所撰写的精华。这不仅能使自己更加容易布道，而且也有利于开启人们的心灵。

The Vision of Mirzah

Joseph Addison

—Omnem, quae nunc obducta tuenti
Mortales hebetat visus tibi, et humida circum
Caligat, nubem eripiam—

When I was at Grand Cairo, I picked up several oriental manuscripts, which I have still by me. Among others I met with one, entitled *The Visions of Mirzah*, which I have read over with great pleasure. I intend to give it to the public when I have no other entertainment for them; and shall begin with the first vision, which I have translated word for word as follows:

'On the fifth day of the moon, which according to the custom of my forefathers I always keep holy, after having washed myself and offered up my morning devotions, I ascended the high hills of **Bagdad**, in order to pass the rest of the day in meditation and prayer. As I was here airing myself on the tops of the mountains, I fell into a profound contemplation on the vanity of human life; and passing from one thought to another, "surely," said I, "**man is** but a shadow, and life a dream." Whilst I was thus musing, I cast my eyes towards the summit of a rock that was not far from me, where I discovered one in the habit of a shepherd, with a little musical instrument in his hand. As I looked upon him he applied it to his lips, and began to play upon it. The sound of it was exceeding sweet, and wrought into a variety of tunes that were inexpressibly melodious, and altogether different from anything I had ever heard. They put me in mind of those heavenly airs that are played to the departed souls of good men upon their first arrival in Paradise, to wear out the impressions of the last agonies, and qualify them for the pleasures of that happy place. My heart melted away in secret raptures.

'I had been often told that the rock before me was the haunt of a **Genius**; and that several had been entertained with music who had passed by it, but never heard that the musician had before made himself visible. When he had raised my thoughts by those transporting airs which he played to taste the pleasures of his conversation, as I looked upon him like one astonished, he beckoned to me, and by the waving of his hand directed me to approach the place where he sat. I drew near with that reverence which is due to a superior nature; and as my heart was entirely subdued by the captivating strains I had heard, I fell down at his feet and wept. The Genius smiled upon me with a look of compassion and affability that familiarized him to my imagination, and at once dispelled all the fears and apprehensions with which I approached him. He lifted me from the ground, and taking me by the hand, "Mirzah," said he, "I have heard thee in thy soliloquies; follow me."

'He then led me to the highest pinnacle of the rock, and placing me on the top of it, "Cast thy eyes eastward," said he, "and tell me what thou seest." "I see," said I, "a huge valley, and a prodigious tide of water rolling through it." "The valley that thou seest," said he, "is the Vale of Misery, and the tide of water that thou seest is part of the great Tide of Eternity." "What is the reason," said I, "that the tide I see rises out of a thick mist at one end, and again loses itself in a thick mist at the other?" "What thou seest," said he, "is that portion of eternity which is called time, measured out by the sun, and reaching from the beginning of the world to its consummation. Examine now," said he, "this sea that is thus bounded with darkness at both ends, and tell me what thou discoverest in it." "I see a **bridge**," said I, "standing in the midst of the tide." "The bridge thou seest," said he, "is human life; consider it attentively." Upon a more leisurely survey of it, I found that it consisted of **threescore and ten** entire arches, with several broken arches, which, added to those that were entire, made up the number about a hundred. As I was counting the arches, the Genius told me that this bridge consisted at first of a thousand arches; but that a great flood swept away the rest, and left the bridge in the ruinous condition I now beheld it. "But tell me further," said he, "what thou discoverest on it." "I see multitudes of people passing over it," said I, "and a black cloud hanging on each end of it." As I looked more attentively, I saw several of the passengers dropping through the bridge into the great tide that flowed underneath it; and upon further examination, perceived there were innumerable trap-doors that lay concealed in the bridge, which the passengers no sooner trod upon but they fell through them into the tide and immediately disappeared. These hidden pit-falls were set very thick at the entrance of the bridge, so that throngs of people no sooner broke through the cloud but many of them fell into them. They grew thinner towards the middle, but multiplied and lay closer together towards the end of the arches that were entire.

'There were indeed some persons, but their number was very small, that continued a kind of hobbling march on the broken arches, but fell through one after another, being quite tired and spent with so long a walk.

'I passed some time in the contemplation of this wonderful structure and the great variety of objects which it presented. My heart was filled with a deep melancholy to see several dropping unexpectedly in the midst of mirth and jollity, and catching at everything that stood by them to save themselves. Some were looking up towards the heavens in a thoughtful posture, and in the midst of a speculation stumbled and fell out of sight. Multitudes were very busy in the pursuit of bubbles that glittered in their eyes and danced before them; but often when they thought themselves within the reach of them, their footing failed and down they sunk. In this confusion of objects, I observed some with **scimitars** in their hands, and others with **urinals**, who ran to and fro upon the bridge, thrusting several persons on trap-doors which did not seem to lie in their way, and which they might have escaped had they not been thus forced upon them.

'The Genius, seeing me indulge myself on this melancholy prospect, told me I had dwelt long enough upon it. "Take thine eyes off the bridge," said he, "and tell me if thou yet seest anything thou dost not comprehend." Upon looking up, "What mean," said I, "those great flights of birds that are perpetually hovering about the bridge, and settling upon it from time to time? I see vultures, harpies, ravens, cormorants; and among many other feathered creatures several little winged boys, that perch in great numbers upon the middle arches." "These," said the Genius, "are Envy, Avarice, Superstition, Despair, Love, with the like cares and passions that infest human life."

'I here fetched a deep sigh. "Alas," said I, "Man was made **in vain**! How is he given away to misery and mortality, tortured in life, and swallowed up in death!" The Genius, being moved with compassion towards me, bid me quit so uncomfortable a prospect. "Look no more," said he, "on man in the first stage of his existence, in his setting out for eternity; but cast thine eye on that thick mist into which the tide bears the several generations of mortals that fall into it." I directed my sight as I was ordered, and (whether or no the good Genius strengthened it with any supernatural force, or dissipated part of the mist that was before too thick for the eye to penetrate) I saw the valley opening at the further end, and spreading forth into an immense ocean, that had a huge rock of adamant running through the midst of it, and dividing it into two equal parts. The clouds still rested on one half of it, insomuch that I could discover nothing in it; but the other appeared to me a vast ocean planted with innumerable islands, that were covered with fruits and flowers, and interwoven with a thousand little shining seas that ran among them. I could see persons dressed in glorious habits, with garlands upon their heads, passing among the trees, lying down by the sides of fountains, or resting on beds of flowers; and could hear a confused harmony of singing birds, falling waters, human voices, and musical instruments.

Gladness grew in me upon the discovery of so delightful a scene. I wished for the wings of an eagle, that I might fly away to those happy seats; but the Genius told me there was no passage to them, except through the gates of death that I saw opening every moment upon the bridge. "The islands," said he, "that lie so fresh and green before thee, and with which the whole face of the ocean appears spotted as far as thou canst see, are more in number than the sands on the seashore; there are myriads of islands behind those which thou here discoverest, reaching further than thine eye or even thine imagination can extend itself. These are the **mansions** of good men after death, who, according to the degree and kinds of virtue in which they excelled, are distributed among these several islands, which abound with pleasures of different kinds and degrees, suitable to the relishes and perfections of those who are settled in them; every island is a Paradise accommodated to its respective inhabitants. Are not these, O Mirzah, habitations worth contending for? Does life appear miserable that gives thee opportunities of earning such a reward? Is death to be feared that will convey thee to so happy an existence? Think not man was made in vain, who has such an eternity reserved for him." I gazed with inexpressible pleasure on these happy islands. At length, said I, "show me now, I beseech thee, the secrets that lie hid under those dark clouds which cover the ocean on the other side of the rock of adamant." The Genius making me no answer, I turned about to address myself to him a second time, but I found that he had left me; I then turned again to the vision which I had been so long contemplating; but instead of the rolling tide, the arched bridge, and the happy islands, I saw nothing but the long hollow valley of

Bagdad, with oxen, sheep, and camels grazing upon the sides of it.'

Notes

From the *Spectator*, No. 159 (September 1, 1711). This is an example of
the narrative essay revealing the vogue of the Oriental tale in England—
a vogue which came with the *Arabian Nights' Entertainment* in the early 18th
century. The '*Oriental manuscript*' here mentioned is a piece of fiction. But
throughout the essay Addison has attempted to retain the flavour of a
translation and the solemn mood that fits the subject. This device appears
frequently in literature, as for example in Charles Lamb's 'Dissertation
upon Roast Pig.'

    Motto, from Virgil, *The Aeneid*, II, 604—606:

    'The cloud, which, intercepting the clear light,

    Hangs o'er thy eyes, and blunts thy mortal sight,

    I will remove.'

    Bagdad, a city in Turkey which figures prominently in the *Arabian Nights'*
Entertainment.

    man is, etc. A familiar conception of life. Compare *I Chronicles*, xxix,
15: 'Our days on the earth are as a shadow, and there is none abiding.'
See also Shakespeare, *The Tempest*, IV, i, 156—158:

    'We are such stuff

    As dreams are made on, and our little life

    Is rounded with a sleep.'

    Genius, one of the spirits of the air, frequently referred to in the *Arabian*
Nights' Entertainment and other oriental literature.

bridge. The representation of life as a bridge over which all must pass appears frequently in mediaeval woodcuts.

threescore and ten, the 'psalmist's span of life.' Compare *Psalms,* xc, 10: 'The days of our years are threescore years and ten; and if by reason of strength they be fourscore years, yet is their strength labour and sorrow; for it is soon cut off, and we fly away.'

scimitars and urinals. Scimitars suggest war; and urinals, the physician's test-tubes, suggest disease.

in vain. 'Vanity of vanities. Saith the Preacher, vanity of vanities; all is vanity.' (*Ecclesiastes,* i, 2).

mansions. 'In my Father's house are many mansions.' (*St. John,* xiv, 2).

【作品简介】

本文选自《旁观者》第 159 期（1711 年 9 月 1 日）。这是叙述性散文中的一个范例，它揭示了当时东方故事在英国的风靡，伴随着 18 世纪早期《天方夜谭》的流行而来。这里提到的"东方手稿"是一个虚构的故事。但在整篇文章中，艾迪生试图保留原文的风格和适合主题的庄重，这种风格在文学作品中比比皆是，例如查尔斯·兰姆的《论烤猪》。

篇首格言出自维吉尔的《埃涅阿斯纪》第二卷："云雾，遮住了明亮的光线／悬挂在你的眼帘，使你凡人的视觉变得愚钝／我要将迷雾拨开。"

【作品解析】

Bagdad：巴格达是土耳其的一座城市（今天的伊拉克历史上曾为土耳其人的奥斯曼帝国所统治——译者注），该城市在《天方夜谭》一书中占有显要地位。

man is, etc.：此句表达了一种常见的人生观。参见《历代志·上》第 29 章："地球上的日子如同影子一般，无人可以永存。"也可参见莎士比亚的《暴风雨》

第4场："我们就是睡梦中的填充物，我们小小的人生，被睡梦环绕着。"

Genius：在《天方夜谭》和其他东方文学作品中常常提到的气态神灵。

bridge：在中世纪的木刻作品中，经常将所有人的生命表现为必须跨越的桥梁。

threescore and ten：即"《诗篇》中所说的人生"。参见《诗篇》："我们的生命大约七十岁；如果有能量可以活到八十岁，但能量却是劳苦和悲伤，那么我们不久将会了断人生，自由地飞翔。"

scimitars and urinals：弯刀暗示着战争，便壶、医用试管暗示着疾病。

in vain："虚空的虚空。传道者说，虚空的虚空；一切皆是虚空。"（《传道书》，第1章）

mansions："在我父亲家里有许多住处。"（《圣约翰》，第14章）

【参考译文】

米尔扎的憧憬

艾迪生

> 云雾，遮住了明亮的光线，
> 悬挂在你的眼帘，使你凡人的视觉变得愚钝，
> 我要将迷雾拨开。

在埃及大开罗，我收集了几本东方文字的手稿，现在仍保存在我这里。其中有一本叫作《米尔扎的憧憬》，我很有兴趣地读完了这本手稿。我想把它介绍给大家，作为茶余饭后的娱乐。下面我就从第一篇开始，逐字逐句地翻译如下：

　　每个月初始的第五天，按照祖先的习俗，我得保持圣洁。早上一起来，我便净了身并做了祷告，然后，登上巴格达的山顶，将在冥想和祷告中度过余下的一天。我顶着风站在山顶上，陷入了深思，深深地感到人生的空虚，脑海中闪现出了各种念头。我自言自语道："天哪！人如同影子一般，而人生不过就是一场梦而已！"我正在沉思，发现离我不远的一块岩石上有位牧羊人，手里拿着一件小乐器。我看着他，他正把乐器放在嘴唇边，开始吹奏起来。吹奏的曲调异常甜美，而且各种音调配合得如此协调、如此完美，与我所听到过的任何曲调都截然不同。这是天籁之音！是那些好人们的灵魂在离开他们的躯体升入天堂时，所能听到的天籁之音；是帮助他们解除最后的痛苦，走向极乐世界，让他们在这块幸福之地获得永生时的天籁之音。我的心，在暗自狂喜中融化了。

　　我听说，眼前的岩石经常会有精灵出现；甚至有些路过那里的人，听到过音乐，但从来没有听说过哪位音乐家曾经现过身。他那优美的音乐旋律激发了我的思绪，让我体会到了与他对话的乐趣。我看着他，目瞪口呆。他向我招招手，示意我走近他坐的地方。当我怀着敬仰之情走近这位精灵时，我的心完全被那优美的音乐征服了，我拜倒在他的脚下，激动得热泪盈眶，泪流满面。这位精灵带着慈善和亲切和蔼的表情向我微笑；与我想象的完全一样，他的微笑立刻打消了我的不安。他把我从地上扶了起来，牵着我的手说："米尔扎，我刚刚听到了你的独白，请跟我来。"

　　他把我领到岩石的最高峰，让我坐下。"现在你向东望，"然后他说，"告诉我，你看到了什么？""我看到一个大山谷，山谷中间有一条汹涌澎湃的大河。"我说。"你看到的山谷是苦难之谷，你看到的大河是永恒之河的一条支流。"他向我解释道。"那么为什么大河的一端从浓雾中升起，而另一端又消失在浓雾之中呢？"我又追问道。"你看到的，"他说，"仅仅是永恒之河中的一部分，称为时间。它是通过日出日落来测量的，从世界开端的初民时期起，将会一直延续到世界末日。"他说："现在你再看看那片处于黑暗之中的大海，请告诉我，你在海上发现了什么？""我看见中间有一座大桥，"我说，"屹立在潮水之中。""你看到的桥梁就是人生，你再仔细看看。"他又说道。我又仔细地看了一遍，发现大桥有七十个完整的拱门和一些破损的拱门，大约共有一百来个拱门。在我数拱门的时候，精灵告诉我，这座桥最初是由一千个拱门组成的；后来由于遭受了一场巨大的洪水，被冲走了其余的部分，桥梁处于毁灭性的状态，变成了现在我所看见的样子。"请再告诉我，"精灵问道，"你还发现了什么？"我说："我看到许多人从桥上走过，而且大桥的两端都笼罩着乌云。"我再仔细看时，还发现有些人从桥上跌了下去，被汹涌的波涛和奔腾不息的激流所吞噬。我还注意到大桥上有无数个暗藏的陷阱，一旦陷了进去，就会落入海里，立即消失。这些暗藏的陷阱密布在大桥的入口；因此，许多人刚穿过云雾，就很快落入了陷阱。大桥中间陷阱少了一些，然而当快靠近完好无损的拱门的尽头时，陷阱又多了起来，而且一个接着一个。

有少数人在破损的拱门上步履蹒跚佝偻着腰前进。由于走了很长的时间，他们相当疲惫，最后，仍然一个接着一个不断地掉进陷阱，坠入大海。

我注视着眼前大桥的精巧结构以及它所呈现的各种与之有关的景象，陷入了沉思。看见那些还在欢乐中就失足而丧生的人，看见那些为了生存而拼命抓住身边任何一根救命稻草来拯救自己的人，我心里充满了伤感。有的人正在仰望着天空，若有所思，蹒跚而行就落入了水中，消失在我们的面前。人们常常为了追求在他们眼前闪闪发光的东西，在漫天飞舞的气泡中，疲于奔命；就在眼看快要唾手可得的时候，却失了足，落了水，丧失了性命。在混乱的人群中，我看到有些人手中拿着象征着战争的弯刀，或者象征着疾病的便壶，在桥上来回奔跑，把那些并不妨碍他们征程的行人推进陷阱；而那些人如果不是硬被推进陷阱，其实也是可以逃脱的。

精灵看我沉浸在伤感之中，告诉我已经待了太长的时间了。他说："够了，别再看大桥了，把你的眼睛从大桥上移开，告诉我，你还有什么地方不懂的？"我抬起头，最后看了一眼，问道："那些一直在桥上徘徊，时而盘旋，时而停下来休息的鸟类，又是怎么回事呢？"我看到了秃鹰、哈比鸟（女人面相的鸟）、乌鸦、鸱鹅等等。在它们中间，除了许多羽翼丰满的鸟儿之外，还有刚刚长出翅膀的小雏鸟，大量栖息在中间的拱门上。"这些，"精灵说，"就是嫉妒、贪婪、迷信、绝望、爱情以及影响整个人类生活的牵挂和激情。"

此时，我深深地叹了一口气，说："人都是虚空，注定要饱受苦难和死亡的折磨！活着的时候要遭受折磨，最终还是要被死亡所吞噬！"精灵对我产生了怜悯之心，要我不必这样想下去。"不要再去想了，"他说，"这是人生的最初阶段，是迈向永恒的第一步。你看水上飘着的那团浓雾，你知道里面承载着从古到今多少代凡人的生命吗？"我按照他指引的方向看了过去，也许是精灵具有超自然的力量增强了我的视力，也许是他驱散了之前挡住我视线的浓雾，我看到了山谷一直延伸到了浩瀚的大海，大海中间有一块巨大而坚硬的岩石，将其分成两个相等的部分。其中一部分仍然有云雾，我看不见里面。另一部分却是一片广阔的海洋，海洋里有无数的岛屿，岛上遍地是水果和鲜花，并与数千个闪闪发光的小海域交织在了一起。我看到人们穿着漂亮，头上戴着花环，或在树丛中行走，或躺在喷泉旁边，或在花坛中休息；我还能模糊地听见鸟儿的歌声、瀑布的水流声、人们的交谈声以及乐器弹奏的优美旋律，各种声音交织在了一起，简直就是一首交响曲！看到这番景象后，我的心情也渐渐地愉悦了起来。我真希望我是一只带有翅膀的鹰，可以立刻飞到幸福的彼岸。然而，精灵告诉我，除了我在桥上每时每刻看到的打开的死亡之门之外，再也没有别的通道。"你所看见的那些清新而翠绿的岛屿，那些点缀大海的岛屿，实际上比海滩上的沙粒还多。岛屿的种类也比你发现的要多，甚至超出了你的想象。这些都是善良的人们死后的宅邸，上苍根据他们所突出的美德的程度和种类，把他们安排在不同的岛屿。岛上充满了各种欢乐，适合岛上的居民生活和享受。每个岛屿都是天堂的一部分，是专门为各种不同的居民设置的。想想吧，米尔扎！有这样的住所难道还不心满意足吗？生命给你创造了这么好的机会，生活是否还会感到痛苦？死亡可以把你变得如此幸福，死亡是否还会令你感到可怕？不要以为人生是虚空的，人生的最后，会获得如此般的永生。"凝视着远方那些幸福的岛屿，我有一种无法言语的喜悦。过了好一会儿，我又问道："我恳请您告诉我，笼罩在岩石另一边海洋上的乌云的秘密是什么？"精灵没有回答。当我转过身来，第二次问他时，才发现他已经离开了我。于是我又回转过身，想再看看那个令我沉思冥想的憧憬；然而，奔腾的大海、筑有拱门的大桥和幸福的岛屿，全都消失了。在我眼前的只有巴格达那又长又凹的山谷，正在山谷两侧吃草并嬉耍的牛、羊和骆驼。

JONATHAN SWIFT (1667—1745)

Jonathan Swift (1667—1745) was born in Dublin of English parents and brought up in extreme poverty. He was educated in Trinity College, Dublin, where he obtained his degree by 'special grace.' In 1689 he entered the household of Sir William Temple, in Surrey, as secretary to the Whig diplomat. There he had access to a well-stocked library and became a close student of classics. He left his service in 1694, took orders in the Church of Ireland, and became Vicar of Laracor in 1699. He made frequent visits to London, and wrote political pamphlets, first for the Whigs, then for the Tories. All this was to end in bitter disappointment. He had hoped for a bishopric, but this high honour was denied him. He had to pocket his pride and accept the deanery of St. Patrick's, Dublin, in 1713. A victim of misanthropy, he became almost insane in his last years.

Swift was called by one of his contemporaries 'the unhappiest man that ever lived.' By nature and temperament, he was perhaps destined to lead a life of misery. He defined happiness as 'a perpetual possession of being well deceived,' and as 'the serene peaceful state of being a fool among knaves.' Refusing to be deceived and scorning to play the fool among knaves, he devoted his colossal genius for satire to the exposing of fools and the lashing of knaves. His representative works are representative works of satire in the English language: *A Tale of a Tub* (1704) is a fierce attack on religious controversies and hypocrisy, and *Gulliver's Travels* (1726) a bitter exposure of the weaknesses of mankind. He was, however, not incapable of tenderness and playful humour, which found expression in his *Journal to Stella* (1710—1713), a series of intimate letters to Esther Johnson.

【作者简介】

乔纳森·斯威夫特（1667—1745），生于都柏林，父母是英国人，成长在一个极度贫穷的家庭里。他在都柏林的三一学院接受教育，并以"特殊恩典"的方式获得了学位。1689 年，他进入萨里郡的威廉·坦普尔爵士的家，担任辉格党外交官的秘书。那里有个藏书丰富的图书馆，他可以经常出入，阅读经典著作。1694 年，他辞去秘书职务，接受了爱尔兰教堂的神职，并于 1699 年担任拉腊柯尔地区的牧师。他经常去伦敦，撰写政治性小册子，最先是为辉格党写，后来又给托利党写。这一切都以失望而告终。他曾希望得到主教的职位，但这个崇高的荣誉被剥夺了。1713 年，他不得不收起傲慢，接受了都柏林圣帕特里克教堂教长的职位。作为愤世嫉俗的受害者，斯威夫特在生命的最后几年几乎精神失常。同时代的人称之为"有史以来最不幸的人"。他的天性和气质或许注定了他要过一种痛苦的生活。他把幸福定义为"永远受人欺骗"，或是"在恶棍中做傻瓜保持宁静平和的状态"。他拒绝受骗，也不屑于在那些恶棍中扮演傻瓜；他把自己巨大的讽刺天赋专门用于揭露傻瓜和鞭挞恶棍。他的代表作也是英语讽刺作品中的代表——《一只桶的故事》（1704）是对宗教争论和虚伪的猛烈抨击，《格列佛游记》（1726）是对人类弱点的深刻揭露。然而，他并不缺乏温柔和幽默，这在他的《致斯特拉的日记》（1710—1713）中得到了体现，这是写给埃丝特·约翰逊的一系列亲密的信件。

A Modest Proposal

**For Preventing the Children of Poor People in Ireland from
Being a Burden to Their Parents or Country, and
for Making Them Beneficial to the Public.**

It is a melancholy object to those who walk through **this great
town** or travel in the country, when they see the streets, the roads,
and cabin-doors crowded with beggars of the female sex, followed
by three, four, or six children, *all in rags* and importuning every
passenger for an alms. These mothers, instead of being able to work
for their honest livelihood, are forced to employ all their time in
strolling, to beg sustenance for their helpless infants, who as they
grow up either turn thieves for want of work, or leave their dear
native country to fight for **the Pretender in Spain**, or **sell themselves
to the Barbados**.

I think it is agreed by all parties that this prodigious number
of children in the arms, or on the backs, or at the heels of their
mothers, and frequently of their fathers, is in the present deplorable
state of the kingdom a very great additional grievance; and therefore

whoever could find out a fair, cheap, and easy method of making these children sound, useful members of the commonwealth would deserve so well of the public as to have his statue set up for a preserver of the nation.

But my intention is very far from being confined to provide only for the children of professed beggars; it is of a much greater extent, and shall take in the whole number of infants at a certain age who are born of parents in effect as little able to support them as those who demand our charity in the streets.

As to my own part, having turned my thoughts for many years upon this important subject, and maturely weighed the several schemes of other projectors, I have always found them grossly mistaken in their computation. It is true, a child just dropped from its dam may be supported by her milk for a solar year, with little other nourishment, at most not above the value of two shillings, which the mother may certainly get, or the value in scraps, by her lawful occupation of begging, and it is exactly at one year old that I propose to provide for them in such a manner as, instead of being a charge upon their parents or the parish, or wanting food and raiment for the rest of their lives, they shall on the contrary contribute to the feeding, and partly to the clothing of many thousands.

There is likewise another great advantage in my scheme, that it will prevent those voluntary abortions, and that horrid practice of women murdering their bastard children, alas, too frequent among us, sacrificing the poor innocent babes, I doubt, more to avoid the expense than the shame, which would move tears and pity in the most savage and inhuman breast.

The number of souls in this kingdom being usually reckoned one million and a half, of these I calculate there may be about two hundred thousand couple whose wives are breeders; from which number I subtract thirty thousand couple who are able to maintain their own children, although I apprehend there cannot be so many under the present distresses of the kingdom; but this being granted, there will remain a hundred and seventy thousand breeders. I again subtract fifty thousand for those women who miscarry, or whose children die by accident or disease within the year. There only remain a hundred and twenty thousand children of poor parents annually born. The question therefore is how this number shall be reared and provided for, which, as I have already said, under the present situation of affairs, is utterly impossible by all the methods hitherto proposed. For we can neither employ them in handicraft or agriculture; we neither build houses (I mean in the country) nor cultivate land: they can very seldom pick up a livelihood by stealing till they arrive at six years old, except where they are of towardly parts, although I confess they learn the rudiments much earlier, during which time they can, however, be properly looked upon only as probationers, as I have been informed by a principal gentleman in the County of Cavan, who protested to me that he never knew above one or two instances under the age of six, even in a part of the kingdom so renowned for the quickest proficiency in that art.

I am assured by our merchants that a boy or a girl before twelve years old is no saleable commodity, and even when they come to this age, they will not yield above three pounds, or three pounds and half-a-crown at most on the exchange, which cannot turn to account either to the parents or kingdom, the charge of nutriment and rags having been at least four times that value.

I shall now therefore humbly propose my own thoughts, which I hope will not be liable to the least objection.

I have been assured by **a very knowing American** of my acquaintance in London that a young healthy child well nursed is at a year old a most delicious, nourishing, and wholesome food, whether stewed, roasted, baked, or boiled, and I make no doubt that it will equally serve in a fricassee or a ragout.

I do therefore humbly offer it to public consideration, that of the hundred and twenty thousand children already computed, twenty thousand may be reserved for breed, whereof only one fourth part to be males, which is more than we allow to sheep, black-cattle, or swine, and my reason is that these children are seldom the fruits of marriage, a circumstance not much regarded by our savages, therefore one male will be sufficient to serve four females. That the remaining hundred thousand may at a year old be offered in sale to the persons of quality and fortune through the kingdom, always advising the mother to let them suck plentifully in the last month, so as to render them plump and fat for a good table. A child will make two dishes at an entertainment for friends, and when the family dines alone, the fore or hind quarter will make a reasonable dish, and seasoned with a little pepper or salt will be very good boiled on the fourth day, especially in winter.

I have reckoned upon a medium that a child just born will weigh 12 pounds, and in a solar year, if tolerably nursed, will increase to 28 pounds.

I grant this food will be somewhat dear, and therefore very

proper for landlords, who, as they have already devoured most of the parents, seem to have the best title to the children.

Infant's flesh will be in season throughout the year, but more plentiful in March, and a little before and after; for we are told by a grave author, **an eminent French physician**, that fish being a prolific diet, there are more children born in Roman Catholic countries about nine months after Lent than at any other season; therefore, reckoning a year after Lent, the markets will be more glutted than usual, because the number of popish infants is at least three to one in this kingdom, and therefore it will have one other collateral advantage, by lessening the number of Papists among us.

I have already computed the charge of nursing a beggar's child (in which list I reckon all cottagers, labourers, and four-fifths of the farmers) to be about two shillings per annum, rags included; and I believe no gentleman would repine to give ten shillings for the carcass of a good fat child, which, as I have said, will make four dishes of excellent nutritive meat when he hath only some particular friend or his own family to dine with him. Thus the squire will learn to be a good landlord, and grow popular among his tenants, the mother will have eight shillings net profit, and be fit for work till she produces another child.

Those who are more thrifty (as I must confess the times require) may flay the carcass; the skin of which, artificially dressed, will make admirable gloves for ladies and summer boots for fine gentlemen.

As to our city of Dublin, shambles may be appointed for this purpose in the most convenient parts of it, and butchers we may be assured will not be wanting; although I rather recommend buying the children alive, and dressing them hot from the knife as we do roasting pigs.

A very worthy person, a true lover of his country, and whose virtues I highly esteem, was lately pleased in discoursing on this matter to offer a refinement upon my scheme. He said that, many gentlemen of this kingdom having of late destroyed their deer, he conceived that the want of venison might be well supplied by the bodies of young lads and maidens, not exceeding fourteen years of age nor under twelve, so great a number of both sexes in every country being now ready to starve for want of work and service; and these to be disposed of by their parents if alive, or otherwise by their nearest relations. But with due deference to so excellent a friend and so deserving a patriot, I cannot be altogether in his sentiments; for as to the males, my American acquaintance assured me, from frequent experience, that their flesh was generally tough and lean like that of our school-boys, by continual exercise, and their taste disagreeable, and to fatten them would not answer the charge. Then as to the females, it would, I think with humble submission, be a loss to the public, because they soon would become breeders themselves; and besides, it is not improbable that some scrupulous people might be apt to censure such a practice (although indeed very unjustly) as a little bordering upon cruelty, which I confess, hath always been with me the strongest objection against any project, how well soever intended.

But in order to justify my friend, he confessed that this expedient was put into his head by the famous **Psalmanazar**, a native of the island Formosa[1], who came from thence to London, above twenty years ago, and in conversation told my friend that in his country when any young person happened to be put to death, the executioner sold the carcass to persons of quality, as a prime dainty; and that in his time the body of a plump girl of fifteen, who was crucified for an attempt to poison the emperor, was sold to his Imperial Majesty's prime minister of state, and other great mandarins of the court in joints from the gibbet, at four hundred crowns. Neither indeed can I deny that if the same use were made of several plump young girls in this town, who, without one single groat to their fortunes, cannot stir abroad without a chair, and appear at a playhouse and assemblies in foreign fineries, which they never will pay for, the kingdom would not be the worse.

Some persons of a desponding spirit are in great concern about that vast number of poor people who are aged, diseased, or maimed, and I have been desired to employ my thoughts what course may be taken to ease the nation of so grievous an encumbrance. But I am not in the least pain upon that matter, because it is very well known that they are everyday dying and rotting by cold and famine, and filth and vermin, as fast as can be reasonably expected. And as to the young labourers, they are now in almost as hopeful a condition. They cannot get work, and consequently pine away for want of nourishment, to a degree that if at any time they are accidentally hired to common labour, they have not strength to perform it; and thus the country and themselves are happily delivered from the evils to

---

1　此为葡萄牙人对中国台湾的旧称。下同。——编注

come.

I have too long digressed, and therefore shall return to my subject. I think the advantages by the proposal which I have made are obvious and many, as well as of the highest importance.

For first, as I have already observed, it would greatly lessen the number of Papists, with whom we are yearly overrun, being the principal breeders of the nation, as well as our most dangerous enemies, and who stay at home on purpose with a design to deliver the kingdom to the Pretender, hoping to take their advantage by the absence of so many good Protestants, who have chosen rather to leave their country than stay at home and pay tithes against their conscience to an episcopal curate.

Secondly, the poorer tenants will have something valuable of their own, which by law may be made liable to distress, and help to pay their landlord's rent, their corn and cattle being already seized, and *money a thing unknown*.

Thirdly, whereas the maintenance of a hundred thousand children from two years old and upwards cannot be computed at less than ten shillings a piece *per annum*, the nation's stock will be thereby increased fifty thousand pounds *per annum*, besides the profit of a new dish introduced to the tables of all gentlemen of fortune in the kingdom who have any refinement in taste, and the money will circulate among ourselves, the goods being entirely of our own growth and manufacture.

Fourthly, the constant breeders, besides the gain of eight shillings sterling *per annum* by the sale of their children, will be rid of the charge of maintaining them after the first year.

Fifthly, this food would likewise bring great custom to taverns, where the vintners will certainly be so prudent as to procure the best receipts for dressing it to perfection, and consequently have their houses frequented by all the fine gentlemen, who justly value themselves upon their knowledge in good eating; and a skilful cook who understands how to oblige his guests will contrive to make it as expensive as they please.

Sixthly, this would be a great inducement to marriage, which all wise nations have either encouraged by rewards or enforced by laws and penalties. It would increase the care and tenderness of mothers toward their children, when they were sure of a settlement for life to the poor babes, provided in some sort by the public to their annual profit, instead of expense. We should see an honest emulation among the married women which of them could bring the fattest child to the market. Men would become as fond of their wives during the time of their pregnancy as they are now of their mares in foal, their cows in calf, or sows when they are ready to farrow, nor offer to beat or kick them (as is too frequent a practice) for fear of a miscarriage.

Many other advantages might be enumerated: for instance, the addition of some thousand carcasses in our exportation of barreled beef; the propagation of swine's flesh, and improvement in the art of making good bacon, so much wanted among us by the great destruction of pigs, too frequent at our tables, which are no way comparable in taste or magnificence to a well-grown, fat, yearling child, which roasted whole will make a considerable figure at a lord mayor's feast or any other public entertainment. But this and many others I omit, being studious of brevity.

Supposing that one thousand families in this city would be constant customers for infants' flesh, besides others who might have it at merry-meetings, particularly at weddings and christenings, I compute that Dublin would take off annually about twenty thousand carcasses, and the rest of the kingdom (where probably they will be sold somewhat cheaper) the remaining eighty thousand.

I can think of no one objection that will possibly be raised against this proposal, unless it should be urged that the number of people will be thereby much lessened in the kingdom. This I freely own, and it was indeed one principal design in offering it to the world. I desire the reader will observe that I calculate my remedy *for this one individual kingdom of Ireland, and for no other that ever was, is, or I think ever can be upon earth.* Therefore let no man talk to me of **other expedients: of taxing our absentees at five shillings a pound**; of using neither clothes nor household furniture except what is of our own growth and manufacture; of utterly rejecting the materials and instruments that promote foreign luxury; of curing the expensiveness of pride, vanity, idleness and gaming in our women; of introducing a vein of parsimony, prudence, and temperance; of learning to love our country, wherein we differ even from Laplanders, and the inhabitants of **Topinamboo**; of quitting our animosities and factions, nor acting any longer like the Jews, who were murdering one another at the very moment their city was taken; of being a little cautious not to sell our country and consciences for nothing; of teaching landlords to have at least one degree of mercy towards their tenants. Lastly, of putting a spirit of honesty, industry, and skill into our shopkeepers, who, if a resolution could now be taken to buy only our native goods, would immediately unite to cheat and exact upon us in the price, the measure, and the goodness, nor could ever yet be brought to make one fair proposal of just dealing, though often and earnestly invited to it.

Therefore I repeat, let no man talk to me of these and the like expedients, till he hath at least some glimpse of hope that there will ever be some hearty and sincere attempt to put them in practice.

But as to myself, having been wearied out for many years with offering vain, idle, visionary thoughts, and at length utterly despairing of success, I fortunately fell upon this proposal, which, as it is wholly new, so it hath something solid and real, of no expense and little trouble, full in our own power, and whereby we can incur **no danger in** *disobliging* **England**. For this kind of commodity will not bear exportation, the flesh being of too tender a consistence to admit a long continuance in salt, *although perhaps I could name a country which would be glad to eat up our whole nation without it*.

After all, I am not so violently bent upon my own opinion as to reject any offer proposed by wise men, which shall be found equally innocent, cheap, easy, and effectual. But before something of that kind shall be advanced in contradiction to my scheme, and offering a better, I desire the author or authors will be pleased maturely to consider two points. First, as things now stand, how they will be able to find food and raiment for a hundred thousand useless mouths and backs. And secondly, there being a round million of creatures in human figure throughout this kingdom, whose whole subsistence put into a common stock would leave them in debt two millions of pounds sterling, adding those who are beggars by profession to the bulk of farmers, cottagers, and labourers, with their wives and children, who are beggars in effect; I desire those politicians who dislike my overture, and may perhaps be so bold as to attempt an answer, that they will first ask the parents of these mortals whether they would not at this day think it a great happiness to have been sold for food at a year old, in the manner I prescribe, and thereby have avoided such a perpetual scene of misfortunes as they have since gone through by the oppression of landlords, the impossibility of paying rent without money or trade, the want of common sustenance, with neither house nor clothes to cover them from the inclemencies of the weather, and the most inevitable prospect of entailing the like or greater miseries upon their breed forever.

I profess, in the sincerity of my heart, that I have not the least personal interest in endeavouring to promote this necessary work, having no other motive than the *public good of my country, by advancing our trade, providing for infants, relieving the poor, and giving some pleasure to the rich*. I have no children by which I can propose to get a single penny; the youngest being nine years old, and my wife past child-bearing.

Notes

One of the most serious problems of Ireland in the time of Swift, and for many years afterwards, was the sharp demarcation between the rich and the poor, i.e. between the rackrenting landlords and the oppressed tenants. When the *Proposal* was published (1729), Ireland was in the throes of a famine, which lasted for three years. Swift denounced the landlords and spoke for the tenants, especially the Catholics, since most tenants were Catholic. It was his love for humanity that prompted the writing of the pamphlet.

this great town, i.e. Dublin, capital of Ireland.

the Pretender in Spain. Probably a reference to the intrigue of Cardinal Alberoni with the Jacobites. Cardinal Giulio Alberoni (1664—1752), Prime Minister of Spain, equipped a small expedition in 1718 to help the Scottish Jacobites against George II, but the fleet was wrecked on its way from Cadiz. The Jacobites were the adherents to the House of Stuarts after the Revolution of 1688. There were many of them in Ireland, especially among the Roman Catholics.

sell themselves to the Barbados. Poor people sometimes went to the colonies by agreeing to work there for some years to pay for their transportation. Barbados is an island and British colony in the West Indies.

a very knowing American, etc. It was believed in some quarters at that time that some of the natives in America were Cannibals.

an eminent French physician, i.e. François Rabelais (1494?—1553), an eminent French physician and author of two entertaining books, *Gargantua* and *Pantagruel*.

Psalmanazar, George (1679?—1763), a famous literary imposter, who pretended to have come to England from Formosa and who described in detail the primitive customs of the 'Formosans' in his *Description of the Island of Formosa* (1705).

other expedients: of taxing our absentees at five shillings a pound, etc. This is a reference to the numerous proposals Swift had written for the improvement of conditions in Ireland.

Topinamboo, a district in Brazil, the inhabitants of which were said to be savages.

no danger in disobliging England. This passage refers to the English prohibition of the exports of Irish produce. All Irish trade was carried in English-built ships sailing from English ports; and the right to export freely live-stock, dead meat, cheese and butter was denied, Swift, though an Englishman, stood for Ireland against England.

【作品简介】

斯威夫特时期以及以后的许多年里，爱尔兰最严重的问题之一就是富人和穷人之间，如高价出租房屋的地主和受压迫的佃户之间的贫富差距十分明显。《一个温和的建议》（1729）发表的时候，爱尔兰正处于持续了三年的饥荒困境之中。斯威夫特谴责地主并为佃户特别是天主教徒说话，因为大多数佃户都是天主教徒。正是他对人性的热爱，促使他撰写了这本小册子。

【作品解析】

this great town：指的是爱尔兰的首都都柏林。

the Pretender in Spain：也许是指红衣主教阿尔贝罗尼和詹姆斯二世党人的阴谋。红衣主教朱利奥·阿尔贝罗尼（1664—1752），同时也是西班牙首相，于1718年装备了一支小型远征军，帮助苏格兰的詹姆斯二世党人推翻乔治二世，然而舰队在离加的斯不远处触礁。詹姆斯二世党人是1688年英国"光荣革命"之后斯图亚特王朝的追随者。在爱尔兰有很多这样的人，特别是在罗马天主教徒中。

sell themselves to the Barbados：穷人往往会同意到殖民地去做几年苦力，以支付他们的交通费用。巴巴多斯是西印度群岛中的一个岛屿，英国的殖民地。

a very knowing American, etc.：此句指当时有人认为美国的土著人是食人族。

an eminent French physician：这里是指弗朗索瓦·拉伯雷（约1494—1553），杰出的法国医生，曾著有两部有趣的小说《卡冈都亚》和《庞大固埃》（全称《巨人传》）。

Psalmanazar：乔治·普萨尔玛纳札（约 1679—1763），著名的文学骗子，自称是从中国台湾来到英国，实际上是来自法国；并在《台湾岛志》[1]（1705）中详尽描述了当地人的原始习俗。

other expedients：of taxing our absentees at five shillings a pound, etc.：这里指斯威夫特为改善爱尔兰状况而撰写的众多政治建议的参考檄文。

Topinamboo：托平兰布，是巴西的一个地区，据说那里的居民都是野蛮人。

no danger in disobliging England：这段文字指的是英国禁止爱尔兰产品出口的规定。所有爱尔兰的贸易货物都必须用英国制造的船只从英国港口运出，并且爱尔兰没有权利自由出口活牲畜、生肉、奶酪和黄油。斯威夫特虽然是一名英国人，却代表爱尔兰反对英国的这一条禁令。

【参考译文】

一个温和的建议

为了不让爱尔兰的贫穷孩子成为父母和国家的负担
并使他们有利于人民大众

凡是路过这座大城镇，或者是在乡间旅游的人们，每当他们看到街边、马路上、茅舍屋内挤满了女乞丐，后面跟着三四个或者更多的衣衫褴褛的孩子，纠缠过路的行人乞求施舍的情景，就会感到忧郁。这些母亲无法以体面的劳作谋求正当的生计，为了养活她们的孩子，不得不沿街乞

---

1 此书为历史上一部有名的伪书，书中对中国台湾地区人民和风俗的描绘，对动物与植物的叙述全属凭空捏造。他本人并未去过台湾，书中所述荒诞、野蛮，却让他成为英国文坛的焦点。斯威夫特也曾听过他讲的离奇故事，并引用到自己的文章中。——编注

讨。而她们的孩子长大后，由于缺少工作机会，要么沦为窃贼，要么背井离乡去西班牙为那个假冒国王卖命，或者把自己卖身到巴巴多斯。

我想各方人士都会同意，这些在他们母亲或者父亲手中抱着的、背上背着的以及身后跟着的孩子，数量多得惊人。在当前王国处于可悲的状况下，这将是一个巨大而又沉重的负担。因此，谁能想出一个既公平又廉价，且简单易行的办法，让这些孩子成为国家坚实的有用之才，那么他将会受到人们的尊敬和爱戴，值得人们尊他为护国英雄，并为他竖立雕像。

然而，我的打算却远远不止这些；不仅要供养那些专业乞丐的孩子，而且其范围要广泛得多，包括所有在某个年龄段出生的、父母几乎没有能力供养的孩子，正如那些我们在街上看见的向过路行人强行乞讨的孩子。

至于我的这个想法，已经酝酿了好多年，也曾仔细斟酌过其他人提供的几个方案；然而，却总是发现他们的计算方法很有问题。确实，一个初生的婴儿，在第一年里也许只需要母乳，而不需要其他的辅助营养品也可以养活，费用顶多不会超过两个先令，而这两个先令或者说同等价值的残羹剩饭，母亲一般都可以通过合法的乞讨行为挣得。当他们整一岁时，我提议以这样的方式来供养他们，这些儿童接下来不但不会成为父母或教区的负担，也不会在余生中缺少衣食，相反，他们还可以为成千上万的人提供食物和部分衣物。

我的方案还有个大好处，就是可以阻止妇女私自堕胎和谋杀私生子女的可怕行径。天哪，这类事件在我们的国家真是司空见惯。我敢说她们牺牲那些无辜可怜的婴儿不是为了逃避耻辱，而更多的是为了逃避抚养的费用。即便是那些心如铁石的蛮凶之徒，也会为此情此景洒一掬怜悯之泪吧。

在这个王国里，人口大约为一百五十万，我估计大约有二十万对夫妇有生育能力，其中最多只有三万对夫妇有能力抚养孩子，虽然我知道这个国家在目前的困境下，不可能有这么多人有抚养能力；但是即使如此，仍将会有十七万对夫妇只有生育能力而没有能力抚养。再减去五万因为流产或者在一年以内死于意外和疾病的孩子，每年出生在贫困家庭中的孩子，大约仍有十二万。问题是如何抚养这么多的孩子。正如我前面所提到的，迄今为止，还没有一个能够解决这个问题的方案。我们不能雇用这些孩子去从事手工业或者农业，我们不能雇用他们去建造房屋（我的意思是在乡下），也不能雇用他们开耕土地。这些孩子也不可能在六岁之前学会小偷小摸，自谋生计，除非他们有帮派团伙的帮衬。尽管我承认，这些孩子很小就开始学偷，但只不过是见习罢了。正如卡文郡一位颇有地位的绅士对我说的，据他所知，即使是在这个王国以最快通晓这门手艺而闻名的某个地区，在六岁以下精通偷窃技艺的儿童，也不会超过一两个。

商人们也确定地对我说，十二岁以下的男女儿童是不能作为商品交易的，因为年龄太小卖不上好的价钱；即便是到了十二岁，在大多数的交易市场里，他们的利润也不会超过三英镑，最多也不过是三镑五先令。这些钱远远不足以补偿他们的父母和国家抚养他们的费用。他们吃过的辅助营养品和穿戴过的衣物的费用，至少是这个价钱的四倍。

在此，我想说说我的想法，希望不会遭到任何异议和反对。

伦敦有一位颇有学识的美国朋友告诉我，一岁的孩子如果健康、营养良好的话，是味道鲜美、营养丰富、延年益寿的美食；焖、烤、焙、煮皆无不可。我相信做成焖肉和蔬菜炖肉也同样可口。

因此，我谨把我的建议提出，请大家考虑：在已经计算出的十二万儿童中，也许可以留下两万名用于进行繁殖，其中雄性应当只需占其中的四分之一；这已经比我们允许用在猪、牛、羊身上的比例大多了。我的理由是：这些孩子并不是正常婚姻的产物，对于这一点我们这样的野蛮人根本就不在乎，因此，一雄足以配对四雌。剩下的十万名，在满周岁时，可以卖给国内有权有势的富贵人士。在卖之前，得叮嘱他们的母亲，在最后一个月里用奶水喂饱他们，把他们养得丰满、肥腻，好做饭桌上最美味的佳肴。在招待朋友的筵席上，一个婴儿可以做成两道菜；如果家庭聚餐，孩子的一条前腿或一条后腿，就可以做成一道美味的佳肴；如果再加点胡椒粉或盐，腌制四天后再煮，味道将会更加鲜美，尤其是在冬天。

我曾经算过，一般来说，刚出生的孩子重十二磅，照料得好一点的话，一年以后就可长到二十八磅。

我承认这种食物多少有点昂贵，因此非常适合地主们享用。因为他们已经基本上吞噬了孩子们的父母，似乎也最有资格吃掉他们的孩子。

婴儿的鲜肉一年四季皆有供应，但在三月份前后最为充足。一位严肃、不苟言笑的作家同时又是一位著名的法国外科大夫告诉我们，由于鱼类是促进生育的最佳食物，在信仰罗马天主教的国家里，在四旬斋后九个月左右，即将出生的婴儿会比其他任何时期都多；因此估计在大斋节后一年的这个时节，市场上婴儿的鲜肉供应将比平常充足，而且由于我国天主教派里的婴儿数量与其他教派里的婴儿数量的比例至少是三比一，所以这个方案还有一个附带的好处，那就是可以减少我们天主教徒的数量。

我已经算过，照料一个乞丐乳婴的费用（其中包括了所有的佃农、劳工和五分之四农民的婴儿），以及他们所穿的衣物的费用，每年大约需要两先令。我相信没有一个绅士会在乎花上十先令买一个优质多肉婴儿的胴体；他可以做四样美味的佳肴来招待朋友或者是与家人品尝。这样，乡绅们就会学着去做一个好东家，并受到佃户们的爱戴。而婴儿的母亲们将会有八先令的净利润收入，之后可以继续工作，直到生下第二胎。

那些节俭的人（我必须承认这是由于时代所迫），可能会剥下婴儿胴体的皮，经过手工加工处理，将它制成品质极好的女士手套和绅士们穿着的夏季靴。

至于我们的都柏林市，为了这一目的，可以在城市中最便利的地方设立屠宰场，而且可以肯定有的是屠夫。尽管这样，我还是建议大家都去买活婴，就像我们烤乳猪一样，备好调料，再把刀加热。

一位德高望重、我很尊敬的爱国人士，最近对我的提案很感兴趣，并主动要求加以改进。他说，近来我国许多绅士捕猎野鹿无度导致鹿肉匮之。他认为，人们对鹿肉的需求可以由十二周岁以上、十四周岁以下少男少女的鲜肉来填补，眼下在这个国度，这个年龄段的少男少女由于找不到工作而在挨饿的数不胜数；如果他们的父母还活着，将由他们的父母处理，或由他们的亲人处理。但是，对于这位我很尊重的德高望重的爱国人士的建议，我却不能完全苟同。我的一位美国朋友告诉我，根据他的丰富经验，男孩子由于经常活动，就像我们学校里不停运动的男学生一样，一般肉都是又瘦又硬，而且味道也很糟，养肥之后卖出去，根本赚不到抚养他们的费用。至于女孩子，我认为那么做对国家将是一笔损失，因为她们很快便会到育龄期，生儿育女。此外，一些谨小慎微的人可能会对此提出责难（尽管确实很不公正），认为这种做法近乎有些残忍。但我必须坦白地说，我一直强烈反对任何残忍的提案，无论其动机是多么好。

为了证明我的朋友不是无中生有，他承认，这个权宜之计是从著名的普萨尔玛纳札那里得来的。普萨尔玛纳札是一个土生土长的台湾人，二十多年前，他来到伦敦。在一次谈话中，他告诉我的朋友，在他们那里，当一个年轻人被处以死刑以后，躯体的肉便会被刽子手卖给有权势的人，作为上等的美味。那时，就有一个十五岁体态丰满圆润的女孩蓄意谋弒皇帝，被钉死在了十字架上，绞架上的肉块以四百克朗的价钱卖给了皇帝的宰相，还有其他的宫廷大臣。确实我也不能否认，如果在我们这个城镇，将那些丰满圆润的姑娘采用同样的方法来处理的话——她们身无分文，不坐在车椅上就无法外出活动，穿着不用自己去付出代价就获得的外国时装出现在戏院里和集会上——这个王国也就不会每况愈下了。

一些心灰意冷的人士对那些年迈、患病或残疾的数量巨大的穷人感到担忧，要求我考虑怎样为国家排忧解难。但在这件事上我没有感觉到一点痛苦，因为这是众所周知的，他们每天都因寒冷、饥饿、污秽、害虫而死亡，并腐烂发臭，速度之快正如我们所预期的那样。至于年轻的劳动者，他们目前也处于差不多同样乐观的状态。他们如果长期找不到工作，就会因为缺乏营养而身体虚弱；一旦有了工作，也会因没有力量而无法胜任。

因此，国家也好，个人也好，都乐于从这样的厄运中摆脱出来。

扯得太远了，还是回到正题吧。显而易见，我的提议有很多的好处，而且也十分重要。

第一，正如我已经提到的那样，我的方案将会大大地减少天主教徒的数量。这些天主教徒每年都在迅速增长，已经成了国家的主要生育者，是我们最危险的敌人。他们整天闭门不出，趁着众多优秀的新教徒离家出走之际，阴谋怎样把国家卖给那个假冒国王，而这些新教徒宁愿离开自己的国家，也不愿意待在家里，昧着自己的良心向圣公会助理牧师支付什一税。

第二，贫困的佃户会有一些自己值钱的物品，按照法律规定，这些物品很可能会被抵押，用以帮助向地主支付租金；他们的庄稼和牲畜早已被没收了，而钱是一种未知的东西。

第三，供养十万个两岁和两岁以上的儿童，每人每年的花费以不少于十先令计算，本计划实施后除了可以给国内所有食不厌精的富绅们的饭桌上添加一碟新鲜佳肴外，国库还会因此每年增加五万英镑的额外收入。而这笔收入将会在我们之间流通，因为货物完全由我们自己生产。

第四，那些常年生育的妇女，除了每年卖孩子可以挣得八个先令外，她们只需要把孩子抚养到一岁，以后也就免去了抚养子女的费用和责任。

第五，这些食品还可为酒馆招徕大批主顾。酒馆老板必将悉心寻觅最好的食谱，使自己的酒馆成为那些美食家、富绅频频光临之地；而熟知顾客心理、手艺娴熟的厨师，便会想方设法把它做成一道价格昂贵的佳肴。

第六，促进婚姻。所有明智的国家要么通过奖励来鼓励婚姻，要么通过法律和刑罚来强迫婚姻。我的提案可以增进母亲对孩子的关爱和呵护，因为当她们确定这些可怜孩子的去向时，她们所得到的都是收入，而没有任何的花费。我们可以看到已婚妇女中有了一种正当的竞争，看谁能养出最胖的孩子送到市场上去。在女人怀孕期间，男人们也会十分爱护他们的妻子，就像他们现在爱护怀着小马驹的母马，爱护怀着牛犊的母牛，爱护即将临盆的母猪一样，他们不会对她们拳打脚踢，使之流产；而这种情况平时则是司空见惯的。

我的这一提案还有许多其他的好处，诸如，除了出口桶装牛肉外，我们还可以增加出口畜体千具左右；有利于猪肉的推销，以及改进上好的火腿制作工艺。因为猪肉是我们餐桌上经常出现的大众食品，现在却因为猪的大量死亡而变得奇缺；但在味道和色泽上都无法与一岁健康多肉的乳婴相媲美。如果在市长大人的宴席上或者在任何其他公共娱乐活动中，有一整只烤乳婴，将会成为宴席中相当重要的部分。除了这些，我的提案还有其他一些优点，但为了不耽搁各位的时间，我就不赘述了。

假如这个城市中有一千个家庭会是婴儿胴体购买的固定客户，再加上某些宴会，特别是在婚宴和洗礼仪式上可能会需要，我估计都柏林每年需要消费大约两万具乳婴，在这个王国的其他区域，还可以消费其余的八万具（也许价格会卖得便宜些）。

我想象不出对这个提案会有什么样的反对意见，除非有人说这会使国家人口大大减少。坦白说，这也是我将这一方案公之于世的目的。我衷心希望读者能意识到这是我专为爱尔兰王国开立的一个补救办法，对于地球上存在的任何国家来说，过去、现在和将来都不需要这剂良方。因此，不要让任何人和我谈论其他的权宜之计，例如，以每磅五先令的价格向我们住在国外的人征收税赋；使用自己种植和生产的东西而不去用进口的布料和家具；彻底拒绝使用那些宣扬、推动外国奢侈之风的材料和器具；积极医治女性骄傲、虚荣、懒惰和豪赌的毛病，遏止浪费；提倡节约、谨慎和节制的精神；学会爱我们的国家，在这方面我们甚至还不如那些拉普兰和托平兰布的居民；放下仇恨和宗教派系，不要像犹太人那样，在他们的城市被攻占的时候，还在自相残杀；谨慎一点，不要把我们的国家和自己的良心也变卖得一钱不值；教导地主对他们的佃户至少要有一点怜悯之心。最后，将诚信、勤奋的精神以及技能灌输给我们的店主，如果现在规定人人都只能买国货，他们就会立即联合起来欺骗我们，确切地说是在价格、数量、质量上对我们进行敲诈，而且也绝对不可能做到公平交易，尽管我们经常恳请他们这样做。

因此，我再说一遍，不要让任何人与我谈论这些和类似的权宜之计，除非至少有那么一丁点一眼能看得见的希望，直到真的会有人诚心诚意把这些提案付诸实践。

就我自己而言，多年来一直在为社会提供各种徒有虚名的、没有实际意义的憧憬和设想，因而感到疲惫不堪，而且没有任何实质性成功的希望。有幸的是，我想出了这么一个全新的切实可行的提案，我们可以充分发挥我们自己的力量，毫无花费而且简单易行，这样我们就免除得罪英国的危险。这种商品不适合出口，因为肉太嫩不适合长期用盐腌制。不过我也许能给出一个国家的名字，这个国家即使不用盐也会很高兴地吞噬我们整个民族。

然而，我并非固执己见，反对任何明智之士提出的建议，只要这些建议与我的提案同样大公无私，同样简单易行，同样行之有效。在明智之士提出更加完善的建议，并且能够更好地解决问题之前，我想请各位注意两个问题。首先，现在的情况是，怎样为这十万个只能吃而不能工作的孩子提供食物和衣服？其次，这个国家里有数以百万计的人口，如果将他们的生计全部纳入国库，我们将背负二百万英镑的债务，其中包括大量的职业乞丐以及农民、作坊工人、劳动者和他们的妻子与孩子；其实他们也都等同于乞丐。我希望那些不喜欢我提案的政治家，或者是那些大胆试图反驳我的人，去问问那些孩子的父母，是否像我描述的那样，为了食物能够把一岁大的婴儿卖掉不是件非常高兴的事？这样，以我提供的方式，他们可以避免历来遭受地主压迫的痛苦，避免没钱交纳房租和缺乏食品的痛苦，避免在恶劣的气候下没有住处藏身、没有足够的衣物裹身的痛苦；然而，更重要的是可以避免把这种痛苦世代相传。

其实，我推动这项工作，完全是为了国家的公共利益，向国家供应婴幼儿是为了促进贸易，解救穷人，同时也为富人提供一些享受，并不带有丝毫的个人利益。按照我的提案，我自己没有一个孩子符合买卖标准；我最小的孩子已经九岁，而我的妻子也早已过了生育的年龄。

LORD CHESTERFIELD (1694—1773)

Philip Dormer Stanhope, Fourth Earl of Chesterfield (1694—1773) was one of the ablest diplomats and statesmen of his time. He entered the House of Commons in 1715 and the House of Lords in 1726. He spent a number of years on foreign embassies: served as ambassador at The Hague from 1728 to 1732, and was appointed Lord Lieutenant of Ireland in 1745. Partly because of growing deafness, he withdrew from public life while still in his prime, and thereafter played the part of a shrewd observer.

【作者简介】

菲利普·多默·斯坦霍普，第四任切斯特菲尔德勋爵（1694—1773）是那个年代最有能力的外交官和政治家之一。他 1715 年进入下议院，1726 年进入上议院。他在外国大使馆工作多年，1728 年至 1732 年在海牙担任大使，1745 年被任命为爱尔兰总督。他在其事业鼎盛时期退出了公众视野，部分原因是其日益严重的耳聋。之后，他在生活中扮演了一个敏锐的观察者。

Letters to His Son

Bath, October 4, **O. S.** 1746.

Dear Boy,

Though I employ so much of my time in writing to you, I confess I have often my doubts whether it is to any purpose. I know how unwelcome advice generally is; I know that those who want it most like it and follow it least; and I know, too, that the advice of parents, more particularly, is ascribed to the moroseness, the imperiousness, or the garrulity of old age. But then, on the other hand, I flatter myself, that as your own reason, though too young as yet to suggest much to you of itself, is however, strong enough to enable you, both to judge of and receive plain truths: I flatter myself (I say) that your own reason, young as it is, must tell you, that I can have no interest but yours in the advice I give you; and that consequently, you will at least weigh and consider it well: in which case, some of it will, I hope, have its effect. Do not think that I mean to dictate as a parent; I only mean to advise as a friend, and an indulgent one too: and do not apprehend that I mean to check your pleasures, of which, on the contrary, I only desire to be the guide, not the censor. Let my experience supply your want of it, and clear your way, in the progress of your youth, of those thorns and briars which scratched and disfigured me in the course of mine. I do not, therefore, so much as hint to you how absolutely dependent you are upon me; that you neither have nor can have a shilling in the world but from me; and that, as I have no womanish weakness for your person, your merit must and will be the only measure of my kindness. I say, I do not hint these things to you, because I am convinced that you will act right upon more noble and generous principles; I mean for the sake of doing right, and out of affection and gratitude to me.

I have so often recommended to you attention and application to whatever you learn that I do not mention them now as duties; but I point them out to you as conducive, nay, absolutely necessary, to your pleasures; for can there be a greater pleasure than to be universally allowed to excel those of one's own age and manner of life? And, consequently, can there be anything more mortifying than to be excelled by them? In this latter case, your shame and regret must be greater than anybody's, because every person knows the uncommon care which has been taken of your education and the opportunities you have had of knowing more than others of your age. I do not confine the application which I recommend singly to the view and emulation of excelling others (though that is a very sensible pleasure and a very warrantable pride); but I mean likewise to excel in the thing itself; for in my mind, one may as well not know a thing at all as know it but imperfectly. To know a little of anything gives neither satisfaction nor credit; but often brings disgrace or ridicule.

Mr. Pope says, very truly,

A little knowledge is a dangerous thing;
Drink deep or taste not the Castalian spring.

And what is called a *smattering* of everything infallibly constitutes a coxcomb. I have often, of late, reflected what an unhappy man I must now have been if I had not acquired in my youth some fund and taste of learning. What could I have done with myself at this age without them? I must, as many ignorant people do, have destroyed my health and faculties by sotting away the evenings; or, by wasting them frivolously in the tattle of women's company, must have exposed myself to the ridicule and contempt of those very women; or, lastly, I must have hanged myself, as a man once did, for weariness of putting on and pulling off his shoes and stockings every day. My books, and only my books, are now left me: and I daily find what **Cicero** says of learning to be true: *Haec studia* (says he) *adolescentiam alunt, senectutem oblectant, secundas res ornant, adversis perfugium ac solatium praebent, delectant domi, non impediunt foris, pernoctant nobiscum, peregrinantur, rusticantur.*

I do not mean, by this, to exclude conversation out of the pleasures of an advanced age; on the contrary, it is a very great and a very rational pleasure, at all ages; but the conversation of the ignorant is no conversation, and gives even them no pleasure; they tire of their own sterility, and have not matter enough to furnish them with words to keep up a conversation.

Let me, therefore, most earnestly recommend to you to hoard up, while you can, a great stock of knowledge; for though, during the dissipation of your youth, you may not have occasion to spend much of it, yet you may depend upon it that a time will come when you will want it to maintain you. Public granaries are filled in plentiful years, not that it is known that the next, or the second, or third year will prove a scarce one; but because it is known that, sooner or later, such a year will come, in which the grain will be wanted.

l will say no more to you upon this subject; you have **Mr. Harte** with you to enforce it; you have reason to assent to the truth of it; so that, in short, 'you have Moses and the Prophets; if you will not believe them, neither will you believe though one rose from the dead.' Do not imagine that the knowledge which I so much recommend to you is confined to books, pleasing, useful, and necessary as that knowledge is, but I comprehend in it the great knowledge of the world, still more necessary than that of books. In truth, they assist one another reciprocally; and no man will have either perfectly who has not both. The knowledge of the world is only to be acquired in the world, and not in a closet. Books alone will never teach it you; but they will suggest many things to your observation which might otherwise escape you; and your own observations upon mankind, when compared with those which you will find in books, will help you to fix the true point.

To know mankind well requires full as much attention and application as to know books, and, it may be, more sagacity and discernment. I am, at this time, acquainted with many elderly people who have all passed their whole lives in the great world, but with such levity and inattention that they know no more of it now than they did at fifteen. Do not flatter yourself, therefore, with the thoughts that you can acquire this knowledge in the frivolous chit-chat of idle companies; no, you must go much deeper than that.

You must look into people, as well as at them. Almost all people are born with all the passions, to a certain degree; but almost every man has a prevailing one, to which the others are subordinate. Search everyone for that **ruling passion**; pry into the recesses of his heart, and observe the different workings of the same passion in different people; and when you have found out the prevailing passion of any man, remember never to trust him where that passion is concerned. Work upon him by it, if you please; but be upon your guard yourself against it, whatever professions he may make you.

I would desire you to read this letter twice over, but that I much doubt whether you will read once to the end of it. I will trouble you no longer now; but we will have more upon this subject hereafter. Adieu.

I have this moment received your letter from **Schaffhausen**; in the date of it you forgot the month.

London, October 16, O. S. 1747

Dear Boy,

The art of pleasing is a very necessary one to possess; but a very difficult one to acquire. It can hardly be reduced to rules; and your own good sense and observation will teach you more of it than I can. Do as you would be done by is the surest method that I know of pleasing. Observe carefully what pleases you in others, and probably the same things in you will please others. If you are pleased with the complaisance and attention of others to your humours, your tastes, or your weaknesses, depend upon it the same complaisance and attention on your part to theirs will equally please them. Take the tone of the company that you are in, and do not pretend to give it; be serious, gay, or even trifling, as you find the present humour of the company; this is an attention due from every individual to the majority. Do not tell stories in company; there is nothing more tedious and disagreeable; if by chance you know a very short story, and exceedingly applicable to the present subject of conversation, tell it in as few words as possible; and even then, throw out that you do not love to tell stories, but that the shortness of it tempted you. Of all things, banish the egotism out of your conversation, and never think of entertaining people with your own personal concerns or private affairs; though they are interesting to you, they are tedious and impertinent to everybody else; besides that, one cannot keep one's own private affairs too secret. Whatever you think your own excellencies may be, do not affectedly display them in company; nor labour, as many people do, to give that turn to the conversation which may supply you with an opportunity of exhibiting them. If they are real, they will infallibly be discovered, without your pointing them out yourself, and with much more advantage. Never maintain an argument with heat and clamour, though you think or know yourself to be in the right; but give your opinion modestly and coolly, which is the only way to convince; and, if that does not do, try to change the conversation, by saying, with good humour, 'We shall hardly convince one another; nor is it necessary that we should, so let us talk of something else.'

Remember that there is a local propriety to be observed in all companies; and that what is extremely proper in one company, may be, and often is, highly improper in another.

The jokes, the *bons mots*, the little adventures, which may do very well in one company, will seem flat and tedious when related in another. The particular characters, the habits, the cant of one company, may give credit to a word or a gesture which would have none at all if divested of those accidental circumstances. Here people very commonly err; and fond of something that has entertained them in one company and in certain circumstances, repeat it with emphasis in another, where it is either insipid, or, it may be, offensive, by being ill-timed or misplaced. Nay, they often do it with this silly preamble; 'I will tell you an excellent thing'; or 'I will tell you the best thing in the world.' This raises expectations, which when absolutely disappointed, make the relator of this excellent thing look, very deservedly, like a fool.

If you would particularly gain the affection and friendship of particular people, whether men or women, endeavour to find out their predominant excellency, if they have one, and their prevailing weakness, which everybody has; and do justice to the one and something more than justice to the other. Men have various objects in which they may excel, or at least would be thought to excel; and, though they love to hear justice done to them where they know that they excel, yet they are most and best flattered upon those points where they wish to excel and yet are doubtful whether they do or not. As for example: **Cardinal Richelieu**, who was undoubtedly the ablest statesman of his time or perhaps of any other, had the

idle vanity of being thought the best poet too; he envied the great
Corneille his reputation, and ordered a criticism to be written upon
the *Cid*. Those therefore, who flattered skillfully, said little to him of
his abilities in state affairs, or at least but *en passant*, and as it might
naturally occur. But the incense which they gave him, the smoke
of which they knew would turn his head in their favour, was as a
bel esprit and a poet. Why? Because he was sure of one excellency
and distrustful as to the other. You will easily discover every man's
prevailing vanity by observing his favourite topic of conversation; for
every man talks most of what he has most a mind to be thought to
excel in. Touch him but there, and you touch him to the quick. The
late **Sir Robert Walpole** (who was certainly an able man) was little
open to flattery upon that head; for he was in no doubt himself about
it; but his prevailing weakness was to be thought to have a polite and
happy turn to gallantry—of which he had undoubtedly less than any
man living: it was his favourite and frequent subject of conversation;
which proved, to those who had any penetration, that it was his
prevailing weakness. And they applied to it with success.

Women have, in general, but one object, which is their beauty;
upon which, scarce any flattery is too gross for them to swallow.
Nature has hardly formed a woman ugly enough to be insensible
to flattery upon her person; if her face is so shocking that she must
in some degree be conscious of it, her figure and air, she trusts,
make ample amends for it. If her figure is deformed, her face, she
thinks, counterbalances it. If they are both bad, she comforts herself
that she has graces; a certain manner, a *je ne sais quoi*, still more
engaging than beauty. This truth is evident from the studied and

elaborate dress of the ugliest women in the world. An undoubted, uncontested, conscious beauty is, of all women, the least sensible of flattery upon that head; she knows that it is her due and is therefore obliged to nobody for giving it her. She must be flattered upon her understanding, which, though she may possibly not doubt of herself, yet she suspects that men may distrust.

Do not mistake me and think that I mean to recommend to you abject and criminal flattery; no; flatter nobody's vices or crimes: on the contrary, abhor and discourage them. But there is no living in the world without a complaisant indulgence for people's weaknesses and innocent, though ridiculous, vanities. If a man has a mind to be thought wiser, and a woman handsomer, than they really are, their error is a comfortable one to themselves and an innocent one with regard to other people; and I would rather make them my friends by indulging them in it than my enemies by endeavouring (and that to no purpose) to undeceive them.

There are little attentions likewise which are infinitely engaging, and which sensibly affect that degree of pride and self-love which is inseparable from human nature; as they are unquestionable proofs of the regard and consideration which we have for the person to whom we pay them. As, for example, to observe the little habits, the likings, the antipathies, and the tastes of those whom we would gain; and then take care to provide them with the one, and to secure them from the other; giving them, genteelly, to understand that you had observed that they liked such a dish or such a room; for which reason you had prepared it: or, on the contrary, that having observed they had an aversion to such a dish, a dislike to such a person, etc., you had taken care to avoid presenting them. Such attention to such trifles flatters self-love much more than greater things, as it makes people think themselves almost the only objects of your thoughts and care.

These are some of the *arcana* necessary for your initiation in the great society of the world. I wish I had known them better at your age; I have paid the price of three-and-fifty years for them, and shall not grudge it if you reap the advantage. Adieu.

Notes

Lord Chesterfield is now chiefly known as the author of *Letters*, addressed to his natural son, Philip Stanhope. It was Chesterfield's ambition to endow his illegitimate son with the learning of the scholar and the manners of the courtier and thus to equip him for a career in diplomacy. For this purpose, he began his series of instructive letters when the boy was only five years old. His assiduity, however, was ill-rewarded. Young Stanhope was 'boorish' and 'loutish,' and turned out a middling figure in public life. In 1763, young Stanhope died. The *Letters* passed into the hands of Mrs. Eugenia Stanhope, the widow, and they were published in 1774, soon after the death of the writer.

For many years Chesterfield's work was the object of adverse criticism. When his letters to his natural son were published, Johnson observed that 'they teach the morals of a whore and the manners of a dancing master.' A hue and cry was raised against the memory of the lord. On the whole, his *Letters to His Son* may be regarded as the best embodiment of worldly wisdom in the most brilliant and persuasive style,—only they are sometimes a bit too worldly.

Bath, a city in Somersetshire, England, well-known for its hot springs and baths.

O.S., 'Old Style,' i.e. the Julian Calendar, introduced by Julius Caesar in 46 B.C. In 1582 Pope Gregory XIII introduced a modified form of the Calendar. This, known as 'New Style,' was not adopted in Great Britain until 1752.

Mr. Pope, Alexander (1688—1744), English poet and critic. The two lines are quoted, inaccurately, from his *Essay on Criticism*, lines 215—216. The original reads:

> 'A little learning is a dangerous thing;
>
> Drink deep or taste not the Pierian spring.'

Cicero, Marcus Tullius (106—43 B.C.), Roman philosopher and orator. The passage about learning, quoted from his *Pro Archia*, VII, 16, may be rendered thus: These studies educate youth, please old age, are ornaments to favourable circumstances, afford a flight and a solace in misfortune, delight at home, are no impediment in the world; they attend us through the night, become our travelling companions, and sweeten solitude.

Mr. Harte, Walter (1709—1774), Stanhope's tutor, who was said to be 'an Oxford pedant.'

ruling passion, prevailing or predominating passion. Men are born with certain leanings and are drawn to those who have the same leanings and repelled by those whose leanings are too different. Such leanings were called humours in the Renaissance and ruling passions in the 17th and 18th centuries.

Schaffhausen, in north Switzerland. Young Stanhope was then having a 'grand tour' on the Continent.

bons mots (French), witty remarks.

Cardinal Richelieu, Armand Jean du Plessis (1585—1642), was bishop of

Lucon in 1607, and became prime minister of Louis XIII's in 1624. He was one of the greatest of French statesmen.

Corneille, Pierre (1606—1684), French dramatist. *Le Cid* (1636), one of his masterpieces, is based on the legends and plays concerning the Spanish hero Rodrigo Díaz de Vivar el Cid Campeador ('el Cid' the lord; 'Campeador', champion).

en passant (French), by the way, incidentally.

bel esprit (French), a wit.

Sir Robert Walpole (1676—1745), the most important English political leader in the first half of the 18th century. He remained in office for twenty-one years (1721—1742). Chesterfield was one of his political opponents.

je ne sais quoi (French), literally, 'I know not what.' —a phrase which came into fashion in the early 18th century. It was used to indicate something strange, fine, or pretty, yet hard to define. It was sometimes rendered 'somethingness.'

arcana (plural of *arcanum*), secrets.

【作品简介 】

切斯特菲尔德勋爵主要是以"书信"出名，这些都是他写给亲生儿子菲利普·斯坦霍普的家书。切斯特菲尔德勋爵想通过书信教导他的私生子，使他具有学者的学识和朝臣的礼仪，为外交官生涯做准备。因此，当他的儿子只有五岁的时候，切斯特菲尔德勋爵就开始给他写了一系列指导性的信件。然而，他的勤勉却没有得到应有的回报。年轻的斯坦霍普"举止粗俗""放荡不羁"，在公众眼里不过是个二流人物而已。1763 年，年轻的斯坦霍普去世。于是这些信件就交到了遗孀尤金妮娅·斯坦霍普夫人手中。在作者去世后不久，这些信件于 1774 年出版。

多年来，切斯特菲尔德勋爵的作品一直是公众批评的对象。当他写给亲生儿子的信件出版以后，塞缪尔·约翰逊评论说："这些信所教导的是妓女的道德品行和舞蹈大师的行为举止。"于是，人们强烈反对纪念勋爵。总的来说，人们认为他写给儿子的信，可以说是把世俗的聪明才智用最完美、最富有说服力的文风体现了出来，只是有时过于世俗了。

【作品解析】

Bath：巴斯，英格兰萨默塞特郡的一座城市，以其温泉和浴池而闻名。

O.S.："旧历"，即儒略历，由儒略·恺撒于公元前46年引入。1582年，教皇格列高利十三世引进了一种改良的历法。这就是所谓的"新历"，直到1752年才在英国被采用。

Mr. Pope：亚历山大·蒲柏（1688—1744），英国诗人和评论家。文中所引的两行诗出自《批评论》，第215—216行，并不确切。原文是"A little learning is a dangerous thing；Drink deep or taste not the Pierian spring"。译为："一知半解是危险的；要么痛饮，否则就不能品尝比埃里亚的圣泉。"

Cicero：马库斯·图留斯·西塞罗（前106—前43），罗马哲学家和演说家。文中关于学习的段落引自他的《为诗人阿奇亚辩护》。这段引文也许可以这样表述：这些书可以教育年轻人，也可以愉悦老年人；这些书是顺境中的装饰品，也是逆境中的庇护所；是居家的欢乐，不是世上的障碍。这些书整夜陪伴着我们，也是我们旅途中的伴侣，让我们的孤独的夜晚变得甜蜜而愉快。

Mr. Harte：沃尔特·哈特先生（1709—1774），斯坦霍普的家庭教师，据说是"牛津大学的学究"。

ruling passion：唯一的或占主导地位的激情。人天生就带有某种倾向，被具有相同倾向的人所吸引，而受到那些倾向迥然不同人的排斥。这种倾向在文艺复兴时期被称为性情，在17和18世纪被称为主导激情。

Schaffhausen：沙夫豪森，位于瑞士北部。年轻的斯坦霍普当时正在欧洲大陆进行"盛大之旅"。

bons mots（法语）：诙谐的言论，即俏皮话。

Cardinal Richelieu：红衣主教黎塞留，阿尔芒·让·迪普莱西·德·黎塞留（1585—1642），1607年曾担任吕松主教，并于1624年成为路易十三的首相。他是法国最伟大的政治家之一。

Corneille：皮埃尔·高乃依（1606—1684），法国剧作家。他的代表作之一《熙德》（1636），是根据西班牙英雄罗德里克·迪亚兹·德·比瓦尔勋爵（人称熙德"El Cid"）的传说和戏剧改编的。

en passant（法语）：顺便提一下。

bel esprit（法语）：才子，机智的人。

Sir Robert Walpole：罗伯特·沃波尔爵士（1676—1745），是 18 世纪上半叶最重要的英国政治领袖。他任职二十一年（1721—1742）。切斯特菲尔德是他的政治对手之一。

je ne sais quoi（法语）：直译为"我不知道是什么"。这是在 18 世纪初开始流行起来的一个短语，指某些奇怪、精致或漂亮的事物，但又很难定义。有时被译为"某种事物"。

arcana（arcanum 的复数）：奥秘、机密。

【参考译文】

给儿子的家书

亲爱的孩子：

　　虽然我花了很多的时间给你写信，但我必须承认，我经常会怀疑自己这样做究竟有什么意图。我知道，建议和忠告一般来说是不受欢迎的；而且我也知道，那些最需要建议和忠告的人，却很少愿意去接受或遵循这些建议和忠告；并且我还知道，特别是父母的建议和忠告，往往被认为是老年人的抑郁、专横跋扈和喋喋不休的产物。但是从另一方面，我自以为你自身的理智虽然尚不够成熟，不能让你从中获取很多教益，但是却足以使你能够辨明并接受这些真实的情况：我自以为（听着！）你自身的理智虽然还不够练达，却一定能告诉你，我给你的忠告都是为了你好而不是为了我的利益。因此，你起码应该对之做认真权衡和考虑。如果是那样，其中的一些建议才有望取得成效。不要把我看作像独裁者那样的父亲；我只是想以一个朋友的身份给你一些建议和忠告，同时还是一个宽容的朋友。不要以为我会限制你的自由和快乐；恰恰相反，我只是想做一个向导，而不是做一个稽查员来监督你。让我的经验来满足你的需求，弥补你的不足，并在你青春成长的过程中，帮你清除路途中曾经在我成长过程中深深刺伤过和毁坏过我的那些灌木丛和荆棘。但是，以上所述不是在向你暗示，你完全可以依赖我；在这个世界上除了从我这里，你得不到也不可能得到一个先令；而且，我对你没有女人的优柔寡断，你的优点美德将是衡量我仁慈善良的唯一标准。我是说，我不会向你暗示这些事情，因为，我深信你的言行举止具有更加高尚和慷慨的规范与准则。我的意思是说，你的行为举止应当出自正义，而并非出自对我的真情和感恩。

我经常建议你，无论学习什么都要专注和勤奋用功；我现在不是把这当作责任来说，而是要向你指出，这对你的快乐是有益的，不仅仅是有益，而且绝对是必要的；因为，除了可以使你超越周围的同龄人和他们现有的生活方式之外，还有比这更大的乐趣吗？那么同样，还有什么比被他人超越更加令人难堪和伤心的呢？在这种情况下，你的羞愧和遗憾也许比任何人都要多，因为每个人都知道你成长的特殊环境，你所受过的教育和非同寻常的关爱，使你有机遇比同龄人知道得更多。我所建议的勤奋用功并不局限于观察模仿或者超越他人（尽管这可以给人带来一种非常明智的快乐，也是一件值得骄傲的事）；但我的意思是，应当探本溯源，并要在这件事上出类拔萃。在我看来，一个人对某件事情一知半解，就等于他对那件事情全然无知。对任何事情如果只是一知半解，既不能满足自己也不能取信于他人，而且常常会带来耻辱和嘲笑。

蒲柏曾经真诚地告诫我们：一知半解是危险的；要么痛饮，否则就不能品尝比埃里亚的圣泉。所谓一知半解，绝对是纨绔子弟的特点。最近我常想，如果我年轻时，没有获得一些资助，没有感受到学习的乐趣，那么现在的我，必定会是一个非常不幸的人！如果没有这些，我又能去做些什么呢？也许我会像许多无知的人一样，整夜酗酒，酩酊大醉，毁了自己的健康和才干；或者，浪费在与轻浮女人的厮混之中，让自己饱受那些女人的讥笑和蔑视；或者，最后我会像某个男人一样厌倦了每天穿脱鞋袜而把自己吊死。现在我只有书了，因为，除了我的书以外，我什么都没有了。我每天都在回顾西塞罗对学问的探讨，发现他的研究是千真万确的：这些书可以教育年轻人，也可以愉悦老年人；这些书是顺境中的装饰品，也是逆境中的庇护所；是居家的快乐，不是世上的障碍。这些书整夜陪伴着我们，也是我们旅途中的伴侣，让我们的孤独的夜晚变得甜蜜而愉快。

我这么说吧，与老年人的谈话并非就一点乐趣都没有；恰恰相反，交谈对所有年龄段的人来说，都是莫大的、富于理性的快乐之事。至于与无知者的交谈，那简直就不是交谈了，因为连他们自己也没有感觉到一点点快乐。他们言辞匮乏，语竭词穷，也没有足够的知识将交谈继续下去。

所以，我诚恳地建议你，尽可能地多学习，多积累知识。也许这些知识在你年轻时还来不及运用，但请你相信，总有一天你会用得到。我希望这些知识能让你享用一生。在丰收年代，公共粮仓里储藏了供多年食用的粮食，这并不意味着人们都会预先知道接下来的一年、第二年或第三年会缺乏粮食；但是，人们都知道，总会有这么一年。

关于这个话题，我将不用对你说得太多。你身旁有哈特先生的敦促，你有理由相信这是对的。所以，简而言之，"你有摩西和先知；如果你不相信他们，即使他们中有一人死而复生，你也不会相信的"。不要以为我推荐给你的仅仅限于书本知识，尽管这些知识令人愉快、行之有效，而且很有必要，但我领悟到在现实世界里获得渊博知识，远远要比在书本上获得知识显得重要。事实上，这两种知识相辅相成，没有任何人会对其中一种知识完全精通而对另一种知识一无所知。现实世界的知识只能在现实世界里获得，不可能在家中的衣柜里获得。书本本身可能教会不了你现实世界里的知识，然而，书本却可以给你许多建议，建议你去观察以前可能忽略的细节；书本还可以让你对观察到的东西，与你在书本中所看到的相同事物做比较，有助于你筛选出真正有用的观点和方法。

要充分了解人类，就像掌握书本知识一样需要全神贯注和勤奋用功。但这还不够，也许还需要更多的睿智和洞察力。最近，我认识了许多老人，他们在这个伟大的世界里几乎度过了整个人生，但由于他们心浮气躁、三心二意，以至于他们对这方面的认知并不比他们十五岁时知道得多。因此，不要以为在与无所事事的老人们的闲聊中，就能获得这些知识，这是不可能的。你必须下功夫观察人类，你得下大功夫去深入研究他们。从某种意义上说，几乎所有的人天生都具有各种激情，但几乎每个人只有一种激情占据主导地位，其他都是次要的。只有找到了占主导地位的激情，才能窥探到他的内心深处，观察具有同样激情的不同人的不同生活方式。一旦你发现任何一个人的激情占主导地位时，你得千万记住，在与这种情感有关的事情上永远不要相信他。如果你愿意，你可以用他的激情来对付他，但要小心保护好自己免受伤害，无论他对你承诺过什么。

我希望你能把这封信认真地阅读两遍。但我怀疑，你是否能从头到尾阅读一遍。我就此搁笔，关于这类问题以后再聊。再见。

刚刚收到你来自瑞士沙夫豪森的信；但在写日期的时候，你忘记写月份了。

旧历 1746 年 10 月 4 日于巴斯

亲爱的孩子：

讨人喜欢是每个人必备的技能之一；然而，这又是一门很难学到的艺术。讨人喜欢几乎没有规律可循，而你自己的观察和判断能力则是你最好的老师，比我教给你的要强得多。待人如待己，是我坚信的一条信念。仔细观察别人做的让你高兴的事，也许你做同样的事也会让别人高兴。如果你的气质、你的品位，甚至你的弱点都能够受到别人的恭维和关注，而你又感到高兴，那么有鉴于此，你对他们表现出同样程度的恭维和关注，也可以让他们感到高兴。与人来往时，应注意氛围，切勿矫揉造作；要配合你的同伴当时的心境，表现出严肃、欢快，甚至是无聊的样子；这是从个体到大多数人在社交时都应该引起注意的。在人前不要夸夸其谈，没有比这更让人乏味和讨厌的事了。如果你恰好知道一些与话题有关的短小精悍的故事，而且非常适合现在谈话的主题，就用简短的语言来陈述；即使这样，你也要说，你不擅长言语，而那仅仅是因为与话题有关而且非常简短，才吸引了你。最重要的一点，就是在与人交谈时，要摆脱自我为中心的癖好，绝不要用你自己关心的或者个人的私事来取悦别人。虽然这些事对你来说很有趣，但在别人看来却毫无兴趣，甚至显得没有礼貌。除此之外，也没有必要暴露自己的隐私。无论你自以为有多么优秀，都不要在人前装模作样地炫耀自己的才华！不要像许多人那样，挖空心思地引导话题，伺机自我表现一番。如果你确实有真才实学，必会被人发现，不必自己显露，这样对自己有利。当与人争辩时，绝不要激动地大喊大叫，即使你认为或知道自己是正确的，也要谦虚、冷静地说出自己的观点和意见，这是说服他人的唯一方法。如果这样仍不奏效，就试着变个话题，心情愉悦地说："我俩谁也说服不了谁，而且也没必要非得说服对方不可，我们还是谈谈别的吧。"

与人交往时，我们得遵守当地的礼仪；有些行为举止在某种场合下很适宜，但在另外的场合下，却常常显得不得体。

适合于某些场合的幽默、俏皮话，甚至小小的出格行为，换个场合会显得平庸，单调乏味。在某些场合，某种性格、习惯、行话，可能会使某个词或某个手势表达得恰到好处；一旦离开那种特定的氛围，这些词和手势就会变得没有任何意义。这是人们的通病，他们喜欢把在某种特定的环境中得意的言行套用到其他的场合，要么很不合时宜，要么是放错了地方，其结果要么使人兴味索然，要么无礼甚至冒犯他人。不仅如此，他们还经常使用这样可笑的开场白："告诉你一件无与伦比的事……"或者"我要讲个这世上最美妙的事情……"这就引起了对方的期待，然而，其结果往往却是让人彻底失望，使得这个兜售新闻的人看起来像个十足的傻瓜。

　　如果你特别想赢得某人的喜爱和友谊，无论男女，尽量去寻找他们突出的优点（如果他们有的话），和他们主要的弱点（当然每个人都会有弱点）。一方面要公正对待他们的优点，而另一方面更要公正地对待他们的弱点，或者说仅仅公正还不够。人们也许擅长各种各样的技能，他们可以在竞技中胜出，或者至少他们希望自己被认为是优胜者；尽管他们乐于听到人们对他们的过人之处进行公允的评价，但是，他们在企图出人头地却又缺乏自信的方面获得他人赞扬时，才最为志得意满。例如：红衣主教黎塞留，毋庸置疑，在他那个时代，或者也许在所有的时代，是公认的最有能力的政治家。但他爱慕虚荣，也想被认为是最出色的诗人。他嫉妒当时伟大的剧作家皮埃尔·高乃依的声誉，于是下令让人撰写对高乃依作品《熙德》的批评文章。所以，那些善于奉承拍马的人很少提及他处理政务方面的能力，或者一带而过，认为这些都是自然而然的事。他们知道用才子和诗人这样的溢美之词会使黎塞留飘飘然，然后他们可以得到他的青睐。为什么呢？因为黎塞留确信自己是一个卓越的政治家，而对自己才子和诗人的冠名却没有坚定的信心。通过观察每个人最喜欢谈论的话题，你将会轻而易举地发现他们普遍存在的虚荣心。因为，每个人最喜欢谈论和炫耀自己的就是最希望被认可的擅长的技能，一旦被你发现了，你很快就触碰到他的虚荣心。已故的罗伯特·沃波尔爵士（确实是一位很有才干的人）是一个不太愿意听别人在这方面对他奉承的人，因为他丝毫不怀疑自己在这方面的能力。但是，他的主要弱点却在于他希望人们认为他具有彬彬有礼和勇敢的骑士风范。毫无疑问，他在这方面的表现不及当时任何一个活着的人。这也是他最喜爱和最经常谈论的话题。事实证明，那些善于观察的人都知道这是他的主要弱点。因此，他们成功地利用了他的这一弱点。

通常来说，女性所关心的只有一个话题，那就是她们的美貌。在这个方面，无论什么恭维的话对她来说都不过分。大自然几乎从来没有造出过一个丑陋的女性，丑到连听到别人对她外表的阿谀奉承都无动于衷。如果她的脸长得难看，那么她自己肯定会在某种程度上意识到这一点。于是，她便相信她的身材和气质在某种程度上可以弥补这一缺陷。如果她的身材很糟糕，那么她认为她的长相可以弥补。如果身材和长相都很糟糕，那么她会安慰自己，认为自己具有某种"不知道是什么"的比美丽更加迷人的高贵优雅的气质。这个真理从世界上最丑的女性考究的穿着上，就可以得到证实。在所有的女人中，一个深知自己的美貌无可争议、毋庸置疑、无人可以媲美的女性，觉得这是她应得的"天赋"，因此对一般相貌上的奉承并不在意。于是你得奉承她的思维能力，尽管她对自己的思维能力毫不怀疑，但她还是担心男人们可能并不会相信这一点。

请不要误解我的意思，不要以为我是想让你去学那种卑躬屈膝、厚颜无耻的阿谀奉承。绝对不是。绝不可以吹捧别人的恶习或罪行；正相反，对此要深恶痛绝，尽力阻止。但生活在这个世界上，总是会有人想方设法去讨好别人，迁就他人的弱点，迎合他们虽然荒谬却无害的虚荣。如果一位男士希望人们认为他有一颗更聪明的头脑，而一位女士希望人们认可自己的容颜比实际中更漂亮，那么，他们的这种错误想法也只是对他们自己来说是一种自我安慰，对于其他人来说并没有什么伤害。我宁可宽容他们，与他们交朋友，也不愿意想方设法地揭示真相，与他们为敌；这样做是毫无意义的。

同样，对细微处的关注也是极其令人愉快的。因为这些小小的关注会明显影响一个人的自尊和自爱的程度，而这两点与人性密不可分。因为这种关注毫无疑问地证实了我们对关注对象的关心和尊重。例如，观察我们想要结交的那些人在某些细小方面的习惯、喜好、厌恶以及他们的品味，然后注意投其所好，避免让他们不悦，并以某种优雅的方式让他们知道，你注意到他们喜欢这样的菜肴或者这样的房间，正因为他们喜欢，所以你这样安排了。或者相反，你注意到他们讨厌这类菜肴，甚至于不喜欢这种类型的人等，你就会尽量注意避免让其出现。对于这类琐碎事务的关注，比那些大事更能满足人们的自爱心理，因为这样做会让他们觉得，他们几乎是你所考虑和关心的唯一对象。

这些人生的秘诀，对于刚刚踏入这个社会的你来说，是非常必要的。我多么希望我能在你这个年纪时，就能知道这些；然而，我却为了这些付出了五十三年的代价，如果你能从中受益，我会毫不吝啬地告诉你。再见。

旧历 1747 年 10 月 16 日于伦敦

OLIVER GOLDSMITH (1730?—1774)

Oliver Goldsmith (1730?—1774), the son of a clergyman, was born in Ireland. Upon his graduation from Trinity College, Dublin (February, 1749), he spent some years of adventures in Ireland, in Scotland, and on the Continent, where he got along by disputing at universities and playing the flute. In 1756 he went to London, almost penniless; and having tried his hands without success at teaching and pharmacy, he began his career as a journalist. His first substantial reputation arose from a series of imaginary letters of a Chinese philosopher, which he wrote for the *Public Ledger* between January 4, 1760 and August 14, 1761. These letters, 123 in all, took so well with the public that they were collected and republished in two volumes as *The Citizen of the World* (1762).

When Johnson's famous Club was organized in 1764, afterwards called the Literary Club, Goldsmith was admitted to membership. In the company of the most gifted talkers of the time, he did not always appear at an advantage. He lacked the readiness of tongue, which is indispensable for incessant combats of wit. But he knew how to write, and he wrote well. In the decade between the founding of the Club and his death he published *The Traveller* (1764), *The Vicar of Wakefield* (1766), *The Good-Natured Man* (1768), *The Deserted Village* (1770), and *She Stoops to Conquer* (1773). No contemporary of his ever wrote so many pieces of permanent value in the same length of time. The unique charm of his work lies in the fact that, whatever the subject or the form, it is impregnated with his own rich and wholesome personality—a personality in which humour and pathos, tears and laughter, worldly shrewdness and childlike simplicity are strangely mixed. In 1774, worn out with overwork and anxiety, he died. Johnson wrote his epitaph, which contains these lines:

Qui nullum fere scribendi genus non tetigit,

Nullum quod tetigit non ornavit.

— 'There is almost no kind of composition which he did not touch, and nothing he touched which he did not adorn.'

【作者简介】

奥利弗·哥尔德斯密斯（约 1730—1774），一位牧师的儿子，出生于爱尔兰。他从都柏林三一学院毕业后（1749 年 2 月），用了几年的时间在爱尔兰、苏格兰和欧洲大陆游历；游历时，他以在大学辩论和演奏长笛为生。1756 年，他到了伦敦，几乎身无分文；他尝试以教师和药剂师为职业，但均未成功，于是他开始了记者的职业生涯。他最初的主要声誉来自他以一位中国哲学家的身份撰写的一系列虚构的随笔信件，于 1760 年 1 月 4 日至 1761 年 8 月 14 日间连载在《大众纪事报》上。这些信件共有 123 封，受到公众的好评，后来集结成册重新出版，分为两卷，取名为《世界公民》(1762)。

　　1764 年，约翰逊开创了著名的俱乐部，即后来所称的"文学俱乐部"，哥尔德斯密斯是会员之一。在那些当时最有天赋的、善于言辞的会员中，他并不能充分展示他的才华。他缺乏能言善辩的才能，而这对于无休止的斗智斗勇是不可缺少的。然而他知道如何写作，而且写得很好。在俱乐部成立到他去世之间的十年间，他出版了《旅行者》(1764)、《威克菲尔德牧师传》(1766)、《好心人》(1768)、《荒村》(1770) 和《屈身求爱》(1773)。在同时期的当代作家里，没有一位能像他一样在相同的时间内，创作出如此之多并富有永恒价值的文学作品。他作品的独特魅力在于，无论什么主题或者形式，都充满了他自己丰富而又健全的个性——幽默与伤感，泪水与笑声，世俗的精明与孩子般的单纯奇妙地交织在一起。1774 年，由于工作过度劳累和焦虑，他疲惫不堪，与世长辞了。约翰逊为他写了墓志铭，其中有这样几行："几乎没有一种文学创作他未曾涉猎过，凡是他涉猎过的无处没有他的点缀。"

The English Character

The English seem as silent as the Japanese, yet vainer than the inhabitants of Siam. Upon my arrival I attributed that reserve to modesty, which, I now find, has its origin in pride. Condescend to address them first, and you are sure of their acquaintance; stoop to flattery, and you conciliate their friendship and esteem. They bear hunger, cold, fatigue, and all the miseries of life without shrinking; danger only calls forth their fortitude; they even exult in calamity; but contempt is what they cannot bear. An Englishman fears contempt more than death; he often flies to death as a refuge from its pressure; and dies when he fancies the world has ceased to esteem him.

Pride seems the source not only of their national vices, but of their national virtues also. An Englishman is taught to love his king as his friend, but to acknowledge no other master than the laws which himself has contributed to enact. He despises those nations who, that one may be free, are all content to be slaves; who first lift a tyrant into terror, and then shrink under his power as if delegated from Heaven. Liberty is echoed in all their assemblies; and thousands might be found ready to offer up their lives for the sound, though perhaps not one of all the number understands its meaning. The lowest mechanic, however, looks upon it as his duty to be a watchful guardian of his country's freedom, and often uses a language that might seem haughty, even in the mouth of the Great Emperor who traces his ancestry to the moon.

A few days ago, passing by one of their prisons, I could not avoid stopping, in order to listen to a dialogue which I thought might afford me some entertainment. The conversation was carried on between a debtor, through the grate of his prison, a porter who had stopped to rest his burden, and a soldier at the window. The subject was upon a **threatened invasion from France**, and each seemed extremely anxious to rescue his country from the impending danger. 'For my part,' cries the prisoner, 'the greatest of my apprehensions is for our freedom; if the French should conquer, what would become of English liberty? My dear friends, liberty is the Englishman's prerogative; we must preserve that at the expense of our lives; of that the French shall never deprive us. It is not to be expected that men who are slaves themselves would preserve our freedom should they happen to conquer.' — 'Ay, slaves,' cries the porter, 'they are all slaves, fit only to carry burdens, every one of them. Before I would stoop to slavery, may this be my poison,' (and he held the goblet in his hand) 'may this be my poison—but I would sooner **'list** for a soldier.'

The soldier, taking the goblet from his friend, with much awe, fervently cried out, 'It is not so much our liberties, as our religion, that would suffer by such a change : ay, our religion, my lads. May the devil sink me into flames,' (such was the solemnity of his adjuration) 'if the French should come over, but our religion would be utterly undone!' —So saying, instead of a libation, he applied the goblet to his lips, and confirmed his sentiments with a ceremony of the most persevering devotion.

In short, every man here pretends to be a politician; even the fair sex are sometimes found to mix the severity of national altercation with the blandishments of love, and often become conquerors, by more weapons of destruction than their eyes.

This universal passion for politics is gratified by **Daily Gazettes**, as with us **in China**. But as in ours the Emperor endeavours to instruct his people, in theirs the people endeavour to instruct the administration. You must not, however, imagine, that they who compile these papers have any actual knowledge of the politics, or the government, of a state; they only collect their materials from the oracle of some coffee-house, which oracle has himself gathered them the night before from a beau at a gaming-table, who has pillaged his knowledge from a great man's porter, who has had his information from the great man's gentleman, who has invented the whole story for his own amusement the night preceding.

The English, in general, seem fonder of gaining the esteem than the love of those they converse with. This gives a formality to their amusements; their gayest conversations have something too wise for innocent relaxation; though in company you are seldom disgusted with the absurdity of a fool, you are seldom lifted into rapture by those strokes of vivacity, which give instant, though not permanent, pleasure.

What they want, however, in gaiety, they make up in politeness. You smile at hearing me praise the English for their politeness; you who have heard very different accounts from the missionaries at Peking, who have seen such a different behaviour in their merchants and seamen at home.

But I must still repeat it, the English seem more polite than any of their neighbours: their great art in this respect lies in endeavouring, while they oblige, to lessen the force of the favour. Other countries are fond of obliging a stranger; but seem desirous that he should be sensible of the obligation. The English confer their kindness with an appearance of indifference, and give away benefits with an air as if they despised them.

Walking, a few days ago, between an English and a Frenchman, in the suburbs of the city, we were overtaken by a heavy shower of rain. I was unprepared; but they had each large coats, which defended them from what seemed to me a perfect inundation. The Englishman, seeing me shrink from the weather, accosted me thus: 'Pshaw, man, what dost shrink at? Here, take this coat; I don't want it; I find it no way useful to me, I had as lief be without it.' The Frenchman began to show his politeness in turn. 'My dear friend,' cries he, 'why won't you oblige me by making use of my coat? You see how well it defends me from the rain; I should not choose to part with it to others, but to such a friend as you I could even part with my skin to do him service.'

From such minute instances as these, most reverend Fum Hoam, I am sensible your sagacity will collect instruction. The volume of nature is the book of knowledge; and he becomes most wise who makes the most judicious selection. Farewell.

Notes

This is Letter IV of *The Citizen of the World*, supposed to be written by Lien Chi Altangi, a Chinese philosopher in London, to his friend Fum

Hoam, First President of the Ceremonial Academy in Peking. The Chinese colouring in this letter, as in many others, is slight, and Goldsmith speaks too clearly in his own character. But much of the peculiar charm of the satire would be lost without the fiction of the foreign traveler.

threatened invasion from France. A reference to the Seven Years War, 1756—1763. The English and French were then engaged in a struggle for colonies in America and India.

'list, enlist, enter as a soldier (archaic).

Daily Gazettes in China. It was almost universally known that public gazettes in China were exemplary. In the *Bee* for 1733, for instance, Eustace Budgell wrote: 'They (Chinese gazettes) are just the reverse of our European newspapers, which are a medley of truth and falsehood, blended together without any distinction, and often containing more of the latter than the former; whereas these are so strictly tied down to truth and fact that to deviate from them is a capital crime... These gazettes are presented to the Emperor, and they often contain pieces of his own composition.'

【作品简介】

本文选自《世界公民》第4封信，据说是借旅居在伦敦的一位中国哲学家李安济的身份写给他的朋友——北京任礼部官员的冯皇。与其他书信一样，这封信的中国文化色彩也很淡，哥尔德斯密斯在他自己的人物描述里清楚地说明了这一点。但是，如果没有虚构的外国旅行者，这部作品就会失去其独特的讽刺魅力。

【作品解析】

threatened invasion from France：这里指的是七年战争（1756—1763），英

国和法国为了争夺在美国和印度的殖民地而发生的一场争斗。

'list：今多用"enlist"，征召士兵（古义）。

Daily Gazettes in China：众所周知，中国的公报堪称典范。例如，在 1733 年《蜜蜂》周刊中，尤斯塔斯·巴杰尔曾写道："它们（中国的公报）正好与我们的欧洲报纸相反；我们的报纸是真理和谬误的混合物，将真理和谬误毫无区分地混合在了一起，而且后者往往比前者多。而中国的公报却紧紧围绕着真理（和事实），一旦有所偏离，就是重罪……这些公报是呈送给皇帝的，其中经常包含一些他自己的作品。"

【参考译文】

英国人的性格

英国人看起来似乎与日本人一样沉默寡言，然而却比泰国人更加虚荣。初来英国时，我把这种虚荣看作谦虚，现在我才发现，这种谦虚其实来源于傲慢。要是你愿意屈尊先与他们打招呼，你肯定会与他们相识。要是你对他们阿谀奉承，你就会赢得他们的友谊和尊重。他们可以忍受饥饿、寒冷、疲劳，面对生活中的苦难，他们从不退缩；危机只会让他们更加坚毅。即便是身处逆境，他们仍然能欣然面对。然而，他们决不能忍受蔑视。一个英国人害怕蔑视胜过死亡，他们常常会因为承受不了人们的蔑视，而向死神寻求解脱。当他们觉得不受人们尊重时，就会抑郁而亡。

傲慢似乎不仅是他们国家恶习的来源，也是他们民族美德的源泉。一个英国人所受的教育，是要像爱他们的朋友一样爱戴他们的国王，但是他们只认可自己参与和制定过的宪法。英国人鄙视那些为了获得自由，而心甘情愿受奴役、受压迫的民族；鄙视那些似乎是受了神的旨意，先是举起反对暴君的旗帜，制造恐怖，然后又畏缩在君王的集权之下的人。他们在所有的集会上呼吁自由；数千人已经做好了为之献出自己生命的准备，尽管也许不是所有人都能真正懂得它其中的意义。就连社会底层的技工，也认为他们有义务成为国家自由的守护者。因此，他们经常会使用一种即便是在先祖大帝时代，听起来也有几分傲慢的言语。

几天前，我路过一个监狱，听到了一段谈话，我不由自主地停下了脚步，因为这段谈话给我带来了乐趣。谈话是在一个监狱护栏内的债务人、一个停下来休息的搬运工、一个站在窗边的士兵之间进行的。谈话的主题是来自法国的侵略威胁，他们每个人似乎都急不可待地想将他们的国家从迫在眉睫的危机中拯救出来。"就我而言，"囚犯说道，"我最大的担忧就是自由。如果法国人征服了英国，那我们英国还会有什么样的自由？我亲爱的朋友们，自由是英国人的特权！我们必须以自己的生命为代价来维护它，法国人绝不能剥夺我们享有自由的权利！如果他们碰巧征服了英国，我们不能幻想，本身就是被奴役的法国人，会保护我们的自由吗？""唉，奴隶们！"搬运工叫道，"他们都是奴隶，只配做搬运工。在我被迫屈服于奴隶之前，但愿这就是我的毒药，"他拿着高脚酒杯比画着，"但愿这就是我的毒药——我宁愿早点成为一名士兵。"

士兵从搬运工手中接过高脚酒杯，满怀激情并非常严肃地说："不仅我们的自由，而且我们的宗教都要遭到迫害。唉，我们的宗教，我的伙计们！愿魔鬼把我燃烧成灰烬，"这是他庄严的恳求，"如果法国人打了过来，我们的宗教就彻底毁灭了！"说完后，他并没有将酒一饮而尽，而是将酒杯贴在嘴唇上，并用这样一个最虔诚的仪式来证明他的感情。

简而言之，这里谈话中的每个人都假装自己是个政治家。甚至有时人们发现，即使美丽的女工们在打情骂俏时也掺杂着严肃的民族争论，这比她们的眼睛更具有杀伤力，常常使她们成为征服者。

《每日公报》满足了人们普遍的政治热情，就像我们在中国一样。然而，如同我们的皇帝努力教导他的人民一样，同时，人民也努力指导他们的政府。可你无论如何想象不到，那些编撰这些稿件的人，对国家的政治或政府没有任何实际的了解或者这方面的知识；他们只不过是从某个咖啡馆的通讯员那里收集了情报，而通讯员的情报又是他前一天晚上从一张赌桌上某个花花公子的嘴里收集到的，那个花花公子则又是从某位有识之士的门卫那里偷听到的，而这位有识之士只是为了自己的一时高兴自娱自乐，在前一天晚上编撰了整个故事。

一般来说，英国人似乎比较喜欢在交谈中赢得对方的尊重而不仅仅是喜爱。这就给他们娱乐消遣的谈话赋予了一种形式；他们最快乐的谈话蕴藏着机智，绝不是一般放松的闲聊。虽然，在谈话中你很少会对愚蠢荒谬的言论感到厌恶，但你也很少会被那些充满活力的语言所陶醉，那些只能给你带来一时的欢乐，而绝不可能带来永久的享受。

他们想要的就是皆大欢喜，而彬彬有礼则是他们达到这一目的的方式和方法。听到我对英国人的礼貌表示赞美时，你也许会发笑，你从到过北京的传教士那儿听到过不同的说法吗？他们在英国国内的商人和海员身上看到了完全不同的行为。但我还是要重申一遍，英国人似乎比邻国的任何人都要彬彬有礼：他们在这方面极其丰富的技巧在于不断地努力，他们认为有义务去帮助他人，他们也尽量不让受助人感觉到是施舍和恩惠。而其他国家的人也喜欢乐于助人，但似乎希望受助人能意识到这一点。英国人以冷漠的态度来表达他们的善意，并以毫不在意的态度去帮助他人。

几天前，在城市的郊区，我同一个英国人和一个法国人在一起散步，突然一阵瓢泼大雨。我一点准备都没有，而他们每个人都穿着防雨外套，躲过了这场大雨。英国人看我冷得发抖，就跟我搭讪说："哎呀，老兄，你都发抖了？给你，穿上这件外套吧！我真的不需要，我觉得它对我没有多大的用处。没有了这件外套，我倒反而少了个累赘。"而法国人却显得彬彬有礼，"我亲爱的朋友，"他嚷道，"你为什么不让我用大衣来为你遮雨呢？你看它有多好，把我从雨中解救了出来！我不应该选择把它留给别人，而应该留给你这样的朋友，我自己淋雨也心甘情愿。"

最尊敬的冯皇大人，从这些微小的事例中，我意识到以您的聪明才智，一定会从中汲取精华并有所启迪。无限广阔的大自然便是书本知识的源泉；而最聪明的人，就是做出明智选择的人。

就此搁笔。

Westminster Abbey

I am just returned from **Westminster Abbey**, the place of sepulture for the philosophers, heroes, and kings of England. What a gloom do monumental inscriptions, and all the venerable remains of deceased merit inspire? Imagine a temple marked with the hand of antiquity, solemn as religious awe, adorned with all the magnificence of barbarous profusion, dim windows, fretted pillars, long colonnades and dark ceilings. Think, then, what were my sensations at being introduced to such a scene. I stood in the midst of the temple, and threw my eyes round on the walls, filled with the statues, the inscriptions, and the monuments of the dead.

Alas! I said to myself, how does pride attend the puny child of dust even to the grave! Even humble as I am, I possess more consequence in the present scene than greatest hero of them all: they have toiled for an hour to gain a transient immortality, and are at length retired to the grave, where they have no attendant but the worm, none to flatter but the epitaph.

As I was indulging such reflections, a gentleman dressed in black, perceiving me to be a stranger, came up, entered into conversation, and politely offered to be my instructor and guide through the temple. 'If any monument,' said he, 'should particularly excite your curiosity, I shall endeavour to satisfy your demands.' I accepted, with thanks, the gentleman's offer, adding that 'I was come to observe the policy, the wisdom, and the justice of the English, in conferring rewards upon deceased merit. If adulation like this,' continued I, 'be properly conducted, as it can no ways injure those who are flattered, so it may be a glorious incentive to those who are now capable of enjoying it. It is the duty of every good government to turn this monumental pride to its own advantage; to become strong in the aggregate from the weakness of the individual. If none but the truly great have a place in this awful repository, a temple like this will give the finest lessons of morality, and be a strong incentive to true ambition. I am told that none have a place here but characters of the most distinguished merit.' **The Man in Black** seemed impatient at my observations; so I discontinued my remarks, and we walked on together to take a view of every particular monument in order as it lay.

As the eye is naturally caught by the finest objects, I could not avoid being particularly curious about one monument, which appeared more beautiful than the rest. 'That,' said I to my guide, 'I take to be the tomb of some very great man. By the peculiar excellence of the workmanship, and the magnificence of the design, this must be a trophy raised to the memory of some king who has saved his country from ruin, or law-giver who has reduced his fellow-citizens from anarchy into just subjection.' — 'It is not requisite,' replied my companion, smiling, 'to have such qualifications in order to have a very fine monument here: more humble abilities will suffice.' —

'What! I suppose, then, the gaining two or three battles, or the taking half a score towns, is thought a sufficient qualification?' — 'Gaining battles, or taking towns,' replied the Man in Black, 'may be of service; but a gentleman may have a very fine monument here without ever seeing a battle or a siege.' — 'This, then, is the monument of some poet, I presume—of one whose wit has gained him immortality?' — 'No, sir,' replied my guide, 'the gentleman who lies here never made verses; and as for wit, he despised it in others, because he had none himself.' — 'Pray tell me, then, in a word,' said I, peevishly, 'what is the great man who lies here particularly remarkable for?' — 'Remarkable, sir?' said my companion; 'why, sir, the gentleman that lies here is remarkable, very remarkable—for a tomb in Westminster Abbey.' — 'But, **head of my ancestors**! How has he got here? I fancy he could never bribe the guardians of the temple to give him a place. Should he not be ashamed to be seen among company where even moderate merit would look like infamy?' — 'I suppose,' replied the Man in Black, 'the gentleman was rich, and his friends, as is usual in such a case, told him he was great. He readily believed them; the guardians of the temple, as they got by the self-delusion, were ready to believe him too; so he paid his money for a fine monument; and the workman, as you see, has made him one of the most beautiful. Think not, however, that this gentleman is singular in his desire of being buried among the great; there are several others in the temple, who, hated and shunned by the great while alive, have come here, fully resolved to keep them company now they are dead.'

As we walked along to a particular part of the temple, 'There,' says the gentleman, pointing with his finger, 'that is the **Poets'**

Corner; there you see the monuments of Shakespeare, and Milton, and Prior, and Drayton.' — 'Drayton!' I replied; 'I never heard of him before; but I have been told of one **Pope**—is he there?' — 'It is time enough,' replied my guide, 'these hundred years; he is not long dead; people have not done hating him yet.' — 'Strange,' cried I, 'can any be found to hate a man whose life was wholly spent in entertaining and instructing his fellow-creatures?' — 'Yes,' says my guide, 'they hate him for that very reason. There are a set of men called answerers of books, who take upon them to watch the republic of letters, and distribute reputation by the sheet, they somewhat resemble the eunuchs in a seraglio, who are incapable of giving pleasure themselves, and hinder those that would. These answerers have no other employment but to cry out Dunce and Scribbler; to praise the dead, and revile the living; to grant a man of confessed abilities some small share of merit; to applaud twenty blockheads in order to gain the reputation of candour; and to revile the moral character of the man whose writings they cannot injure. Such wretches are kept in pay by some mercenary bookseller, or more frequently the bookseller himself takes this dirty work off their hands, as all that is required is to be very abusive and very dull. Every poet of any genius is sure to find such enemies; he feels, though he seems to despise, their malice; they make him miserable here, and in the pursuit of empty fame, at last he gains solid anxiety.'

'Has this been the case with every poet I see here?' cried I. 'Yes, with very mother's son of them,' replied he, 'except he happened to be born a mandarin. If he has much money, he may buy reputation from your book-answerers, as well as a monument from the guardians of the temple.'

'But are there not some men of distinguished taste, as in China, who are willing to patronize men of merit, and soften the rancour of malevolent dullness?' 'I own there are many,' replied the Man in Black; 'but, alas! sir, the book-answerers crowd about them, and call themselves the writers of books; and the patron is too indolent to distinguish: thus poets are kept at a distance, while their enemies eat up all their rewards at the mandarin's table.'

Leaving this part of the temple, we made up to an iron gate, through which my companion told me we were to pass, in order to see the monuments of the kings. Accordingly, I marched up without further ceremony, and was going to enter, when a person who held the gate in his hand told me I must pay first. I was surprised at such a demand; and asked the man, whether the people of England kept a show?—Whether the paltry sum he demanded was not a national reproach?—Whether it was not more to the honour of the country to let their magnificence, or their antiquities be openly seen than thus meanly to tax a curiosity which tended to their own honour? 'As for your questions,' replied the gate-keeper, 'to be sure they may be very right, because I don't understand them; but, as for that there threepence, I farm it from one—who rents it from another— who hires it from a third—who leases it from the guardians of the temple,—and we all must live.' I expected, upon paying here, to see something extraordinary, since what I had seen for nothing filled me with so much surprise: but in this I was disappointed; there was little more within than black coffins, rusty armour, tattered standards, and some few slovenly figures in wax. I was sorry I had paid, but

I comforted myself by considering it would be my last payment. A person attended us who, without once blushing, told a hundred lies: he talked of a lady who died by pricking her finger; of a king with a golden head, and twenty such pieces of absurdity. 'Look ye there, gentlemen,' says he, pointing to **an old oak chair**, 'there's a curiosity for ye; in that chair the kings of England were crowned: you see also a stone underneath, and that stone is Jacob's pillow.' I could see no curiosity either in the oak chair or the stone: could I, indeed, behold one of the old kings of England seated in this, or Jacob's head laid upon the other, there might be something curious in the sight; but in the present case, there was no more reason for my surprise, than if I should pick a stone from their streets, and call it a curiosity, merely because one of the kings happened to tread upon it as he passed in a procession.

From hence our conductor led us through several dark walks and winding ways, uttering lies, talking to himself, and flourishing a wand which he held in his hand. He reminded me of the black magicians of **Kobi**. After we had been almost fatigued with a variety of objects, he at last desired me to consider attentively a certain suit of armour, which seemed to show nothing remarkable. 'This armour,' said he, 'belonged to **General Monk**.' — 'Very surprising that a general should wear armour!' — 'And pray,' added he, 'observe this cap; this is General Monk's cap.' — 'Very strange indeed, very strange, that a general should have a cap also! Pray, friend, what might this cap have cost originally?' — 'That, sir,' says he, 'I don't know; but this cap is all the wages I have for my trouble.' — 'A very small recompense, truly,' said I. 'Not so very small.' replied he, 'for every gentleman puts some money into it, and

I spend, the money.' — 'What, more money! Still more money!' — 'Every gentleman gives something, sir.' — 'I'll give thee nothing,' returned I; 'the guardians of the temple should pay you your wages, friend, and not permit you to squeeze thus from every spectator. When we pay our money at the door to see a show, we never give more as we are going out. Sure, the guardians of the temple can never think they get enough. Show me the gate; if I stay longer, I may probably meet with more of those ecclesiastical beggars.'

Thus leaving the temple precipitately, I returned to my lodgings, in order to ruminate over what was great and to despise what was mean in the occurrences of the day.

Notes

This is Letter XIII of *The Citizen of the World*.

Westminster Abbey, the famous cathedral in London, certain sections of which were built during the reign of Henry III (1216—1272). Many kings and queens of England were buried there.

The Man in Black, one of the notable characters in *The Citizen of the World*. In Letter XXVII Goldsmith says that he was a very 'good-natured and had not the least share of harm in him.'

head of my ancestors, supposed to be a form of Chinese swearing.

Poets' Corner, in the south transept of Westminster Abbey, contains the monuments or other memorials of Shakespeare, Milton, and other British authors. Michael Drayton (1563—1631) was an author of sonnets and historical poems, and Matthew Prior (1664—1721) was one of the best

English epigrammatists; both of them were buried in Westminster Abbey.

Pope, Alexander (1688—1744), was for many years the object of hostile comment; he was hated as he had hated most of his contemporaries.

an old oak chair, i.e. the coronation chair in the Confessor's Chapel, Westminster Abbey. It contains beneath its seat the stone of Scone, on which Scottish kings were crowned. It is of Scottish origin, but tradition identifies it with Jacob's pillow at Bethel.

Kobi, i.e. Gobi Desert, in Mongolia.

General Monk, i.e. George Monk (or Monck), First Duke of Albemarle (1608—1670), who figured prominently in military and political affairs in the Commonwealth and the Restoration. He defeated the Dutch fleet in 1667.

【作品简介】

本文选自《世界公民》第 13 封信。

【作品解析】

Westminster Abbey：伦敦著名的大教堂，其中某些部分是在亨利三世统治期间（1216—1272）建造的。英国的许多国王和王后都被埋葬在那里。

The Man in Black：黑衣人，《世界公民》中最著名的人物之一。在第 27 封信中，哥尔德斯密斯说他是一个"天性非常善良，最不可能伤害别人的人"。

head of my ancestors：意指中国人的口头语，一种惊讶但又无奈的表达方式。

Poets' Corner：诗人之角，位于西敏寺南侧，其中有莎士比亚、弥尔顿和其他英国作家的纪念碑或其他纪念物。迈克尔·德雷顿（1563—1631）一生致力于创作十四行诗和史诗，马修·普赖尔（1664—1721）是英国最优秀的讽刺诗人之一：他们俩都葬在西敏寺。

Pope：亚历山大·蒲柏（1688—1744），多年来一直是公众颇有敌意的评论对象，人们憎恨他如同他憎恨大多数与他同时代的人物一样。

an old oak chair：指的是西敏寺忏悔室里的加冕椅。它的座位下面乃是苏格兰历代国王加冕时使用的一块斯昆石。这块石头来源于苏格兰，但传统上却把它和雅各在伯特利枕过的枕石联系在了一起。

Kobi：指蒙古戈壁沙漠。

General Monk：蒙克将军，即乔治·蒙克，阿尔比马尔第一任公爵（1608—1670），他在英格兰联邦和王政复辟时期的军事以及政治事务中表现突出，并于1667年击败了荷兰舰队。

【参考译文】

西敏寺

我刚从西敏寺回来，那里是英国哲学家们、英雄们和国王们的安息之地。那里不朽的铭文以及德高望重的前辈们的遗骸，将会激发人们怎样的伤感和沮丧？设想一下，一座古色古香的殿宇，有着宗教的敬畏和庄严，殿宇里的装饰充满了初民时代的宏伟；幽暗的窗户、雕花的柱子、长长的柱廊和昏暗的天花板。我站在殿宇的中央，环顾四周，这里处处都是雕像、铭文和死者的纪念碑。设身处地想一想，您的感觉会是怎样？

天哪！我对自己说，虚荣甚至在坟墓里还侍奉着可怜的尘埃之子！尽管我身份卑微，但至少现在的我，要比他们中间最伟大的英雄对于这个世界更具有影响力。他们辛辛苦苦奋斗了短暂的一生，永生之后才获得了不朽，最终还是隐退到了坟墓。在那里，他们除了蠕虫之外，没有随从陪伴；除了墓志铭之外，再也不会有人阿谀奉承。

正当我沉思时，一位身着黑衣的绅士向我走了过来并与我攀谈了起来。他看出来我不是本地人，便很有礼貌地提出想做我的向导，带我参观这里。"如果您对哪一座墓碑感兴趣，"他说，"我会尽力向您解释。"我非常感谢并接受了这位先生的提议，我还告诉他："我来此地，是考察英国是以什么样的公正公平的睿智政策，为已故者加冠进爵。好像这样的赞美之词，"我接着说，"只要处理得当，既不会伤害那些被赞美的已故者，同时对于那些现在有资格可以享受这些赞美的人来说，它可能会是一种极为光荣的激励。每一个好的政府都有责任把这种永生不朽的荣誉转变成国家的优势，将个人微弱的荣誉汇集起来，形成一股强大的力量。如果只有真正的伟人才能葬在这里的话，那么这座寺院将是最好的道德教育场所，也可以成为激发人们雄心壮志的强大动力。有人告诉我，除了最杰出的人物，没有其他人能在这里占有一席之地。"黑衣人似乎对我的议论有点不耐烦；于是，我便停了下来，不再多说什么了。我们一边往前走，一边依次阅览每座纪念碑。

人们的眼睛总是自然地会被最好看的事物所吸引，我也无法摆脱这种好奇心，不由自主对其中一座纪念碑产生了特别的好奇，它看起来比其他的更漂亮。"那个，"我对我的向导说，"我想那里一定是个非常伟大的人物的墓地。从独特的工艺和雄伟的设计上看，那一定是为了纪念某位拯救过国家免于毁灭的国王，或者是为了纪念哪位把他的同胞从无政府状态中挽救出来，带来正义的法律制定者。""并非如此，"我的同伴微笑着说，"为了在这里有一座非常精美、漂亮的纪念碑，并非要有这样的资格，能力差的也可以拥有。""什么！照这样说，难道参加并获得过两三次战役的胜利者，或者攻占过十来个城镇的人，也有资格享受这种待遇？""参加过战役或者夺取过城镇的，"黑衣人说，"可能有用；但是，从来没有参加过战役或者夺取过城镇的人，在这里也可以有座非常好的纪念碑。""这也许是某位诗人的纪念碑，我猜想——是他的智慧让他永生不朽，获得了纪念碑吧？""不是的，先生，"我的向导回答说，"这位躺在这里的先生从来没有创作过诗文；至于智慧嘛，他经常受到别人的藐视，因为他并没有什么智慧。""那么，请你用一句话告诉我，"我生气地说，简直不敢相信，"这里躺着的伟人到底有什么样的过人之处？""过人之处，先生？"我的向导说道，"为什么，先生，能躺在这里的人都非得了不起吗？非得要有过人之处吗？不就是在西敏寺有一座坟墓吗！""天哪，我的个祖宗！他到底是怎么弄进来的？我想他不至于是贿赂寺院里的守护人给了他一个位置吧。在这里，即使是中等的功绩也会被同伴们视为耻辱，他难道不应该感到羞耻吗？""我猜想大概就是这样吧，"黑衣人回答道，"这位先生很富有，而他的朋友们，就像常人对待富人一样，告诉他很棒，确实很了不起。这位先生就欣然地相信了，寺院的守护人也自欺欺人地跟着相信了；于是他付了钱买了一座精美的纪念碑；正如你所看见的那样，雕碑工人将他的墓碑雕成了最漂亮的墓碑之一。然而，这位先生并不是唯一的一位想同伟人们葬在一起的人。在寺院里还有其他几位，他们活着的时候受到伟人们的憎恨和躲避，在他们死了以后，却决定来到这里，现在永远地和伟人们做伴了。"

我们走到了西敏寺的某个区域，"这，"我的向导用手指了指说，"这是诗人之角；这儿有莎士比亚、弥尔顿、普赖尔和德雷顿的纪念碑。""德雷顿！"我惊讶地说，"之前，我没有听说过他，但我听说过蒲柏——他也埋在这里吗？""这是个时间问题，"我的向导说，"这里需要百年之后；蒲柏才去世不久，人们还没有恨够他呢！""这真是有点怪了，"我提高了声音，"难道人们会憎恨一位一辈子以指导别人并以使别人快乐为己任的人吗？""是啊，"我的向导说，"人们正是因为这个才恨他。有一群人，他们把自己称为书评家，审阅出版的作品，通过书的简评散布名誉。他们有点像掌握内务的太监，自己无法享受快乐，还要千方百计阻挠别人去享受。这群人自称为书评家，没有什么职业，只会叫嚣这个是蠢材，那个是蹩脚文人；他们赞美死者，辱骂生者；对公认有能力的人他们只会说一点点好话，而为了沽名钓誉居然能为二十个傻瓜鼓掌叫好；他们无法伤害名作家的作品，只能辱骂他们个人的声誉。这些可怜虫往往是受某些唯利是图的书商雇用，更加常见的是，书商们亲自参与这些肮脏的勾当，因为唯一的要求就是书评要具有侮辱性的语言和枯燥无味的文字。任何一位天才的诗人都会有这样的敌人；诗人感受到了他们的恶意，尽管他看起来对之不屑一顾。他们让诗人从此痛苦不堪；在追求虚名的过程中，诗人最终得到的是与日俱增的焦虑。"

"这里安息的每位诗人都是这样吗？"我问道。"是的，每一位诗人都一样，"他答道，"除非他出生在一个官僚家庭。如果他很有钱，他可以从书评家那里买到名声，也可以从寺院的守护人那里买到纪念碑。"

"难道他们中间就没有一些品位出众的绅士，愿意赞助有识之士，从而抵消书评人的仇恨和恶意吗？就像在中国那样。""我承认有许多这样的人，"黑衣人说，"但是，唉，书评家成群结队地围绕在诗人的身边，也把自己称为著作者，而那些赞助者又懒得去分辨真假；于是，诗人就被隔离开来并抛在了一边，无人理睬，而他们的冤家则享尽了诗人的荣耀。"

出了西敏寺的这个区域，我们来到了一扇铁门前。我的向导告诉我穿过这扇铁门，我们就可以看到国王们的纪念碑。于是，我不再客套直接走上前去，正要进去，看门人告诉我，必须先付钱。我对这样的要求感到很吃惊，于是便问他，难道英国人就是用这种方式做宣传的吗？收取如此微不足道的钱财是否有损国家的体面？难道向公众公开展示辉煌的历史古迹，不是为了国家的荣誉，而是以卑劣的手段利用人们对他们荣誉的好奇心收费吗？"至于你的问题，"看门人回答道，"虽然我不明白你说的道理，但我肯定它们可能都是对的。但是，门票是三个便士，这个场地是我从一个人手里租来的，此人是从另一个人手里租来的，而另一个人，又是从第三个人手里租来的，那第三个人则是从西敏寺看护人那里租来的，我们都得靠这个生活。"我想，在这里付了钱之后，我就能看到些新鲜的东西，因为到此时为止，还没有什么能让我印象深刻的。然而，我失望了。四周除了黑色棺木，生锈的盔甲，破烂的锦旗，和几尊蓬头垢面、披头散发的蜡像以外，什么都没有。我很后悔我付了门票钱，只好自己安慰自己，这也许是最后一次付钱了。我的向导向我们编造了一百多个谎言，从不脸红。他说一个女子因手指被刺而亡，有个国王的头是用金子铸成的，等等；还有二十多个这样荒谬的故事。"先生们，请看，"他指着一张古老的橡木椅说，"这儿有个稀罕之物，英格兰国王就是坐在那张椅子上加冕的，椅子下面有一块石头，那块石头叫作雅各的枕头。"然而，对古老的橡木椅和那块石头，我却看不出有什么稀奇之处。如果眼前我真的能看见古代英国国王坐在那里加冕的情景，或者雅各的头枕在石头上的情景，那倒会激起我的一些好奇。但在目前的情况下，没有任何理由让我感到惊讶，就像我在街上捡了一块石头，之所以称之为稀罕之物，那仅仅是因为某位国王在行走时，曾经碰巧踩到了它。

从那以后，我们的向导领着我们走过了几条又昏暗又弯曲的小道，时常自言自语，神神道道，挥舞着手中的拐杖讲述着没有一点根据的故事。他让我想起了蒙古戈壁沙漠中的黑魔法师。在我们几乎被参观各种各样的东西弄得疲惫不堪之后，他终于要求我仔细观看一件盔甲，但对我来说，这件盔甲并没有什么特别之处。"这件盔甲，"他说，"是蒙克将军披戴过的。""这也太奇怪了吧，将军还要披盔戴甲！""请相信我，"他补充道，"这顶便帽，也是将军戴过的。""这着实太奇怪了，真是太奇怪了，将军也得戴顶便帽！请问朋友，这顶便帽当时值多少钱？""这个，先生，"他说，"我不知道，但这顶便帽却是我带领你们一路走过来的报酬。""这真是非常少的报酬。"我说。"不少，"他回答说，"每个绅士都会在里面放些钱，这就足够我花的了。""什么，你还要钱？想要更多的钱？""先生，每个绅士都会施舍一点的。""我什么都不会给你，"我回答道，"朋友，西敏寺应该付给你工资，而不是允许你从每个参观者的身上骗取钱财。我们进来时，就已经付过了门票钱，出门时，我们再也不会付给你钱了。当然，寺院守护人永远不会认为，他们得到的已经足够多了。告诉我大门在哪儿？如果我在这里再多停留点时间我可能会遇到更多的教会乞丐。"

　　于是，我急急匆匆地离开了西敏寺，回到我的住处。我得回顾这一天所发生的事情，思考一下什么是伟大的，什么应该遭到鄙视。

Beau Tibbs at Home

I am apt to fancy I have contracted a new acquaintance whom it will be no easy matter to shake off. My little Beau yesterday overtook me again in one of the public walks and, slapping me on the shoulder, saluted me with an air of the most perfect familiarity. His dress was the same as usual, except that he had more powder in his hair, wore a dirtier shirt, a pair of **temple spectacles**, and his hat under his arm.

As I knew him to be a harmless, amusing little thing, I could not return his smiles with any degree of severity; so we walked forward on terms of the utmost intimacy, and in a few minutes discussed all the usual topics preliminary to particular conversation. The oddities that marked his character, however, soon began to appear; he bowed to several well-dressed persons who, by their manner of returning the compliment, appeared perfect strangers. At intervals he drew out a **pocket-book**, seeming to take memorandums, before all the company, with much importance and assiduity. In this manner he led me through the length of the whole walk, fretting at his absurdities, and fancying myself laughed at not less than him by every spectator.

When we were got to the end of our procession, 'Blast me,'

cries he, with an air of vivacity, 'I never saw **the Park** so thin in my life before! There's no company at all to-day; not a single face to be seen.' — 'No company!' interrupted I, peevishly; 'no company where there is such a crowd? Why, man, there's too much. What are the thousands that have been laughing at us but company?' — 'Lord, my dear,' returned he, with the utmost good humour, 'you seem immensely chagrined; but, blast me, when the world laughs at me, I laugh at the world, and so we are even. My **Lord Trip**, Bill Squash the **Creolian**, and I sometimes make a party at being ridiculous; and so we say and do a thousand things for the joke's sake. But I see you are grave, and if you are for a fine grave sentimental companion, you shall dine with me and my wife to-day; I must insist on't. I'll introduce you to Mrs. Tibbs, a lady of as elegant qualifications as any in nature; she was bred (but that's between ourselves) under the inspection of the Countess of All-night. A charming body of voice; but no more of that—she will give us a song. You shall see my little girl too, Carolina Wilhelmina Amelia Tibbs, a sweet pretty creature! I design her for my Lord Drumstick's eldest son; but that's in friendship, let it go no further: she's but six years old, and yet she **walks a minuet**, and plays on the guitar immensely already. I intend she shall be as perfect as possible in every accomplishment. In the first place, I'll make her a scholar: I'll teach her Greek myself, and learn that language purposely to instruct her; but let that be a secret.'

Thus saying, without waiting for a reply, he took me by the arm and hauled me along. We passed through many dark alleys and winding ways; for, from some motives to me unknown, he seemed to have a particular aversion to every frequented street; at last, however, we got to the door of a dismal-looking house in the outlets of the town, where he informed me he chose to reside for the benefit of the air.

We entered the lower door, which ever seemed to lie most hospitably open; and I began to ascend an old and creaking staircase, when, as he mounted to show me the way, he demanded whether I delighted in prospects; to which answering in the affirmative; 'Then,' says he, 'I shall show you one of the most charming in the world out of my windows; we shall see the ships sailing and the whole country for twenty miles round, tip top, quite high. My Lord Swamp would give ten thousand guineas for such a one; but, as I sometimes pleasantly tell him, I always love to keep my prospects at home, that my friends may see me the oftener.'

By this time we were arrived as high as the stairs would permit us to ascend, till we came to what he was facetiously pleased to call the first floor down the chimney; and knocking at the door, a voice from within demanded, 'Who's there?' My conductor answered that it was him. But this not satisfying the querist, the voice again repeated the demand; to which he answered louder than before; and now the door was opened by an old woman with cautious reluctance.

When we were got in, he welcomed me to his house with great ceremony, and turning to the old woman, asked where was her lady? 'Good troth,' replied she in a peculiar dialect, 'she's washing your twa shirts at the next door, because they have taken an oath against lending out the tub any longer.' — 'My two shirts!' cried he in a tone that faltered with confusion; 'what does the idiot mean?' — '**I ken what I mean weel enough**,' replied the other; 'she's washing your twa shirts at the next door, because —' 'Fire and fury, no more of thy stupid explanations!' cried he; 'go and inform her we have got company. Were that Scotch hag,' continued he, turning to me, 'to be forever in my family, she would never learn politeness, nor forget that absurd poisonous accent of hers, or testify the smallest specimen of breeding or high life; and yet it is very surprising too, as I had her from a Parliament man, a friend of mine from the Highlands, one of the politest men in the world; but that's a secret.'

We waited some time for Mrs. Tibbs' arrival, during which interval I had a full opportunity of surveying the chamber and all its furniture, which consisted of four chairs with old wrought bottoms, that he assured me were his wife's embroidery; a square table that had been once japanned; a cradle in one corner, a lumbering cabinet in the other; a broken shepherdess and a mandarin without a head were stuck over the chimney; and round the walls several paltry unframed pictures, which, he observed, were all his own drawing. 'What do you think, sir, of that head in the corner, done in the manner of **Grisoni**? **There's the true keeping in it**; it is my own face, and though there happens to be no likeness, a Countess offered me a hundred for its fellow. I refused her, for, hang it, that would be **mechanical**, you know.'

The wife at last made her appearance, at once a slattern and a coquette; much emaciated, but still carrying the remains of beauty. She made twenty apologies for being seen in such odious dishabille, but hoped to be excused, as she had stayed out all night at **the gardens** with the Countess, who was excessively fond of **the horns**. 'And indeed, my dear,' added she, turning to her husband, 'his lordship drank your health in a bumper.' — 'Poor Jack!' cries he; 'a dear good-natured creature, I know he loves me. But I hope, my dear, you have given orders for dinner; you need make no great preparations neither, there are but three of us; something elegant and little will do,—**a turbot, an ortolan**, or a—' 'Or what do you think, mydear,' interrupts the wife, 'of a nice pretty bit of ox-cheek, piping hot, and dressed with a little of my own sauce?' — 'The very thing!' replies he; 'it will eat best with some smart bottled beer: but be sure to let us have the sauce his Grace was so fond of. I hate your immense loads of meat; that is country all over; extremely disgusting to those who are in the least acquainted with high life.'

By this time my curiosity began to abate, and my appetite to increase; the company of fools may at first make us smile, but at last never fails of rendering us melancholy. I, therefore, pretended to recollect a prior engagement, and, after having shown my respect to the house, according to the fashion of the English, by giving the old servant a piece of money at the door, I took my leave; Mrs. Tibbs assuring me that dinner, if I stayed, would be ready at least in less than two hours.

Notes

This is Letter LV of *The Citizen of the World*. Beau Tibbs, the tarnished but gay gentleman, is one of the entertaining pretenders to position and respectability in English fiction (cf. Dickens' Micawber and Mark Twain's Colonel Sellers).

temple spectacles, i.e. spectacles; the temples are the side bars passing behind the ears.

pocket-book, memorandum book.

the Park, probably Hyde Park, a fashionable resort in London.

Creolian, i.e. creole, a person of European blood born in the West Indies or Spanish America.

Lord Trip, etc. Notice the names of the comic characters: Lord Trip, Bill Squash, Countess All-night, Lord Drumstick, and the pretty name of Tibbs' daughter, Carolina Wilhelmina Amelia Tibbs.

walks a minuet. The minuet was always 'walked' and not 'danced,' at it was a very slow dance.

'*I ken what I mean weel enough*' (Scotch), I know what I mean well enough. The 'hag' talks broad Scotch: she says 'twa' instead of 'two.'

Grisoni, Giuseppe (1699 —1769), a popular Florentine portraitpainter.

There's the true keeping in it. Here 'keeping' means harmony; it is a technical term in painting.

mechanical, i.e. like a common workman.

the gardens, i.e. Vauxhall Gardens, a fashionable pleasure resort on the south bank of the Thames, which was opened in 1661 and closed in 1859.

the horns, the wind instrument in the orchestra.

a turbot, an ortolan. Turbot 'a flat fish' and ortolan (garden bunting) were highly esteemed table delicacies.

Oliver Goldsmith

【作品简介】

本文选自《世界公民》第 55 封信。花花公子蒂布斯，一个名声不是太好，却成天无忧无虑的先生，是英国小说中的那些有趣而又假装体面、追求地位的人物之一（参见狄更斯塑造的人物米考伯先生和马克·吐温笔下的塞勒斯上校）。

【作品解析】

temple spectacles：即眼镜，其镜架绕过耳背。

pocket-book：这里指袖珍本备忘录。

the Park：也许是指海德公园，伦敦的一个时尚的度假胜地。

Creolian：即克里奥尔人，出生于西印度群岛或西班牙在美洲殖民地的具有欧洲血统的人。

Lord Trip, etc.：在这段话中，请注意这些喜剧性人物的名字：特里普勋爵，比尔·南瓜，通宵伯爵夫人，鼓槌勋爵，还有蒂布斯的美丽女儿卡罗琳娜·威廉米娜·阿梅莉亚·蒂布斯。

walks a minuet：小步舞曲总是"走"而不是"跳"，是一种非常缓慢的舞蹈。

"I ken what I mean weel enough"（苏格兰语）：英语为"I know what I mean well enough"，即我很明白我的意思；文中那个"苏格兰老妇"常常说的是苏格兰土话：她把"two"说成了"twa"。

Grisoni：朱塞佩·格里索尼（1699—1769），一位受欢迎的佛罗伦萨肖像画家。

There's the true keeping in it：此处"keeping"是指绘画中的和谐，是绘画中的一个技术术语。

mechanical：文中是指绘画显得太没有特色了。

the gardens：即沃克斯豪尔花园，泰晤士河南岸一个时尚的度假胜地，于 1661 年开放，1859 年关闭。

the horns：号角，管弦乐队中的管乐器。

a turbot, an ortolan：大菱鲆（又名"比目鱼"）和食米鸟（花园中的圃鹀），它们都是备受推崇的美食。

【参考译文】

家中的花花公子蒂布斯

我以为我结交了一位刚认识不久的新朋友，要想摆脱他可不是一件容易的事。我的这位小公子哥昨天在公共场合散步时，又一次追赶上了我。他拍拍我的肩膀，并以非常熟悉的神情向我行了个礼。他的衣着和往常一样，只是头发上涂了更多的粉。他穿着一件脏兮兮的衬衫，戴着一副眼镜，胳膊下夹着一顶帽子。

我知道他是一个无伤大雅，而且十分有趣的小人物，所以面对他的微笑，我也无法以任何严肃的态度予以回应。于是，我们走在了一起，亲密地交谈起来，几分钟内就谈完了所有的客套话题。很快，他性格中怪僻的地方就显露了出来，他向几位衣冠楚楚的人鞠躬致敬，然而从他们回敬的姿势上看，显然是完全不认识的陌生人。他每隔一段时间，就会抽出一本袖珍手册，显得非常认真地记下一段备忘录，他的行为似乎有点做作，似乎是专门做给同伴看的。就这样，他带我走过了一段长路。我对他的荒诞举止感到烦躁不安，认为每个过路人都在嘲笑我，甚至超过于他。

在我们散步快结束时，"天哪！"他带着一种活泼天真的神情喊道，"我以前从来没有见过公园这么冷清！今天根本没有游客，连个人影都没有！""没人！"我不耐烦地打断了他的话说，"周围这么多人你说没人？是不是太夸张了，朋友？难道那些一直在嘲笑我们的不是人吗？""我亲爱的大人，"他带着极其愉快的心情对我说，"看起来，您为此非常烦恼；但是，该死的，对我而言，当这个世界嘲笑我时，我就嘲笑这个世界，这样我们就扯平，互不相欠了。尊敬的特里普勋爵、克里奥尔人比尔·南瓜，还有我，有时会开一个派对做些荒诞可笑的事；为了开玩笑取悦，我们甚至可以说上千个笑话做上千件可笑的事情。但我觉得您比较严肃，如果您想结交一个严肃而又多愁善感的好朋友，今天您就应该和我还有我的妻子一起共进晚餐，我必须要邀请您。我会把您介绍给蒂布斯夫人，她天性优雅，一直在受到通宵伯爵夫人的保护（但这是我们之间的秘密）。她的声音甜美迷人，这个就不用多说了——她一定会为我们演唱一首歌曲。您也会见到我的小女儿，卡罗琳娜·威廉米娜·阿梅莉亚·蒂布斯，一个甜美而又漂亮的孩子！我想让她嫁给鼓槌勋爵的大少爷，但目前还只是朋友，顺其自然，以后再说吧。她现在只有六岁，就会跳小步舞，而且吉他已经弹得很好了。我希望她在每项技能上，都能尽善尽美。然而最主要的是，我想让她成为一名学者：我会亲自教她希腊语，并且会有目的地学习这种语言去指导她，这就算是个秘密吧！"

他就这样说着，还没等我回话，就挎着我的胳膊，拽着我向前走。我们穿过了一些又黑又暗的小巷和弯弯曲曲的小路，我不知道他是出于什么原因，他似乎对每一条繁忙的大街都特别反感。最后，我们终于到了市镇出口处一栋看上去有点阴沉并带有一种凄凉感的住宅门口，他告诉我，他之所以选择居住在这里是因为这儿空气新鲜。

我们走进了楼下的门，那扇门似乎总是敞开着的，好像在友好地欢迎着我们。他在前面领着我上楼，当我踏着那陈旧的吱吱作响的楼梯时，他问我是否对即将展现的风景感兴趣，我告诉他，我的确很有兴趣。"那么，"他说，"我将从我的窗口向您展示世界上最迷人的景色之一，我们将会看到船舶航行和本镇方圆二十英里的风景，这是顶层，相当高。为了这个迷人的景色，斯旺普伯爵愿意出一万个基尼；然而我用平常和蔼的口吻告诉他，我喜欢把这样的景色留在家中，这样我的朋友们就会经常来看望我了。"

这时，我们已经登到了楼梯的顶层，也就是蒂布斯戏谑时所说的烟囱下的一楼。蒂布斯敲了敲门，里面传出来一个声音："谁呀？"我的向导蒂布斯说是他。里面的人似乎不太满意这样的回答，于是又重复问了一遍，蒂布斯又重复回答了一次，这次比前一次声音要高。最后，一位老妇人终于小心翼翼地开了门，一脸的不高兴。

我们进到屋里，他以极大的热情欢迎我的到来，然后转向老妇人，问他的太太在哪里。"说真的，"她用一种特殊的方言说，"她正在隔壁，洗您的两件衬衫，因为他们发誓不再把木盆借出去了。""我的两件衬衫！"蒂布斯完全被弄糊涂了，不由得惊叫起来，"你这个蠢货到底是什么意思？""我说的已经够清楚了，"老妇人说，"她正在隔壁洗您的两件衬衫，因为……""够了，不要再说了！"蒂布斯叫喊道，"去告诉她，我们家来客人了。那个苏格兰老妇，"蒂布斯转身对我说，"在我家多年了，但她永远也学不会礼貌，也改不掉那荒谬而有害的口音，也无法证明她出身上流社会或者具有高贵的血统。然而这也是非常令人惊讶的，她是我的一位国会议员朋友介绍来的，而我的这位朋友是苏格兰高地人，是世界上最有礼貌的人之一；这也是个秘密。"

我们等了一会儿蒂布斯夫人才来。我利用这段时间，把房间和家具打量了一番。房间里有四把椅子，椅垫早已老旧，每个椅垫都是用刺绣裹着的，蒂布斯告诉我这些都是他夫人绣的。房间里还有一张曾经喷过漆的四方桌，房间的一个角落放着一个摇篮，另一个角落里有一个笨重的柜子，里面乱糟糟的。一个破旧的牧羊女和一个没有了脑袋的官员雕塑被卡在壁炉的上方。房间四周的墙壁上挂着几幅不起眼的没有框架的油画，他见我在看这些画，便告诉我，所有这些画都是他的作品。"先生，您认为角落里的那幅模仿格里索尼风格画的头像怎样？这幅肖像画确实很和谐，那是以我自己的脸模子为原型的，虽然它们之间没有什么相似之处。一位伯爵夫人仍愿意出一百英镑请我画一幅同样类型的画，我拒绝了她，见鬼！您知道，那样做就显得太没有特色了。"

蒂布斯夫人终于露面了，立刻让人感觉她是一个有点邋遢，而又喜欢卖弄风情的女人；虽然有些憔悴，却带着几分没有消失殆尽的美丽。她为自己穿着令人反感讨厌的便服不停地道歉，希望能够得到谅解。因为她整个晚上都在花园里，陪伴喜欢号角的伯爵夫人。"的确是这样的，亲爱的，"她转过身来，对着她的丈夫补充道，"伯爵为了你的身体健康还干了一杯酒。""哦，可怜的杰克！"蒂布斯说，"生性善良的伯爵，我知道他喜欢我。好了，亲爱的，我想你应该让仆人们准备晚餐了；不需要任何特殊的准备，只有我们三个人。少而精——一条大菱鲆，一只食米鸟或者一只……""或者，你觉得怎样，亲爱的，"蒂布斯夫人打断了他的话，"做一点优质的牛面颊肉，热乎乎的，再涂点自制的调味酱？""这样挺好！"蒂布斯说，"搭配一些上等的瓶装啤酒这样会吃得更好一些；但一定要让我们尝尝这位先生所喜爱的调味酱。我讨厌请客时上一大堆的大鱼大肉，那是在乡下；只要对上流社会的生活有一丁点儿了解的人，都会对此感到不愉快。"

这时，我的好奇心渐渐地开始减弱了，而我的食欲却逐渐增强了。与傻瓜们为伍，开始会让我们微笑，但最终也会让我们感到愁眉不展。于是我假装想起还有约，按照英国人的风俗在门口给老仆人一点赏钱，向这家人表示敬意之后，便告辞了。蒂布斯夫人还在向我保证，如果我能留下来的话，用不了两个小时，晚餐就准备好了。

JAMES BOSWELL (1740—1795)

James Boswell (1740—1795) was the son of Alexander Boswell, a prominent member of the landed gentry of Scotland and also a distinguished advocate and judge. Under the paternal influence, he studied law at Edinburgh, Glasgow and Utrecht, and was admitted to the Scottish bar in 1766. From the beginning, however, he had no great zeal for the dry details of law-practice. He was eager 'to share the society of men distinguished either by their rank or their talents.' He was restless, and made frequent visits to London. In 1763 he met for the first time Dr. Johnson, dictator of English letters. The acquaintance developed into a life-long friendship. In 1773 he had the happiness to be admitted to Johnson's Literary Club. To his contemporaries he was known as a man about town, a 'celebrated traveller,' a lion-hunter, and an author of travels and occasional essays (*An Account of Corsica*, 1768; *Journal of a Tour to the Hebrides with Dr. Johnson*, 1785; *The Hypochondriac*, 1777—1783). In 1791 he published his magnum opus, *The Life of Samuel Johnson*, which is not only the best life of Johnson, but the best of all English biographies.

The meeting of Johnson and Boswell must be considered one of the rare accidents in literary history —Johnson, the most picturesque of English men of letters, and Boswell, the most devoted and skilful portrait-painter. According to actual estimate, during the twenty-one years of their acquaintance, Boswell had the opportunity of being in Dr. Johnson's company on only two-hundred and seventy days. But he had studied his master so carefully that he could mimic him to the life, in voice and gesture. *The Life* is more than a biography; it is the diary of one man written by another. Generations of readers have turned to the pages of this great book to enjoy the company of an extraordinary person, perhaps the most representative man of the English people. Lord Macaulay, who was unduly severe on Boswell as a man, did full justice to his skill in biography. He wrote: 'Homer is not more decidedly the first of heroic poets, Shakespeare is not more decidedly the first of dramatists, Demosthenes is not more decidedly the first of orators, than Boswell is the first of biographers. He has no second. He has distanced all the competitors so decidedly that it is not worthwhile to place them. Eclipse is first, and the rest nowhere.'

【作者简介】

詹姆斯·鲍斯威尔（1740—1795）是亚历山大·鲍斯威尔之子，亚历山大·鲍斯威尔是苏格兰乡绅中一位杰出的成员，同时也是一位受人尊敬的辩护律师和法官。在父亲的影响下，詹姆斯·鲍斯威尔在爱丁堡、格拉斯哥和乌得勒支学习法律，并于 1766 年成为一名苏格兰律师协会认可的律师。然而，从一开始他就对法律实务的枯燥细节没有太多的热情。他渴望"与那些有名望或者才华出众的能人们交往，并与他们共享社会地位和才能"。他不安于自己的工作，经常去伦敦。1763 年，他第一次见到英国史上最有名望的文人约翰逊博士。这次见面之后，他们由相识发展成为终身挚友。1773 年，他有幸加入了约翰逊的文学俱乐部。对与詹姆斯·鲍斯威尔同时代的人来说，他是个城里人，一个"著名的旅行者"，一个喜好交攀名流的人，会写游记，偶尔也会写散文（《科西嘉岛纪实》，1768；《赫布里底群岛旅游日记》，1785；《忧郁症患者》，1777—1783）。1791 年，他出版了代表作《约翰逊传》，这不仅是对约翰逊一生最好的记述，也是英国文学史上最好的一部传记。

约翰逊和鲍斯威尔的相遇是文学史上罕见的奇迹之一——约翰逊，当时是英国最生动、最有魅力的文人，而鲍斯威尔是一位最敬业和技艺精湛的肖像画家。按照真实的估计，在他们相识的二十一年间，鲍斯威尔有机会陪伴在约翰逊博士身边只不过二百七十天。然而，鲍斯威尔却非常仔细地研究了约翰逊博士，甚至可以模仿约翰逊博士在生活中的声音和动作。《约翰逊传》不仅仅是一本传记，简直就是鲍斯威尔记录约翰逊博士的日记。每一代读者在翻阅这部伟大的传记时，都在享受着一位非凡伟人的陪伴，也许是英国人中最具有代表性的人物。麦考利勋爵一向对鲍斯威尔过于苛刻，却对鲍斯威尔在传记中的写作技能给予了充分的肯定。他写道："毫无疑问，荷马并非英雄史诗的创始人，莎士比亚并非第一位戏剧家，德摩斯梯尼也并非第一位演说家，而鲍斯威尔却是传记作家第一人；对他来说，没有第二。他的竞争对手与他相差甚远，无法同日而语。日食在先，其余的均无光泽。"

Johnson and Lord Chesterfield

Lord Chesterfield, to whom Johnson had paid the high compliment of addressing to his Lordship the *Plan* **of his** *Dictionary*, had behaved to him in such a manner as to excite his contempt and indignation. The world has been for many years amused with a story confidently told, and as confidently repeated with additional circumstances, that a sudden disgust was taken by Johnson upon occasion of his having been one day kept long in waiting in his Lordship's antechamber, for which the reason assigned was that he had company with him; and that at last, when the door opened, out walked **Colley Cibber**; and that Johnson was so violently provoked when he found for whom he had been so long excluded that he went away in a passion and never would return. I remember having mentioned this story to George Lord Lyttelton, who told me he was very intimate with Lord Chesterfield; and holding it as a well-known truth, defended Lord Chesterfield by saying that 'Cibber, who had been introduced familiarly by the back-stairs, had probably not been there above ten minutes.' It may seem strange even to entertain a doubt concerning a story so long and so widely current and thus implicitly adopted, if not sanctioned, by the authority which I have mentioned; but

Johnson himself assured me that there was not the least foundation for it. He told me, that there never was any particular incident which produced a quarrel between Lord Chesterfield and him; but that his Lordship's continued neglect was the reason why he resolved to have no connection with him. When the *Dictionary* was upon the eve of publication, Lord Chesterfield, who, it is said, had flattered himself with expectations that Johnson would dedicate the work to him, attempted, in a courtly manner, to soothe and insinuate himself with the Sage, conscious, as it should seem, of the cold indifference with which he had treated its learned author; and further attempted to conciliate him, by writing two papers in **The World**, in recommendation of the work; and it must be confessed that they contain some studied compliments, so finely turned that if there had been no previous offence it is probable that Johnson would have been highly delighted. Praise, in general, was pleasing to him; but by praise from a man of rank and elegant accomplishments he was peculiarly gratified...

This courtly device failed of its effect. Johnson, who thought that 'all was false and hollow,' despised the honeyed words, and was even indignant that Lord Chesterfield should for a moment imagine that he could be the dupe of such an artifice. His expression to me concerning Lord Chesterfield upon this occasion was, 'Sir, after making great professions, he had, for many years, taken no notice of me; but when my *Dictionary* was coming out, he fell a scribbling in *The World* about it. Upon which, I wrote him a letter expressed in civil terms, but such as might show him that I did not mind what he said or wrote, and that I had done with him.'

This is that celebrated letter of which so much has been said, and about which curiosity has been so long excited, without being gratified. I for many years solicited Johnson to favour me with a copy of it, that so excellent a composition might not be lost to posterity. He delayed from time to time to give it me; till at last in 1781, when we were on a visit at **Mr. Dilly**'s, at Southhill in Bedfordshire, he was pleased to dictate it to me from memory. He afterwards found among his papers a copy of it, which he had dictated to **Mr. Baretti**, with its title and corrections, in his own handwriting. This he gave to **Mr. Langton**; adding that if it were to come into print, he wished it to be from that copy. By Mr. Langton's kindness, I am enabled to enrich my work with a perfect transcript of what the world has so eagerly desired to see.

To the Right Honourable the Earl of Chesterfield.

February 7, 1755.

My Lord,

I have been lately informed, by the proprietor of The World, that two papers, in which my Dictionary is recommended to the public, were written by your Lordship. To be so distinguished, is an honour, which, being very little accustomed to favours from the great, I know not well how to receive, or in what terms to acknowledge.

When, upon some slight encouragement, I first visited your Lordship, I was overpowered, like the rest of mankind, by the enchantment of your address; and could not forbear to wish that I might boast myself **Le vainqueur du vainqueur de la terre;**—*that I might obtain that regard for which I saw the world contending; but I found my attendance so little encouraged, that neither pride nor modesty would suffer me to continue it. When I had once addressed your Lordship in public,*

I had exhausted all the art of pleasing which a retired and uncourtly scholar can possess. I had done all that I could; and no man is well pleased to have his all neglected, be it ever so little.

*Seven years, my Lord, have now passed, since I waited in your outward rooms, or was repulsed from your door; during which time I have been pushing on my work through difficulties, of which it is useless to complain, and have brought it, at last, to the verge of publication, without one act of assistance, one word of encouragement, or one smile of favour. Such treatment I did not expect, for I never had a **Patron** before.*

*The shepherd in **Virgil** grew at last acquainted with Love; and found him a native of the rocks.*

*Is not a Patron, my Lord, one who looks with unconcern on a man struggling for life in the water, and, when he has reached ground, encumbers him with help? The notice which you have been pleased to take of my labours, had it been early, had been kind; but it has been delayed till I am indifferent, and cannot enjoy it; till **I am solitary**, and cannot impart it; till I am known, and do not want it. I hope it is no very cynical asperity not to confess obligations where no benefit has been received, or to be unwilling that the public should consider me as owing that to a Patron, which Providence has enabled me to do for myself.*

Having carried on my work thus far with so little obligation to any favourer of learning, I shall not be disappointed though I should conclude it, if less be possible, with less; for I have been long wakened from that dream of hope, in which I once boasted myself with so much exultation.

My Lord,
Your Lordship's most humble
Most obedient servant,
Sam. Johnson.

Notes

This selection, from *The Life of Johnson* (under the year 1754), contains Johnson's famous letter to Lord Chesterfield. Johnson's life (1709—1784), before the publication of his *Dictionary* in 1755, was one of extreme obscurity: it was a long and proud struggle against poverty, melancholy, and disease. The *Dictionary* established his reputation, but did not increase his means; and he never ceased to struggle until he was given a pension by the government in 1762. The letter to Lord Chesterfield is 'the voice of all the poor and proud men of the world.' For the life and works of Chesterfield, see page 93.

Plan of his Dictionary, i.e. the prospect of the *Dictionary*, addressed to Lord Chesterfield and published in 1747. Johnson's object was to fix the pronunciation and preserve the purity of the English language. And he was eminently successful. For about a century his *Dictionary* was regarded as the highest court of appeal in English usage.

Colley Cibber (1671—1757), playwright, actor, and poet laureate. He is now remembered for his *Apology for the Life of Colley Cibber, Comedian,* which contains portraits of actors and actresses of his time. Johnson never spoke of him but with contempt.

The World, a popular periodical (1753—1756), edited by Edward Moore. Chesterfield was among the contributors.

Mr. Dilly, Charles, bookseller and publisher in London.

Mr. Baretti, Giuseppe, Marc' Antonio (1719—1789), a friend of Johnson's, was born in Italy. He opened a school for teaching Italian in 1751, and published an *Italian and English Dictionary* in 1760.

Mr. Langton, Bennet, a much valued friend of Johnson's, and one of the original members of the Club.

Le vainqueur du vainqueur de la terre (French), the conqueror of the conqueror of the world.

Seven years, my Lord, etc. The most moving passage in the letter. Johnson began his work on the *Dictionary* in 1747 and brought it to completion in 1754. It was published in two folio volumes in 1755.

Patron. In the *Dictionary* Johnson defined 'patron' as 'commonly a wretch who supports with insolence and is paid with flattery.' He had probably Chesterfield in his mind. Boswell notes that in *The Vanity of Human Wishes* (1749) one of the couplets about men of letters stood thus:

'Yet think what ills the scholar's life assail.

Toil envy, want, the *garret*, and the jail.'

After the Chesterfield episode, Johnson dismissed the word *garret*, and in all subsequent editions the second line of the couplet stands:

'Toil, envy, the *Patron*, and the jail.'

Virgil, Publius Vergilius Maro (70 B.C.—19 B.C.), Roman poet, author of *Aeneid*, *Georgics* and *Eclogues*. The 'shepherd' in this passage is a reference to his *Eclogues* VIII, 44—46.

I am solitary. Boswell's note: 'In this passage Dr. Johnson alludes to the loss of his wife.' Johnson's wife, formerly Mrs. Porter, who was twenty years his senior, died in 1752. In spite of the disparity in age, the marriage seems to have been a happy one.

【作品简介】

本文选自《约翰逊传》（1754 年之后），其中含有约翰逊致切斯特菲尔德勋爵那封著名的信。约翰逊（1709—1784）在 1755 年他的《英语词典》出版之前，一直默默无闻，处在与贫穷、忧郁和疾病做漫长而又自豪的斗争之中。这部约翰逊编纂的《英语词典》的出版，奠定了他的声誉，但并没有增加他的收入；但他也从未停止过在穷困潦倒中抗争，直到 1762 年获得了政府的养老金。致切斯特菲尔德勋爵的信是"世界上所有贫穷且骄傲者的声音"。有关切斯特菲尔德的生平与作品，参见本书切斯特菲尔德勋爵章节。

【作品解析】

Plan of his *Dictionary*：即《英语词典》的前景，约翰逊曾将此写进致切斯特菲尔德勋爵的信中，并于 1747 年出版。约翰逊编纂这部《英语词典》的目的是修正英语发音并保持其英语的纯粹。他非常成功。大约一个世纪以来，他的《英语词典》被公认为英语用法的最高权威。

Colley Cibber：科利·西伯（1671—1757），剧作家、演员，也是桂冠诗人。他因代表作《为喜剧演员科利·西伯的一生道歉》而被人们铭记，里面有他对那个时代男女演员的详细描述。约翰逊提起他时总是带有轻蔑的语气。

The World：《世界报》（1753—1756），当时的流行期刊，由爱德华·莫尔主编。切斯特菲尔德是撰稿人之一。

Mr. Dilly：查尔斯·迪利先生，伦敦的书商和出版商。

Mr. Baretti：朱塞佩·马可·安东尼奥·巴雷蒂先生（1719—1789），约翰逊的朋友，出生于意大利。1751 年，他开设了一所意大利语言学校，并于 1760 年出版了一本《意大利语和英语词典》。

Mr. Langton：贝内特·兰顿先生，约翰逊一位受尊敬的朋友，也是约翰逊俱乐部开创时的成员之一。

Le vainqueur du vainqueur de la terre（法语）：世界征服者的征服者。

Seven years, my Lord, etc.：这是信中最感人的一段。约翰逊于 1747 年开始了他的《英语词典》编纂工作，并于 1754 年完成，1755 年以对开本的形式出版了两卷本。

Patron：在《英语词典》里，约翰逊把"赞助人"定义为"通常是傲慢无礼、盛气凌人的无耻之徒，以通过提供资助从中索取人们的阿谀奉承"。也许他当时想到了切斯特菲尔德。鲍斯威尔指出，在《人类欲望的虚幻》（1749）中，有一副关于文人的对句，是这样写的：

　　"然而，想想吧，是什么使这位学者终身受到伤害，

　　　辛劳，嫉妒，欲望，阁楼和监狱。"

在经历了切斯特菲尔德这一事件之后，约翰逊从《英语词典》里把"阁楼"一词换掉了，于是在后来的版本中，对句的第二行就变成了下面这一句："辛劳，嫉妒，欲望，赞助人和监狱。"

　　Virgil：普布留斯·维吉留斯·马罗，通称维吉尔（前 70—前 19），古罗马诗人，著有《埃涅阿斯纪》《农事诗集》《牧歌集》。文中的"牧羊人"是指他的《牧歌集》第八首。

　　I am solitary：鲍斯威尔注："在这段文字里，约翰逊博士暗示他失去了妻子。"约翰逊的妻子，曾是波特太太，比约翰逊大二十岁，1752 年去世。尽管年龄悬殊，他们的婚姻似乎也很幸福。

【参考译文】

约翰逊和切斯特菲尔德勋爵

　　约翰逊在向切斯特菲尔德勋爵陈述他的《英语词典编写计划》时，对切斯特菲尔德勋爵大加赞美。然而，切斯特菲尔德勋爵对他的态度，激起了约翰逊的轻蔑和愤慨。多年来，这个故事一直广为流传，人们很自信地讲述这个故事，在相互传播中添加了一些自以为是的情节。约翰逊之所以突然被切斯特菲尔德勋爵激怒，是因为有一天他在勋爵的前客厅里等待会见，他等了很长时间，因为切斯特菲尔德勋爵正和他的同伴在一起。最后门开了，从里面走出来的却是科利·西伯。约翰逊发现自己受到切斯特菲尔德勋爵的冷落并长时间被排斥在外，竟然是因为科利·西伯，于是他被激怒了，激愤地走出了客厅，发誓永远不再回来。我记得，我曾经向

乔治·利特尔顿勋爵提起过这个故事，他告诉我，他与切斯特菲尔德勋爵非常亲密；他认为这是一个众所周知的事实，为切斯特菲尔德勋爵辩解道："科利·西伯，只是熟悉从客厅后面的楼梯进去，大概待了还不到十分钟。"对这个长期以来广为流传并得到人们默认的故事，如果没有我之前提到的权威人士的认可，而心生疑惑，似乎有点奇怪；但约翰逊本人向我证实，这个故事没有一点事实基础。他告诉我，他和切斯特菲尔德勋爵之间，从来没有发生过任何不和。但切斯特菲尔德勋爵的一再冷落，是他没有和勋爵继续联系的主要原因。在《英语词典》出版前夕，据说切斯特菲尔德勋爵自鸣得意地以为约翰逊会将这部词典题献给自己，因此，他自以为是，试图以一种谦恭的态度、礼貌的方式，去抚慰和暗示这位似乎已经意识到受冷落的清高而有学问的作者，以缓和他们之间的关系；甚至在《世界报》上撰写了两篇文章，赞扬和推荐约翰逊的《英语词典》。必须承认，这两篇文章有一些深思熟虑的赞美之词。如果之前切斯特菲尔德勋爵没有激怒过约翰逊，那么约翰逊很可能会非常高兴。一般来说，赞美之词是约翰逊所喜欢的，尤其是出自一位既有名望而又高雅、有成就的达官贵人之口的赞美之词，约翰逊应当会感到特别的满足和荣耀……

然而，切斯特菲尔德勋爵的这两篇吹捧的文章没有收到应有的效果。约翰逊认为"一切都是虚假空洞之词"，他不仅鄙视切斯特菲尔德勋爵的这些甜言蜜语，甚至一想起切斯特菲尔德勋爵会用这种诡计来愚弄自己就怒不可遏。他对我谈到切斯特菲尔德勋爵时，评论道："先生，在他对我信誓旦旦之后，多年来对我不闻不问，非常冷落。然而，在我做了大量的工作，当我的《英语词典》即将出版之时，他却在《世界报》上随便写了两篇文章，敷衍两句。为此，我便用文明的语言给他写了一封信，告诉他我丝毫不关心他所说的或所写的任何内容，我与他没有任何关系。"

这就是上面所提到的那封著名的信，对于这封信，许多人一直满怀好奇，却难以得到满足。多年来，我一直恳请约翰逊给我一份这封信的副本，让这样一篇优秀的作品，得以世世代代流传下去。他却迟迟没有给我，直到 1781 年，在我们去贝德福德郡南山的迪利先生家拜访时，他才高兴地凭着记忆，向我口授了这封信。后来，他又在文件中找到了这封信的手抄本，是他口述给巴雷蒂先生的，其中标题和几处的更正，全是约翰逊自己的笔迹。之后，他又把手抄本送给了兰顿先生，并补充说，如果日后出版，希望以此文本为准。多谢兰顿先生的好意，我才可以用这完美的文字记录来充实丰富我的作品，满足人们渴望读到这世界上最完美的书信的心愿。

致尊敬的切斯特菲尔德勋爵阁下

我尊敬的阁下：

近日从《世界报》主编那里知悉，该报刊载了大人两篇文章，向公众推荐我编纂的《英语词典》，这是一种荣耀。然而，一向不习惯接受大人物恩宠的我，不知道如何去接受这份殊荣，也不知道应该用什么样的言辞来表达谢意。

回顾当年，我像所有人一样，为大人言谈的风采所倾倒，我无法克制自己并异想天开可以炫耀自己是"世界征服者的征服者"——也许，我可以得到这份人们都在相争的殊荣。我第一次拜访了您大人阁下，但我很快发现，我的拜访并没有得到任何鼓励，无论是出于骄傲还是谦卑，都无法让我再继续下去。起初，当我在公开场合提到大人您的时候，我已经竭尽全力，用尽了一个退隐的卑微学者所能拥有的一切赞美艺术。然而，我所做的这一切却被大人您冷落了，没有人会为此而感到高兴，尽管这一切都微不足道。

大人阁下，自从我在贵府会客厅等待接见，或者说是被您拒之于门外，到现在已经过去七年了。在这七年的时间里，我一直在困境中继续着我的编纂工作。这些痛苦，现在再来倾诉，已经毫无意义。所幸的是，我的《英语词典》就要出版了。在这七年里，我没有得到过任何一点赞助，没有得到过任何一句鼓励，也没有见到过任何一丝称赞的微笑。我从来也没指望过能有那样的待遇，因为我从来没有过赞助人。

维吉尔诗中的牧羊人，最后终于和爱神相识；那时他才发现，所谓的爱神不过是一个身居岩石堆中的土著人。

大人阁下，如果有人看着在水中挣扎求生存的人漠不关心，而就在他已经爬上岸时，却以援助去拖累他，难道这就是赞助人？大人阁下，您对我的工作如果能早一点关注，也许还是仁慈的；可是现在已经太晚了，我对此已经漠然，无法消受您的帮助；现在，我已经孑然一身，无法与他人分享；现在，我已经有点名气，无须您的恩典。坦白地说，我从来没有得到过任何恩惠，也不必感恩；在没有得到任何好处的情况下，我也不愿意让公众认为我曾经受惠于某位赞助人，而这正是上苍的旨意，让我孤身一人独自完成这一使命。但愿，我不承认自己有义务去感恩不是一种愤世嫉俗的无礼行为。

迄今为止，我的《英语词典》编纂工作很少得到过任何著名学者资助的承诺，今后也许会更少。如果，还有可能更少的话，即便是这样，我也会更加努力去完成它，绝不会因此而感到失望。因为，我早已从那个希望得到赞助的美梦中幡然醒悟；虽然在那个梦里，我曾经是那么得意地炫耀自己。

> 我尊敬的阁下
> 您最谦卑的
> 最顺从的仆人
> 塞缪尔·约翰逊
> 1755 年 2 月 7 日

Boswell's Introduction to Johnson

Mr. **Thomas Davies** the actor, who then kept a bookseller's shop in Russell Street, Covent Garden, told me that Johnson was very much his friend, and came frequently to his house, where he more than once invited me to meet him; but by some unlucky accident or other he was prevented from coming to us.

Mr. Thomas Davies was a man of good understanding and talents, with the advantage of a liberal education. Though somewhat pompous, he was an entertaining companion; and his literary performances have no inconsiderable share of merit. He was a friendly and very hospitable man. Both he and his wife (who has been celebrated for her beauty), though upon the stage for many years, maintained an uniform decency of character; and Johnson esteemed them, and lived in as easy an intimacy with them as with any family which he used to visit. Mr. Davies recollected several of Johnson's remarkable sayings, and was one of the best of the many imitators of his voice and manner, while relating them. He increased my impatience more and more to see the extraordinary man whose works I highly valued, and whose conversation was reported to be so peculiarly excellent.

At last, on Monday the 16th of May, when I was sitting in Mr. Davies' back-parlour, after having drunk tea with him and Mrs. Davies, Johnson unexpectedly came into the shop; and Mr. Davies having perceived him through the glass-door in the room in which we were sitting, advancing towards us,—he announced his awful approach to me, somewhat in the manner of an actor in the part of Horatio, when he addresses Hamlet on the appearance of his father's ghost, '**Look, my Lord, it comes**.' I found that I had a very perfect idea of Johnson's figure, from the portrait of him painted by **Sir Joshua Reynolds** soon after he had published his *Dictionary,* in the attitude of sitting in his easy chair in deep meditation, which was the first picture his friend did for him, which Sir Joshua very kindly presented to me, and from which an engraving has been made for this work. Mr. Davies mentioned my name, and respectfully introduced me to him. I was much agitated; and recollecting his **prejudice against the Scotch**, of which I had heard much, I said to Davies, 'Don't tell where I come from.' — 'From Scotland,' cried Davies roguishly. 'Mr. Johnson,' said I, 'I do indeed come from Scotland, but I cannot help it.' I am willing to flatter myself that I meant this as light pleasantry to soothe and conciliate him, and not as a humiliating abasement at the expense of my country. But however that might be, this speech was somewhat unlucky; for with that quickness of wit for which he was so remarkable, he seized the expression 'come from Scotland,' which I used in the sense of being of that country; and, as if I had said that I had come away from it or left it, retorted, 'That, sir, I find, is what a very great many of your countrymen cannot help.'

This stroke stunned me a good deal; and when we had sat down, I felt myself not a little embarrassed, and apprehensive of what might come next. He then addressed himself to Davies: 'What do you think of Garrick? He has refused me an order for the play for **Miss Williams**, because he knows the house will be full, and that an order would be worth three shillings.' Eager to take any opening to get into conversation with him, I ventured to say, 'Oh, sir, I cannot think Mr. Garrick would grudge such a trifle to you.' 'Sir,' said he, with a stern look, 'I have known **David Garrick** longer than you have done; and I know no right you have to talk to me on the subject.' Perhaps I deserved this check; for it was rather presumptuous in me, an entire stranger, to express any doubt of the justice of his animadversion upon his old acquaintance and pupil. I now felt myself much mortified, and began to think that the hope which I had long indulged of obtaining his acquaintance was blasted. And, in truth, had not my ardour been uncommonly strong, and my resolution uncommonly persevering, so rough a reception might have deterred me for ever from making any further attempts. Fortunately, however, I remained upon the field not wholly discomfited; and was soon rewarded by hearing some of his conversation.

Notes

This extract; from *The Life of Johnson* (under the year 1763), reveals Boswell's characteristic traits: sympathy, perseverance, and deftness in story-telling. Here, as elsewhere, he writes with his youthful enthusiasm even at his own expense.

Thomas Davies (1712?—1785), an actor at Drury Lane. He was driven from the stage by the verse of Charles Churchill: 'He mouths a sentence as curs mouth a bone.' Later he became a bookseller and publisher, and set himself up as patron and critic.

'*Look, my Lord, it comes.*' A reference to the appearance of the ghost in Shakespeare's *Hamlet*, Act I, scene iv. Hamlet, Horatio and Marcellus stand on the platform of the battlements. At midnight the ghost appears. Horatio says to Hamlet, 'Look, my Lord, it comes.'

Sir Joshua Reynolds (1723—1792), an eminent portrait-painter and art critic, one of the founders of the Club. He is said to have declared that he founded the Club in order to give Dr. Johnson abundant opportunity for talking.

prejudice against the Scotch. Johnson never loved any other people than the English, and was never tired of making fun of the Scotch. On one occasion, for instance, he says: 'The noblest prospect which a Scotchman ever sees is the high road that leads him to England.'

Miss Williams, Anna, daughter of a Welsh physician. She came to London to cure a cataract in her eyes and became a friend of Mrs. Johnson's. Later she became blind, and Johnson gave her an apartment in his house during the rest of his life. She died in 1783.

David Garrick (1717—1779), Johnson's pupil, playwright and actor. In 1747 he became manager of Drury Lane and produced a large number of Shakespearian plays. Johnson and Garrick attracted and repelled each other in a very peculiar manner. From time to time Johnson attacked his pupil, and yet never allowed anyone else to abuse him.

【作品简介】

本文选自《约翰逊传》（1763 年之后），文章揭示了鲍斯威尔的个性特征：富有同情心、拥有顽强的毅力、善于讲故事。在这里，和其他文章一样，他以自己年轻的热情来写作，甚至不惜一切代价，哪怕自己承担费用。

【作品解析】

Thomas Davies：托马斯·戴维斯（约 1712—1785），德鲁里街剧院的一名演员。由于查尔斯·丘吉尔在诗句中说"他读台词时，就像野狗在啃骨头"，他因此被驱逐出了舞台。后来他成了书商和出版商，自称为赞助人和评论家。

"Look, my Lord, it comes."：参见莎士比亚《哈姆雷特》剧中第一幕第四场，鬼魂的出现。哈姆雷特、霍拉肖和马塞勒斯站在城墙的平台上。午夜时分，幽灵出现了。霍拉肖对哈姆雷特说："看哪，大人，他现身了。"

Sir Joshua Reynolds：乔舒亚·雷诺兹爵士（1723—1792），著名的肖像画家和艺术评论家，也是文学俱乐部创始人之一。据说，他创建这个俱乐部的目的就是为了给约翰逊博士有充分的谈话机会。

prejudice against the Scotch：约翰逊从来没有喜欢过英国人以外的其他任何人，也从未厌倦过取笑苏格兰人。例如，他有一次说："苏格兰人所能展望的最壮丽的前景就是通往英格兰的大道。"

Miss Williams：安娜·威廉姆斯小姐，一位威尔士医生的女儿。她到伦敦治疗白内障，并成为约翰逊夫人的朋友。后来她失明了，约翰逊在他的别墅里给了她一套单间，让她安度余生。安娜·威廉姆斯小姐于 1783 年去世。

David Garrick：大卫·加里克（1717—1779），约翰逊的学生、剧作家和演员。1747 年，他成为德鲁里街剧院的经理，创作了大量的莎士比亚戏剧。约翰逊和加里克既相互吸引又相互排斥，关系奇特。约翰逊常常攻击他的学生，却又不允许其他人批评他。

【参考译文】

鲍斯威尔对约翰逊的介绍

托马斯·戴维斯先生是一位演员，并且在考文特花园罗素街开了一家书店，他告诉我，约翰逊是他的好友，经常到他家做客，并不止一次地邀请我与约翰逊见面。但不巧的是要么我有事，要么他有事，我始终没能如愿。

托马斯·戴维斯先生是一个通情达理、才华横溢的人，受过良好的教育。他尽管有点言辞浮夸，但却是个有趣的同伴。他的文学表演无不蕴藏着智慧和美德。他为人热情好客。他和他那美貌出众的妻子，虽然在舞台上多年，但始终保持着一种端庄的品格；约翰逊很尊重他们，和他们相处得非常融洽，与他们保持着一种亲密无间的关系，就像他曾经拜访过的任何家庭一样。每当戴维斯先生背诵起约翰逊的几句名言时，他的语音语调和神情举止都是众多模仿者当中最好的一个。他让我急切地期待见到约翰逊这位非凡的人物。我对约翰逊的作品评价颇高，而人们都说他的言谈非常美妙。

机会终于来了。5月16日，星期一，在戴维斯先生书店的后客厅里，我和他以及戴维斯夫人坐在一起喝茶时，约翰逊意外地走进了书店。戴维斯先生已经透过我们坐的房间玻璃门看到了他正向我们走来——戴维斯先生向我宣布他即将到来，那架势有点像扮演霍拉肖的演员在向哈姆雷特描述他父亲亡灵再现时的样子，"看哪，大人，他现身了！"我对约翰逊的形象印象深刻，那是在他的《英语词典》出版后不久，在乔舒亚·雷诺兹爵士那里看到的约翰逊画像。画像中的约翰逊坐在安乐椅上，陷入了沉思。这是他的朋友为他画的第一幅画像，乔舒亚爵士非常友好地把它赠送给了我，并根据这幅作品雕刻了一幅版画。戴维斯先生提到我的名字，并恭敬地把我介绍给了他。我非常激动，但同时想起约翰逊对苏格兰人有偏见，于是就对戴维斯说："不要告诉他我是从哪里来的。""从苏格兰来的。"戴维斯不无幽默地大声说道。"约翰逊先生，"我只好说，"我确实来自苏格兰，但我也没有办法。"我本想用这样的自嘲来缓和一下气氛，以保全苏格兰人的荣誉。然而，没想到反而弄巧成拙；约翰逊以他超人的机敏，紧紧抓住了"来自苏格兰"这句话。我的原意是我出生在苏格兰，但他却让我觉得仿佛我是在说：我已经离开了苏格兰。约翰逊立刻反唇相讥，并说道："一点不错，我发现对此你的许多同胞也都无能为力。"他的这番话让我始料未及。当我们坐下时，我感觉有点尴尬，为不知道下面还会发生什么而感到不安。约翰逊对戴维斯说："你觉得加里克这人怎样？他拒绝帮我给威廉姆斯小姐订一张戏票，因为他知道那时一定会满场，会有许多观众，而且一张票需要三个先令。"为了急于同约翰逊说上话，我就冒昧大胆地说："哦，先生，我想加里克先生不会不情愿为您做这样一件小事。""先生，"他神情严肃地说，"我认识大卫·加里克的时间比你要长，我不知道你有什么权利和我谈论这个问题。"这也许是我应得的报应，我确实相当冒昧。我这个陌生人，居然为他的老熟人和学生打抱不平，对约翰逊的批评表示质疑，我感到非常窘迫，以为长期以来沉溺于想与约翰逊相识的愿望就要化为泡影了。事实上，如果我的热情不那么强烈，如果我的决心没有那么坚定，这样不友好的初次见面，很可能会让我永远不敢再做任何去和他相识的进一步尝试。不过，幸运的是，我留了下来，他也并没有使我太难堪；而且，很快我便得到了回报，听到了他的一些谈话。

Oliver Goldsmith

As Dr. Oliver Goldsmith will frequently appear in this narrative, I shall endeavour to make my readers in some degree acquainted with his singular character. He was a native of Ireland, and a contemporary with **Mr. Burke**, at Trinity College, Dublin, but did not then give much promise of future celebrity. He, however, observed to **Mr. Malone** that, 'though he made no great figure in mathematics, which was a study in much repute there, he could turn an Ode of **Horace** into English better than any of them.' He afterwards studied physic at Edinburgh, and upon the Continent; and I have been informed, was enabled to pursue his travels on foot, partly by demanding at universities to enter the lists as a disputant, by which, according to the custom of many of them, he was entitled to the premium of a crown, when luckily for him his challenge was not accepted; so that, as I once observed to Dr. Johnson, he *disputed* his passage through Europe. He then came to England, and was employed successively in the capacities of an usher to an academy, a corrector of the press, a reviewer, and a writer for a newspaper. He had sagacity enough to cultivate assiduously the acquaintance of Johnson, and his faculties were gradually enlarged by the contemplation of such a model. To me and many others it appeared that he studiously copied the manner of Johnson, though, indeed, upon a smaller scale.

At this time I think he had published nothing with his name, though it was pretty generally known that one Dr. Goldsmith was the author of *An Enquiry into the Present State of Polite Learning in Europe*, and of *The Citizen of the World*, a series of letters supposed to be written from London by a Chinese. No man had the art of displaying with more advantage as a writer, whatever literary acquisitions he made. '*Nihil quod tetigit non ornavit.*' His mind resembled a fertile, but thin soil. There was a quick, but not a strong vegetation, of whatever chanced to be thrown upon it. No deep root could be struck. The oak of the forest did not grow there; but the elegant shrubbery and the fragrant parterre appeared in gay succession. It has been generally circulated and believed that **he was a mere fool in conversation**; but in truth, this has been greatly exaggerated. He had, no doubt, a more than common share of that hurry of ideas which we often find in his countrymen, and which sometimes produces a laughable confusion in expressing them. He was very much what the French call *un étourdi*, and from vanity and an eager desire of being conspicuous wherever he was, he frequently talked carelessly without knowledge of the subject, or even without thought. His person was short, his countenance coarse and vulgar, his deportment that of a scholar awkwardly affecting the easy gentleman. Those who were in any way distinguished, excited envy in him to so ridiculous an excess, that the instances of it are hardly credible. When accompanying two beautiful young ladies with their mother on a tour in France, he was seriously angry that more attention was paid to them than to him; and once at the exhibition of the *Fantoccini* in London, when those who sat next him observed with what dexterity a puppet was made to toss a pike, he could not bear that it should have such praise, and exclaimed with some warmth, 'Pshaw! I can do it better myself.'

He, I am afraid, had no settled system of any sort, so that his conduct must not be strictly scrutinised; but his affections were social and generous, and when he had money he gave it away very liberally. His desire of imaginary consequence predominated over his attention to truth. When he began to rise into notice, he said he had a brother who was Dean of Durham, a fiction so easily detected, that it is wonderful how he should have been so inconsiderate as to hazard it. He boasted to me at this time of the power of his pen in commanding money, which I believe was true in a certain degree, though in the instance he gave he was by no means correct. He told me that he had sold a novel for four hundred pounds. This was his *Vicar of Wakefield*. But Johnson informed me, that he had made the bargain for Goldsmith, and the price was sixty pounds. 'And, sir,' said he, 'a sufficient price too, when it was sold; for then the fame of Goldsmith had not been elevated, as it afterwards was, by his *Traveller*; and the bookseller had such faint hopes of profit by his bargain that he kept the manuscript by him a long time and did not publish it till after *The Traveller* had appeared. Then, to be sure, it was accidentally worth more money.'

Mrs. Piozzi and **Sir John Hawkins** have strangely misstated the history of Goldsmith's situation and Johnson's friendly interference, when this novel was sold. I shall give it authentically from Johnson's own exact narration:

'I received one morning a message from poor Goldsmith that he was in great distress, and, as it was not in his power to come to me, begging that I would come to him as soon as possible. I sent him a guinea, and promised to come to him directly. I accordingly went as soon as I was dressed, and found that his landlady had arrested him for his rent, at which he was in a violent passion. I perceived that he had already changed my guinea, and had got a bottle of Madeira and a glass before him. I put the cork into the bottle, desired he would be calm, and began to talk to him of the means by which he might be extricated. He then told me that he had a novel ready for the press, which he produced to me. I looked into it, and saw its merit; told the landlady I should soon return, and having gone to a bookseller, sold it for sixty pounds. I brought Goldsmith the money, and he discharged his rent, not without rating his landlady in a high tone for having used him so ill.'

Notes

From *The Life of Johnson* (under the year 1763). In this interesting sketch of Goldsmith, Boswell shows an evident streak of envy. He always looked upon Goldsmith as a rival in the affection of Dr. Johnson. He was inclined also to use Goldsmith as a foil to bring out the excellences of his hero.

Mr. Burke, Edmund (1729—1797), the great parliamentarian, author of *Reflections on the French Revolution* (1790). He was a member of Johnson's

Club.

Mr. Malone, Edmond (1741—1812), literary critic and Shakespearian scholar. He was a member of Johnson's Club and a friend of Boswell's.

Horace, Quintus Horatius Flaccus (65 B.C.—8 B.C.), Roman poet, and critic, author of *Satires, Odes, Epodes,* and *Ars Poetica* (art of poetry).

'*Nihil quod tetigit non ornavit*' (Latin), 'he adorned whatever he touched,' —quoted, rather inaccurately, from the epitaph Johnson wrote for Goldsmith's monument in Westminster Abbey.

he was a mere fool in conversation. Goldsmith was not a brilliant talker in the company of wits. Probably, Garrick's mock epitaph contained an element of truth:

> 'Here lies Oliver, for short called Noll,
>
> Who wrote like an angel, but talked like poor Poll.'

un étourdi (French), a rattle-brain.

Fantoccini (Italian), puppet show.

Mrs. Piozzi, née Hester Lynch Salusbury (1741—1821), one of the 'bluestockings' of the age. She married Henry Thrale, a brewer. For more than twenty years she was on intimate terms with Dr. Johnson. After Thrale's death she married Gabriel Piozzi, an Italian musician. She was the author of *Anecdotes of the Late Samuel Johnson* (1786), which ran through four editions within a year of publication.

Sir John Hawkins, one of the original members of Johnson's Club, from which he withdrew later. John said that he was 'a most unclubbable man.' He was the author of the *Life of Dr. Samuel Johnson* (1787).

【作品简介】

本文选自《约翰逊传》（1763 年之后）。在这篇对哥尔德斯密斯有趣的描绘中，鲍斯威尔明显表露出了有点嫉妒的意思。在对约翰逊博士的情感中，他总是把哥尔德斯密斯看作是他的竞争对手。他经常用哥尔德斯密斯作为陪衬，展示自己卓越的英雄气概。

【作品解析】

Mr．Burke：埃德蒙·伯克（1729—1797），杰出的国会议员，《法国革命记》（1790）的作者，约翰逊俱乐部成员之一。

Mr．Malone：埃德蒙·马隆（1741—1812），文学批评家，莎士比亚学者，约翰逊俱乐部成员之一，与鲍斯威尔是朋友。

Horace：昆图斯·贺拉斯·弗拉库斯（前65—前8），古罗马诗人和评论家，著有《讽刺诗集》《歌集》《长短句集》《诗艺》。

"Nihil quod tetigit non ornavit"（拉丁语）：即"he adorned whatever he touched"（英文），意思是"凡是他涉猎过的，无处没有他的点缀"。引文出自约翰逊在西敏寺为哥尔德斯密斯纪念碑撰写的墓志铭，引用得相当不准确。

He was a mere fool in conversation：哥尔德斯密斯在聪明人中间，不是个能说会道的人。也许，加里克带有讥笑的墓志铭向我们透露了一点真相："这儿安息的是奥利弗，或称诺尔／他的创作像天使一般，然而交谈起来却像可怜的波尔。"

un étourdi（法语）：一个欠考虑的人，意指头脑糊涂，做事粗心大意。

Fantoccini（意大利语）：木偶戏。

Mrs．Piozzi：原名赫斯特·林奇·索尔兹伯里（1741—1821），是那个时代的女才子之一。她与酿酒商亨利·瑟尔结婚。二十多年来，她与约翰逊博士关系密切。瑟尔去世后，她又与意大利音乐家加布里埃尔·皮奥齐结婚。她是《已故塞缪尔·约翰逊博士最后二十年生活逸事》（1786）的作者，她的这部著作在出版后一年内，连续再版了四次。

Sir John Hawkins：约翰·霍金斯爵士，约翰逊俱乐部的早期成员，后来退出了俱乐部。他说约翰逊是一个"最不爱交际的人"。约翰·霍金斯爵士是《塞缪尔·约翰逊博士传》（1787）的作者。

【参考译文】

奥利弗·哥尔德斯密斯

由于在我的叙述中，经常会提到奥利弗·哥尔德斯密斯博士，为此，我将会努力地使读者在某种程度上了解他的独特性格。他是爱尔兰人，与伯克先生是同时代的人物。他在都柏林三一学院读书时，对未来的成名并没有抱太多的希望。然而，马隆先生却发现："尽管他在享有盛名的数学领域里没有取得什么太好的成绩，但他可以把贺拉斯的颂歌译成英文，而且译得比任何人都好。"他后来在爱丁堡学医，随后去了欧洲大陆。我还听说他徒步旅行，部分原因是为了争取以辩论者的身份进入大学校名册，根据许多大学的惯例，他可以由此获得一银币（英国旧币，相当于五先令）的奖励，幸运的是，他的挑战没有被他人接受。正如我曾经听约翰逊博士所说的那样，奥利弗·哥尔德斯密斯就是以这种辩论的方法穿越欧洲的。他来到英国之后，以工作人员的身份先后当过学院的助理教员、报社校对员、评论员和新闻报刊的撰稿人。他具有足够的聪明才智努力地去培养、维持和发展与约翰逊的友谊；而另一方面，他的睿智也不断地受到他的典范约翰逊的影响，他的能力逐渐提高了。对于我和许多人来说，奥利弗·哥尔德斯密斯在某些地方，似乎是刻意地去模仿约翰逊，尽管模仿的范围不大。

到目前为止，我没有看到过用他自己的名字发表过的任何文章。尽管众所周知，哥尔德斯密斯博士是《关于欧洲高雅文学现状的探讨》和《世界公民》的作者，其中《世界公民》是假托一名住在伦敦的中国人撰写的信札合集。作为一名作家，无论他有多好的文学修养，没有一个能超越哥尔德斯密斯的才华，他善于修饰任何他所触及过的事物。他的思想就像施于贫瘠土地上的沃肥，偶然被扔到上面的植物会长得很快，但不够强壮。由于根基不深，森林里的橡树难以在这里生长，却能培养出优雅的灌木丛和令人赏心悦目的芳香花坛。一般来说，人们都以为他不善于言谈，但事实上，这是言过其实。毫无疑问，他和常人一样，经常能看到他有更多的想法急于表达，而往往在表达时，又会出现某种可笑的混乱。他非常像法国人所说的是一个欠考虑的人——头脑糊涂，做事粗心，也许是虚荣心驱使他渴望在任何一个地方都能得到人们的关注，他经常会漫不经心地谈论某个话题，甚至不假思索，而他对这个话题又一无所知。他个子不高，面容粗俗，本有学者的风度，却笨拙地装出一副随和的绅士的样子，略显尴尬。那些不论在任何方面都很杰出的人，会激起他强烈且荒唐可笑的嫉妒心，简直难以置信。当他陪伴两位美丽年轻的女士与她们的母亲一起去法国旅行时，他非常生气，因为人们对她们的关注要比对他多得多。在伦敦的一次木偶戏展览会上，当身旁的观众称赞木偶对长矛娴熟使用的表演技巧时，他忍受不了如此的赞扬，激动地叫道："哼！要是我的话，做得比这要好的多得多！"

他没有任何陈规戒律，因而他的行为举止也不受任何约束。但是，他喜欢社交，喜欢慷慨解囊；只要有钱，他就会捐助给别人。他过于期待想象中的结果，很少关注现实。在他开始引起你注意时，他会告诉你，他有个哥哥是达勒姆教长。这是一个很容易被戳穿的假话，但说来也很不可思议，他居然如此冒失地说出此言，完全不顾及他人。他曾经向我吹嘘他的钢笔在支配金钱方面的力量，我相信在某种程度上他是对的，然而他的例子没有一个可以得到验证。他告诉我他的一部小说卖了四百英镑，这就是他的《威克菲尔德牧师传》。但约翰逊告诉我，他曾经帮哥尔德斯密斯讨价还价卖了那本书，价格应该是六十英镑。"而且，先生，"约翰逊说，"这个价钱就算不错了，当时哥尔德斯密斯并没有像后来他的《旅行者》出版以后那么有名；而书商也没有指望凭借这部小说赚钱，于是就把哥尔德斯密斯的手稿压了很长一段时间，等到《旅行者》问世后才出版。然而，可以肯定的是，这本书意外地卖了更多的钱。"

在出售这本小说时，皮奥齐太太和约翰·霍金斯爵士不知道为什么误述了哥尔德斯密斯的处境和约翰逊友好介入的这段历史。从约翰逊本人确切的叙述中，我获知真实情况如下：

"一天早上，我收到可怜的哥尔德斯密斯给我的口信，说他遇到了麻烦，但又不能到我这儿来，请求我尽快去他那里。我给送信的人一基尼，并答应哥尔德斯密斯直接去他那里。我穿上衣服就出了门，发现他的房东因为他拖欠房租而把他拘留在了那里，哥尔德斯密斯当时极其愤怒。他一定是花光了我给他的基尼，他面前摆着一瓶马德拉白葡萄酒和一只酒杯。我用软木塞把酒瓶口塞住，希望他能冷静下来，然后开始和他商谈补救措施。他告诉我，他有一本小说可以出版，并给我看了小说的原稿。我看了看，认为有价值，就对房东太太说去去就来。于是，我急忙赶到书商那里，将这本小说卖了六十英镑。我把钱给了哥尔德斯密斯，他付了房租，并高声谴责了房东太太对他的无礼行为，从而平息了这场风波。"

CHARLES LAMB (1775—1834)

Charles Lamb (1775—1834), the son of John Lamb, was born and bred a Londoner. He was educated at Christ's Hospital, a charity school for poor children, where he formed a lasting friendship with young Coleridge. At the age of fifteen, he left school to serve as a junior clerk in the South Sea House. Thence he was transferred to the East India House in 1792, and remained there for the next thirty-three years until he retired with a pension offered him by the directors for his long and faithful service. Lamb once said humourously that his true work might be found on the shelves of the company, filling some hundred folios; but it was his 'literary recreations' that have endeared him to posterity. *The Tales from Shakespeare* (1807), compiled in collaboration with his sister Mary, and the *Specimens of English Dramatic Poets Contemporary with Shakespeare* (1808) are both worthy contributions to a revival of interest in the old Elizabethan playwrights. Lamb's fame as a writer rests chiefly on his essays, most of which first appeared in the *London Magazine* and were later collected in the *Essays of Elia* (1823) and *Last Essays of Elia* (1833).

Lamb's essays are largely personal, full of reminiscences and anecdotes, descriptions of local scenes connected with his childhood and later life. He is frank in self-revelation; he has said of himself as consisting of a bundle of prejudices—made up of likings and dislikings. It is no exaggeration to say that it is the man Lamb that constitutes the enduring charm of his written words. His humour, which sparkles in every page of his work, is inseparable from his personality. Whimsical and gesticulating all the time, he plays the harlequin to amuse the reader; but even where his laughter is the loudest, there runs an undercurrent of fellow feeling that flows in all his writings. Just as his humour tickles us, so his pathos touches our heart with sympathy and affection. To form an acquaintance with his essays is to cement a lasting friendship with their author who is certainly the gentlest, the quaintest, and the most charming of the English men of letters.

【作者简介】

查尔斯·兰姆（1775—1834），约翰·兰姆之子，出生于伦敦并在伦敦长大。他曾在基督医院接受过教育，那是一所为贫困儿童开办的慈善学校，在那里他与年轻的柯勒律治建立了长久的友谊。十五岁那年，他便离开了学校，到南海公司担任初级文书。1792 年他被调到东印度公司，并在那里一直工作了三十三年直到退休，董事们考虑到他长期忠诚的服务，向他提供了养老金。兰姆曾经幽默地说，他真正的作品可能会在公司的书架上找到，里面足足有数百本的对开本；然而，正是这种"文学娱乐"使他深受后人爱戴。他与姐姐玛丽共同编纂的《莎士比亚戏剧故事集》(1807)，以及他自己的《莎士比亚同时代英国戏剧诗人之范作及注》(1808)，对于重新唤起人们对伊丽莎白时期老剧作家们的兴趣做出了有价值的贡献。然而，兰姆作为一名作家的声誉主要取决于他的散文，其中大部分散文最早出现在《伦敦杂志》上，后来被收集在《伊利亚随笔集》(1823)和《伊利亚随笔续集》(1833)中。

兰姆的散文主要是以个人为主体，充满了回忆和逸事，描写与他的童年和晚年生活有关的地方场景。他的自我揭露很坦率，他说自己是由一系列偏见组成的，这些偏见左右了他的好恶。可以毫不夸张地说，正是兰姆这种男子气概，使他的文字充满了持久的魅力。他作品中的每一页都闪烁着幽默，这与他的个性是分不开的。他总是异想天开，打着手势扮演滑稽角色来取悦读者；然而，即使在他笑声最爽朗的地方，也有一种潜在的同情之情在他所有的作品中流淌。就像他的幽默逗乐了我们一样，他的悲怆也以同情和深情深深触动了我们的心。专心品读兰姆的散文，就能与作者相识并建立一种持久而牢固的友谊。无可置疑，兰姆是英国文坛中最具有绅士风度、最古朴典雅、最迷人的作家。

Dream-Children: A Reverie

Children love to listen to stories about their elders, when *they* were children; to stretch their imagination to the conception of a traditionary great-uncle or grandame, whom they never saw. It was in this spirit that my little ones crept about me the other evening to hear about their **great-grandmother Field**, who lived in **a great house in Norfolk** (a hundred times bigger than that in which they and papa lived) which had been the scene—so at least it was generally believed in that part of the country—of the tragic incidents which they had lately become familiar with from the ballad of the '**Children in the Wood**'. Certain it is that the whole story of the children and their cruel uncle was to be seen fairly carved out in wood upon the chimney-piece of the great hall, the whole story down to the Robin Redbreasts, till a foolish rich person pulled it down to set up a marble one of modern invention in its stead, with no story upon it. Here Alice put out one of her dear mother's looks, too tender to be called upbraiding. Then I went on to say, how religious and how good their great-grandmother Field was, how beloved and respected by everybody, though she was not indeed the mistress of this great house, but had only the charge of it (and yet in some respects she might be said to be the mistress of it too) committed to her by the owner, who preferred living in a **newer and more fashionable mansion** which he had purchased somewhere in the adjoining county; but still she lived in it in a manner as if it had been her own, and kept up the dignity of the great house **in a sort** while she lived, which afterwards came to decay, and was nearly pulled down, and all its old ornaments stripped and carried away to the owner's other house, where they were set up, and looked as awkward as if someone were to carry away the old tombs they had seen lately at the **Abbey**, and stick them up in Lady C.'s tawdry gilt drawing-room. Here John smiled, as much as to say, 'that would be foolish indeed.' And then I told how, when she came to die, her funeral was attended by a concourse of all the poor, and some of the gentry too, of the neighbourhood for many miles round, to show their respect for her memory, because she had been such a good and religious woman; so good indeed that she knew all the **Psaltery** by heart, ay, and a great part of the Testament besides. Here little Alice spread her hands. Then I told what a tall, upright, graceful person their great-grandmother Field once was; and how in her youth she was esteemed the best dancer— here Alice's little right foot played an involuntary movement, till upon my looking grave, it desisted—the best dancer, I was saying, in the county, till a cruel disease, called a cancer, came, and bowed her down with pain; but it could never bend her good spirits, or make them stoop, but they were still upright, because she was so good and religious. Then I told how she was used to sleep by herself in a lone chamber of the great lone house; and how she believed that an apparition of two infants was to be seen at midnight gliding up and down the great staircase near where she slept, but she said those innocents would do her no harm; and how frightened I used to be, though in those days I had my maid to sleep with me, because I was never half so good or religious as she—and yet I never saw the infants. Here John **expanded all his eyebrows** and tried to look courageous. Then I told how good she was to all her grandchildren, having us to the great house in the **holydays**, where I in particular used to spend many hours by myself, in gazing upon the old busts of the **Twelve Caesars,** that had been Emperors of Rome, till the old marble heads would seem to live again, or I to be turned into marble with them; how I never could be tired with roaming about that huge mansion with its vast empty rooms, with their worn-out hangings, fluttering tapestry, and carved oaken panels, with the gilding almost rubbed out—sometimes in the spacious, old-fashioned gardens, which I had almost to myself, unless when now and then a solitary gardening man would cross me—and how the nectarines and peaches hung upon the walls, without my ever offering to pluck them, because they were **forbidden fruit,** unless now and then,—and because I had more pleasure in strolling about among the old melancholy-looking yew trees, or the firs, and picking up the red berries, and the **fir apples**, which were good for nothing but to look at—or in lying about upon the fresh grass, with all the fine garden smells around me—or basking in the orangery, till I could almost fancy myself ripening too along with the oranges and the limes in that grateful warmth—or in watching the dace that darted to and fro in the fish-pond, at the bottom of the garden, with here and there a great sulky pike hanging midway down the water in silent state, as if it mocked at their impertinent friskings,—I had more pleasure in these busy-idle diversions than in all the sweet flavours of peaches, nectarines, oranges, and such like common baits of children. Here John slyly deposited back upon the plate a bunch of grapes, which, not unobserved by Alice, he had meditated dividing with her, and both seemed willing to relinquish them for the present as irrelevant. Then in somewhat a more heightened tone, I told how, though their great-grandmother Field loved all her grandchildren, yet in an especial manner she might be said to love their uncle, **John L—**, because he was so handsome and spirited a youth, and a king to the rest of us; and, instead of moping about in solitary corners, like some of us, he would mount the most mettlesome horse he could get, when but an imp no bigger than themselves, and make it carry him half over the county in a morning, and join the hunters when there were any out—and yet he loved the old great house and gardens too, but had too much spirit to be always pent up within their boundaries— and how their uncle grew up to man's estate as brave as he was handsome, to the admiration of everybody, but of their great- grandmother Field most especially; and how he used to carry me upon his back **when I was a lame-footed boy**—for **he was a good bit older than me**—many a mile when I could not walk for pain;—and how in after life he became lame-footed too, and I did not always (I fear) make allowances enough for him when he was impatient, and in pain, nor remember sufficiently how considerate he had been to me when I was lame-footed; and how when he died, though he had not been dead an hour, it seemed as if he had died a great while ago, such a distance there is betwixt life and death; and how I bore his death as I thought pretty well at first, but afterwards it haunted and haunted me; and though I did not cry or take it to heart as some do, and as I think he would have done if I had died, yet I missed him all day long, and knew not till then how much I had loved him. I missed his kindness, and I missed his crossness, and wished him to be alive again, to be quarrelling with him (for we quarrelled sometimes), rather than not have him again, and was as uneasy without him as he, their poor uncle, must have been when the doctor took off his limb. Here the children fell a crying, and asked if their little mourning which they had on was not for uncle John, and they looked up, and prayed me not to go on about their uncle, but to tell them some stories about their pretty dead mother. Then I told how for seven long years, in hope sometimes, sometimes in despair, yet persisting ever, I courted the **fair Alice W—n**; and, as much as children could understand, I explained to them what coyness, and difficulty, and denial meant in maidens—when suddenly, turning to Alice, the soul of the first Alice looked out at her eyes with such a reality of **re-presentment**, that I became in doubt which of them stood there before me, or whose that bright hair was; and while I stood gazing, both the children gradually grew fainter to my view, receding, and still receding till nothing at last but two mournful features were seen in the uttermost distance, which, without speech, strangely impressed upon me the effects of speech; 'We are not of Alice, nor of thee, nor are we children at all. The children of Alice call **Bartrum** father. We are nothing; less than nothing, and dreams. We are only what might have been, and must wait upon **the tedious shores of Lethe** millions of ages before we have existence, and a name.' —and immediately awaking, I found myself quietly seated in my bachelor armchair, where I had fallen asleep, with the faithful **Bridget** unchanged by my side—but John L. (**or James Elia**) was gone forever.

Notes

The 'Dream Children' was published in the *London Magazine* in January, 1822 and collected in the *Essays of Elia*. It is a piece of tender and pathetic prose, with rich, imaginative, and dream-like qualities, written on the occasion of the recent death of his brother John. It shows that our bachelor author was by no means insensitive to the comforts of family life, and he must have yearned sometimes for the dear little ones who would have crept about him to listen to his stories, if he were married to his early love. As it was, he could only console himself with the bare semblance of a home kept by him and his faithful sister. The essay was written from his heart and the sincerity of his feelings makes it one of the most poignantly touching of English prose writings.

great-grandmother Field. This refers to Mary Field, Lamb's maternal grandmother, hence great-grandmother to the dream children. Mrs. Field was housekeeper to the Plumer family at Blakesware.

a great house in Norfolk. Norfolk is a county in eastern England. The great house, however, was really at Blakesware in Hertfordshire. It belonged to the Plumers, a rich family, who had two residences in the district. After they had moved over to their new mansion, the old house was left to the care of Mrs. Field, who kept up its dignity while she lived.

'*Children in the Wood*', the subject of an old ballad (apparently written in 1595), which is included in Bishop Percy's *Reliques of Ancient English Poetry*. A gentleman of Norfolk on his death-bed leaves his property to his infant son and daughter, and gives the charge of them to his brother. The brother designs to get possession of the property by making away with the children. He hires two ruffians to slay them in a wood. One of these, more tender-hearted than the other, repents and kills his fellow, and abandons the children in the wood. The children perish, and the Robin-redbreast covers them with leaves. The wrath of God falls upon the wicked uncle, who loses his son and his goods, and dies in goal. The surviving ruffian is arrested for robbery, condemned to death, and confesses the deed.

newer and more fashionable mansion, the Plumers' new residence in Gilston, a few miles distant from the old house.

in a sort, in a respectable manner.

Abbey, Westminster Abbey, where the celebrities were buried.

Psaltery, the Psalter or Book of Psalms.

expanded all his eyebrows, i.e. to look brave and elate.

holydays. Holidays were originally holy days.

Twelve Caesars, the first twelve Roman emperors from Julius Caesar to Domitian, whose busts were frequently used to decorate bookcases.

forbidden fruit, the thing desired because not allowed—a reference to *Genesis* ii, 16—17.

fir apples, fir cones.

John L—, John Lamb, Charles Lamb's brother, who died a short time before this essay was written. John's death brought home to Charles a sense of his loneliness.

when I was a lame-footed boy, of Lamb's lameness when a child, this is the only reference.

he was a good bit older than me. John Lamb, born in June 1763, was twelve years Charles senior.

fair Alice W—n, Winterton, a feigned name, vaguely identified with Ann Simmons whom Lamb may have courted.

re-presentment, re-appearance, re-incarnation.

Bartrum, Mr. Bartrum, a London pawnbroker, who married Ann Simmons, and had several children by her.

the tedious shores of Lethe. In Greek and Roman legends, it is said that souls, after a cycle of a thousand years, assemble in Hades upon the banks of Lethe, the river of forgetfulness, before they again become embodied upon earth.

Bridget ... (or James Elia). Bridget and James Elia were the names Lamb gave to his sister Mary and brother John in his essays.

【作品简介】

《梦幻中的孩子们》于 1822 年 1 月在《伦敦杂志》上发表，后来编入《伊利亚随笔集》。这是一篇充满柔情又凄婉的散文，具有丰富的想象力和梦幻般的特点，是兰姆在他哥哥约翰去世后不久写的。此文表明了我们的单身汉作者，对家庭生活的安乐舒适并不是不向往，如果他与他的初恋结了婚，他一定会时常希望有一群可爱的小孩围绕在他的膝旁，聆听他讲述的故事。事实上，他只能靠他和他忠实的姐姐所拥有的形同虚设的一个家来安慰自己。这篇文章是发自内心的，感情之真切使之成为英国散文中最感人的作品之一。

【作品解析】

great-grandmother Field：这是指玛丽·菲尔德，兰姆的外祖母，也是梦幻中的孩子们伟大的曾祖母。菲尔德太太曾是布拉科斯威尔镇（英国伦敦）普卢默家里的女管家。

a great house in Norfolk：诺福克是英格兰东部的一个郡（县）。这座大房子实际上是在赫特福德郡的布拉科斯威尔镇，属于当地的富豪普卢默家族，他们在这个地区有两处豪宅。他们搬到新宅邸后，这所老宅子就留给菲尔德太太照管，她居住在那儿时，仍保持着这所老宅子的庄重。

"Children in the Wood"：《森林里的孩子》（也许创作于1595年），是一首古老的民谣，收录在珀西主教的《英诗辑古》中。一位诺福克郡的绅士临终前躺在病榻上，把他的财产留给了还是婴儿的儿子和女儿，并把监护权交给了自己的兄弟。这个兄弟企图把孩子们弄走，以此来获得财产。他雇用了两名歹徒要把孩子们杀死在森林里。其中一个歹徒比较心软，良心发现，杀死了他的同伴，并把孩子们抛弃在了森林里。孩子们死了，红胸知更鸟用树叶把孩子们的尸体掩埋了。上帝的愤怒降临到邪恶叔叔的身上，他失去了他自己的儿子和财物，也被死神射中了。那个幸存的歹徒也因抢劫被捕，被判处死刑，对其罪责供认不讳。

newer and more fashionable mansion：这里是指普卢默家在盖尔斯顿的新豪宅，离旧豪宅只有几英里远。

in a sort：以某种得体的方式。

Abbey：指西敏寺，名人显贵们的安息之地。

Psaltery：《圣经》里的《诗篇》。

expanded all his eyebrows：即看起来勇敢且快乐。

holydays：假日（holidays）起初是指神圣的日子（holy days）。

Twelve Caesars：从儒略·恺撒大帝到图密善期间的前十二位罗马皇帝，他们的半身像经常被用于装饰书柜。

forbidden fruit：禁果，不可拥有却又想得到的东西，参见《创世记》第2卷。

fir apples：冷杉果。

John L—：指约翰·兰姆，查尔斯·兰姆的哥哥，在查尔斯写这篇散文前不久去世了。约翰的去世给查尔斯带来了孤独感。

when I was a lame-footed boy：这是兰姆儿童时期跛足的唯一参考。

he was a good bit older than me：约翰·兰姆，生于 1763 年 6 月，比查尔斯大十二岁。

Alice W—n：艾丽丝·温特顿，一个假名，可能是安·西蒙斯，兰姆曾经追求过她。

re-presentment：重现，化身。

Bartrum：巴特鲁姆先生，伦敦当铺（典当行）的老板，与安·西蒙斯结婚，并生了几个孩子。

the tedious shores of Lethe：在希腊和罗马的神话里，传说魂灵经过一千年的循环之后，可在冥府里聚集在忘川河畔，然后再次轮回到地球上。

Bridget... (or James Elia)：布里奇特和詹姆斯·埃利亚是查尔斯·兰姆在散文中给他的姐姐玛丽和哥哥约翰起的笔名。

【参考译文】

梦幻中的孩子们：一段遐想

小时候的孩子们都喜欢聆听有关长辈们的故事，他们想象力丰富，幻想着从来没有见过面的、传说中的叔祖父或祖母的伟大形象。正是由于这样的灵感，那天晚上，我的孩子们悄悄地围拢了过来，坐在我的身边，想聆听我讲述他们曾祖母菲尔德的故事。曾祖母菲尔德住在诺福克的一座大房子里（比现在他们和爸爸居住的房子还要大上一百倍），当地的人们都认为那里曾经是民谣《森林里的孩子》一系列悲剧事件的发源地。可以肯定的是，孩子们和他们邪恶叔叔的传说，这整个故事的细节，甚至红胸知更鸟，都雕刻在了大厅壁炉墙上的木板上。后来，某个愚蠢的富人把壁炉上的木刻拉了下来，换成了现代时髦的大理石，却没有了故事。这时，艾丽丝流露出了一副神情，像极了她的母亲，她是那么娇嫩温柔，没有一点像是在责备的意思。于是，我继续向他们讲述着曾祖母菲尔德的故事。菲尔德既虔诚又善良，每个人都爱戴和尊重她。虽然她并不是这座大宅子里的真正女主人，只是向主人承诺照料管理这座房子而已，房屋的主人更喜欢居住在邻县购买的那个更新、更加时髦的豪宅里，因此在某种程度上，也不妨说她就是这座大房子的女主人。曾祖母尔德在这座宅子居住生活的一段时间里，把它当作了自己的家，以她自己的方式来保持这座宅子的庄严。后来，这座宅子破旧了，差一点就倒塌了下来，宅子里所有的装饰品统统都卸了下来，打包运到主人另一座新的豪宅里。这些装饰品放在那里看起来有些不大协调，就好像有人把西敏寺里的古墓搬进某位夫人那装潢俗气、四面镀金、华丽的客厅里一样。此时，约翰笑了笑，好像在说："这的确是太愚蠢了。"我继续讲述着，曾祖母菲尔德去世的时候，方圆数英里的许多穷人，还有一些绅士和好友，都来参加她的葬礼，表示对她的怀念和尊敬。因为曾祖母菲尔德是一个非常善良和虔诚的妇人；她真的是太好了，她能把所有的《诗篇》都牢牢地记住，嗯，还有大部分的《圣约》。这时，小艾丽丝摊开了双手。我接着说，曾祖母菲尔德曾经是一个身材高挑、性格正直、举止优雅的女人。她年轻时，是人们公认的最好的舞者。这时，艾丽丝的小右脚不由自主地摆动着，做了个舞蹈的动作，后来她看到我神情严肃，也就没有继续下去了。我接着说，她是这个郡里最好的舞者，不幸的是，曾祖母菲尔德后来得了一种残酷的疾病，人们称之为癌症，她疼痛不堪，病魔把她折磨得连腰都直不起来了；然而，癌症却战胜不了她的意志，也不能使她善良的灵魂屈服，或者让她的情绪低落，她始终是个精神饱满的人，因为她善良虔诚。我继续讲述着，曾祖母菲尔德是如何习惯独自一人睡在这座孤零零的大宅子里的；又如何总是觉得有两个婴儿的幽灵每天在午夜时分，在她卧房附近的楼梯上爬上爬下。但她却说，那些无辜的孩子是不会伤及她的。虽然当时有位女仆陪伴着我一起睡觉，可我还是挺害怕的，也许我没有曾祖母那么善良，也没有她那么虔诚吧！——不过，我也从来没有见到过那两个婴儿。这时，约翰展开了眉毛，显得很勇敢的样子。然后，我告诉他们，曾祖母菲尔德对每个孙子孙女都很好，在假日里，她带着我们到这座大房子里度假。在那里，我总是独自待上几小时，凝视着十二座古罗马恺撒的半身塑像，一直看到那些用大理石雕刻的头像似乎活了过来，而自己似乎就快要变成大理石像了，才肯罢休。我在那座巨大空旷的宅邸里闲逛，从不感到厌倦，那些空荡荡的房间，挂着破旧不堪的帷幔和摇摇欲坠的挂毯，还有雕花的橡木板，上面的镀金几乎都快被磨掉了。我有时待在宽敞的老式花园里，整个花园几乎就只有我一人，偶尔会碰到一个孤独的园丁路过。花园的墙上挂满了油桃和桃子，而我从来没有想过要去摘下它们，因为它们是禁果，只能在某些特殊的情况下才可以采摘。而我更喜欢漫步在看似忧郁的紫杉树和冷杉树之间，采摘一些红浆果和冷杉果，这些果子只为了被欣赏而并没有其他的用处。有时，我也喜欢躺在鲜嫩的草坪上，闻着萦绕在美丽花园里的芳香；有时，我在橘园里晒太阳，直到我觉得温暖的阳光快要把我和橘子、柠檬一起晒熟了才肯离开；有时，我在鱼塘边观看鲮鱼，看着它们在鱼塘底部匆匆忙忙地游来游去，蹿上蹿下，时不时还会有一两条体形较大的梭鱼默默地潜伏在鱼塘的中层，似乎在嘲笑鲮鱼鲁莽和笨拙的动作。一般来说，那些桃子和橘子之类的甜味都是吸引孩子们兴趣的诱饵，然而我却更加喜欢这些忙碌而闲暇的消遣。这时，艾丽丝注意到约翰偷偷地将一串葡萄放到了盘子里，约翰原本想与艾丽丝分享来着，现在他们两人似乎都愿意暂时放弃。因为现在这些对他们来说，都已无关紧要了。我提高了声调告诉他们，曾祖母菲尔德虽然喜欢所有的孙子和孙女，但她特别喜欢的是他们的伯伯约翰·兰，因为他潇洒英俊，年轻活泼，充满了激情，对我们来说简直就像是我们的头领。他不喜欢像我们那样躲在孤零零的角落里闷闷不乐地徘徊；而是骑上他能找得到的最强壮的马，当时的他并不比其他孩子大多少，是个小淘气，一大早就骑着马穿过大半个郡，然后当猎人出行打猎时，他就加入他们的行列——不过他也喜欢古老的大房子和花园，然而他那旺盛的精力总是让他不会心甘情愿地被禁锢在疆界之内——后来，伯伯约翰·兰渐渐地长大了，成为庄园里的男子汉。他的潇洒英俊赢得了人们的赞赏，特别是曾祖母菲尔德的赞赏。当我是一个跛脚男孩的时候，他总是背着我——因为他比我大一点——我因脚疼痛走不了路的时候他就背着我走好多英里；——后来他自己的脚也跛了，在他痛苦和不安的时候，我恐怕总是不够宽容和体谅他；也不记得在我跛脚的时候，他对我是有多么体贴入微。后来，他去世的时候，虽然刚走还不到一小时，但我却觉得他死了很久，这就是生与死之间的距离。起初对于他的死，我还能承受，然而到了后来，他的死却一直萦绕着我；虽然我没有像其他的人那样哭泣，也没有久久不能释怀，我想如果我死了，他也会这么做的，但是我整天都在思念他，直到那时我才知道我有多么地爱他。我怀念他对我的好，怀念他固执的坏脾气，希望他能再次地活过来，和他争吵（因为有时我们也会吵架），也比没有了他要好得多。没有了他，我就像孩子们可怜的伯伯当年被医生截肢时一样感到不安。这时，孩子们哭了起来，询问他们刚刚的伤心落泪是因为约翰伯伯而难过吗？他们抬起了头，请求我不要再继续谈论他们的伯伯，而给他们讲讲已故漂亮母亲的故事。于是，我向他们讲述了在漫长的七年里，我是怎样追求美丽的艾丽丝·温特顿并向她求婚的，有时我满怀着希望，有时我却感到很绝望，但不管怎样，我坚持了下来。我尽量用孩子们所能理解的语言向他们描述纯情少女的羞怯、为难以及拒绝将会意味着什么——当我突然间转向小艾丽丝时，之前那个艾丽丝的灵魂从她的双眼显露了出来，真实的表情犹如现世一般。她俩如此相像，我简直分不清站在我面前的是哪一个艾丽丝，那满头金发的又会是谁呢？在我凝视着陷入沉思时，两个孩子却在我的视线里逐渐模糊，渐渐地退去，他们无声无息，而且越退越远，直到最后，在很远的地方留下了两张悲哀的面容，无声无息。然而奇怪的是，无声的语言却给我留下了深刻的印象，好像是在说："我们不属于艾丽丝，也不属于你，我们也根本不是什么孩子，艾丽丝孩子的父亲叫巴特鲁姆。我们什么都不是，或者说，实际上根本不存在，只是个梦幻而已。我们也许曾经存在过；但现在必须在乏味的忘川河畔等待数百万年才能还世，有自己的名字。"——我，这才惊醒，发现自己静静地坐在单人扶手椅上睡着了，只有忠实的布里奇特仍守候在我的身边——而约翰·兰（又名詹姆斯·埃利亚）却已经永远地消失了。

A Bachelor's Complaint of the
Behaviour of Married People

As a single man, I have spent a good deal of my time in noting down the infirmities of Married People, to console myself for those superior pleasures, which they tell me I have lost by remaining as I am.

I cannot say that the quarrels of men and their wives ever made any great impression upon me, or had much tendency to strengthen me in those **antisocial resolutions**, which I took up long ago upon more substantial considerations. What oftenest offends me at the houses of married persons where I visit, is an error of quite a different description;—it is that they are too loving.

Not too loving neither: that does not explain my meaning. Besides, why should that offend me? The very act of separating themselves from the rest of the world, to have the fuller enjoyment of each other's society, implies that they prefer one another to all the world.

But what I complain of is, that they carry this preference so undisguisedly, they perk it up in the faces of us single people so shamelessly, you cannot be in their company a moment without being made to feel, by some indirect hint or open avowal, that *you* are not the object of this preference. Now there are some things which give no offense, while implied or taken for granted merely; but expressed, there is much offence in them. If a man were to accost the first homely-featured or plain-dressed young woman of his acquaintance, and tell her bluntly, that she was not handsome or rich enough for him, and he could not marry her, he would deserve to be kicked for his ill manners; yet no less is implied in the fact, that having access and opportunity of **putting the question to her**, he has never yet thought fit to do it. The young woman understands this as clearly as if it were put into words; but no reasonable young woman would think of making this the ground of a quarrel. Just as little right have a married couple to tell me by speeches and looks that are scarce less plain than speeches, that I am not the happy man,—the lady's choice. It is enough that I know I am not: I do not want this perpetual reminding.

The display of superior knowledge or riches may be made sufficiently mortifying; but these admit of a palliative. The knowledge which is brought out to insult me, may accidentally improve me; and in the rich man's houses and pictures,—his parks and gardens, I have a temporary **usufruct** at least. But the display of married happiness has none of these palliatives: it is throughout pure, unrecompensed, unqualified insult.

Marriage by its best title is a monopoly, and not of the least invidious sort. It is the cunning of most possessors of any exclusive privilege to keep their advantage as much out of sight as possible, that their less favoured neighbours, seeing little of the benefit, may the less be disposed to question the right. But these married monopolists thrust the most obnoxious part of their patent into our faces.

Nothing is to me more distasteful than that entire complacency and satisfaction which beam in the countenances of a new-married couple,—in that of the lady particularly; it tells you, that her lot is disposed of in this world: that *you* can have no hopes of her. It is true, I have none; nor wishes either, perhaps; but this is one of those truths which ought, as I said before, to be taken for granted, not expressed.

The excessive airs which those people give themselves, founded on the ignorance of us unmarried people, would be more offensive if they were less irrational. We will allow them to understand the mysteries belonging to their own craft better than we who have not had the happiness to be made free of the company: but their arrogance is not content within these limits. If a single person presumes to offer his opinion in their presence, though upon the most indifferent subject, he is immediately silenced as an incompetent person. Nay, a young married lady of my acquaintance who, the best of the jest was, had not changed her condition above a fortnight before, in a question on which I had the misfortune to differ from her, respecting the properest mode of breeding oysters for the London market, had the assurance to ask with a sneer, how such an old Bachelor as I could pretend to know anything about such matters.

But what I have spoken of hitherto is nothing to the airs which these creatures give themselves when they come, as they generally do, to have children. When I consider how little of a rarity children are,—that every street and blind alley swarms with them,—that the poorest people commonly have them in most abundance,—that there are few marriages that are not blest with at least one of these bargains,—how often they turn out ill, and defeat the fond hopes of their parents, taking to vicious courses, which end in poverty, disgrace, the gallows, etc.—I cannot for my life tell what cause for pride there can possibly be in having them. If they were young phoenixes, indeed, that were born but one in a year, there might be a pretext. But when they are so common—

I do not advert to the insolent merit which they assume with their husbands on these occasions. Let them look to that. But why *we*, who are not their natural-born subjects, should be expected to bring our spices, myrrh, and incense,—our tribute and homage of admiration,—I do not see.

'**Like as the arrows** in the hand of the giant, even so are the young children' : so says the excellent **office** in our Prayer-book appointed for the **churching of women**. 'Happy is the man that hath his quiver full of them' : So say I; but then don't let him discharge his quiver upon us that are weaponless;—let them be arrows, but not to gall and stick us. I have generally observed that these arrows are double-headed; they have two forks, to be sure to hit with one or the other. As for instance, where you come into a house which is full of children, if you happen to take no notice of them (you are thinking of something else, perhaps, and turn a deaf ear to their innocent caresses), you are set down as untractable, morose, a hater of children. On the other hand, if you find them more than usually engaging,—if you are taken with their pretty manners, and set about in earnest to romp and play with them, some pretext or other is sure to be found for sending them out of the room: they are too noisy or boisterous, or Mr.—does not like children. With one or other of these forks the arrow is sure to hit you.

I could forgive their jealousy, and dispense with toying with their brats, if it gives them any pain; but I think it unreasonable to be called upon to *love* them, where I see no occasion,—to love a whole family, perhaps, eight, nine, or ten, indiscriminately,—to love all the pretty dears, because children are so engaging.

I know there is a proverb, 'Love me, love my dog' : that is not always so very practicable, particularly if the dog be set upon you to tease you or snap at you in sport. But a dog, or a lesser thing,—any inanimate substance, as a keepsake, a watch or a ring, a tree, or the place where we last parted when my friend went away upon a long absence, I can make shift to love, because I love him, and anything that reminds me of him; provided it be in its nature indifferent, and apt to receive whatever hue fancy can give it. But children have a real character and an essential being of themselves: they are amiable or unamiable *per se*; I must love or hate them, as I see cause for either in their qualities. A child's nature is too serious a thing to admit of its being regarded as a mere appendage to another being, and to be loved or hated accordingly: they stand with me upon their own stock, as much as men and women do. Oh! but you will say, sure it is an attractive age,—there is something in the tender years of infancy that of itself charms us. That is the very reason why I am more **nice** about them. I know that a sweet child is the sweetest thing in nature, not even excepting the delicate creatures which bear them, but the prettier the kind of a thing is, the more desirable it is that it should be pretty of its kind. **One daisy differs not** much from another in glory;

but a violet should look and smell the daintiest.—I was always rather squeamish in my women and children.

But this is not the worst: one must be admitted into their familiarity at least, before they can complain of inattention. It implies visits, and some kind of intercourse. But if the husband be a man with whom you have lived on a friendly footing before marriage,—if you did not come in on the wife's side,—if you did not sneak into the house in her train, but were an old friend in fast habits of intimacy before their courtship was so much as thought on,—look about you— your tenure is precarious—before a twelve month shall roll over your head, you shall find your old friend gradually grow cool and altered towards you, and at last seek opportunities of breaking with you. I have scarce a married friend of my acquaintance, upon whose firm faith I can rely, whose friendship did not commence *after the period of his marriage*. With some limitations they can endure that: but that the good man should have dared to enter into a solemn league of friendship in which they were not consulted, though it happened before they knew him,—before they that are now man and wife ever met,—this is intolerable to them. Every long friendship, every old authentic intimacy, must be brought into their office to be new stamped with their currency, as a sovereign Prince calls in the good old money that was coined in some reign before he was born or thought of, to be new marked and minted with the stamp of his authority, before he will let it pass current in the world. You may guess what luck generally befalls such a rusty piece of metal as I am in these *new mintings*.

Innumerable are the ways which they take to insult and worm

you out of their husband's confidence. Laughing at all you say with a kind of wonder, as if you were a queer kind of fellow that said good things, *but an oddity*, is one of the ways;—they have a particular kind of stare for the purpose;—till at last the husband, who used to defer to your judgment, and would pass over some **excrescences** of understanding and manner for the sake of a general vein of observation (not quite vulgar) which he perceived in you, begins to suspect whether you are not altogether a humourist,—a fellow well enough to have consorted with in his bachelor days, but not quite so proper to be introduced to ladies. This may be called the staring way; and is that which has oftenest been put in practice against me.

Then there is the exaggerating way, or the way of irony; that is, where they find you an object of especial regard with their husband, who is not so easily to be shaken from the lasting attachment founded on esteem which he has conceived towards you; by never-qualified exaggerations to cry up all that you say or do, till the good man, who understands well enough that it is all done in compliment to him, grows weary of the debt of gratitude which is due to so much candour, and by relaxing a little on his part, and taking down a peg or two in his enthusiasm, sinks at length to that kindly level of moderate esteem,—that '**decent affection** and complacent kindness' towards you, where she herself can join in sympathy with him without much stretch and violence to her sincerity.

Another way (for the ways they have to accomplish so desirable a purpose are infinite) is, with a kind of innocent simplicity, continually to mistake what it was which first made their husband fond of you. If an esteem for something excellent in your moral character was that which riveted the chain which she is to break, upon any imaginary discovery of a want of poignancy in your conversation, she will cry, 'I thought my dear, you described your friend, Mr. —, as a great wit.' If, on the other hand, it was for some supposed charm in your conversation, that he first grew to like you, and was content for this to overlook some trifling irregularities in your moral deportment, upon the first notice of any of these she as readily exclaims, 'This, my dear, is your good Mr. —.' One good lady whom I took the liberty of expostulating with for not showing me quite so much respect as I thought due to her husband's old friend, had the candour to confess to me that she had often heard Mr.—speak of me before marriage, and that she had conceived a great desire to be acquainted with me, but that the sight of me had very much disappointed her expectations; for from her husband's representations of me, she had formed a notion that she was to see a fine, tall, officer-like looking man (I use her very words); the very reverse of which proved to be the truth. This was candid; and I had the civility not to ask her in return, how she came to pitch upon a standard of personal accomplishments for her husband's friends which differed so much from his own; for my friend's dimensions as near as possible approximate to mine; he standing five feet five in his shoes, in which I have the advantage of him by about half an inch; and he no more than myself exhibiting any indications of a martial character in his air or countenance.

These are some of the mortifications which I have encountered in the absurd attempt to visit at their houses. To enumerate them all would be a vain endeavour; I shall therefore just glance at the very common impropriety of which married ladies are guilty,—of treating us as if we were their husbands, and *vice versa*. I mean, when they use us with familiarity, and their husbands with ceremony. **Testacea**, for instance, kept me the other night two or three hours beyond my usual time of supping, while she was fretting because Mr.—did not come home, till the oysters were all spoiled, rather than she would be guilty of the impoliteness of touching one in his absence. This was reversing the point of good manners: for ceremony is an invention to take off the uneasy feeling which we derive from knowing ourselves to be less the object of love and esteem with a fellow creature than some other person is. It endeavours to make up, by superior attentions in little points, for that invidious preference which it is forced to deny in the greater. Had *Testacea* kept the oysters back for me, and withstood her husband's importunities to go to supper, she would have acted according to the strict rules of propriety. I know no ceremony that ladies are bound to observe to their husbands, beyond the point of a modest behaviour and decorum: therefore I must protest against the vicarious gluttony of **Cerasia**, who at her own table sent away a dish of **Morellas**, which I was applying to with great good will, to her husband at the other end of the table, and recommended a plate of less extraordinary gooseberries to my unwedded palate in their stead. Neither can I excuse the wanton affront of —.

But I am weary of stringing up all my married acquaintances by Roman denominations. Let them amend and change their manners, or I promise to record the full-length English of their names, to the terror of all such desperate offenders in future.

<u>Notes</u>

This, the earliest of the *Elia* essays, first appeared in *The Reflector,* No. 4, in 1811 and was reprinted in the *London Magazine* for Sept. 1822. It was included in the *Essays of Elia,* from which the present text is taken. It shows Lamb as a humourist in the fullest sense of the word. Here is a perfect specimen of that peculiar brand of Lamb's wit which is more good-natured than pungent. The essay itself is neither boisterously farcial nor extravagantly ironical, but is full of delightful and exquisite humour, tinged with a touch of gentle pathos.

antisocial resolutions, i.e. resolutions to remain in bachelorhood.

putting the question to her, courting her.

usufruct, right of enjoyment without ownership; a term derived from Roman law.

'*Like as the arrows,*' etc. From Psalm cxxvii, 5,6.

office, prayer.

churching of women, performing a church service for women after recovery from child birth.

per se (Latin), in themselves.

nice, fastidious.

One daisy differs not, etc. A reminiscence of *I Corinthians* xv, 41.

excrescences, outgrowth, in the sense of oddities.

'*decent affection,*' etc. From John Home's (1722—1808) tragedy *Douglas,* Act I, scene i.

Testacea. Lamb humourously forms the name from the Latin for shell-fish.

Cerasia. From cerasus, the Latin word for cherry. Lamb invented these names to express the 'shelly' and 'cherry' ladies whom he connected with the oyster and cherry stories.

Morellas, morello cherries, so called from their dark (It. *morello*) colour.

【作品简介】

这是《伊利亚随笔集》中最早的一篇散文，最初于 1811 年发表在《反光镜》第 4 期，后来于 1822 年 9 月在《伦敦杂志》上重新再版。之后被收录在《伊利亚随笔集》中，本文选自于此。这篇散文充分显示了兰姆是个地地道道的幽默作家，是展现兰姆独特机智的典范，全文充满着善意的幽默而不是辛辣的讽刺。这篇文章本身既不是吵吵嚷嚷的闹剧，也没有过激的讽刺，而是充满了令人愉悦和细腻的幽默，略带一丝温柔的伤感。

【作品解析】

antisocial resolutions：这里即保持单身的决心。

putting the question to her：向她求爱。

usufruct：使用权，没有所有权；这个术语源于罗马法律。

"Like as the arrows," etc.：此句出自《诗篇》。

office：祷告。

churching of women：为生完孩子后的妇女做礼拜。

per se（拉丁语）：他们自己。

nice：这里指很挑剔。

One daisy differs not, etc.：此句让人想起《哥林多前书》第十五章。

excrescences：多余累赘的东西。

"decent affection," etc.：此句出自约翰·霍姆（1722—1808）的悲剧《道格拉斯》，第一幕，第一场。

Testacea：泰斯泰莎，这是兰姆幽默地从拉丁语创造出的人名，拉丁语的原意是贝类。

Cerasia：塞拉西亚，来自拉丁语（Cerasus），意为樱桃。兰姆创造了这些名字，用来表达"贝壳"和"樱桃"女士，是他在牡蛎和樱桃故事中的人物。

Morellas：黑樱桃，这个名字由樱桃的颜色引申而来。

【参考译文】

单身汉对已婚人士行为的抱怨

作为单身男人，我用了大量的时间来记录已婚人士的各种弱点借以宽慰自己，因为他们总是在训斥我，说我保持单身状态，从而失去了已婚人士才能享有的高级快乐。

我说不上丈夫和妻子之间的争吵，曾经给我留下过什么样的深刻印象，也不是说这就坚定了我保持单身的决心。对于单身，我是在很久以前经过更实质性的考虑后才做出决定的。在我拜访已婚人士的家庭时，让我最不愉快的并非是他们夫妻之间的争吵，而恰恰相反，是他们太相爱了。

也不是说他们彼此之间太相爱了，这并不能说明我的意思。再说了，为什么会冒犯到我呢？那是因为他们将自己与外界分离开来，以便有足够的时间去享受他们彼此之间的世界。这就恰恰意味着：他们只关心彼此，而对其他外界的事物，则漠不关心。

然而我抱怨的是，在我们单身汉的面前，他们对这种偏好毫不掩饰，一点也不害羞。如果与他们为伴，你就会感觉到，他们要么在暗示你，要么直接告诉你，让你时时刻刻感觉到，你并非是他们所钟爱的人。有些事情如果只是暗示或认为是理所当然的，那当然算不上是冒犯；然而只要一经表达，就成了诸多有意的冒犯。如果一个男子向一位他认识的相貌平平或穿着朴素的年轻女子搭讪，并直言不讳地告诉她，她长得不够漂亮也不算富有，所以他不能娶她，那么这个男子就理所应当因为他的粗鲁行为而被踢上一脚。但事实上，他既有机会与她见面，也有机会向她求婚，他也从未想过这样做是件合适的事情，每位年轻女子都很清楚这种暗示，就好像是用语言表达出来一样清晰。即便是这样，没有一个有理智的年轻女子会以此作为争吵的理由。如此说来，正如一对已婚夫妇也没有权利可以用言语甚至比言语更清楚的眼神来告诉我，我不是一个幸福的男人——不是女子的意中人。够了，我知道我不是，不需要别人这样不断地提醒。

在别人面前炫耀自己的学识渊博或者是财大气粗，已经够令人反感了；然而这些，尚且还能忍受。用知识渊博来羞辱我，可能会意外地激励我；而富人的豪宅和名画，他的庭院和花园，至少我还可以暂时地享用一番。而已婚者所表现出来的婚姻幸福，使我无法忍受；它自始至终是一种完全无法补偿的、绝对的冒犯。

婚姻本身就是一种垄断，这是对它最好的诠释，并且是相当令人讨厌的那种。特权拥有者的狡诈之处在于他们尽可能隐匿他们的优越，这样一来，那些没有他们那样幸运的邻居看不到他们的享乐，也就不那么想质疑他们的权利了。然而，这些已婚的垄断者，却把他们特权中最令人讨厌的那部分抛到了我们单身汉的面前。

对我来说，新婚夫妇脸上洋溢着那种沾沾自喜和自我满足的得意神情，是最令人讨厌的，尤其是在女士的脸上。她的这种表情似乎在告诉你，今生她已名花有主了，你在她那里一点希望也没有了。这是真的，我确实没有，也不希望有。正如我之前所说的，这应该被认为是理所当然的真实情况，无须表达出来。

那些已婚人士基于我们未婚者对婚姻的无知，故意在我们面前装腔作势，如果他们失去理性的话，就会越发表现得更加无礼。我们承认已婚人士要比我们这些未能拥有过幸福伴侣的人更了解属于他们行业的奥秘。然而，他们的傲慢和盛气凌人并不仅限于这些。比如，如果一个单身汉在他们面前发表自己的观点，即便是最无关紧要的问题，作为一个单身汉就会被当作一个不够资格的人，立刻遭受到他们的冷漠和压制。不仅仅这些，我所认识的一位年轻的已婚女士，最好笑的是，两周前她还是单身，我不幸与她在关于伦敦市场上牡蛎最佳的养殖方式上意见有所不一。她对我嗤之以鼻，竟敢轻蔑地问我，像我这样一个老光棍，怎么可能知道这些事情，只不过是装腔作势罢了。

至此，我所谈论的这些比起已婚夫妇在有了孩子之后所表现出来的那种神态简直算不了什么。所有的已婚夫妇通常都会有孩子。我时常在想，有孩子并非是件稀奇的事——我们在每一条大街小巷，常常都会看到成群结队的孩子，通常越是贫穷人家孩子就越多。每个婚姻至少有一个孩子，只有很少的婚姻得不到上帝的恩典，没有孩子。但是这些孩子常常不走正道，辜负了他们父母的美好希望，最终贫困潦倒，受人羞辱，有的甚至犯罪，走向绞架——我这一辈子也不会明白拥有这样的孩子有什么好值得骄傲的呢？实际上，如果这些孩子是年幼的凤凰，每年只生一个，那也许还情有可原。可是，像这样平庸的孩子太多，太普遍了。

我还没有提及在某种场合下，已婚女士对丈夫的傲慢举止，这只能让他们自己去面对。然而，我所不明白的是，我们不是她们天生的臣民，她们却期望我们单身汉带上作料、没药和贡香向她们进贡，并表示崇拜和敬仰。

"年幼的孩子就像巨人手中的箭一样。"这是为生完孩子的妇女做礼拜时所说的祈祷词。我这么说："如果他的箭袋装满了箭，他就是一个幸福的人。"让孩子们成为箭，但不要让这些箭伤及我们，不要让巨人的箭射向我们这些手无寸铁的单身汉。然而，我却发现这些箭是双向的；它们有两个箭头，其中一个箭头总是会射中你的。比如，当你在拜访一个有孩子的家庭时，碰巧你正在想着其他的事情，而忽视了对天真烂漫孩子的爱，那么，他们的家长就会认为你是一个难以捉摸、脾气不好，甚至讨厌孩子的人。另一方面，如果你发现孩子们比平时更加吸引人，被他们可爱的举止所吸引，并且你开始认真地和他们的孩子一起嬉戏玩耍，那么，这个家庭的女主人就一定会找到一些借口把孩子们赶出房间：比如孩子们太吵、太闹腾了，或者会说某某先生不喜欢孩子。总之，这些箭中的一头或者另一头一定会射中你的。

　　我可以原谅他们的这种嫉妒，如果和他们调皮捣蛋的孩子玩耍，在那种场合会给他们带来任何痛苦，我可以不和他们的孩子玩耍。可是我认为没有理由被要求去爱他们家中所有的孩子，那是荒谬的——去爱整个家庭中的八个、九个，甚至十个孩子而不加以区别对待——去爱所有可爱漂亮的孩子，就是因为他们太迷人了——我认为，这是不合乎常理的爱。

　　我知道，有一句谚语叫作"爱我，即爱我的狗"，特别是当这条狗踩了你一脚，爬到你的身上捉弄你，或者突然向你猛扑过来的时候，这句谚语并非总是那么切实可行。但是，一条狗或者任何一件较小的东西——任何没有生命的东西，如一件纪念品、一块手表、一枚戒指、一棵树，或者和朋友最后一次分手的地方，我都可以想尽办法去爱；因为我爱他，所有能让我想起他的事与物，我都会去爱。至于东西本身并无所谓，只要去接受所赋予它的任何色彩和幻想，这就足够了，我做到了。然而，孩子们却有他们自己的性格和个性，有着真实的自我存在。孩子们要么亲切友好，要么很难以相处；这就决定了我要么去爱他们，要么去恨他们。因为，我认为这与他们的品行是相关的。孩子们的天性是件严肃认真的事，不可能把他们作为某些人的附属品由此来决定是爱还是恨。他们就像其他男人和女人一样，和我是平等的。哦！你也许会说，这确实是一个引人注目的年龄——婴幼儿时期的娇嫩，正是吸引我们的魅力所在，这也正是我会对他们更加友好的原因。我知道，一个可爱的孩子是自然界中最甜美的生物，甚至连哺育他们的母亲也不例外；越是漂亮的东西就越具有吸引力，就越希望它是那种出类拔萃的漂亮。一朵雏菊与另一朵雏菊不尽相同，没有什么差别；然而一朵紫罗兰无论是在外观还是气味上，应该都是最娇俏的。因此，对于我熟悉的妇女和儿童，我总是过于拘谨。

　　这倒不是最糟糕的。在他们抱怨你对他们不闻不问之前，至少他们承认自己和你还是很熟悉的。这就意味着你们之前有过来往，有过某种交流。但是，如果她的丈夫在结婚之前，曾经与你生活在一起，是友好相处的朋友；如果你不站在他妻子那一边；如果你不是紧紧跟随着他的妻子溜进这个家，而是作为他求婚之前有着亲密关系的老朋友——那么，你就等着瞧吧！你们的友谊岌岌可危。不到一年，你就会发现你的老朋友对你逐渐变得冷淡，改变了对你的态度，最后甚至会寻找机会与你绝交。我很少有熟悉的、可以信赖的已婚朋友是在他结婚之前就与他建立了友谊。已婚妻子可以在一定的范围内容忍一些事情；但是，一个好男人竟然不征求她们的意见就加入某个庄严的友谊同盟，即便这种友谊同盟是在他们还没有相遇、成为夫妻之前就已经加入了——这对于妻子们来说，也是无法容忍的。任何一段长期的友谊，任何一段以往的亲密关系，都必须送进她们的办公室，在她们友谊的"货币上"加盖新的印记，就像新执政的君主，将前王朝统治时期铸造好的旧钱币回收，在让它到市面上流通之前，必须要用她们权威的印记重新标记和铸造。你可以想象，像我这样一块生了锈的金属片，在这些"新币值"的工厂里，通常会遭遇到什么样的命运。

她们会用无数种方式侮辱你，使你慢慢失去她们的丈夫对你的信任。她们对你所说的每一句话会感到惊讶和好笑，会嘲笑你，仿佛你是一个只会说好话的稀奇古怪的家伙，这是其中的一种方法——为了某种目的，她们带着一种特殊的目光凝视着你——直到最后，她们那个曾经对你言听计从的丈夫，之前为了顾全大局，只要你的言谈举止不是太粗俗，他们会忽略你身上的一些异常行为；但是，现在他们也开始怀疑起你是否完全是个性情乖张者——也许在他单身的日子里可以混得很熟，但不太适合将你介绍给女士们吧。这也许就是所谓的"注视法"，这也是她们经常用来对付我的方法。

还有一种就是夸张的方式，或者说是富有讽刺意味的方法。也就是说，当她们发现你和她们丈夫的关系比较特殊，难以动摇她们丈夫长期以来与你建立起来的尊重的根基，于是她们对你所说的话或所做的事会表现出过度的夸张和赞扬，直到心地善良的丈夫认为他的太太所做的一切都是为了恭维自己，并渐渐地厌烦了由于坦诚而欠下的感激之情。他稍微放松了一下，这就大大降低了对你的热情和尊重的程度；最终，保持了一种既沉默又温和的态度——她们的丈夫即以"体面的情感和自以为荣的博爱"来对待你，而她本人也有同感，这样可以和她的丈夫一起维持这种关系，而无须付出太多的诚意，也不会受到太多的指责。

而另一种方法（她们想要达到目的，方法是无穷无尽的），就是以一种天真单纯的态度，不断地想方设法让她们的丈夫意识到，当初喜欢你是错误的。如果她们的丈夫尊重你的优良美德，这个优良美德就是她们想要挣脱的枷锁，那她就会在你的谈话中吹毛求疵。在和你的交谈中，一旦她发现了臆想中她想捕捉的任何尖酸犀利的语言，就会尖叫起来："亲爱的，我以为你的朋友——某某先生，像你所描述的那样是个很机智的人。"反过来说，如果正是因为你的谈话中有一些魅力，她们的丈夫才会渐渐地喜欢上你，并不在乎你谈话中略带一些微不足道的不得体的行为举止，然而一旦她们注意到这种举止，就会很容易随口嚷起来："亲爱的，这就是你说的那位好先生吗？"我曾经冒昧地规劝过一位好太太，因为她没有像我想象的那样，对我这样的她丈夫的老朋友表现出应有的尊重。她坦率地向我承认，结婚前，她经常听到某某先生说起我，并且她怀着一种强烈的愿望想和我认识。然而，一见到我就大失所望。原来，从她丈夫对我的描述中，使她早已形成了一种观念，以为她将会见到的是一个英俊、身材高大、像军官一样的男人（我用她的话说）；然而，事实却大相径庭。这番话是坦诚的，出于礼貌我不便反问她，她是以什么样的标准来衡量她丈夫的朋友以及个人的天赋的？为什么这一标准与衡量她丈夫的标准相差甚远？我朋友的身材和我差不多，如果穿着鞋站立着他也只有五英尺五英寸高，然而我还比他高出半英寸，而他的神态和面容显露出来的军人气质丝毫也不比我强多少。

　　这些都是我在荒谬地试图去拜访已婚家庭时遭遇到的一些屈辱。现在我把它们列举出来都是徒劳的，没有任何意义。因此，我只是想提一提已婚女士常犯的一种不当行为——她们把我们这些客人当作丈夫来对待，反之亦然，对待她们的丈夫倒像个客人。我的意思是，她们在我们面前肆无忌惮，而在丈夫面前却举止文雅。比如，那天晚上，泰斯泰莎让我比平时吃饭的时间多等了两到三个小时，因为她的丈夫没有回来。直到牡蛎都变质了，她却要讲究礼节，等到她丈夫回来才能开饭。其实，这已颠倒了礼节的意义，礼节被发明出来是用来弥补、消除、减缓我们受到别人冷落时那种令人不安的情绪；这种不安的情绪源于我们了解自己与其他人相比，不太容易成为受人爱戴和尊敬的对象。只有试图努力通过对一些微小细节的高度关注，才会弥补在更大的事情上处于被动的那种令人讨厌的偏爱。如果泰斯泰莎坚持把牡蛎留给了我，而不去理睬她的丈夫硬要回家吃晚餐的要求，她就是严格按照礼仪行事了。除了谦虚恭敬的举止和礼仪之外，我真不知道女士们还有什么样的礼仪必须要对她们的丈夫遵守；因此，我绝不能容忍赛拉西亚女士替人做主的行为。她在自己的餐桌上，把一盘我正想要品尝的黑樱桃递给了坐在餐桌另一端的丈夫，而向我推荐了一盘我并没有什么胃口，也没有什么特色的醋栗取而代之。无论怎样，我都不能原谅这种肆意的冒犯……

　　我已厌倦了按照罗马字号对我认识的已婚人士分群别类。他们应当改善自己的言行举止；否则，我将会把他们的英文全名记录下来，以警示日后所有这些不择手段的冒犯者。

Old China

I have an almost feminine partiality for old china. When I go to see any great house, I inquire for the china-closet, and next for the picture gallery. I cannot defend the order of preference, but by saying, that we have all some taste or other, of too ancient a date to admit of our remembering distinctly that it was an acquired one. I can call to mind **the first play**, and the first exhibition, that I was taken to; but I am not conscious of a time when china jars and saucers were introduced into my imagination.

I had no repugnance then—why should I now have?—to those little, lawless, azure-tinctured grotesques, that under the notion of men and women, float about, uncircumscirbed by any element, in that world before perspective—a china tea-cup.

I like to see my old friends—whom distance cannot diminish—figuring up in the air (so they appear to our optics), yet on **terra firma** still—for so we must in courtesy interpret that speck of deeper blue,—which the decorous artist, to prevent absurdity, had made to spring up beneath their sandals.

I love the men with women's faces, and the women, if possible, with still more womanish expressions.

Here is a young and courtly Mandarin, handing tea to a lady from a salver—two miles off. See how distance seems to set off respect! And here the same lady, or another—for likeness is identity on tea-cups—is stepping into a little fairy boat, moored on the hither side of this calm garden river, with a dainty mincing foot, which in a right **angle of incidence** (as angles go in our world) must infallibly land her in the midst of a flowery mead—a furlong off on the other side of the same strange stream!

Farther on—if far or near can be predicated of their world—see horses, trees, pagodas, dancing **the hays**.

Here—a cow and rabbit **couchant**, and co-extensive—so objects show, seen through the lucid atmosphere of fine **Cathay**.

I was pointing out to my cousin last evening, over our **Hyson** (which we are old fashioned enough to drink unmixed still of an afternoon), some of these *speciosa miracula* upon a set of extraordinary old blue china (a recent purchase) which we were now for the first time using; and could not help remarking, how favourable circumstances had been to us of late years, that we could afford to please the eye sometimes with trifles of this sort—when a passing sentiment seemed to overshade the brows of my companion. I am quick at detecting these summer clouds in Bridget.

'I wish the good old times would come again,' she said, 'when we were not quite so rich. I do not mean, that I want to be poor; but there was a middle state' —so she was pleased to ramble on,— 'in which I am sure we were a great deal happier. A purchase is but a purchase, now that you have money enough and to spare. Formerly it used to be a triumph. When we coveted a cheap luxury (and, Oh!

how much ado I had to get you to consent in those times!)—we were used to have a debate two or three days before, and to weigh the *for* and *against*, and think what we might spare it out of, and what saving we could hit upon, that should be an equivalent. A thing was worth buying then, when we felt the money that we paid for it.

'Do you remember the brown suit, which you made to hang upon you, till all your friends cried shame upon you, it grew so threadbare—and all because of that **folio Beaumont and Fletcher**, which you dragged home late at night from Barker's in **Covent Garden**? Do you remember how we eyed it for weeks before we could make up our minds to the purchase, and had not come to a determination till it was near ten o'clock of the Saturday night, when you set off from **Islington**, fearing you should be too late—and when the old bookseller with some grumbling opened his shop, and by the twinkling taper (for he was setting bedwards) lighted out the relic from his dusty treasures—and when you lugged it home, wishing it were twice as cumbersome—and when you presented it to me—and when we were exploring the perfectness of it (*collating* you called it)—and while I was repairing some of the loose leaves with paste, which your impatience would not suffer to be left till daybreak—was there no pleasure in being a poor man? or can those neat black clothes which you wear now, and are so careful to keep brushed, since we have become rich and finical, give you half the honest vanity, with which you flaunted it about in that over-worn suit—your old **corbeau**—for four or five weeks longer than you should have done, to pacify your conscience for the mighty sum of fifteen—or sixteen shillings was it?—a great affair we thought it then—which you had lavished on the old folio. Now you can afford to buy any book that pleases you, but I do not see that you ever bring me home any nice old purchases now.

'When you came home with twenty apologies for laying out a less number of shillings upon that print after **Lionardo**, which we christened the "Lady Blanch;" when you looked at the purchase, and thought of the money—and thought of the money, and looked again at the picture—was there no pleasure in being a poor man? Now, you have nothing to do but to walk into **Colnaghi's**, and buy a wilderness of Lionardos. Yet do you?

'Then, do you remember our pleasant walks to **Enfield**, and **Potter's Bar**, and **Waltham**, when we had a holyday—holydays, and all other fun, are gone, now we are rich—and the little hand-basket in which I used to deposit our day's fare of savoury cold lamb and salad—and how you would pry about at noontide for some decent house, where we might go in, and produce our store—only paying for the ale that you must call for—and speculate upon the looks of the landlady, and whether she was likely to allow us a tablecloth—and wish for such another honest hostess, as Izaak Walton had described many a one on the pleasant banks of the Lea, when he went a-fishing—and sometimes they would prove obliging enough, and sometimes they would look grudgingly upon us—but we had cheerful looks still for one another, and would eat our plain food savourily, scarcely grudging **Piscator** his **Trout Hall**? Now,—when we go out a day's pleasuring, which is seldom moreover, we *ride* part of the way—and go into a fine inn, and order the best of dinners, never debating the expense—which, after all, never has half the relish of those chance country snaps, when we were at the mercy of uncertain usage, and a precarious welcome.

'You are too proud to see a play anywhere now but in the pit. Do you remember where it was we used to sit, when we saw the **Battle of Hexham**, and the **Surrender of Calais**, and Bannister and Mrs. Bland in the **Children in the Wood**—when we squeezed out our shillings apiece to sit three or four times in a season in the one-shilling gallery— where you felt all the time that you ought not to have brought me— and more strongly I felt obligation to you for having brought me— and the pleasure was the better for a little shame—and when the curtain drew up, what cared we for our place in the house, or what mattered it where we were sitting, when our thoughts were with **Rosalind** in Arden, or with **Viola** at the Court of Illyria? You used to say, that the Gallery was the best place of all for enjoying a play socially—that the relish of such exhibitions must be in proportion to the infrequency of going—that the company we met there, not being in general readers of plays, were obliged to attend the more, and did attend, to what was going on, on the stage—because a word lost would have been a chasm, which it was impossible for them to fill up. With such reflections we consoled our pride then—and I appeal to you, whether, as a woman, I met generally with less attention and accommodation, than I have done since in more expensive situations in the house? The getting in indeed, and the crowding up those inconvenient staircases, was bad enough,—but there was still a law of civility to woman recognised to quite as great an extent as we ever found in the other passages—and how a little difficulty overcome heightened the snug seat, and the play, afterwards! Now we can only pay our money and walk in. You cannot see, you say, in the galleries now. I am sure we saw, and heard too, well enough then—but sight, and all, I think is gone with our poverty.

'There was pleasure in eating strawberries, before they became quite common—in the first dish of peas, while they were yet dear— to have them for a nice supper, a treat. What treat can we have now? If we were to treat ourselves now—that is, to have dainties a little above our means, it would be selfish and wicked. It is very little more that we allow ourselves beyond what the actual poor can get at, that makes what I call a treat—when two people living together, as we have done, now and then indulge themselves in a cheap luxury, which both like; while each apologises, and is willing to take both halves of the blame to his single share. I see no harm in people making much of themselves in that sense of the word. It may give them a hint how to make much of others. But now—what I mean by the word—we never do make much of ourselves. None but the poor can do it. I do not mean the veriest poor of all, but persons as we were, just above poverty.

'l know what you were going to say, that it is mighty pleasant at the end of the year to make all meet,—and much ado we used to have every Thirty-first Night of December to account for our exceedings—many a long face did you make over your puzzled accounts, and in contriving to make it out how we had spent so much— or that we had not spent so much—or that is was impossible we should spend so much next year—and still we found our slender capital decreasing—but then, betwixt ways, and projects, and compromises of one sort or another, and talk of curtailing this charge, and doing without that for the future—and the hope that youth brings, and laughing spirits (in which you were never poor till now) we pocketed up our loss, and in conclusion, with "lusty brimmers" (as you used to quote it out of **hearty cheerful Mr. Cotton**, as you called him), we used to welcome in the "**coming guest.**" Now we have no reckoning at all at the end of the old year—no flattering promises about the new year doing better for us.'

Bridget is so sparing of her speech on most occasions, that when she gets into a rhetorical vein, I am careful how I interrupt it. I could not help, however, smiling at the phantom of wealth which her dear imagination had conjured up out of a clear income of poor—hundred pounds a year. 'It is true we were happier when we were poor, but we were also younger, my cousin. I am afraid we must put up with the excess, for if we were to shake the **superflux** into the sea, we should not much mend ourselves. That we had much to struggle with, as we grew up together, we have reason to be most thankful. It strengthened, and knit our compact closer. We could never have been what we have been to each other, if we had always had the sufficiency which you now complain of. The resisting power—those natural dilations of the youthful spirit, which circumstances cannot straiten—with us are long since passed away. Competence to age is supplementary youth, a sorry supplement indeed, but I fear the best that is to be had. We must ride, where we formerly walked: live better, and lie softer—and shall be wise to do so—than we had means to do in those good old days you speak of. Yet could those days return—could you and I once more walk our thirty miles a day—could Bannister, and Mrs. Bland again be young, and you and I be young to see them—could the good old one-shilling gallery days return—they are dreams, my cousin, now—but could you and I at this moment, instead of this quiet argument, by our well-carpeted fireside, sitting on this luxurious sofa—be once more struggling up those inconvenient staircases, pushed about, and squeezed, and elbowed by the poorest rabble of poor gallery scramblers—could I once more hear those anxious shrieks of yours—and the delicious *Thank God, we are safe*, which always followed when the topmost stair, conquered, let in the first light of the whole cheerful theatre down beneath us—I know not the fathom line that ever touched a descent so deep as I would be willing to bury more wealth in than **Croesus** had, or the **great Jew R**—is supposed to have, to purchase it. And now do just look at that merry little Chinese waiter holding an umbrella, big enough for a **bed-tester**, over the head of that pretty insipid **half Madonna-ish chit of a lady** in that very blue summer house.'

Notes

This essay, published in the *London Magazine* for March, 1823 and collected in the *Last Essays of Elia*, is an excellent illustration of Lamb's method of merging fact, fancy, and philosophy of life. It shows the author's life-long devotion to his sister Mary, with whom he lived together for the thirty-eight years after the unfortunate death of their parents. Mary suffered at intervals from violent attacks of insanity and it was to keep her company that Lamb remained a bachelor throughout life. Though poor and lonely, they had moments of brightness in their strange household, when the two would sit cozily by the hearth fire to chat pleasantly on the beauties of old china tea-cups and the pleasures of modest poverty, as if they were unwilling to be rich. Together they read and wrote, visited playhouses, undertook excursions and entertained companies, for when sane, Mary was a good hostess. Their joint work, *The Tales from Shakespeare*, is a lasting memorial to the beautiful relationship that existed between them.

the first play that Lamb was taken to was *Artaxerxes*, an opera with music by Thomas Augustine Arne (1710—1778), performed posthumously at Drury Lane 1 Dec. 1780, when Lamb was in his sixth year.

terra firma (Latin), solid earth.

angle of incidence, the angle which any line, as of a ray of light, falling on a surface, makes with a perpendicular to the surface at the point of incidence. (Webster)

the hays, an old English-country dance.

couchant, and co-extensive, reclining and of the same size.

Cathay, the old name for China, derived from *Khitai* 契丹 .

Hyson, a species of green tea from China. Hyson was regarded as a choice tea in England from the early eighteenth century. The Chinese characters from which it is formed are 熙春 .

speciosa miracula (Latin), brilliant wonders. Horace uses this phrase in *Ars Poetica*, line 144, to describe the stories of the *Iliad*.

folio Beaumont and Fletcher. The first folio of the plays of Francis Beaumont (1584?—1616) and John Fletcher (1579—1625) was published in 1647.

Covent Garden, a section of London known for its theaters and market places.

Islington, a borough in London; in 1799—1800 the Lambs lived at 36, Chapel Street, Pentonville.

corbeau, a phrase for a black suit, from French *corbeau* = a raven.

Lionardo, Leonardo da Vinci (1452—1519), an Italian painter. The picture referred to is 'Modesty and Vanity' and is the subject of a poem by Mary Lamb.

Colnaghi's, the famous print shop in Pall Mall East, founded by Paul Colnaghi (1751—1833), a native of Milan.

Enfield, Potter's Bar, Waltham, towns not far from London, in Middlesex and Hertford counties.

Piscator...Trout Hall. Piscator is the fisherman in Izaak Walton's *The Complete Angler* (1653); his favourite inn was Trout Hall, which is supposed to have been on the river Lea, near Edmonton.

Battle of Hexham, Surrender of Calais, Children in the Wood. The first two are comedies by George Colman the Younger (1762—1836); the third is a musical play by Thomas Morton (1764—1838). John Bannister was a noted comedian and Maria Theresa Bland a popular actress—both of them friends of the Lambs.

Rosalind ... Viola, the heroines of Shakespeare's *As You Like It* and *Twelfth Night* respectively.

hearty cheerful Mr. Cotton. Charles Cotton (1630—1687) was a miscellaneous writer who added a second part to Walton's *The Complete Angler*. His poem 'The New Year' contains these lines:

'Then let us welcome the New Guest

With lusty brimmers of the best.'

'*coming guest*', a phrase taken from Pope's translation of Homer's *Odyssey*, xv, 34, which reads:

'Welcome the coming, speed the parting guest.'

superflux, overflow, surplus.

Croesus, an ancient king of Lydia, reigned 560—546 B.C., famous for his fabulous wealth.

Great Jew R—, Nathan Meyer, Baron de Rothschild (1777—1836), a famous London banker.

bed-tester, a canopy over a four-poster bed.

half Madonna-ish chit of a lady, small slender lady who looks somewhat like a Madonna.

【作品简介】

这篇散文于 1823 年 3 月发表在《伦敦杂志》上，后来被收录在《伊利亚随笔续集》中，是兰姆把事实、幻想和人生的哲学方法融合为一体的典范。这篇散文展示了作者对姐姐玛丽一生的忠诚和挚爱，自从他们的父母不幸去世之后，兰姆和他的姐姐在一起生活了 38 年。每隔一段时间，玛丽就会因受到强烈的刺激而精神失常，为了陪伴在她的身边，兰姆终生保持单身。虽然他们贫穷、寂寞，然而在他们奇特的家庭里，也有光明的时刻。那时候，他俩会舒适地坐在壁炉旁，愉快地谈论着茶杯这种古瓷器的精美和贫穷时的乐趣，好像他们不愿意变得富有似的。他们一起阅读，一起写作，一起看戏，一起看展，一起进行短途旅行，一起相互逗乐，玛丽在神志清醒时，是一位优秀的女主人。他们共同的作品《莎士比亚戏剧故事集》，就是他们之间美好关系的永恒纪念。

【作品解析】

the first play：兰姆看的第一出戏是《阿尔塔薛西斯》，这是托马斯·奥古斯丁·阿恩（1710—1778）作曲的歌剧，在他去世后，于 1780 年 12 月 1 日才在德鲁里街剧院公演，当时兰姆才六岁。

terra firma（拉丁语）：坚实的大地。

angle of incidence：入射光线与入射表面法线的夹角。（英文释义参见《韦氏大词典》。)

the hays：一种古老的英格兰乡村舞蹈。

couchant，and co-extensive：俯卧着，并共处在同样大小的地方。

Cathay：古代中国，一般用于古英语的诗歌中；来源于 Khitai（契丹）音译。

Hyson：熙春，即中国出产的一种绿茶，从 18 世纪初期起，熙春就被英国人认为是一种精选的茶叶。

speciosa miracula（拉丁语）：奇观。贺拉斯在《诗艺》第 144 行中，使用了这个短语来赞美《伊利亚特》故事。

folio Beaumont and Fletcher：弗朗西斯·博蒙特（约 1584—1616）和约翰·弗莱彻（1579—1625）戏剧集最原始的对开本，出版于 1647 年。

Covent Garden：考文特花园，伦敦一个以剧院和小市场出名的地区。

Islington：伊斯灵顿，伦敦的一个地区；1799—1800 年，兰姆就住在那里的本顿维尔教会街 36 号。

corbeau：黑色西装，这个词来自法语 corbeau（乌鸦）。

Lionardo：莱昂纳多·达·芬奇（1452—1519），意大利画家。文中所说的这幅画被命名为《谦虚与虚荣》，同样这也是玛丽·兰姆一首诗歌的主题。

Colnaghi's：蓓尔美尔东街一个著名的画廊，由米兰人保罗·科尔纳吉（1751—1833）创建。

Enfield，Potter's Bar，Waltham：恩菲尔德、波特斯巴、沃尔瑟姆，这些城镇离伦敦不远，在米德尔塞克斯郡和赫特福德郡。

Piscator...Trout Hall：皮斯卡托是艾萨克·沃尔顿《钓客清话》（1653）中的渔夫，他最喜欢的旅馆是鳟鱼旅馆，据说它是在埃德蒙顿附近的利河河畔。

Battle of Hexham，*Surrender of Calais*，*Children in the Wood*：《赫克瑟姆战役》《加莱的投降》是由小乔治·科尔曼（1762—1836）创作的喜剧；《森林里的孩子》是托马斯·莫顿（1764—1838）创作的音乐剧。约翰·班尼斯特是一名著名的喜剧演员，玛丽亚·特雷莎·布兰德是一位受人们喜爱的女演员——他们两位都是兰姆的朋友。

Rosalind ... Viola：罗莎琳德和薇奥拉是莎士比亚《皆大欢喜》和《第十二夜》中的女主人公。

hearty cheerful Mr. Cotton：查尔斯·科顿（1630—1687）是一位趣闻杂谈作家，他曾为沃尔顿的《钓客清话》增写了第二部分。他的诗歌《新年》中有如下几行："那么，让我们欢迎新客人／带着最好的烈酒。"（寓意：满怀着美好的希望。）

"coming guest"：这个短语出自蒲柏对荷马《奥德赛》的翻译；参见第 15 章，第 34 页，原文如下："Welcome the coming, speed the parting guest.（欢迎来宾，欢送匆匆临别的客人。）"

superflux：过剩、溢出、盈余。

Croesus：克罗伊斯，小亚细亚古国吕底亚末代国王，执政于约公元前 560—前 546 年，以其惊人的财富而闻名。

Great Jew R—：内森·梅耶·罗斯柴尔德男爵（1777—1836），著名的伦敦银行家。

bed-tester：一个带有顶篷的四帷柱大床。

half Madonna-ish chit of a lady：身材较小的女士，看上去有点像圣母玛利亚。

【参考译文】

古　瓷

对于古瓷，我近乎有一种女性化的偏爱。每当我去参观大宅屋时，我总是要先去看看瓷器壁橱，然后再去看看画廊。我无法对这种偏爱的先后顺序做出任何解释，但我要说的是，我们每个人都有不同的喜好，由于年代久远，我已无法清楚地记得这样一个喜好是何时形成的。我能回忆起看过的第一出戏和第一次参观过的展览，但我却无法回忆起茶具这种瓷器是何时进入我的脑海的。

当时，我一点也没有觉得反感或有什么不协调——那么现在，我会觉得它不协调了吗？——瓷器茶杯上面呈现的那些小巧玲珑的、湛蓝色的、样子怪异的男人和女人的图案，雕刻得不合章法，不讲透视，好像不受任何因素的限制。

我喜看到我的这些老朋友——这中间的距离没有使它们缩小——似乎是悬在空中（至少他们在我们的视觉中呈现的是这样），然而却又好像是踏踏实实地站在坚实的大地上。这样，我们就可以礼貌地去诠释那个深湛蓝色的斑点——这也许是一位高雅的艺术家，为了避免图案过分荒诞，特意在他们的凉鞋下添加了一笔。

我喜欢那些有女人面相的男人；如果可能的话，我更希望这里的女人可以具有更多的女人表情。

茶杯上，一位彬彬有礼、温文尔雅的中国衙门官吏，端着一个金属托盘给一位女士敬茶——相距大约两英里。可见，距离似乎意味着尊重！这里同样是这位女士，也许是另一位女士——因为从茶杯上看，她们的形象几乎一模一样——这位女士正踏上停泊在静谧花园小河这边的一艘小渡船，她抬起了那只精致纤嫩而灵巧的小脚，按照她抬脚的角度（就像我们现实世界中的角度一样），她一定会在大约一弗隆（约 201 米）远的地方，在同一条奇特小溪的对岸，在绚丽多彩鲜花盛开的草坪上，稳稳地上岸。

再往远些，如果以他们世界的视觉远近去看，你就会看到马、树、宝塔，好像在草地上跳着乡村舞蹈。

这上面，有一头母牛和蹲着的一只兔子，它们同处一处——这些画面呈现了透过晴朗的天空看到的美好中国的景象。

昨天傍晚，在品尝熙春茶的时候（我们喝下午茶还保留着原有的习惯，什么都不加），我向表姐指了指我们第一次使用的一套令人惊叹的古老的青花瓷（最近刚买来的）上面呈现的一些特有的奇观。我忍不住要告诉她，近几年来，我们的状况不错，可以负担得起购买这种赏心悦目的小坑意儿。此时，表姐的眉宇之间闪现出了一丝伤感，我很快就在布里奇特的眼里探测到了一片夏天的乌云。

"我希望过去美好的时光能够重新再现，"她说，"那时，我们并不这么富有。当然，我不是说我想变穷。应当有一个中间的状态，"她兴致勃勃地继续往下说了，"我确信在那种状态下，我们会更加快乐。现在你有足够的钱去花，东西买了就是买了。以前，每次购买东西都是一件大喜事。当我们觊觎廉价的奢侈品时（哎，要是在以前，我得费多大的劲才能让你同意），在购买前两三天，我们通常会进行辩论，权衡利弊得出赞成或反对的意见，想想我们从哪里可以节省下来，又能从中省多少钱，才能刚好抵得上那个需要花费的数额。当我们觉得物有所值时，我们才会去购买这件东西。

"你还记得你做的那套棕色的西装吗？你一直穿在身上，你所有的朋友都在为你穿着这套如此破旧不堪的西装感到羞愧，这一切不都是因为你在深夜时分，从考文特花园的巴克书店里拖回那套沉重的作品——博蒙特和弗莱彻的那套对开本戏剧集吗？你还记得，我们盯了好几个星期，都还没有做出决定是否要去购买这套作品集。直到周六晚上十点钟左右，你才下定决心，你从伊斯灵顿起程出发，担心为时已晚，害怕错过了购买的时机——那个老书商满腹牢骚，唠唠叨叨地打开店铺门（因为他正在整理床铺准备睡觉），借着闪烁的烛光，从他那尘封已久的宝藏中，找出了这件遗留的宝物——当你用尽全力把它拖回家时，似乎希望它能再有两倍的重量。后来，你把它展示给我看时，我们一起探讨它的完美之处，你把这个过程称为校勘。我用糨糊修复一些松散的书页，这样你就不会在天亮之前一直忍受烦躁不安的情绪的煎熬了——你能说，当穷人就真的没有乐趣了吗？或者说，自从我们变得富有，你现在穿着这身整洁的黑色西装，天天小心翼翼地刷来刷去，它现在带给你的能有曾经穿上那件破旧棕色西服到处炫耀时，那种纯朴自豪感的一半吗？——那套旧西服你多穿了四五个星期，为了安抚你的良心不安，因为当时你购买那套旧作品花费了不少钱，花了十五或十六个先令，是吗？这对我们来说是一笔巨款。现在，你可以买得起任何你喜欢的书籍，但是，我却看不出你现在带回家的旧书要比你以前买的更精致更有价值。

"有一次，当你回到家的时候，不停地道歉，因为你花费了几个先令购买了一幅莱昂纳多画作的复制品，这幅画作我们称之为《布兰奇夫人》。你一会儿看看购买的复制品，一会儿又想想花费的钱；一会儿想想钱，一会儿又看看购买的复制品；你能说当穷人就真的没有乐趣了吗？而现在呢，你成天有事没事都去逛科尔纳吉画廊，买上一大堆莱昂纳多（的画）。是这样吗？

"还有，你还记得我们步行去恩菲尔德、波特斯巴和沃尔瑟姆度假时那段愉快的日子吗？现在我们有钱富裕了，然而所有的这些乐趣都消失了——以前，我有一个小手提篮，专门用来存放每天的美味，有冷羊肉和沙拉。你每天中午都在寻找体面的房子，我们就好进去摆出我们自己制作的美食享用，这样你就只需要支付你必须要点的啤酒所花费的钱。那时，你得看女主人的脸色，她是否愿意让我们铺放一块桌布——希望她是一位淳朴的女主人，就像艾萨克·沃尔顿笔下描述的当他去钓鱼时，在宜人的利河河畔上遇到的许许多多女主人一样——有时她们对我们和蔼可亲，有时却有些勉强不情愿。但我们仍然保持着高兴的样子面带喜悦，虽然只是粗茶淡饭，却吃得津津有味，几乎很少会想到皮斯卡托的鳟鱼馆。然而现在，我们外出度假的次数愈来愈少，当我们偶尔出去游玩一天，也很少走路，都是开车，半路上在高级旅馆里歇脚，点最好的晚餐，从来不会为费用发愁。然而这些，终究不及我们偶然品尝到的乡村粗茶淡饭的一半美味，尽管乡村不确定的习俗和不周全的接待往往令我们不知所措。

"现在你太高傲了，只会坐在包厢里看戏。你还记得，当时我们看《赫克瑟姆战役》、《加莱的投降》、班尼斯特和布兰德夫人演的《森林里的孩子》时坐过的地方吗？——当时我们每人用节省下来的钱，坐在一先令的顶层楼座上，这样我们就可以在一个季度里，一起看上三到四场戏剧。那时，你一直觉得不应该带我去那个场所——我却因为你带我去而愈发感激你——而我得到的愉悦远远要比这点小小的有失体面要多得多。每当幕布拉开时，谁会注意到我们在戏院里坐的位置，我们坐在哪里也都无关紧要。我们的注意力全都集中在阿尔登森林的罗莎琳德身上，或者是在伊利里亚宫廷中的薇奥拉身上——你曾经常说，剧院顶层楼座是所有人享受戏剧的最佳场所，而这种看戏的趣味性程度一定是与不常去看戏成反比的。我们在那里遇到的观众，一般都没有阅读过戏剧剧本，他们格外全神贯注地观看舞台上的表演，而且确实需要这样做——因为如果漏掉了一句台词，就像是遇到一个鸿沟，剧情的衔接将会无法弥补。当时，我们用这样的想法来安抚我们的自尊心——然而我想问，现在家里条件好了，有了更多的消费，可是作为一个女人，我之前得到的关注就更少、待遇就更差吗？确实，我们挤进门，挤上拥挤不堪的楼梯，这是够糟糕的——但正如我们在其他的通道中所遇到的那样，在很大的程度上，对于女人仍然有一种公认的礼貌法则——而在这之后，我们只要花上一点力气最终克服这个小小的困难之后，座位显得更加舒适并能更好地享受戏剧。现在，我们只要付了钱，就直接走了进去。你说，你现在无法在顶层楼座上看戏了。我相信我们当时的所见所闻都是很好的，这就足够了——然而，我认为那里所有的原汁原味，都已经随着我们的贫穷从视线中一并消失了。

"在草莓还没有普遍上市之前，能吃上草莓就是一件快乐之事；同样，当豌豆还很昂贵的时候，将豌豆作为第一道菜，那就是一顿丰盛的晚餐，一种享受。可是现在，我们还能有什么样的享受？如果我们现在要好好地款待我们自己——也就是说，吃一点超出我们收入范畴的美味佳肴，那会显得自私和任性。我所说的享受，不过是指能够允许自己超出一点点实际的生活水平——当两个人生活在一起时，就像我们曾经那样，偶尔地放纵一下自己，沉溺于两个人都喜欢的一种廉价奢侈品之中；然后，两个人都道歉，并愿意将两人各占一半的责任全部归咎于自己。我认为，从这个意义上讲，人们重视自己并没有什么不好，这也许会给其他人一种暗示：要懂得如何去对待别人。但是现在——我的意思是，就这个词来说——我们从来没有重视过我们自己，而这只有穷人才能做得到。我指的并不是真正的最贫穷的那类人，而是像我们曾经那样处于贫困线上的人。

"我知道你要说什么，在年底的时候，所有的收支平衡是件最快乐的事。过去每到 12 月 31 日的晚上，我们都会聚集在一起探讨我们超支的部分，那些困惑不解的账目弄得你拉长了脸，满脸愁容，并且千方百计想弄清楚我们是怎样花掉了这么多的钱，或者说，也许我们没有花费这么多的钱，又或者，我们明年绝不能再花掉这么多的钱。同时，我们还发现本来就微薄的资金又在减少。接下来，就是在各种计划和各种方案之间进行协调，大谈在将来的各个计划中如何削减开支、避免来年再次亏空。年轻赋予我们的希望和欢乐的精神（直到现在，你也从未失去过这点）使我们接受了这个现实并把损失装进了衣袋。'以几杯烈酒'（你会引用性格开朗活泼的科顿先生的话，正如你从前这样称呼他），我们'欢迎来宾'作为结束语。现在年终时，我们不会再有以往旧年的年终结算——对于新的一年，既没有美好的承诺，也没有振奋人心的展望。"

布里奇特在大多数的场合不爱说话，在她打开话匣滔滔不绝时，我得注意怎样去打断她的话。然而，我却忍不住笑了，笑她那可爱的想象力，那是从一个穷人每年一百英镑纯收入中所幻想出来的财富。"一点也不错，穷的时候，我们感到更快乐；但那时，我们也更年轻啊，我的姐姐。现在，我们恐怕必须得忍受这多余的财富，如果我们把这些都扔进了大海，我们就无法照顾好自己。为此，我们努力奋斗，我们一起长大，我们应当感恩。这些努力和奋斗使我们之间的关系更加紧密，并把我们凝聚在了一起。如果我们一直都有你现在所抱怨的那种富有的满足感，我们的关系就永远不可能像现在这样亲密融洽。我们身上那种抗争力——那种青春活力的一次次自然地膨胀是环境所不能束缚的——早就消失殆尽了。对于上了年龄的人来说，财富是对青春的一种补偿，这的确是一种令人遗憾的补偿，但恐怕这也是我们有望得到的最好的补偿了。现在，我们必须开车出行，去我们以往走过的地方；将生活过得比过去（你所说的那种美好但贫穷的日子）更加美好，睡得比过去更加柔软，这才是明智的做法。然而，如果时光可以倒流——你和我还能不能一天步行三十英里；班尼斯特和布兰德夫人能不能再回到年轻时的样子；你和我还能不能再年轻一点，去剧院看他们演戏；那美好顶层楼座上看戏的日子，还能否重现——然而，这一切现在都已经成了梦幻，我亲爱的姐姐，此时此刻，你和我，能不能不要再坐在我们铺着地毯的壁炉旁，坐在靠着墙边这豪华的沙发上，进行这种安静的争论，而是再一次艰难地去争着爬上那个推来推去、挤着压着、拥挤不堪的楼梯，我们还会弯着腰在通道里，被那些最贫穷的人挤来挤去——我还能再次听到你那焦虑不安的尖叫声——直到我们终于成功地爬到剧场最高一层的座位，当整个欢腾的剧场的第一缕亮光在我们的脚下照亮，我还能听到你那句令人开心的'谢天谢地，我们总算安全了！'——假如这一切真能重现，我不知道那深不可测的万丈深渊有多深，但我愿意用比克罗伊斯更多的财富，或者说比犹太人银行家罗氏拥有更多的财富去填埋其中，换取这一切欢乐。现在，让我们来看看那位快乐的中国小侍从，他手里拿着一把伞，大得像床架上的顶篷一般，罩在了湛蓝色避暑别墅里那位颇有点圣母玛利亚风格的女士的头上。"

WILLIAM HAZLITT (1778—1830)

William Hazlitt (1778—1830), the son of a Unitarian minister, was born at Maidstone and spent most of his youth at the secluded village of Wem, near Shrewsbury. He was educated for the ministry, but was more interested in philosophy and literature. His love of art almost prompted him to become, like his brother, a painter. He finally took up the pen instead of the brush. He was parliamentary reporter, dramatic critic, and magazine writer. He held strong political views and was associated with the liberal writers of the time, In literary criticism, he belonged to the impressionistic, romantic school of Coleridge, and like Lamb contributed to the recovery of the great Elizabethans in a series of lectures on the *Characters of Shakespeare's Plays* (1817—1818), *The Dramatic Literature of the Age of Elizabeth* (1820), etc. He is chiefly remembered, however, for his miscellaneous essays, collected in *Table Talk* (1821—1822), *The Plain Speaker* (1826), and the posthumous *Literary Remains* (1836) and *Winterslow* (1850). They reveal his many-sided interests in life and the infinite gusto with which he discoursed on his favourite subjects.

In place of the sweet humanity that gives Lamb such an ineffable charm, there are a touch of misanthropy, a sound taste and an understanding of ultra-masculine strength in Hazlitt's writings. They have a frankness and virility peculiarly his own. But like Lamb, he was personal and intimately confidential. The secret of his charms lies in his ability to weave all the elements of reading, observation, and disposition into one web of superb experience. He grappled valiantly with the problems of composition and became in time so lucid and polished a writer that he could proudly declare that he 'never wrote a line that licked the dust.' Hazlitt is the best example in English literature of a writer who has deliberately developed his own art of writing.

【作者简介】

威廉·赫兹里特 (1778—1830)，父亲是神体一位派的牧师，出生于英格兰东南部城市梅德斯通（肯特郡首府），他青年时代的大部分时间是在什鲁斯伯里附近的一个僻静的韦姆镇度过的。他受过牧师培训，但对哲学和文学更感兴趣。他对艺术的热爱几乎促使他像他哥哥一样，成为一名画家。但他最终还是拿起钢笔替代了画笔。他曾经当过议会记者，写过戏剧评论，为杂志撰过稿。他具有强烈的政治主张，并与当时的自由派作家有联系。在文学评论方面，他属于印象派、柯勒律治的浪漫主义学派。像兰姆一样，他的《莎士比亚戏剧中的人物》(1817—1818)、《论伊丽莎白时代戏剧文学》(1820) 等系列讲座，为伟大的伊丽莎白时代的文学复兴做出了贡献。然而，他最为人们所熟知的是他的随笔散文，这些杂文被收录在《席间闲谈》(1821—1822)、《直言者》(1826)，以及遗著《文学遗产》

（1836）和《温特斯洛》（1850）中。这些散文揭示了他对生活多方面的兴趣，他将自己喜爱的或感兴趣的主题论述得津津有味。

在赫兹里特的作品中，有一种愤世嫉俗的情绪，一种纯正的品位，以及一种超强的阳刚之气，取代了兰姆以甜美的人性赋予作品的那种不可言喻的魅力。他的作品坦诚直率而富有男子气概，特别是谈到他自己的时候。他与兰姆一样，都是很自信的人。他的魅力在于他能将阅读、观察以及自身的性情与丰富的经验融为一体。他勇于纠正写作中的问题，最终成为一名思绪清晰、文笔优雅娴熟的作家，他甚至可以自豪地说他"从未写过一句败笔"。赫兹里特是英国文学史上作家有意识地发展自己写作艺术的最好实例。

My First Acquaintance with Poets

My father was a Dissenting Minister at Wem in Shropshire; and in **the year 1798** (the figures that compose that date are to me like the 'dreaded name of **Demogorgon**'), Mr. Coleridge came to Shrewsbury, to succeed Mr. Rowe in the spiritual charge of a Unitarian congregation there. He did not come till late on the Saturday afternoon before he was to preach; and Mr. Rowe, who himself went down to the coach in a state of anxiety and expectation, to look for the arrival of his successor, could find no one at all answering the description but a round-faced man in a short black coat (like a shooting-jacket) which hardly seemed to have been made for him, but who seemed to be talking at a great rate to his fellow passengers. Mr. Rowe had scarce returned to give an account of his disappointment, when the round-faced man in black entered, and dissipated all doubts on the subject, by beginning to talk. He did not cease while he stayed; nor has he since, that I know of. He held the good town of Shrewsbury in delightful suspense for three weeks that he remained there, '**fluttering the** *proud Salopians*, like an eagle in a dove-cote;' and the Welsh mountains that skirt the horizon with their tempestuous confusion, agree to have heard no such mystic sounds since the days of

High-born Hoel's harp *or soft Llewellyn's lay!*

As we passed along between Wem and Shrewsbury, and I eyed their blue tops seen through the wintry branches, or the red rustling leaves of the sturdy oak trees by the roadside, a sound was in my ears as of a Siren's song; I was stunned, startled with it, as from deep sleep; but I had no notion then that I should ever be able to express my admiration to others in motley imagery or quaint allusion, till the light of his genius shone into my soul, like the sun's rays glittering in the puddles of the road. I was at that time dumb, inarticulate, helpless, like a worm by the wayside, crushed, bleeding, lifeless; but now, bursting from the deadly bands that

> **bound them**
> **With Styx** *nine times round them,*

my ideas float on winged words, and as they expand their plumes, catch the golden light of other years. My soul has indeed remained in its original bondage, dark, obscure, with longings infinite and unsatisfied; my heart, shut up in the prison-house of this rude clay, has never found, nor will it ever find, a heart to speak to; but that my understanding also did not remain dumb and brutish, or at length found a language to express itself, I owe to Coleridge. But this is not to my purpose.

My father lived ten miles from Shrewsbury, and was in the habit of exchanging visits with Mr. Rowe, and with Mr. Jenkins of Whitchurch (nine miles farther on) according to the custom of Dissenting Ministers in each other's neighbourhood. A line of communication is thus established, by which the flame of civil and religious liberty is kept alive, and nourishes its smouldering fire unquenchable, like **the fires in the** *Agamemnon* **of Aeschylus**, placed at different stations, that waited for ten long years to announce with their blazing pyramids the destruction of Troy. Coleridge had agreed to come over and see my father, according to the courtesy of the country, as Mr. Rowe's probable successor; but in the meantime I had gone to hear him preach the Sunday after his arrival. A poet and a philosopher getting up into a Unitarian pulpit to preach the Gospel, was a romance in these degenerate days, a sort of revival of the primitive spirit of Christianity, which was not to be resisted.

It was in January of 1798, that I rose one morning before daylight, to walk ten miles in the mud, to hear this celebrated person preach. Never, the longest day I have to live, shall I have such another walk as this cold, raw, comfortless one, in the winter of the year 1798... When I got there, the organ was playing the 100th Psalm, and, when it was done, Mr. Coleridge rose and gave out **his text**, 'And he went up into the mountain to pray, *himself, alone.*' As he gave out this text, his voice '**rose like a steam** of rich distilled perfumes,' and when he came to the two last words, which he pronounced loud, deep, and distinct, it seemed to me, who was then young, as if the sounds had echoed from the bottom of the human heart, and as if that prayer might have floated in solemn silence through the universe. The idea of **St. John** came into mind, '**of one crying in the wilderness**, who had his loins girt about, and whose food was locusts and wild honey.' The preacher then launched into his subject, like an eagle dallying with the wind. The sermon was upon peace and war; upon church and state—not their alliance, but their separation—on the spirit of the world and the spirit of Christianity, not as the same, but as opposed to one another. He talked of those who had 'inscribed the cross of Christ on banners dripping with human gore.' He made a poetical and pastoral excursion,—and to show the fatal effects of war, drew a striking contrast between the simple shepherd boy, driving his team afield, or sitting under the hawthorn, piping to his flock, 'as though he should never been old,' and the same poor country lad, **crimped**, kidnapped, brought into town, made drunk at an alehouse, turned into a wretched drummer boy, with his hair sticking on end with powder and pomatum, a long cue at his back, and tricked out in the loathsome finery of the profession of blood:

> **Such were the notes** *our once-loved poet sung.*

And for myself, I could not have been more delighted if I had heard the music of the spheres. Poetry and Philosophy had met together. Truth and Genius had embraced, under the eye and with the sanction of Religion. This was even beyond my hopes. I returned home well satisfied. The sun that was still labouring pale and wan through the sky, obscured by thick mists, seemed an emblem of the *good cause*; and the cold dank drop of dew that hung half melted on the beard of the thistle, had something genial and refreshing in them; for there was a spirit of hope and youth in all nature, that turned everything into good. The face of nature had not then the brand of *jus divinum* on it:

Like to that sanguine flower inscribed with woe.

On the Tuesday following, the half-inspired speaker came. I was called down into the room where he was, and went half-hoping, half-afraid. He received me very graciously, and I listened for a long time without uttering a word. I did not suffer in his opinion by my silence. 'For those two hours,' he afterwards was pleased to say, 'he was conversing with William Hazlitt's forehead!' His appearance was different from what I had anticipated from seeing him before. At a distance, and in the dim light of the chapel, there was to me a strange wildness in his aspect, a dusky obscurity, and I thought him pitted with the small-pox. His complexion was at that time clear, and even bright—

As are the children of yon azure sheen.

His forehead was broad and high, light as if built of ivory, with large projecting eyebrows, and his eyes rolling beneath them like a sea with darkened lustre. 'A certain tender bloom his face o'erspread,' a purple tinge as we see it in the pale thoughtful complexions of the Spanish portrait-painters, **Murillo and Velázquez**. His mouth was gross, voluptuous, open, eloquent; his chin good-humoured and round; but his nose, the rudder of the face, the index of the will, was small, feeble, nothing-like what he has done. It might seem that the genius of his face as from a height surveyed and projected him (with sufficient capacity and huge aspiration) into the world unknown of thought and imagination, with nothing to support or guide his veering purpose, as if Columbus had launched his adventurous course for the New World in a scallop, without oars or compass. So, at least, I comment on it after the event. Coleridge in his person was rather above the common size, inclining to the corpulent, or **like Lord Hamlet**, 'somewhat fat and **pursy**.' His hair (now, alas! Gray) was then black and glossy as the raven's, and fell in smooth masses over his forehead...

No two individuals were ever more unlike than were the host and his guest. A poet was to my father a sort of nondescript; yet whatever added grace to the Unitarian cause was to him welcome. He could hardly have been more surprised or pleased, if our visitor had worn wings. Indeed, his thoughts had wings; and as the silken sound rustled round our little wainscoted parlour, my father threw back his spectacles over his forehead, his white hairs mixing with its sanguine hue; and a smile of delight beamed across his rugged cordial face, to think that Truth had found a new ally in Fancy... The day passed off pleasantly, and the next morning Mr. Coleridge was to return to Shrewsbury. When I came down to breakfast, I found that he had just received a letter from his friend **T. Wedgwood**, making him an offer of £150 a year if he chose to waive his present pursuit, and devote himself entirely to the study of poetry and philosophy. Coleridge seemed to make up his mind to close with this proposal in the act of tying on one of his shoes. It threw an additional damp on his departure. It took the wayward enthusiast quite from us to cast him into **Deva**'s winding vales, or by the shores of old romance.

Instead of living at ten miles' distance, of being the pastor of a Dissenting congregation at Shrewsbury, he was henceforth to inhabit the **Hill of Parnassus**, to be a Shepherd on the **Delectable Mountains**. Alas! I knew not the way thither, and felt very little gratitude for Mr. Wedgwood's bounty. I was presently relieved from this dilemma; for Mr. Coleridge, asking for a pen and ink, and going to a table to write something on a bit of card, advanced towards me with undulating step, and giving me the precious document, said that that was his address, *Mr. Coleridge, Nether-Stowey, Somersetshire*; and that he should be glad to see me there in a few weeks' time, and, if I chose, would come half-way to meet me. I was not less surprised than the shepherd-boy (this simile is to be found in **Cassandra**) when he sees a thunderbolt fall close at his feet. I stammered out my acknowledgments and acceptance of this offer (I thought Mr. Wedgwood's annuity a trifle to it) as well as I could; and this mighty business being settled, the poet-preacher took leave, and I accompanied him six miles on the road. It was a fine morning in the middle of winter, and he talked the whole way. **The scholar in Chaucer** is described as going 'sounding on his way.' So Coleridge went on his. In digressing, in dilating, in passing from subject to subject, he appeared to me to float in air, to slide on ice... I observed that he continually crossed me on the way by shifting from one side of the footpath to the other. This struck me as an odd movement; but I did not at that time connect it with any instability of purpose or involuntary change of principle, as I have done since. He seemed unable to keep on in a straight line...

On my way back, I had a sound in my ears—it was the voice of Fancy; I had a light before me—it was the face of Poetry. The one still lingers there, the other has not quitted my side! Coleridge in truth met me half-way on the ground of philosophy, or I should not have been won over to his imaginative creed. I had an uneasy, pleasurable sensation all the time, till I was to visit him. During those months the chill breath of winter gave me a welcoming; the vernal air was balm and inspiration to me. The golden sunsets, the silver star of evening, lighted me on my way to new hopes and prospects. *I was to visit Coleridge in the spring.* This circumstance was never absent from my thoughts, and mingled with all my feelings. I wrote to him at the time proposed, and received an answer postponing my intended visit for a week or two, but very cordially urging me to complete my promise then. This delay did not damp, but rather increased my ardour. In the meantime I went to **Llangollen Vale**, by way of initiating myself in the mysteries of natural scenery and I must say I was enchanted with it. I had been reading Coleridge's description of England in his fine 'Ode on the Departing Year,' and I applied it, *con amore*, to the objects before me. That valley was to me (in a manner) the cradle of a new existence: in the river that winds through it, my spirit was baptized in the waters of **Helicon**!

I returned home, and soon after set out on my journey with unworn heart and untired feet. My way lay through **Worcester** and **Gloucester**, and by **Upton**, where I thought of Tom Jones and the **adventure of the muff**. I remember getting completely wet through one day, and stopping at an inn (I think it was at **Tewkesbury**), where I sat up all night to read *Paul and Virginia*. Sweet were the showers in early youth that drenched my body, and sweet the drops of pity that fell upon the books I read! ... I was still two days before the time fixed for my arrival, for I had taken care to set out early enough. I stopped these two days at **Bridgewater**, and when I was tired of sauntering on the banks of its muddy river, returned to the inn, and read *Camilla*. So have I loitered my life away, reading books, looking at pictures, going to plays, hearing, thinking, writing on what pleased me best. I have wanted only one thing to make me happy; but wanting that, have wanted everything!

I arrived, and was well received. The country about **Nether Stowey** is beautiful, green and hilly, and near the seashore. I saw it but the other day, after an interval of twenty years, from a hill near **Taunton**. How was the map of my life spread out before me, as the map of the country lay at my feet! In the afternoon, Coleridge took me over to **Alfoxden**, a romantic old family mansion of the St. Aubins, where Wordsworth lived. It was then in the possession of a friend of the poet's, who gave him the free use of it. Somehow that period (the time just after the French Revolution) was not a time when *nothing was given for nothing*. The mind opened, and a softness might be perceived coming over the heart of individuals, beneath 'the scales that fence' our self-interest. Wordsworth himself was from home, but his sister kept house, and set before us a frugal repast; and we had free access to her brother's poems, the *Lyrical Ballads*, which were still in manuscript, or in the form of **Sybilline Leaves**, I dipped into a few of these with great satisfaction, and with the faith of a novice. I slept that night in an old room with blue hangings, and covered with the round-faced family portraits of the **age of George I and II**, and from the wooded declivity of the adjoining park that overlooked my window, at the dawn of day, could 'hear the loud stag speak.' ...

That morning, as soon as breakfast was over, we strolled out into the park, and seating ourselves on the trunk of an old ash tree that stretched along the ground, Coleridge read aloud, with a sonorous and musical voice, the ballad of '**Betty Foy**.' I was not critically or sceptically inclined. I saw touches of truth and nature, and took the rest for granted. But in the 'Thorn,' the 'Mad Mother,' and the 'Complaint of a Poor Indian Woman,' I felt that deeper power and pathos which have been since acknowledged,

In spite of pride, *in erring reason's spite,*

as the characteristics of this author; and the sense of a new style and a new spirit in poetry came over me. It had to me something of the effect that arises from the turning up of the fresh soil, or of the first welcome breath of spring;

While yet the trembling year *is unconfirmed.*

Coleridge and myself walked back to Stowey that evening, and his voice sounded high

Of Providence, foreknowledge, *will, and fate,*
Fix'd fate, free-will, foreknowledge absolute,

as we passed through echoing grove, by fairy stream or waterfall, gleaming in the summer moonlight! He lamented that Wordsworth was not prone enough to believe in the traditional superstitions of the place, and that there was a something corporeal, a *matter-of-factness*, a clinging to the palpable, or often to the petty, in his poetry, in consequence. His genius was not a spirit that descended to him through the air; it sprung out of the ground like a flower, or unfolded itself from a green spray, on which the goldfinch sang. He said, however (if I remember right), that this objection must be confined to his descriptive pieces, that his philosophic poetry had a grand and comprehensive spirit in it, so that his soul seemed to inhabit the universe like a palace, and to discover truth by intuition rather than by deduction. The next day Wordsworth arrived from Bristol at Coleridge's cottage. I think I see him now. He answered in some degree to his friend's description of him, but was more gaunt and Don Quixote-like. He was quaintly dressed, according to the *costume* of that unconstrained period, in a brown fustian jacket and striped pantaloons. There was something of a **roll**, a lounge in his gait, not unlike his own **Peter Bell**. There was a severe, worn pressure of thought about his temples, a fire in his eye (as if he saw something in objects more than the outward appearance), an intense high narrow forehead, a Roman nose, cheeks furrowed by strong purpose and feeling, and a convulsive inclination to laughter about the mouth, a good deal at variance with the solemn, stately expression of the rest of his face. **Chantrey's bust** wants the marking traits; but he was teased into making it regular and heavy; **Haydon's head of him**, introduced into the 'Entrance of Christ into Jerusalem,' is the most like his drooping weight of thought and expression. He sat down and talked very naturally and freely, with a mixture of clear gushing accents in his voice, a deep guttural intonation, and a strong tincture of the northern *burr,* like the crust on wine...

We went over to Alfoxden again the day following, and Wordsworth read us the story of *Peter Bell* in the open air; and the comment made upon it by his face and voice was very different from that of **some later critics**! Whatever might be thought of the poem, 'his face was as a book where men might read strange matters,' and he announced the fate of his hero in prophetic tones. There is a *chaunt* in the recitation both of Coleridge and Wordsworth, which acts as a spell upon the hearer, and disarms the judgment. Perhaps they have deceived themselves by making habitual use of this ambiguous accompaniment. Coleridge's manner is more full, animated, and varied; Wordsworth's more equable, sustained, and internal. The one might be termed more *dramatic,* the other more *lyrical.* Coleridge has told me that he himself liked to compose in walking over uneven ground, or breaking through the straggling branches of a copse-wood; whereas Wordsworth always wrote, if he could, walking up and down a straight gravel walk, or in some spot where the continuity of his verse met with no collateral interruption...

Notes

This was first published in Leigh Hunt's journal, *The Liberal,* 1822, and later in *Winterslow* (1850). Few of the contemporary sketches of Coleridge can be compared in brilliancy and vividness to this account of the 'poet-preacher' given here by his former votary. Hazlitt was early acquainted with the Lake poets and had a great admiration for Coleridge who started him on his career as a writer on art, literature, and metaphysics. But this youthful enthusiasm did not last long. Violent in political sympathies and antipathies, Hazlitt quarrelled with most of his friends. He, too, was estranged from his Lake friends because of their changed political views, he himself remaining a radical to the end of his life. This explains the caustic reference to Coleridge's 'instability of purpose or involuntary change of principle' in this essay.

the year 1798. In the same year was also published *The Lyrical Ballads*, a collection of poems by Wordsworth and Coleridge.

Demogorgon, name of a mysterious and terrible infernal deity; one of the fallen angels in Milton's *Paradise Lost*.

'fluttering the proud Salopians,' etc. Adapted from Shakespeare's *Coriolanus*, Act V, scene vi, line 116. Salop is another name for Shropshire, hence Salopians are the people of that county. To flutter the dove-cote means to alarm quiet people.

'High-born Hoel's harp,' etc. From Thomas Gray's poem 'The Bard.' According to Rev.E. Evans' 'Dissertatio de Bardis,' Hoel was a Welsh prince; and Llewellyn, last king of North Wales. They were both Welsh poets. In the Arthurian legend, Hoel was duke of Brittany and cousin of King Arthur.

'bound them, With Styx,' etc. From Pope's 'Ode for St. Cecilia's Day.' Styx, 'the flood of deadly hate,' is a river encompassing Hades or the lower world.

the fires in the Agamemnon of Aeschylus. See the opening scene of Aeschylus' tragedy *Agamemnon*, especially the Watch man's soliloquy and Clytemnestra's explanation of the workings of the beacon system that brought to her the happy tiding of Troy's fall.

his text. See *Matthew*, xiv, 23.

'rose like a steam,' etc. From Milton's *Comus*.

St. John, the Baptist, forerunner of Christ.

'of one crying in the wilderness,' etc. See *Matthew*, iii, 3—4.

crimped, entrapped (into military service).

'Such were the notes,' etc. From Pope's 'Epistle to Oxford.'

jus divinum, divine right (of kings).

'Like to that sanguine flower,' etc. From Milton's *Lycidas*, line 107. The sanguine flower is the hyacinth, whose petals the Greeks fancied to be marked with the word meaning *alas*.

'As are the children,' etc. From Thomson's *Castle of Indolence*.

Murillo and Velázquez. Murillo, Bartolomé Esteban (1617—1682), the celebrated Spanish painter of religious pictures; Velázquez, Diego Rodriguez (1599—1660), the great Spanish painter in the court of Philip IV.

like Lord Hamlet, as played by the famous Elizabethan actor, Richard Burbage, a heavy man.

pursy, short winded. The phrase 'somewhat fat and pursy' is an adaptation from *Hamlet*, Act III, scene iv, line 153: 'in the fatness of these pursy times.'

T. Wedgwood, Thomas Wedgwood (1771—1805), the first photographer, and a generous patron of Coleridge.

Deva, the river Dee in Cheshire.

Hill of Parnassus, a mountain in Greece, a few miles north of Delphi, sacred to the Muses.

Delectable Mountains, in Bunyan's *Pilgrim's Progress*, within sight of the Celestial City.

Cassandra, i.e. *Cassandre*, a romance by the French novelist La Calprenède (1609?—1663).

The scholar in Chaucer, etc. A reference to the 'clerk' of Oxford in

Chaucer's Canterbury Tales.

Llangollen Vale, in northern Wales.

con amore (Latin), with love; earnestly; heartily.

Helicon, a mountain of Boeotia sacred to the Muses, and famous for its fountains.

Worcester, Gloucester, Upton. Worcester and Upton in Worcestershire, and Gloucester, in Gloucestershire, are all cities in southwestern England.

adventure of the muff, in *Tom Jones*, a novel by Fielding (1707—1754).

Tewkesbury, a town in Gloucestetshire.

Paul and Virginia, a love romance by Bernardin de Saint-Pierre (1737—1814), a French writer and follower of Rousseau.

Bridgewater, a town in Somersetshire.

Camilla, a realistic novel by Frances Burney (1752—1840), an English woman novelist.

Nether Stowey, Taunton, Alfoxden, all located near together in Somersetshire in the southwest of England.

Sybilline Leaves, 'Prophetic Books;' Coleridge published a collection of poems entitled *Sybilline Leaves* in 1817.

age of George I and II, i.e. 1714—1760.

'Betty Foy,' etc, are poems by Wordsworth.

'In spite of pride,' etc. From Pope's *Essay on Man*.

'While yet the trembling year,' etc. From James Thomson's *Seasons*.

'Of Providence, foreknowledge,' etc. From Milton's *Paradise Lost*.

roll, swaying movement of the body.

Peter Bell, the character in Wordsworth's poem of that name.

Chantrey's bust, by Sir Francis L. Chantrey (1781—1841), English sculptor.

Haydon's head of him, by Benjamin R. Haydon (1786—1846), English painter, in his picture 'The Entrance of Christ in Jerusalem.'

some later critics. The publication of the poem *Peter Bell* (written in 1798) in 1819 met with much harsh criticism; it was made the subject of many parodies (among others one by Shelley).

'his face was a book,' etc. From *Macbeth*, Act l, scene v, line 63.

【作品简介】

这篇散文最初于 1822 年发表在利·亨特的《自由主义者》刊物上，随后被收录于《温特斯洛》(1850)。赫兹里特对柯勒律治这位"诗人传教士"的描绘栩栩如生、光彩照人，当代作家很少有可以与赫兹里特相媲美的。赫兹里特很早就与湖畔诗人相识，并对柯勒律治非常钦佩，柯勒律治使他开始了艺术、文学和形而上学方面的写作生涯；然而，这种年轻的热情并没有使他持续多久。赫兹里特由于在政治观点上持有强烈的不同见解，他几乎与所有的朋友吵翻了。他也与湖畔诗人朋友们疏远了，因为他们的政治观点发生了变化。直到生命的尽头，他仍然是一个激进派。这就解释了本文中他对柯勒律治的讥讽"目的性不明确，或无原则的变更"。

【作品解析】

the year 1798：同年也出版了《抒情歌谣集》，这是华兹华斯和柯勒律治的诗歌合集。

Demogorgon：神秘而又可怕的地狱之神的名字；弥尔顿《失乐园》中的一个堕落天使。

"fluttering the proud Salopians,"etc.：此句出自莎士比亚改编的《科里奥兰纳斯》，第五幕，第六场，第 116 行。萨洛普郡是什罗普郡的另一个名字，因此，萨洛普人是该郡的居民。"To flutter the dove-cote"意味着惊动安静的人们。

"High-born Hoel's harp,"etc.：此句出自托马斯·格雷的诗《吟游诗人》。根据埃文斯牧师的拉丁文论文《吟游诗人研究》，霍尔是威尔士王子，卢埃林是北威尔士最后一位国王。他们都是北威尔士诗人。在有关亚瑟王的传说中，霍尔是布列塔尼公爵和亚瑟王的表亲。

"bound them, With Styx," etc.：此句出自蒲柏的《圣塞西莉亚日的颂歌》。冥河（styx），"致命仇恨的洪水"，是一条环绕着冥府或者地狱的河流。

the fires in the Agamemnon of Aeschylus：参见埃斯库罗斯的悲剧《阿伽门农》的开场白，尤其是守夜人的独白和克吕泰墨斯特拉对烽火台系统工作原理的解释，这给她带来了特洛伊陷落的喜讯。

his text：参见《马太福音》十四，23。

"rose like a steam," etc.：此句出自弥尔顿的《科马斯》。

St. John：施洗者圣约翰，基督教的先驱。

"of one crying in the wilderness," etc.：此句参见《马太福音》三，3—4。

crimped：被困在服兵役中。

"Such were the notes," etc.：此句出自蒲柏《致牛津的信》。

jus divinum：君权神授。

"Like to that sanguine flower," etc.：此句出自弥尔顿《利西达斯》第107行。血红色的花朵是指风信子，风信子的花瓣被希腊人想象标有"唉"的意思。

"As are the children," etc.：此句出自汤姆逊的《懒惰城堡》。

Murillo and Velázquez：巴托洛梅·埃斯特万·牟利罗（1617—1682），著名的西班牙画家，尤其以宗教题材的画著名。迭戈·罗德里格斯·委拉斯开兹（1599—1660），是西班牙国王腓力四世时期著名的宫廷画家。

like Lord Hamlet：就像伊丽莎白时代著名演员理查德·伯比奇扮演的哈姆雷特勋爵一样，他是个大块头。

pursy：短促的。短语"somewhat fat and pursy"（胖得连喘气也困难）改编自《哈姆雷特》，第三幕，第四场，第153行："in the fatness of these pursy times."。

T．Wedgwood：托马斯·韦奇伍德（1771—1805），第一位摄影师，也是柯勒律治慷慨的赞助人。

Deva：柴郡的迪尔河。

Hill of Parnassus：帕尔纳索斯山，希腊的一座山，在德尔斐（希腊古都）以北几英里，是缪斯女神的圣地。

Delectable Mountains：在班扬的《天路历程》中，离天国之城不远，可遥望天城。

Cassandra：即 *Cassandre*（《卡桑德拉》），法国小说家拉·卡尔普勒内德（约1609—1663）的浪漫小说。

The scholar in Chaucer, etc.：指乔叟《坎特伯雷故事集》中所提到的牛津的"职员"。

Llangollen Vale：兰戈伦河谷，位于威尔士北部。

con amore（拉丁语）：充满爱的；真诚的，衷心的。

Helicon：希腊维奥蒂亚山，尊为缪斯女神的圣地，以其山泉而著名。

Worcester, Gloucester, Upton：伍斯特郡的伍斯特、阿普顿，以及格洛斯特郡的格洛斯特，都是英格兰西南部的城市。

adventure of the muff：出自亨利·菲尔丁（1707—1754）的小说《汤姆·琼斯》。

Tewkesbury：蒂克斯伯里，格洛斯特郡的一个小镇。

Paul and Virginia：《保罗和薇吉妮》，法国作家贝尔纳丹·德·圣皮埃尔（1737—1814）的爱情浪漫小说，他受卢梭影响很深。

Bridgewater：布里奇沃特，萨默塞特郡的一个小城镇。

Camilla：《卡米拉》，英国女小说家弗朗西斯·伯尼（1752—1840）的现实主义小说。

Nether Stowey, Taunton, Alfoxden：下斯托伊、汤顿、埃尔福克斯顿，它们都位于英国西南部的萨默塞特郡附近。

Sybilline Leaves：原意为"预言书"；1817 年，柯勒律治出版了一本诗集，将其题名为《西比林树叶》。

age of George I and II：乔治一世和二世时期，即 1714—1760 年。

"Betty Foy,"etc.：这些都是华兹华斯的诗。

"In spite of pride,"etc.：此句出自蒲柏《人论》。

"While yet the trembling year,"etc.：此句出自詹姆斯·汤姆逊《四季》。

"Of Providence, foreknowledge,"etc.：此句出自弥尔顿《失乐园》。

roll：摆动身体的运动。

Peter Bell：彼得·贝尔，华兹华斯同名诗歌中的人物。

Chantrey's bust：英国雕塑家弗朗西斯·勒加特·钱特里爵士（1781—1841）创作。

Haydon's head of him：英国画家本杰明·罗伯特·海登（1786—1846）创作，画名为《基督进入耶路撒冷》。

some later critics：《彼得·贝尔》（华兹华斯作于 1798 年）在 1819 年出版后，遭受到严厉的批评，而且这首叙事诗后来被许多人戏仿（雪莱的一首诗就是其中之一）。

"his face was a book，" etc.：此句出自《麦克白》，第一幕，第五场，第 63 行。

【参考译文】

与诗人的初次相识

我父亲是一名什罗普郡韦姆镇的非国教派牧师。1798 年（这个数字对我来说就像"魔鬼"一样可怕），柯勒律治先生来到了什鲁斯伯里接替罗先生，负责神体一位派信徒的宗教事务。柯勒律治先生直到星期六下午，在布道会之前才到。罗先生亲自走到马车前，带着焦急不安和期待的心情，迎接他那位接班人的到来。他没有发现符合他接班人外貌特征的来客，附近只有一位圆脸男子，穿着一件似乎不太合身的黑色短外套（像一件打猎穿的夹克衫），正在以极快的语速与同行的乘客交谈。正当罗先生几乎还没有来得及回来说明自己的失望时，这位穿着黑色衣服的圆脸男子走了过来，他一开口，消除了众人对这个问题所有的疑虑。在他停留期间，就没有停止过说话；据我所知，从那之后，他就没有停歇过。他在什鲁斯伯里停留的三个星期里，令人愉快和兴奋，"就像鸽子笼里的老鹰一样，惊动了骄傲的萨洛普人"。环绕在地平线上的威尔士山脉，山间的狂风暴雨，似乎也认同我们从来没有听到过这般如此神秘的声音，自从

> 出身高贵的霍尔抚摸着竖琴，
> 还有温柔的卢埃林吟诗歌唱！

当我们在韦姆镇和什鲁斯伯里之间穿行时，我透过冬日的树梢看到蔚蓝色的天空，还有那在路旁高大挺拔的橡树上沙沙作响的红树叶，一个声音在我耳旁回荡，仿佛是塞壬的美妙歌声；我被如此迷人的歌声吓了一跳，我惊呆了，仿佛是从沉睡中惊醒。然而，我并没有意识到，我可以用五彩斑斓的意象或古雅的典故向他人表达我的钦佩之情；直到他天才的光芒照亮了我的心灵，犹如一缕阳光洒落在路旁的水洼里。那时的我，目瞪口呆，笨口拙舌，手足无措，就像是路边的蠕虫，破碎的躯体流淌着鲜血，奄奄一息。然而现在，我却从这致命的锁链中挣脱了出来，这个致命的锁链如同

> 冥河之水把我重重围了九道。

我的思想飘浮在长有翅膀的文字上，每当展开羽翼的时候，就会捕捉到岁月中金色的光芒。我的灵魂却依然处在原有锁链的束缚之中，黑暗，晦涩，依然充满了无限的渴望并处在毫无满足的追索之中。我的心就像是被锁在这粗俗的泥土牢笼里，从来没有打开过，好像永远找不到这样一个可以敞开倾诉的心房。然而，我现在的认知却不像以前那样保持着沉默、笨拙和愚钝，我终于找到了一种语言来表达自己；我得感谢柯勒律治，但这却不是我的目的。

我父亲居住在离什鲁斯伯里十英里的地方，按照附近的非国教派牧师互访的惯例，他经常与罗先生和住在九英里之外惠特教堂的詹金斯先生相

互拜访。这样他们就建立起了一种沟通的渠道，通过这个渠道，他们把民间文明和宗教自由的火种保存了下来，并维护和滋养着燃烧的火焰，生生不息，使之愈烧愈烈，就像古希腊埃斯库罗斯《阿伽门农》中的火焰，放置各处让其自由蔓延；足足等待了十年之久，才用像金字塔一般熊熊燃烧的火焰，向世人宣告特洛伊的毁灭。出于当地的礼节，作为罗先生的接班人，柯勒律治答应前来拜访我父亲；与此同时，在柯勒律治到达后的第一个星期天，我得去听他的布道。在这些颓废的日子里，一位诗人或者说是哲学家走上神体一位派的讲坛传播福音，这是一种浪漫，是对原始基督教精神的一种复兴，是不可抗拒的。

那是 1798 年 1 月一个冬天的清晨，天还没亮，我就起来了，在泥泞中走了十英里，去听这位名人布道。这是我一生中从来没有过的最漫长的一天，我再也不会像在 1798 年的冬天那样寒冷的天气里，在郊外进行如此极不舒服的徒步行走了……当我到达目的地的时候，管风琴正在演奏赞美诗篇第 100 首。唱诗完毕，柯勒律治先生起身，拿着准备好的经文，"他独自走进山里去祷告"。当他诵读经文时，他的声音犹如"一股浓郁而又纯正浓烈的香水"。当他说到最后"独自"两个字的时候，他声音洪亮、深沉，而且异常清晰。对那时还是个年轻人的我来说，这两个字的声音仿佛是发自心底深处的回响，他的祈祷仿佛是在寂静而又庄严的宇宙中飘荡。圣约翰的形象浮现在了我的脑海中，"一个人在旷野里哭泣，他的腰部系着腰带，他的食物是蝗虫和野蜂蜜"。接着，牧师就像一只鹰在风中嬉戏，很快便进入了主题。布道是关于和平与战争，教会与国家的——不是关于他们的联盟，而是关于他们的分离。因为，世俗的精神和基督教的精神——不是彼此相同，而是背道而驰的。他谈到了那些人"在血淋淋的旗帜上，把基督的十字架雕刻在上面"。他把我们带进了一个富有诗情画意的田园牧歌般的境界，为了向我们展示由于战争带来的致命影响，他用了一个鲜活的对比：一个天真的牧童驱赶着他的羊群来到了野外，坐在山茶树下，对着他的羊群吹着笛子，"好像他永远不会变老似的"；然而，就是这个可怜的乡下牧童，被绑架后带到了城里，在一家酒馆里被灌醉，后来变成了一个可怜的鼓手。他的头发上沾满了粉末和润发香油，在他的背后梳着一条长长的发辫；他穿着令人厌恶的华丽服饰，被这血腥行业的外表所欺骗了。

　　这就是我们曾经爱戴过的诗人所唱的词曲。

对我来说，倘若这时听到了天籁之音，我也不会有比这更加高兴的了。诗学与哲学相遇了，真理和天才在宗教管制的眼皮底下拥抱了。这甚至超出了我的希望，我非常满意地回到了家。太阳依旧挂在空中，似乎已经疲倦，显得苍白和暗淡，浓密的云雾遮挡住了太阳；这似乎是正义事业的象征。半挂在蓟叶上冷冰冰的露水珠，散发着亲切、清新的气息。大自然中，充满着青春的活力和希望，一切都将变得美好。当时，在大自然的面貌上并没有打上君权神授的烙印：

　　就像在那鲜艳的花朵上镌刻着悲伤。

　　接下来的星期二，这位颇有灵感的布道者来访了。我被召进他所在的房间，我去时，心里既高兴又害怕。他和蔼可亲地接待了我，我倾听着他的讲话，很长时间没有说一句话。在他看来，我的沉默并不是在受折磨。"那两个小时，"他后来高兴地说，"他是在和威廉·赫兹里特的前额交谈！"他的外表与我之前见到过的他似乎不一样。当时在远处，在教堂昏暗的灯光下，我觉得他身上有一种奇怪的野性，一种朦胧的晦涩，我还以为他得过天花。这次，他的皮肤又白又嫩，甚至还有光泽——

　　就像是那个在蔚蓝色光泽下的孩子。

他的前额又宽又高，像象牙制品一样光亮；他有一双凸出的大眉毛，在眉毛下面，滚动着一双深邃的黑眸，就像黑暗中闪烁着光泽的大海。"他的脸上洋溢着温柔"，正如我们在西班牙肖像画家牟利罗和委拉斯开兹所画的肖像画中看到的，在那苍白若有所思的脸上，有一种紫色的色调。他的嘴唇肥厚、丰满而且开阔，能言善辩；他的下巴圆得可爱；然而他的鼻子，作为脸部的主体和意志的标志，又小又软弱，与他的所作所为完全不相符合。他脸上显露出的才能似乎是从某一个观察的高度投射到了他的身上，并把他（具有的足够的能力和巨大的抱负）投射到了一个尚未开垦不为人知的思维和想象的世界里；在那里，没有任何东西可以支持和引导他，他的意志发挥不了任何的作用；就好像是哥伦布乘坐着大扇贝为新世界开辟一条冒险之路，既没有船桨也没有指南针。事后，我对此发表了一番评论。柯勒律治比一般人都要高，倾向于有点肥胖，或者像哈姆雷特勋爵一样，"有点胖，有点喘不过气来"。他的头发（当然现在，唉！已经变成灰白色的了），当时却是黑色的，就像乌鸦羽毛一般有光泽，整整齐齐地覆盖在他光滑的额头上⋯⋯

　　世上没有比主人和客人更加截然不同的两种人了。诗人对我父亲来说，并不是一种正当的职业；然而，任何能为神体一位派争光的人，对他来说他都欢迎。即使我们的客人长着翅膀，他也不会感到更加惊讶或更加高兴。其实，柯勒律治的思想就有一双翅膀。他柔和的声音在我们装饰着壁板的小客厅中回荡，我父亲摘下眼镜放在额头上，他那花白的头发和他的神采奕奕交融在了一起，还有他那粗犷而亲切的脸庞也露出了喜悦的微笑，以为真理在幻想中又找到了一个新的盟友⋯⋯这一天过得非常愉快。第二天早上，柯勒律治先生就要返回什鲁斯伯里了。当我下楼吃早餐时，发现他刚刚收到了他的朋友托马斯·韦奇伍德寄来的一封信，劝他放弃目前的选择以及现在的追求，让柯勒律治全身心投入到诗歌和哲学的研究中，他将会每年给他一百五十英镑的报酬。柯勒律治在系上一只鞋带时，仔细考虑着这个建议，似乎对这个提议已经做出了决定。这给他的离开更增添了一层阴影。这位任性的宗教的狂热者即将彻底地离开我们，他被抛进了迪尔河蜿蜒的山谷之中，或者说是古老浪漫的海岸上。他不再居住在附近十英里左右的地方，不再是什鲁斯伯里的一个非国教派牧师，从此以后，他就要居住在帕尔纳索斯山上，在这美丽的山中，成为一个牧羊人。唉！我真的不知道去那里的路，而且对韦奇伍德先生的慷慨并没有什么感激之情。但我很快就摆脱了困境，柯勒律治先生问我要了钢笔和墨水，然后走到一张桌子前，在一张卡片上写了点东西，迈着欢快的步伐向我走了过来，递给我这一珍贵的文件，并说这是他的地址：萨默塞特郡，下斯托伊，柯勒律治先生。他高兴地表示，愿意在几周后，在那里，能再次见到我，如果我愿意的话，他会到半途来接我。我当时的惊讶不亚于牧童看见一道霹雳落在他的脚下（借用《卡桑德拉》的比喻）。我结结巴巴尽量表达我的谢意，愉快地接受了他的邀请（我认为韦奇伍德先生的年薪和这比起来算不了什么，简直是微不足道）。把这件大事安排妥当以后，这位诗人传教士起身告辞了，我陪他走了六英里。这是一个隆冬美好晴朗的早晨，他一路走一路讲。乔叟笔下的学者被描述为"一路走一路唱"，柯勒律治也是这样。他从一个主题谈到另一个主题，时而高谈阔论，时而又有点走题，他仿佛飘游在空中，又仿佛在冰上滑行……我观察到他行走时，不断在人行道上从我的一侧越过我走到另一侧，这种奇怪的举动让我目瞪口呆。当时，我并没有把他与任何什么目的性不明确，以及不自觉的改变原则联系起来；从那以后，我才发现他似乎无法保持着直线行走……

在回来的路上，我耳旁有一种声音，那是幻想的声音；在我面前有一道光，闪现出诗歌的容貌；声音依然在我耳旁回响，而诗歌一直都没有离开过我的身边！柯勒律治实际上是在哲学基础层面上与我不期而遇，否则我就不应该会信服于他富有想象力的信条和教义。在我去拜访柯勒律治之前，我一直有种不安但却是愉快的感觉。在那几个月里，冬天的寒冷似乎是在欢迎着我；而春天的气息对我来说是如此清新，给我带来了安慰和不朽的灵感。金色的夕阳，夜晚的银星，照亮了我前行的方向，给了我新的希望和前景。我打算春天去拜访柯勒律治。这个想法一直在我的脑海里，从未忘记过，并与我所有的情感交织在了一起。在约定的时间快要到来的时候，我给他写了封信，并收到了他的回信，他要我把访问推迟一两个星期，并非常诚恳地教促我届时要履行诺言。他的推迟并没有使我垂头丧气，反而更加燃起了我的热情。与此同时，我去了兰戈伦谷，通过探索自然风景的奥秘来启迪自己，我必须说我对兰戈伦谷很着迷。我还读了柯勒律治那首优美的诗歌《告别颂》，我把他诗歌中对英格兰精彩的描述，应用在了我眼前的事物上，充满了爱意和亲切感。在某种意义上，那个河谷对我来说，就是新意识的摇篮；我的灵魂穿过那条蜿蜒曲折的环抱着兰戈伦谷的河流，在赫利孔山的山泉中接受了洗礼！

我回到家之后，兴致依然很高，很快就迈着轻盈的步伐又开始了新的旅程。我要穿过伍斯特和格洛斯特，经过阿普顿，在那里，我想到了汤姆·琼斯和他的"袖筒历险记"。我记得有一天，我浑身淋得透湿，在一家旅店住了下来（我记得是在蒂克斯伯里），然后彻夜坐在那里，阅读《保罗和薇吉妮》。阵雨淋湿了我年少青春的身体，那是多么惬意，就连滴落在我阅读过的书页上那可怜的水珠，也是甜蜜的……我比预定到达的时间早到了两天，因为我很早就动身了，为了给自己留有足够的时间。我在布里奇沃特逗留了两天，在泥泞的河岸上闲逛，累了就回到旅店，埋头阅读《卡米拉》。这些天，我逍遥自在地生活，阅读书籍，看看画册，欣赏戏剧；倾听、思考，并记下最让我高兴的事情。我只想要一件事让我快乐；实际上，想要得到那件事就是想要得到一切！

我到了柯勒律治那里，受到了很好的款待。下斯托伊附近的乡村很美，那儿有绿色的原野和连绵起伏的丘陵，靠近海滨。时隔二十年之后，就在几天前，我又从汤顿附近的一座小山上与之遥遥相望了。我人生的蓝图就如同我脚下这片乡村的地图，展现在眼前，如此相像！下午，柯勒律治带我去了埃尔福克斯顿，这是圣·奥宾斯家族一处浪漫主义风格的古老宅邸，诗人华兹华斯就住在这里，当时是诗人的一位朋友拥有的私人财产，这位朋友让诗人自由使用家中所有的一切。不知何故，那个时期正值法国大革命刚刚结束不久，并不是一个什么都免费给予的时代。随着思想的放开，在我们的私利掩饰下，那些柔弱的一面可能就会从每个人的内心深处显露出来。华兹华斯本人不在家，由他的妹妹负责管家，她为我们安排了一顿简单的饭菜。我们可以随便翻阅欣赏她哥哥的诗歌集《抒情歌谣集》，这些还只是手稿或者说像《西比林树叶》那样的形式；我带着一个初学者的信仰，仔细翻阅了其中几首，心满意足。那天晚上，我睡在一间挂着蓝色帷幔的旧式房间里，墙上挂着乔治一世和二世时代圆形家庭肖像画。我透过窗户，可以俯瞰相邻公园里树木茂密的斜坡，黎明时分，可以"听到雄鹿的大声交谈"……

那天早上，一用完早餐，我们就到公园里漫步，坐在一棵沿着地面伸展的老梣树的树干上，柯勒律治用那铿锵有力而悦耳的声音大声朗读华兹华斯的诗歌《贝蒂·福伊》。对此，我没有做任何的评论也没有任何的怀疑。当我从诗歌中看到了对真理和自然的探讨时，其余的一切都是那么顺理成章。然而，在《荆棘》《疯狂的母亲》《一个可怜的印度女人的抱怨》中，我感受到了更深层次的力量和悲怆，这一点后来得到了公认：

尽管如此骄傲，但却在违背着真理。

这才是这个作者的特点。诗歌中出现了一种新的风格和一种新的精神，我感受到了。这对我来说是从新鲜土壤里滋生的，带来了新春令人愉快的气息。

虽然，这是翻天覆地的一年，
还未经验证。

那天傍晚，柯勒律治和我，在走回斯托伊的路上，他高声朗诵着：

天意，预知，意志和命运；

命运是注定的，意志是自由的，预知是绝对的。

我们穿过充满着回声的小树林，经过仙境般的溪流和瀑布，在夏日的月光下，像一条银色的绸带在闪烁！柯勒律治感叹华兹华斯并不太愿意相信这个地方的迷信传说，因此在他的诗歌里，总是带有那么一些真实存在的物质，常常依附于可以看得见也可以触摸得到的东西，或是琐碎的细节。他的天才并不是从天而降，由上帝赐给他的灵感；而是像花朵一样从大地上生长出来的，在绿色的花枝上绽放，上面还有飞舞的金翅雀在歌唱。然后，他接着说（如果我没有记错的话），华兹华斯这种缺陷仅局限于他的描述性的文章，在他的哲理性的诗歌中，却带有一种宏伟而又完整的精神。所以，这就使他的灵魂似乎像宫殿一样栖息在宇宙之中，他是通过直觉而不是通过演绎去发现真理的。第二天，华兹华斯从布里斯托尔来到柯勒律治的小别墅。至今，我想我还记得当时见到他的情景。华兹华斯的外表在某种程度上，很像柯勒律治描述的那样，然而他却显得更加憔悴，像堂吉诃德。在那个服装不受拘束的时代，他的穿着显得古怪离奇，他穿着一件棕色的绒布夹克和有条纹的长裤。他走路时有点左右摇晃，走走停停，和他诗歌中的人物彼得·贝尔没什么两样。他的两鬓由于承受着沉重的思想压力而显得疲惫不堪，他的眼睛闪烁着光芒（好像可以透过事物的外表看到内在的本质），他的前额又高又窄，还有一个罗马人的鼻子，他的脸颊由于强烈的意志和情感而布满皱纹，嘴角带有一种抽搐，似乎在微笑，与脸上那庄严肃穆的神态大不一样。在钱特里为他雕塑的半身塑像中，本想有着这些标志性的特征，却被他戏弄并制作成了中规中矩和笨拙的形象。在《基督进入耶路撒冷》这幅画中，海登所画的他的头像最能表现他那低头深思的神情。他端坐着，自然而又毫无拘束地说着话，在他的声音里夹杂着一种清晰、热情洋溢混合的口音；一种厚重的喉音并带有一种浓重的北方特有的小舌音，就像是葡萄酒里掺杂了葡萄皮……

　　第二天，我们又去了埃尔福克斯顿。华兹华斯在户外露天的场地为我们朗读了《彼得·贝尔》的故事。他的评价呈现在他的脸上和声音之中，与后来的一些评论家的评论截然不同！无论人们对这首诗歌的想法怎样，"他的面部表情就是一本书，人们可以从他的面部表情里，读到各种稀奇古怪的故事"，他的语调预示了他诗中这位主人公的命运。在柯勒律治和华兹华斯的朗诵中，都有一种神圣感，像咒语一样，常常会使听众着迷，从而失去了自己的判断力。也许，他们习惯用这种模棱两可的方式来欺骗自己。柯勒律治的风格充满了热情，更有生气，富于变化；而华兹华斯则比较稳重平和，持久和内敛。前者可能被称为更富于戏剧性，而另一位则更富于抒情。柯勒律治曾经告诉我，他喜欢在崎岖不平坦的地面上行走，或者在灌木丛中行走作诗；然而，华兹华斯在创作时，如果可以的话，他总是会在一条笔直平坦的砾石小路上徘徊着，或者就是在某个不受任何干扰、可以连续创作的地方……

On the Feeling of Immortality in Youth

No young man believes he shall ever die. It was a saying of my brother's, and a fine one. There is a feeling of Eternity in youth, which makes us amends for everything. To be young is to be as one of the Immortals. One half of time indeed is spent—the other half remains in store for us, with all its countless treasures, for there is no line drawn, and we see no limit to our hopes and wishes. We make the coming age our own—

'**The vast, the unbounded** prospect lies before us.'

Death, old age, are words without a meaning, a dream, a fiction, with which we have nothing to do. Others may have undergone, or may still undergo them—we '**bear a charmed life**,' which laughs to scorn all such idle fancies. As, in setting out on a delightful journey, we strain our eager sight forward,

'**Bidding the lovely scenes** at distance hail,'

and see no end to prospect after prospect, new objects presenting themselves as we advance, in the outset of life we see no end to our desires nor to the opportunities of gratifying them. We have as yet found no obstacle, no disposition to flag, and it seems that we can go on so for ever. We look round in a new world, full of life and motion, and ceaseless progress, and feel in ourselves all the vigour and spirit to keep pace with it, and do not foresee from any present signs how we shall be left behind in the race, decline into old age, and drop into the grave. It is the simplicity and, as it were, abstractedness of our feelings in youth that (so to speak) identifies us with nature and (our experience being weak and our passions strong) makes us fancy ourselves immortal like it. Our short-lived connection with being, we fondly flatter ourselves, is an indissoluble and lasting union. As infants smile and sleep, we are rocked in the cradle of our desires, and hushed into fancied security by the roar of the universe around us—we quaff the cup of life with eager thirst without draining it, and joy and hope seem ever mantling to the brim—objects press around us, filling the mind with their magnitude and with the throng of desires that wait upon them, so that there is no room for the thoughts of death. We are too much dazzled by the gorgeousness and novelty of the bright waking dream about us to discern the dim shadow lingering for us in the distance. Nor would the hold that life has taken of us permit us to detach our thoughts that way, even if we could. We are too much absorbed in present objects and pursuits. While the spirit of youth remains unimpaired, ere '**the wine of life is drunk**,' we are like people intoxicated or in a fever, who are hurried away by the violence of their own sensations: it is only as present objects begin to pall upon the sense, as we have been disappointed in our favourite pursuits, cut off from our closest ties, that we by degrees become weaned from the world, that passion loosens its hold upon futurity, and that we begin to contemplate **as in a glass darkly** the possibility of parting with it for good. Till then, the example of others has no effect upon us. Casualties we avoid; the slow approaches of age we play at *hide and seek* with. Like **the foolish fat scullion** in Sterne, who hears that Master Bobby is dead, our only reflection is, 'so am not I!' The idea of death, instead of staggering our confidence, only seems to strengthen and enhance our sense of the possession and enjoyment of life. Others may fall around us like leaves, or be mowed down by the scythe of Time like grass: these are but metaphors to the unreflecting, buoyant ears and overweening presumption of youth. It is not till we see the flowers of Love, Hope, and Joy withering around us, that we give up the flattering delusions that before led us on, and that the emptiness and dreariness of the prospect before us reconciles us hypothetically to the silence of the grave.

Life is indeed a strange gift, and its privileges are most mysterious. No wonder when it is first granted to us, that our gratitude, our admiration, and our delight should prevent us from reflecting on our own nothingness, or from thinking it will ever be recalled. Our first and strongest impressions are borrowed from the mighty scene that is opened to us, and we unconsciously transfer its durability as well as its splendour to ourselves. So newly found, we cannot think of parting with it yet, or at least put off that consideration ***sine die***. Like a rustic at a fair, we are full of amazement and rapture, and have no thought of going home, or that it will soon be night. We know our existence only by ourselves and confound our knowledge with the objects of it. We and Nature are therefore one. Otherwise the illusion, the '**feast of reason** and the flow of soul,' to which we are invited, is a mockery and a cruel insult. We do not go from a play till the last act is ended, and the lights are about to be extinguished. But the fairy face of Nature still shines on: shall we be called away before the curtain falls, or ere we have scarce had a glimpse of what is going on? Like children, our stepmother Nature holds us up to see the **raree-show** of the universe, and then, as if we were a burden to her to support, lets us fall down again. Yet what **brave sublunary things** does not this pageant present, like a ball or *fête* of the universe!

To see the golden sun, the azure sky, the outstretched ocean; to walk upon the green earth, and be lord of a thousand creatures; to look down yawning precipices or over distant sunny vales; to see the world spread out under one's feet on a map; to bring the stars near; to view the smallest insects through a microscope; to read history, and consider the revolutions of empire and the successions of generations; to hear of the glory of **Tyre**, of **Sidon**, of **Babylon**, and of **Susa**, and to say all these were before me and are now nothing; to say I exist in such a point of time, and in such a point of space; to be a spectator and a part of its ever-moving scene; to witness the change of seasons, of spring and autumn, of winter and summer; to feel hot and cold, pleasure and pain, beauty and deformity, right and wrong; to be sensible to the accidents of nature; to consider **the mighty world of eye and ear**; to listen to **the stock-dove's notes** amid the forest deep; to journey over moor and mountain; to hear the midnight sainted choir; to visit lighted halls, or the cathedral's gloom, or sit in crowded theatres and see life itself mocked; to study the works of art and refine the sense of beauty to agony; to worship fame, and to dream of immortality; to look upon the Vatican, and to read Shakespeare; to gather up the wisdom of the ancients, and to pry into the future; to listen to the trump of war, the shout of victory; to question history as to the movements of the human heart; to seek for truth; to plead the cause of humanity; to **overlook the world** as if time and Nature poured their treasures at our feet—to be and to do all this, and then in a moment to be nothing—to have it all snatched from us as by a juggler's trick or a phantasmagoria! There is something in this transition from all to nothing that shocks us and damps the enthusiasm of youth new flushed with hope and pleasure, and we cast the comfortless thought as far from us as we can. In the first enjoyment of the estate of life we discard the fear of debts and duns, and never think of the final payment of out great debt to Nature. **Art**, we know, **is long**; life, we flatter ourselves, should be so too. We see no end of the difficulties and delays we have to encounter: perfection is slow of attainment, and we must have time to accomplish it in. The fame of the great names we look up to is immortal: and shall not we who contemplate it imbibe a portion of ethereal fire, the *divina particula aurae*, which nothing can extinguish? A wrinkle in **Rembrandt** or in Nature takes whole days to **resolve itself** into its component parts, its softenings and its sharpnesses; we refine upon our perfections, and unfold the intricacies of Nature. What a prospect for the future! What a task have we not begun! And shall we be arrested in the middle of it? We do not count our time thus employed lost, or our pains thrown away; we do not flag or grow tired, but gain new vigour at our endless task. Shall Time, then, grudge us to finish what we have begun, and have formed a compact with Nature to do? Why not fill up the blank that is left us in this manner? I have looked for hours at a Rembrandt without being conscious of the flight of time, but with ever new wonder and delight, have thought that not only my own but another existence I could pass in the same manner. This rarefied, refined existence seemed to have no end, nor stint, nor principle of decay in it. The print would remain long after I who looked on it had become the prey of worms. The thing seems in itself out of all reason: health, strength, appetite are opposed to the idea of death, and we are not ready to credit it till we have found our illusions vanished and our hopes grown cold. Objects in youth, from novelty, etc., are stamped upon the brain with such force and integrity that one thinks nothing can remove or obliterate them. They are riveted there, and appear to us as an element of our nature. It must be a mere violence that destroys them, not a natural decay. In the very strength of this persuasion we seem to enjoy an age by anticipation. We melt down years into a single moment of intense sympathy, and by anticipating the fruits defy the ravages of time. If, then, a single moment of our lives is worth years, shall we set any limits to its total value and extent? Again, does it not happen that so secure do we think ourselves of an indefinite period of existence, that at times, when left to ourselves, and impatient of novelty, we feel annoyed at what seems to us the slow and creeping progress of time, and argue that if it always moves at this tedious snail's pace it will never come to an end? How ready are we to sacrifice any space of time which separates us from a favourite object, little thinking that before long we shall find it move too fast.

For my part, **I started in life with the French Revolution**, and I have lived, alas! to see the end of it. But I did not foresee this result. My sun arose with the first dawn of liberty, and I did not think how soon both must set. The new impulse to ardour given to men's minds imparted a congenial warmth and glow to mine; we were strong to run a race together, and I little dreamed that long before mine was set, the sun of liberty would turn to blood, or set once more in the night of despotism. Since then, I confess, I have no longer felt myself young, for with that my hopes fell.

I have since turned my thoughts to gathering up some of the fragments of my early recollections, and putting them into a form to which I might occasionally revert. The future was barred to my progress, and I turned for consolation and encouragement to the past. It is thus that, while we find our personal and substantial identity vanishing from us, we strive to gain a reflected and vicarious one in our thoughts: we do not like to perish wholly, and wish to bequeath our names, at least, to posterity. As long as we can make our cherished thoughts and nearest interests live in the minds of others, we do not appear to have retired altogether from the stage. We still occupy the breasts of others, and exert an influence and power over them, and it is only our bodies that are reduced to dust and powder. Our favourite speculations still find encouragement, and we make as great a figure in the eye of the world, or perhaps a greater, than in our lifetime. The demands of our self-love are thus satisfied, and these are the most imperious and unremitting. Besides, if by our intellectual superiority we survive ourselves in this world, by our virtues and faith we may

attain an interest in another and a higher state of being, and may thus
be recipients at the same time of men and of angels.

> '**E'en from the tomb** the voice of Nature cries.
>
> E'en in our ashes live their wonted fires.'

As we grow old, our sense of the value of time becomes vivid.
Nothing else, indeed, seems of any consequence. We can never
cease wondering that that which has ever been should cease to be.
We find many things remain the same: why, then, should there be
change in us. This adds a convulsive grasp of whatever is, a sense
of a fallacious hollowness in all we see. Instead of the full, pulpy
feeling of youth, tasting existence and every object in it, all is flat
and vapid,—a whited sepulchre, fair without, but full of ravening
and all uncleanness within. The world is a witch that puts us off
with false shows and appearances. The simplicity of youth, the
confiding expectation, the boundless raptures, are gone; we only
think of getting out of it as well as we can, and without any great
mischance or annoyance. The flush of illusion, even the complacent
retrospect of past joys and hopes, is over: if we can slip out of life
without indignity, can escape with little bodily infirmity, and frame
our minds to the calm and respectable composure of *still-life* before
we return to physical nothingness, it is as much as we can expect. We
do not die wholly at our deaths: we have mouldered away gradually
long before. Faculty after faculty, interest after interest, attachment
after attachment, disappear: we are torn from ourselves while living,
year after year sees us no longer the same, and death only consigns

the last fragment of what we were to the grave. That we should wear out by slow stages, and dwindle at last into nothing, is not wonderful, when even in our prime our strongest impressions leave little trace but for the moment, and we are the creatures of petty circumstance. How little effect is made on us in our best days by the books we have read, the scenes we have witnessed, the sensations we have gone through! Think only of the feelings we experience in reading a fine romance (one of **Sir Walter**'s, for instance); what beauty, what sublimity, what interest, what heart-rending emotions! You would suppose the feelings you then experienced would last for ever, or subdue the mind to their own harmony and tone: while we are reading, it seems as if nothing could ever put us out of our way or trouble us:—the first splash of mud that we get on entering the street, the first twopence we are cheated out of, the feeling vanishes clean out of our minds, and we become the prey of petty and annoying circumstance. The mind soars to the lofty: it is at home in the grovelling, the disagreeable, and the little. And yet we wonder that age should be feeble and querulous,—that the freshness of youth should fade away. Both worlds would hardly satisfy the extravagance of our desires and of our presumption.

Notes

This essay exists in two forms. It first appeared in the *Monthly Magazine* for March, 1827 and was revised and republished, after Hazlitt's death, in the *Literary Remains*. Here the revised version is used. One of the most famous of Hazlitt's essays it excels in the beauty of its style, the facility of its expression as well as in the author's glowing sentiments on the question of youth, age, and death.

'The vast, the unbounded,' etc. An adaptation from Addison's *Cato*, Act V, scene i: 'The wide, the unbounded prospect, lies before me.'

'bear a charmed life.' From *Macbeth*, Act V, scene viii, line 12.

'Bidding the lovely scenes,' etc. From Collins' 'Ode on the Passions,' line 32: 'And bade the lovely scenes at distance hail!'

'the wine of life is drunk.' From *Macbeth*, Act II, scene iii, line 100: 'The wine of life is drawn.' It means everything that gives zest to existence is gone.

as in a glass darkly. From *I Corinthians*, xiii, 12.

the foolish fat scullion. From Laurence Sterne, *Tristram Shandy*, Book V, Chapter 7.

sine die (Latin), without date; to an indefinite time.

'feast of reason,' etc. From Pope's *Imitations of Horace*, Satire I, line 128. The whole phrase means intellectual talk and genial conversation.

raree-show, a cheap show carried about in a box and exhibited on streets and at fairs.

brave sublunary things. From Michael Drayton's 'To Henry Reynolds': 'Those brave translunary things.' Here 'brave' means 'splendid.'

Tyre, one of the most important cities of Phoenicia, noted at one time for its magnificence and luxury.

Sidon, or *Saida* in Arabic, an ancient city of Phoenicia.

Babylon, the celebrated city, now in ruins, about 55 miles south of Bagdad.

Susa, the royal Persian palace.

the mighty world of eye and ear. From William Wordsworth, 'Tintern Abbey,' line 105.

the stock-dove's notes, etc. From James Thomson: *The Castle of Indoleuce*,

Book 1, stanza 4:

'Or stockdoves' plain amid the forest deep.'

overlook the world, have prospect of the world from above.

Art is long. Compare the Latin proverb, 'Ars longa, wita breva.' (Art is long, life is short.)

divina particula aurae (Latin), particles of divine air.

Rembrandt (1606—1669), a great Dutch painter; here it refers to his picture.

resolve itself, break up into fragments.

I started in life with the French Revolution. Hazlitt was one of the enthusiastic supporters of the French Revolution and of Napoleon. He was almost heartbroken at the news of Waterloo.

'E'en from the tomb,' etc. From Gray's 'Elegy on a Country Churchyard,' lines 91—92.

Sir Walter, Sir Walter Scott (1771—1832), the greatest English master of historical romance.

【作品简介】

这篇散文有两个版本。1827 年 3 月，初次见于《月刊》杂志，在赫兹里特去世后，又经过修改，由《文学遗产》再版。这里选用的是修订版。这是赫兹里特最著名的散文之一，其优美的风格，娴熟的表现手法，以及作者在讨论青年、老年和死亡问题时所表现出来的炽热的情感都具有代表性。

【作品解析】

"The vast, the unbounded," etc.：此句改编自艾迪生的《卡托》第五幕第一场："展现在我眼前的是广阔无垠的前景。"

"bear a charmed life": "冥冥之中有神灵保佑", 出自《麦克白》第五幕第八场第 12 行。

"Bidding the lovely scenes," etc.: 此句出自柯林斯的《激情颂》第 32 行: "And bade the lovely scenes at distance hail（向远方的美景致敬）!"

"the wine of life is drunk": 此句出自《麦克白》第二幕第三场, 第 100 行: "The wine of life is drawn（生命之酒已经饮尽）。"这里指激情赋予的一切都已消失了。

as in a glass darkly: 此句出自《哥林多前书》第 13 章。

the foolish fat scullion: 愚蠢的胖子。出自劳伦斯·斯特恩的著作《项狄传》第五卷第七章。

sine die（拉丁语）: 没有时间, 永恒。

"feast of reason," etc.: 此句摘自蒲柏的诗集《仿贺拉斯》讽刺诗第一篇第 128 行。整个短语意指理智和友好的交谈。

raree-show: 在街上和集市上展出一种装在盒子里的廉价表演（西洋镜）。

brave sublunary things: 出自迈克尔·德雷顿的《致亨利·雷诺兹》: "Those brave translunary things（那些绚丽璀璨的景象）。"这里"brave"意为灿烂精彩的, 壮观的。

Tyre: 提尔, 腓尼基最重要的城市之一, 曾经以其雄伟和奢华而闻名。

Sidon: 阿拉伯语又作 Saida, 西顿, 腓尼基的一座古城。

Babylon: 巴比伦, 曾经名噪一时的城市, 现已成为一片废墟, 在巴格达以南 55 英里处。

Susa: 苏萨, 波斯皇宫。

the mighty world of eye and ear: 凭视觉和听觉所感受到的强大的世界。出自威廉·华兹华斯《丁登寺》第 105 行。

the stock-dove's notes, etc.: 此句出自詹姆斯·汤姆逊的《懒惰城堡》第一卷第四节: "森林深处鸥鸽在鸣唱。"

overlook the world: 俯瞰世界, 从高处展望世界。

Art is long: 与拉丁谚语 "Ars longa, wita breva"（艺术是无限的, 生命是短暂的）相似。

divina particula aurae（拉丁语）：英文为"particles of divine air"，神灵特有的光环。

Rembrandt：伦勃朗（1606—1669），著名的荷兰画家；这里指的是他的作品。

resolve itself：把自己分解成几个部分。

I started in life with the French Revolution：赫兹里特是法国大革命和拿破仑的狂热支持者之一。听到滑铁卢的消息，他几乎心碎了。

"E'en from the tomb," etc.：此句出自格雷《墓畔哀歌》，第 91—92 行。

Sir Walter：沃尔特·司各特爵士（1771—1832），英国历史上最伟大的浪漫主义大师。

【参考译文】

论青春不朽之感

没有一个年轻人相信他会死去。这是我哥哥的一句话，也是一句很美妙的话。年轻时，有种永恒的感觉，它使我们改变了对一切事物的看法，并让我们觉得有的是时间可以弥补这一切。只要年轻就会充满着活力。确实，我们生命中一半的时间已然飘逝，但还有另一半的时间仍然为我们储备着无数的宝藏，生命没有界限，我们仍然会有无限的希望和愿望。我们将把未来的时代变成属于我们自己的时代——

广阔无垠的前景，就摆在我们的面前。

死亡，老年；这些词对我们来说没有丝毫意义，就像一个梦，一部虚构的小说，都与我们无关。这样的事情其他人可能已经经历过，或许正在经历着，然而，我们在"冥冥之中有神灵保佑"，对于那些虚无缥缈的幻想予以讥讽。我们就像刚刚踏上一段愉快的旅程，把热切的目光投向远方，

> 向远方的美景致敬！

美景一个接着一个，新生事物在我们生命的进程中不断地呈现出来。在生命之初，我们的欲望没有尽头，也没有机会去满足欲望。到目前为止，我们还没有发现有任何迹象可以阻碍我们前进，似乎我们永远都可以这样下去。眺望四周，我们生活在一个充满着生机，有着活力，不断进步的新世界里，我们自信有足够的精力和勇气与之保持一致。我们现在预见不到有任何迹象表明我们会在与大自然的竞赛中落后、衰老，最后坠入坟墓。简而言之，正是我们年轻时情感的专注，把我们与大自然联系在了一起，我们的经验是脆弱的、有限的，我们的情感却是强烈的，让我们幻想自己也像大自然一样，将会不朽和永恒。我们只是短暂的存在，在与大自然的接触中，我们还自鸣得意以为这是牢不可破的持久联盟。我们就像是在这欲望的摇篮里，被轻轻地摇晃着；在周围宇宙的咆哮声中安静下来，进入了梦幻般的平安之中，像婴儿一样带着微笑入睡——我们如饥似渴地捧着生命之杯，也无法饮尽杯中的琼浆玉液；欢乐和希望似乎在不断地溢出杯子的边缘——围绕在我们身边的万物，用它们巨大的琼浆玉液伴随着欲望的涌动，一并充斥着我们的心灵，等待我们去品尝，使我们没有思考死亡的时间和空间。当我们从美梦中清醒之后，华丽和新奇的梦境把我们弄得眼花缭乱，使我们无法分辨远处萦绕着的朦胧的阴影；即使我们可以分辨，生活对我们的束缚也不允许我们分散思想，我们太过于专注和追求眼前的事与物了。当青春的活力依然旺盛没有受到损伤，在"生命之酒"尚未饮尽之前，我们就像是醉汉和发着高烧的人一样，被自己强烈的情感和可怕的力量驱使着；只有当我们对自己喜爱的追求感到失望，对眼前的事

物感到厌倦，切断我们与最亲密关系之间的联系，渐渐地与外界断绝了来往时，我们才会逐渐脱离整个世界，对未来的激情也渐渐地悄然逝去，我们才开始像是在模糊不清的玻璃中一样沉思是否有可能永远离开这个世界。在这之前，其他人的例子对我们没有任何影响。我们竭尽全力躲避伤亡；为了减缓衰老的步伐，我们与年龄玩起了捉迷藏。就像斯特恩笔下那个愚蠢的胖仆人，当她听说主人博比死了，唯一的反应是："我还活着！"死亡的观念不但不会动摇我们的信心，反而会增强我们对生命的占有并提升我们享受生活的乐趣。其他人可能会像树叶一样落在我们的身边，或者像青草一样被时间的镰刀割了下来，这些在那些不思进取、固执己见、狂妄自大的年轻人眼里，不过都是比喻。直到我们看到了爱、希望和欢乐的花朵在我们身边凋谢，我们才会放弃曾经引导我们前行的这般迷人的谄媚妄想；直到想起未来前景的空虚和凄凉，才会使我们勉强想起坟墓里的寂寞。

生命确实是一份奇特的礼物，它的特权又是最不可思议的。难怪当我们第一次被赋予了生命的时候，我们的感激、我们的钦佩和我们的喜悦，使我们忘却了对自己曾经只是虚无的反思，或者说，我们从未思考过被赋予的生命还是会被永远召回。当我们第一次感受到外界最强烈的印象是来自向我们敞开的壮丽景色时，我们无意识地将它的持久和华丽转移到了我们自己的身上。那么新的发现，我们还不能考虑与其分开，或者至少可以把这种考虑无限期推迟。就像在集市上的乡下人一样，我们充满了惊喜，甚至不想回家，不知不觉很快就到了晚上。我们只知道自己的存在，并把我们所了解的知识和大自然中的其他物体混淆了起来。这样说吧，似乎我们和大自然乃为一体。否则，我们受邀参加"理性的盛宴和心灵的交流"就是一种嘲讽，一种残忍的侮辱。我们看戏总是要从第一场戏开始，直到最后一幕结束，灯光即将熄灭，才会离去。然而大自然仙女般的容貌依然闪烁着光芒，我们应该在帷幕落下之前，或者说是在我们还没有看明白剧情之前，就得被召唤离开吗？我们就像孩子一样，在我们的继母大自然的怀抱里，看到了宇宙间各种各样稀有的景象。然后，大自然似乎觉察到我们是她的负担，于是悄然地再次把我们放了下来，不再理睬我们了。还有什么尘世间的炫丽景象没有在这场盛宴上呈现！仿佛就是宇宙中的一场盛装舞会或庆典！

　　我们看着金色的太阳，蔚蓝的天空和一望无际的海洋；我们行走在绿色的大地上，成为万物的主宰；我们俯瞰悬崖峭壁或眺望着阳光明媚的山谷；我们展开地图，去看在脚下延伸的世界；我们把星辰拉近；我们在显微镜下观察微小的昆虫；我们阅读历史，思考着帝国的革命和世代相传；我们倾听提尔、西顿、巴比伦和苏萨的荣耀，它们曾经名噪一时，并向世人感叹：这一切都是发生在我出生之前的，现在早已荡然无存；我们要说，存在于这样一个时代和这样一个空间，我们既是一名旁观者，也是场景变幻中的一分子；我们见证一年四季春夏秋冬的变化更迭；我们感受冷与暖、快乐与痛苦、美丽与丑陋、真理与谬论；我们对大自然意外事件要有敏锐的洞察力，时刻用眼睛和耳朵去感受思考这浩瀚的世界；我们聆听森林深处鸥鸽在鸣唱；我们穿越荒野翻过高山；我们倾听午夜的圣歌；我们参观灯火辉煌的殿堂或幽静而昏暗的教堂；或者我们坐在拥挤的剧院里，体验生活在戏剧中被嘲弄的滋味；我们研究艺术作品，从美感中提炼出痛苦；我们崇拜名望，梦想永生和不朽；我们仰望梵蒂冈，阅读莎士比亚；我们收集古人的智慧，窥探未来；我们倾听战争的号角和胜利的欢呼；我们从探究"人心活动"去质疑历史；我们去寻求真理；去为人类的事业而辩护；我们俯瞰世界，就好像时间和大自然将它们的财富倾注在了我们的脚下，让我们去做并完成这所有的一切；然而，却在瞬间化为乌有，变成虚无缥缈——就像是一个千变万化的魔术师使用神奇的幻觉手法从我们手中夺走了一切！在这种从拥有一切到一无所有的突如其来的转变中，有些东西使我们感到震惊，挫伤了青年人那种充满希望和欢乐的热情，我们只能把各种不安的想法尽可能地抛弃到远离我们的地方。在最初享受生命和财富的欢乐中，我们抛弃了对债务和债主的恐惧，从未思考过最终我们将要偿还给大自然的会有多么庞大。我们知道，艺术是无限的；于是，我们自命不凡地认为，生命也应该如此——是无限的。我们清楚地看到，我们遇到的困难和拖延的时间是无穷无尽的。完美则是一种缓慢造就的过程，我们必须要有足够的时间去完成。我们所敬仰的伟大人物是永垂不朽的，难道我们不应该深思一下，是否可以吸收一部分神圣的火焰？那是神灵特有的光环，任何力量都不可能将它熄灭。在伦勃朗笔下的每一道褶皱，都需要花上一整天的时间才能将其分解成几个部分，有的部分笔锋柔和，有的部分尖锐犀利，或者说自然界中也是这样，我们应当在追求完美、精益求精的过程中，展现大自然的错综复杂。这是多么美好的未来！这项伟大的任务我们尚未开始！难道会在中途被阻止吗？我们不计较由此而浪费的时间，或者，也不计较由此而付出的都是徒劳；我们不会停滞不前或感到厌倦，而是在这项永无止境的任务中，获得新的活力。那么，时间会不会认为我们不应该去完成我们已经开始的并与大自然早已形成一种契约的这项伟大的任务呢？为什么不能像这样去填写留给我们的空白呢？我看着伦勃朗的画，几个小时过去了，没有意识到时间的流逝，却有了前所未有的新的惊奇和喜悦，我认为，我不仅可以让自己存在，而且我还可以通过用同样的方式有另一种存在。这种高深莫测、精致高雅的存在似乎没有尽头，没有限制，也没有腐朽的原则。在看过这幅画的我成为蠕虫的猎物之后，这幅画依然会保存很久。这件事情的本身看起来似乎没有任何理由与其他有紧密的关联，就好像要么是健康，要么是能量，要么是食欲，这些都与死亡的观念相悖，直到我们发现幻想消失，希望变得渺茫时，我们才会有意识地去相信这点。年轻时接触到的新生事物，由于新奇等原因，都会在人们的脑海里留下这样强有力且完整的记忆，以至于人们认为没有任何东西可以将它们消除或将它们抹去。这些事物深深地刻在了我们的心里，成为我们天性中的一部分，它们不会自然消失，必须用纯粹的暴力，才能将其抹去。在这种强有力的说服下，我们似乎是在提前享受着一个即将到来的时代。我们将多年的光阴融进了具有强烈同情心的一瞬间，期待着果实的到来，抵御时间的摧残。如果我们生命中的每一刻都拥有数年的岁月，那么我们是否应该对生命的总价值和范围加以限制呢？同样的道理，难道说我们不也是这样认为自己生命的存在是毫无期限的吗？有时，当我们想要独处并对新鲜事物感到不耐烦时，我们对时间缓慢地行进感到恼怒并为此争论，如果生命总是以这种枯燥乏味蜗牛式的速度前行，那么生命将永远不会结束吗？我们是否已做好了准备割舍任何将我们与我们最喜欢的事物分离开来的那些时空？倘若这样，不久我们就会发现，我们生命中的时空移动得太快了。

就我而言，我是出生在法国大革命的时代。我生存下来了，唉！我一直看到法国大革命的结束。然而，我却没有预见到这个结局。我心中的太阳随着自由的第一缕曙光冉冉升起，但我没想到，这两个太阳很快就落了下来。人们心中新的热情冲动，也赋予了我一种亲切的温暖和阳光。我们变得坚强起来，共同参与了这场角逐，我做梦也没想到，在我心中的太阳没有落下之前，自由的太阳转变成了血色，在专制独裁的黑夜中再次落下。从那时起，我必须承认，我已经不再觉得自己年轻了，因为我的希望随之而破灭了。

从那时起，我把思绪转移到收集一些早期记忆的片段上，并把它们变成一种形式，以便日后可以偶尔回忆。未来阻碍了我向前发展，我就只好转向过去寻找安慰和鼓励。正是这样，当我们发现我们的个性和生命特征就要从我们的身上消失时，我们就会在我们的思想中努力寻找一个有反应的替代品：我们不喜欢彻底消失，至少希望能把我们的名字留给后代。只要我们能够将我们所珍惜的思想和毕生所爱在他人心中留有念想，似乎我们就不会完全退出舞台。我们仍然可以占据着他人的心房，并对他们产生强有力的影响，只有我们的身体才会化为尘埃和灰烬。我们所偏爱的猜想仍然会得到鼓励，我们在世人的眼中还算是一个伟大的人物，或许比我们生前更加伟大。于是，我们的自尊就这样得到了满足，这些是我们最骄傲的，也是我们最坚持不懈的。此外，如果我们凭借智力上的优势就能在这个世界上得以生存，凭借我们的美德和信仰，我们会以另一种更高的形象对他人产生影响，从而可以同时受到人类和天使的青睐。

坟墓里传出大自然的哭泣声，
我们虽然化作了灰烬，生命依然在熊熊的火焰中延续。

随着年龄的增长，我们对时间价值的认知变得越来越真切。确实，其他一切事物似乎对我们没有任何影响。我们永远不会停止怀疑那些曾经存在过的事物会突然消失。我们发现很多事物都是一成不变的，那么我们为什么要改变呢？这让我们对一切事物产生了一种惊慌失措的感觉，想把它们牢牢地抓在手中，我们所看到的一切事物，似乎都有一种虚假的空虚感。年轻时，那种丰满、扬扬得意的感觉不复存在了，现实生活以及所有存在的事物，似乎都是平淡而乏味的——如同伪君子一样外表冠冕堂皇，内心却充满了贪婪和隐藏的污垢。这个世界就是个女巫，用虚假的表演和外表来搪塞我们。青春的纯朴，满心的期待，无限的欣喜，这些统统地消失了；我们只想尽量在没有任何重大的不幸或烦恼的情况下，尽可能地摆脱这些虚假的外表。于是，一个接着一个的幻想，甚至对过去的欢乐和希望而感到沾沾自喜的回忆，也都渐渐地消失殆尽了：如果我们能够在我们的身体还没有完全虚弱之前，在毫无屈辱的情况下逃离生活，置身于平静的思绪之中，在体面中有尊严地离开这个世界，这就是我们所能期待的结局了。其实在死亡降临之时，我们并非会即刻死去，我们在很久以前就已经开始逐步腐烂，逐渐消失殆尽：一个又一个的感官功能，一个又一个的兴趣，一个又一个的依恋，一个接着一个从我们的身旁溜走了。我们在活着的时候，就被自己给撕裂了，年复一年地看到我们自己已不再是原来的样子。而死亡，只会把我们的最后一部分躯壳丢进坟墓里。我们是慢慢地衰老，最终化为乌有。这并不美妙，因为即使在我们的鼎盛时期，我们所烙下的最深刻的印记也只是在片刻留下了一点点痕迹，而我们只不过是在自然环境条件下，一个微不足道的小小的生物而已。在我们风华正茂的日子里，我们所阅读过的书籍，所见证过的情景，所经历过的感受，对我们所造成的影响几乎是微乎其微！想想我们在阅读一部美好的浪漫小说时的感受吧！比如以沃尔特爵士的小说为例：那是多么美丽，多么崇高，多么有趣，而又多么令人心碎的情感！你会以为你当时所经历的感受，会永远地持续下去，或许你可以将自己的思想永远沉浸在这种和谐的气氛与情调之中。当我们阅读时，似乎没有任何东西可以阻止我们或者打扰我们，让我们烦恼。——当我们进入街道第一次被溅到了泥浆，第一次被骗走了两个便士时，这种感觉在我们的脑海中消失得无影无踪了。我们变成了生活环境中各种琐碎和烦人事物的受害者。尽管心灵升华到了崇高的境界，它的归宿还是在卑躬屈膝、令人不悦和琐碎的事物中。然而，令我们感到诧异的是，人到了老年，会变得脆弱爱抱怨——青春的活力也会随着岁月的流逝而逐渐消失。生存与死亡，这两个世界都难以满足我们的欲望和自以为是。

THOMAS DE QUINCEY (1785—1859)

Thomas De Quincey (1785—1859), the son of a rich merchant, was born in Manchester. He was a queer, shy man, dreamy and melancholy from boyhood. An element of romance coloured his early life. When a student at the Manchester Grammar School, he ran away from school to play the vagabond in Wales and London, where he led the strange Bohemian life recorded in his *Confessions of an English Opium Eater* (1822). In 1803, he was sent to Oxford, but made frequent visits to London and began to take opium. He was one of the early admirers of the Lake poets and after leaving college settled at Grasmere for several years. Later he took to journalism to earn a living and started his literary career with the publication of his *Confessions* in the *London Magazine* in 1821—1822. Among his other works are *Suspiria de Profundis* (1845), a sequel to the

Confessions, and *The English Mail Coach* (1849), both of which he wrote in Edinburgh, where he lived with his family for the last thirty years of his life.

De Quincey's chief title to fame rests on his reviving the impassioned prose of the 17th century, especially of Sir Thomas Browne. His essays are characterized by a kind of phantasmagoric imaginings, for as a result of his opium-eating, he was haunted by 'dreams and noon-day visions.' He had infinite sympathy towards the outcast and wretched, whose existence he himself had experienced in the early days of his vagrancy. His feeling for the mysterious and sublime adds to the romantic qualities of his prose, which is marked by a rich, ornate, and sonorous style.

【作者简介】

托马斯·德·昆西（1785—1859），出生于曼彻斯特，是一个富商的儿子。从童年时代起，他就是个怪人、羞羞答答，充满着幻想，常常处于忧郁状态。他的早期生活充满了浪漫色彩。当他还在曼彻斯特语法学校读书时，他就逃学出走，到威尔士和伦敦去流浪，过着一种如他的《一个英国鸦片吸食者的自白》（1822）书中所记载的稀奇古怪的流浪汉的生活。1803 年，他被送到牛津大学，然而他经常访问伦敦并开始吸食鸦片。他是湖畔诗人最早的崇拜者之一，大学毕业后，他在格拉斯米尔居住了几年。后来，他以从事新闻工作为生，并开始了他的文学生涯。他的处女作《一个英国鸦片吸食者的自白》于 1821—1822 年在《伦敦杂志》上发表，其他作品有《来自深处的叹息》（1845）即《一个英国鸦片吸食者的自白》的续集和《英国邮车》（1849），这两部是他在爱丁堡写的，他在那里和家人一起度过了生命中的最后三十年。

德·昆西的成名主要在于其重振了英国 17 世纪，尤其是托马斯·布朗爵士的热情洋溢的散文风格。他散文的特点是充满着一种梦幻般的想象，由于他吸食了鸦片，常常被"梦幻和白日憧憬"萦绕着。他对于那些无家可归的流浪汉深表同情，因为他们的生活正是他早年流浪时所经历过的。他对神秘事物的感觉和对壮丽景象的情感，为他的散文增添了浪漫色彩，表现出内容丰富、辞藻华丽、语言铿锵有力的风格特点。

My Early Life

My father died when I was about seven years old, and left me to the care of **four guardians**. I was sent to **various schools**, great and small; and was very early distinguished for my classical attainments, especially for my knowledge of Greek. At thirteen I wrote Greek with ease; and at fifteen my command of that language was so great that I not only composed Greek verses in lyric metres, but could converse in Greek fluently, and without embarrassment—an accomplishment which I have not since met with in any scholar of my times, and which, in my case, was owing to the practice of daily reading off the newspapers into the best Greek I could furnish *extempore*; for the necessity of ransacking my memory and invention for all sorts and combinations of periphrastic expressions, as equivalents for modern ideas, images, relations of things, etc., gave me a compass of diction which would never have been called out by a dull translation of moral essays, etc. 'That boy,' said **one of my masters**, pointing the attention of a stranger to me, 'that boy could harangue an Athenian mob better than you or I could address an English one.' He who honoured me with this eulogy, was a scholar, '**and a ripe and good one**': and, of all my tutors, was the only one whom I loved or reverenced. Unfortunately for me (and, as I afterwards learned, to this worthy man's great indignation), I was transferred to the care, first of **a blockhead**, who was in a perpetual panic lest I should expose his ignorance; and finally, to that of **a respectable scholar**, at the head of a great school on an ancient foundation. This man had been appointed to his situation by [Brasenose] College, Oxford; and was a sound, well-built scholar, but, like most men whom I have known from that College, coarse, clumsy, and inelegant. A miserable contrast he presented, in my eyes, to the **Etonian brilliancy** of my favourite master: and, besides, he could not disguise from my hourly notice the poverty and meagreness of his understanding. It is a bad thing for a boy to be, and to know himself, far beyond his tutors, whether in knowledge or in power of mind. That was the case, so far as regarded knowledge at least, not with myself only: for the two boys, who jointly with myself composed the first form, were better Grecians than the headmaster, though not more elegant scholars, nor at all more accustomed to sacrifice to the graces. When I first entered, I remember that we read Sophocles; and it was a constant matter of triumph to us, the learned triumvirate of the first form, to see our '**Archididascalus**,' as he loved to be called, conning our lesson before we went up, and laying a regular train, with lexicon and grammar, for blowing up and blasting, as it were, any difficulties he found in the choruses; whilst *we* never condescended to open our books until the moment of going up, and were generally employed in writing epigrams upon his wig, or some such important matter. My two class-fellows were poor, and dependant for their future prospects at the university, on the recommendation of the headmaster: but

I, who had a small patrimonial property, the income of which was sufficient to support me at college, wished to be sent thither immediately. I made earnest representations on the subject to my guardians, but all to no purpose. One, who was more reasonable, and had more knowledge of the world than the rest, lived at a distance: two of the other three resigned all their authority into the hands of the fourth; and this fourth, with whom I had to negotiate, was a worthy man in his way, but haughty, obstinate, and intolerant of all opposition to his will. After a certain number of letters and personal interviews, I found that I had nothing to hope for, not even a compromise of the matter, from my guardian: unconditional submission was what he demanded: and I prepared myself, therefore, for other measures. Summer was now coming on with hasty steps, and my seventeenth birthday was fast approaching; after which day I had sworn within myself that I would no longer be numbered amongst schoolboys. Money being what I chiefly wanted, I wrote to **a woman of high rank**, who, though young herself, had known me from a child, and had latterly treated me with great distinction, requesting that she would 'lend' me five guineas. For upwards of a week no answer came; and I was beginning to despond, when, at length, a servant put into my hands a **double letter**, with a coronet on the seal. The letter was kind and obliging: the fair writer was on the seacoast, and in that way the delay had arisen: she inclosed double of what I had asked, and good-naturedly hinted that if I should *never* repay her it would not absolutely ruin her. Now then, I was prepared for my scheme: ten guineas, added to about two which I had remaining from my pocket money, seemed to me sufficient for an indefinite length of time: and at that happy age, if no *definite* boundary can be assigned to one's power, the spirit of hope and pleasure makes it virtually infinite.

It is **a just remark of Dr. Johnson's**, and, what cannot often be said of his remarks, it is a very feeling one, that we never do anything consciously for the last time—of things, that is, which we have long been in the habit of doing—without sadness of heart. This truth I felt deeply, when I came to leave [Manchester], a place which I did not love, and where I had not been happy. On the evening before I left [Manchester] forever, I grieved when the ancient and lofty schoolroom resounded with the evening service, performed for the last time in my hearing; and at night, when the muster roll of names was called over, and mine, as usual, was called first, I stepped forward, and, passing the headmaster, who was standing by, I bowed to him, and looked earnestly in his face, thinking to myself, 'He is old and infirm, and in this world I shall not see him again.' I was right: I never *did* see him again, nor ever shall. He looked at me complacently, smiled good-naturedly, returned my salutation, or rather my valediction, and we parted though he knew it not, forever. I could not reverence him intellectually: but he had been uniformly kind, to me, and had allowed me many indulgences: and I grieved at the thought of the mortification I should inflict upon him.

The morning came which was to launch me into the world, and from which my whole succeeding life has, in many important points, taken its colouring. I lodged in the headmaster's house, and had been allowed, from my first entrance, the indulgence of a private room, which I used both as a sleeping-room and as a study. At half after three I rose, and gazed with deep emotion at the ancient towers of [the Collegiate Church], 'dressed in earliest light,' and beginning to crimson with the radiant lustre of a cloudless July morning. I was firm and immovable in my purpose: but yet agitated by anticipation of uncertain danger and troubles; and if I could have foreseen the hurricane and perfect hailstorm of affliction which soon fell upon me, well might I have been agitated. To this agitation the deep peace of the morning presented an affecting contrast, and in some degree a medicine. The silence was more profound than that of midnight: and to me the silence of a summer morning is more touching, than all other silence, because, the light being broad and strong, as that of noon-day at other seasons of the year, it seems to differ from perfect day chiefly because man is not yet abroad; and thus the peace of nature, and of the innocent creatures of God, seems to be secure and deep, only so long as the presence of man, and his restless and unquiet spirit, are not there to trouble its sanctity. I dressed myself, took my hat and gloves, and lingered a little in the room. For the last year and a half this room had been my '**pensive citadel**' : here I had read and studied through all the hours of night: and, though true it was that for the latter part of this time I, who was framed for love and gentle affections, had lost my gaiety and happiness, during the strife and fever of contention with my guardian; yet, on the other hand, as a boy so passionately fond of books, and dedicated to intellectual pursuits, I could not fail to have enjoyed many happy hours in the midst of general dejection. I wept as I looked round on the chair, hearth, writing-table, and other familiar objects, knowing too certainly that I looked upon them for the last time. Whilst I write this, it is **eighteen years ago**: and yet, at this moment, I see distinctly as if it were yesterday, the lineaments and expression of the object on which I fixed my parting gaze: it was **a picture of the lovely** —, which hung over the mantelpiece; the eyes and mouth of which were beautiful, and the whole countenance so radiant with benignity and divine tranquillity, that I had a thousand times laid down my pen or my book, to gather consolation from it, as a devotee from his patron saint. Whilst I was yet gazing upon it, the deep tones of [Manchester] clock proclaimed that it was four o'clock. I went up to the picture, kissed it, and then gently walked out, and closed the door forever!

Notes

This is an extract taken from the *Confessions of an English Opium Eater*. The text used here is the briefer early version which appeared in the *London Magazine* for 1821 and was first reprinted in book form in 1822. A new and much enlarged edition of the *Confessions* appeared in 1856.

four guardians. They were Mr. G., a banker in Lincolnshire; 'who was more reasonable, and had more knowledge of the world than the rest;' Mr. B., a merchant, and Mr. E., a rural magistrate, both of whom, being too busy to attend much to the children's affairs 'resigned all their authority into the hands of the fourth;' and this fourth, 'a worthy man in his way, but haughty, obstinate, and intolerant of all opposition to his will,' was the Rev. Samuel Hall, a curate at Salford near Manchester.

various schools, i.e. Bath Grammar School, Winkfield School, and Manchester Grammar School; the second was a small 'private' school in

Wiltshire.

one of my masters, Mr. Morgan of Bath School.

'and a ripe and good one.' Cf. Shakespeare, *Henry VIII*, Act IV, scene ii, lines 51—52.

a blockhead, etc. Mr. Spencer, the master of Winkfield School.

a respectable scholar, Mr. Charles Lawson, headmaster of Manchester School.

Etonian brilliancy. De Quincey referred to the special and almost exclusive care bestowed upon the classical training at Eton.

'Archididascalus,' headmaster.

a woman of high rank, Lady Carbery, an early friend of De Quincey's mother. De Quincey met her at Bath and maintained with her a correspondence upon questions of literature.

double letter, a mail letter requiring double postage.

a just remark of Dr. Johnson's, etc. From Johnson's *The Idler*, No. 103: 'There are few things not purely evil, of which we can say, without some emotion of uneasiness, "this is the last." Those who never could agree together, shed tears when mutual discontent has determined them to final separation; of a place which has been frequently visited, thought without pleasure, the last look is taken with heaviness of heart.'

'pensive citadel.' From Wordsworth's sonnet 'Nuns fret not...,' line 3: 'And students with their pensive citadels.'

eighteen years ago, really nineteen; in the revised edition of the *Confessions*, 1856, De Quincey changed it to 'nineteen,' and appended the following note: 'Written in the August of 1821.'

a picture of the lovely —, 'The picture of a lovely lady,' according to the revised *Confessions*. 'The housekeeper was in the habit of telling me that the lady had *lived* (meaning, perhaps, had been *born*) two centuries ago; that date would better agree with the tradition that the portrait was a copy from Vandyke... She was also a special benefactress to me, through eighteen months, by means of her sweet Madonna countenance.' —De Quincey's note.

【作品简介】

本文选自《一个英国鸦片吸食者的自白》，是 1821 年发表在《伦敦杂志》上的早期简本，并于 1822 年首次以书本形式重印。《一个英国鸦片吸食者的自白》的增订版于 1856 年出版。

【作品解析】

four guardians：这四个监护人分别是林肯郡的银行家 G 先生，"比其他三位监护人更通情达理，更懂人情世故"；商人 B 先生和地方法官 E 先生，这两位都太忙了，没有时间照看孩子，最终他们把所有监护权都交给了第四位；第四位监护人是曼彻斯特附近索尔福德的塞缪尔·霍尔牧师，他受人尊重，但举止傲慢，刚愎自用，不能容忍任何反对他意愿的行为。

various schools：文中指巴斯语法学校、温克菲尔德学校、曼彻斯特语法学校，其中第二所是威尔特郡一所小型的"私立"学校。

one of my masters：指的是巴斯语法学校的摩根先生。

"and a ripe and good one"：这里是指"成熟而优秀的学者"。参见莎士比亚《亨利八世》，第四幕，第二场，第51—52 行。

a blockhead, etc.：一个愚蠢的傻瓜，指斯宾塞先生，温克菲尔德学校的校长。

a respectable scholar：一位受人尊敬的学者，指查尔斯·劳森先生，曼彻斯特语法学校校长。

Etonian brilliancy：德·昆西提到在伊顿公学接受古典教育，受到睿智的老师无微不至的特殊照顾，当时这种照顾几乎是唯一的。

"Archididascalus"：这里是指"主教官"（校长）的意思。

a woman of high rank：一位地位很高的女士，文中是指卡伯里女士，德·昆西母亲的早期朋友。德·昆西在巴斯遇到她，并一直与她就文学问题保持着书信往来。

double letter：一封贴有双倍邮资的信件。

a just remark of Dr. Johnson's, etc.：出自约翰逊主编的杂志《闲人》第103期："世界上只有很少的事情不是纯粹的邪恶，我们可以心安理得地说'这是最后一次了'，即使那些意见不一致的人，在因相互不满而最终分离时，也会流下眼泪；对于一个我们经常光顾的地方，即便一想起就不高兴，最后的一眼，也是带着沉重的心情。"

"pensive citadel"：出自华兹华斯的十四行诗《修女们不烦恼……》第3行："And students with their pensive citadels（学生们带着他们沉思的城堡）。"

eighteen years ago：其实是十九年；在1856年修订版的《一个英国鸦片吸食者的自白》中，德·昆西把它改成了"十九"，并做了加注："写于1821年8月。"

a picture of the lovely ——：估计是《一张可爱女士的画像》，在《一个英国鸦片吸食者的自白》修订版里，德·昆西是这样注释的："女管家经常对我说，这位女士两个世纪前生活在这里（也许意味着出生在这里）；那个日期恰好符合这样一个传说，这幅肖像画是范德克的复制品……在这十八个月中的日日夜夜，画中她那甜美犹如圣母玛利亚的容颜，对我来说是特别的恩赐。"

【参考译文】

我的早期生活

七岁时，我父亲就去世了，把我托付给了四位监护人。他们把我送进各种大大小小的学校去接受教育。我很早就在古典研究领域里崭露头角，尤其是我的希腊文知识。十三岁时，我就能用希腊文书写；十五岁时，我对希腊文更是得心应手，我不仅能用希腊文写抒情散文和诗歌，而且还能用流利的希腊语与人交谈，不会感到丝毫的尴尬或窘迫——这等成就是当时任何一位学者都力所不及的。就我而言，这种成就应该归功于我每天用希腊语练习阅读报刊，我可以即兴把它朗读成最好的希腊文，为此我必须不停地搜索我的记忆，并且用各种各样的创造性的思维和恰如其分的组合来表达，诸如：现代思想、图像与各种事物之间有连带关系的特征以及背景等等；这些对于我来说，相当于用词的指南针，这样的用词在枯燥乏味的道德文章翻译之类的作品中是见不到的。"那个孩子，"我的老师正对着一个我不认识的陌生人说，"他可以面对雅典的公众高谈阔论，他的口才比你和我对英国人演讲还要出色。"称赞我的这个人，是位成熟而优秀的学者。在我所有的导师中，他是我唯一爱戴和尊敬的人。然而，不幸的是（后来我才知道这件事也使这位可敬的大人为之而愤慨），我先是被转送到了一位傻瓜导师那里，他总是惊慌失措，唯恐我会暴露他的无知；最后，我终于被转送到了一位受人尊敬的学者手里，他是一所历史悠久很有名望的学校的校长。他是由牛津大学布利斯诺斯学院任命的，是位学识坚实，受过良好教育的学者，但就像在那所学院里我认识的大多数先生一样，他有点笨拙，粗俗，有失儒雅。在我的眼里，这位校长与我最喜欢的伊顿公学睿智的老师形成了不幸的对比；他在我时时刻刻的关注下，无法掩饰自己理解能力的匮乏。对于一个男孩子来说，知道自己无论是在知识上还是在思维能力上，都远远超出他的导师，这并不是一件好事。至少，就知识而言，不仅仅是我自己，还有另外两个一年级的男孩子，他们的希腊文水平都在这位校长之上。这是事实，虽然他们既不是儒雅的学者，也根本不会为了体面而去舍弃什么。我还记得第一次进入课堂，我们读的是索福克勒斯的著作；对于我们一年级有学识的三人一伙的同盟来说，这是我们一连串成就中的一个，看到我们的"主教官"（他喜欢人们这样称呼他）在我们上课之前就把众多的词典和语法书籍排列好了，用来应对我们集体提问中的各种难题。而我们从来没有在上课之前打开过我们的书本，通常我们都会忙着以他的假发，或者类似一些"重要的事情"为主题，写些诙谐短诗。我的那两个同班同学没有钱，他们将来是否能上大学取决于校长的推荐。而我却有一小笔遗产，这些钱足够支撑并供我上大学，真希望能立刻被送进大学。就这个问题，我向我的监护人做了认真的陈述，然而却是徒劳的。唯一比较通情达理、更懂人情世故的监护人却住得很远。而其他三个人中，有两个人已将所有监护人的权利和义务交到了第四个监护人的手中；于是我不得不找第四位监护人协商，他虽然值得尊敬，却是一个傲慢、刚愎自用、不能容忍一切反对他意愿的人。经过多次的信件来往和面谈之后，我发现对于我的这个监护人不能抱有任何希望，甚至没有任何妥协的余地，他要求我无条件地服从他的旨意。因此，我只好另想别的办法了。夏天即将来临，我的十七岁生日也快要到了。我曾经发过誓：十七岁以后，我不再是中学生中的一员。金钱是我最想要的东西，我便给一位地位很高的女士写信，请求她"借给我"五个基尼。这位女士虽然年纪轻轻，但在我很小的时候就认识我，而且近来对我特别关心。可是过了一个多星期还没有收到回信，我开始感到沮丧。最终，有一位仆人把一封超重的挂号信交到我的手上，信封上还盖着一个冠冕的印戳，信中充满了和蔼可亲的言语。这位漂亮的女士当时正在海边，因此回信耽搁了几天。信中夹着十个基尼，是我要求的双倍，并且带着善意的暗示：如果我不还她，那也绝对不会毁了她的生活。现在，我已经为我的计划做好了准备。十个基尼，加上我口袋里节省下来的零用钱两个基尼，在我看来已经足够维持我一段时间的生活了。在那个快乐的年代，如果一个人的能力没有受到明确的限制，那么满怀希望加上快乐的精神就会使他无所不能。

约翰逊博士曾经有过这样一句公允的评论，而且与他通常说的许多话不同，这句话充满情感。那就是，我们从来不会在最后一次有意识地去做任何我们早已习以为常的事情时，内心深处没有一丝悲伤。这也正是我在离开曼彻斯特的时候真真切切的感受。那是一个我不爱的地方，一个我过得并不快乐的地方。在我即将永远离开曼彻斯特的前一天晚上，当古老而又威严的教室里响起晚间祷告的声音时，我感到悲伤，这也许将是我最后一次聆听晚间祷告。那天晚上，在集合点名时，和往常一样，我的名字第一个被点到。我走上前去，经过站在旁边的校长，我向他鞠躬，认真地看着他的脸，我对自己说："他年老体弱，在这个世界上，也许我再也见不到他了。"我是对的，我再也没有见到过他，以后也不会再见到他了。他得意地看着我，和蔼地笑了笑，算是回礼，或者更确切地说，也算是向我告别。我们分别了，他当时却不知道，这将是永远的分别。我一直无法在学术上敬重他，但他对我一向是善良的，并且很宽容和放纵。一想到这里，我为我曾经给他带来的屈辱而感到羞愧和悲伤。

　　清晨降临，它将把我带到一个崭新的世界。从此，我整个人生中的许多重要的方面，都将染上各种色彩。我当时寄宿在那位校长的家里，我一到就拥有了一个私人的房间，我把它既用作卧室又用作书房。我三点半起床，怀着深情凝视着"披着晨曦霞光"的学院教堂周围古老的塔楼，七月清晨，天空晴朗无云，塔楼在晨曦霞光的照耀下泛着红光。我对我的目标坚定不移，但还是为预见不到的危险和障碍感到烦躁。如果我当时能预见到苦难的飓风和冰雹很快就会降临到我的身上，那我可能会更加焦虑不安。这种焦虑不安的情绪与清晨的宁静呈现出了强烈的反差。在某种程度上，清晨的宁静更像是一剂良药，此时的寂静比午夜更加深邃。对我来说，夏日清晨的寂静比其他任何时候的寂静都更加令人心动，因为阳光如同一年中其他季节中午时候一样强烈，却似乎与美好的正午阳光有所不同，主要是因为人们还没有出门。因此，只要当人类和他们那焦虑不安的灵魂不出现，大自然以及上帝创造出来的无辜生命似乎才会显得安宁，大自然的圣洁才不会被打扰。我穿好了衣服，戴上帽子和手套，在房间里逗留徘徊了一小会儿。在过去的一年半里，这个房间一直是我"沉思的城堡"，我在这里，曾整夜通宵达旦地阅读和研究。的确在最后的一段时间里，我这个本来充满爱心、柔和温情的人，却在与我的监护人激烈的争论中，失去了我应有的快乐和幸福；然而另一方面，作为一个如此热爱读书，热衷于追求知识的男孩，在那段情绪低落、沮丧的日子里，我在这里享受到了许多幸福和欢乐的时光。当我环顾四周的椅子、壁炉、写字台和其他熟悉的东西时，我流下了眼泪，我清楚地知道，这是我最后一次见到它们了。当我写这篇文章的时候，已经过去了十八年。然而，就在此时此刻，我清楚地记得，我当时凝视这些物体的轮廓和流露出来的表情，仿佛是在昨天——那是挂在壁炉架上一幅某某人可爱的画像，她的眼睛和嘴唇都很美丽，整个面容焕发着一种仁慈和神圣的宁静，使整个房间骤然一亮；我曾经无数次放下手中的笔或书，从画像中得到安慰，就好像一个虔诚的信徒从他的守护神那里得到安慰一样。当我还在凝视着她的时候，曼彻斯特深沉的钟声敲响了，已经四点钟了。我走到画像前，吻了它一下，然后轻轻地走了出去，永远地关上了那扇门！

THOMAS CARLYLE (1795—1881)

Thomas Carlyle (l795—1881), the son of a stone-mason, was born at Ecclefechan, Scotland. He was educated at the University of Edinburgh. After trying divinity, school-teaching, and the law, he took up literature, writing for the magazines, translating German novels, and delivering lectures on history and European culture. His chief works in this period include *Sartor Resartus* (1833—1834), *The French Revolution* (1837), *Heroes and Hero-Worship* (1841), *Past and Present* (1843), *Letters and Speeches of Oliver Cromwell* (1845), and *Frederick the Great* (1858—1865). Signal recognition came to him when in 1865 he was chosen Lord Rector of Edinburgh University. After the death of his wife Jane Welsh, who had given him great encouragement and inspiration, Carlyle lived in much solitude, gloom, and ill health, and wrote little of importance.

A reformer and thinker, Carlyle battled against the selfishness and mental torpor of his age. He has been called 'a moral brass band,' preaching fervently the gospels of work and sacrifice with all the fiery intensity of a Hebrew prophet. His insistence on spiritual values provided a strong check to the growing worship of material things, while his sardonic attack upon the shams and pretences of society roused a sluggish public to a new consciousness of its great moral responsibility. With an eccentric and powerful style, Carlyle succeeded more than any other writer in making Victorian literature such a vast, irresistible force in the regeneration of modern industrial world.

【作者简介】

托马斯·卡莱尔（1795—1881），石匠的儿子，出生于苏格兰的埃克尔费亨村。他在爱丁堡大学接受教育。在尝试了神学、中小学教育和法律之后，他决定从事文学工作，为杂志撰稿，翻译德语小说，并开办有关历史和欧洲文化的讲座。他在这一时期的主要著作有《旧衣新裁》（1833—1834）、《法国革命史》（1837）、《论英雄与英雄崇拜》（1841）、《过去与现在》（1843）、《奥利弗·克伦威尔书信演说集》（1845），以及《普鲁士腓特烈大帝史》（1858—1865）。1865年，他被任命为爱丁堡大学名誉校长，并得到了大家的认可。他的妻子曾经给了他极大的鼓励和灵感，在他的妻子简·威尔士去世之后，卡莱尔一直生活在孤独和忧郁之中，健康状况一直不佳，很少写作，再没有出过重要的作品。

作为改革者和思想家，卡莱尔与他那个时代的自私和精神上的麻木不仁做了坚决的斗争。人们称他为"道德的吹鼓手"，他以希伯来先知那种强烈的热情，忘我地传播福音。他对精神价值观的坚持，强有力地抑制了当时日益增长的物质崇拜；而他对社会丑恶和虚伪的讽刺性攻击唤醒了感觉迟钝的公众，使他们重新意识到自己应当承担这伟大道义上的责任。卡莱尔的文风奇特而气势磅礴，成功地使维多利亚时代的文学在现代工业化的世界里，成为一股波澜壮阔、不可抗拒的力量，这是任何作家所不及的。

Marie Antoinette

On Monday the Fourteenth of October 1793, a Cause is pending in the **Palais de Justice**, in the new Revolutionary Court, such as these old stone-walls never witnessed: the Trial of Marie Antoinette. The once brightest of Queens, now tarnished, defaced, forsaken, stands here at **Fouquier-Tinville**'s Judgement-bar; answering for her life. The Indictment was delivered her last night. To such changes of human fortune what words are adequate? Silence alone is adequate.

There are few Printed things one meets with, of such tragic, almost ghastly, significance as those bald Pages of the *Bulletin du Tribunal Révolutionnaire*, which bear Title, *Trial of the* **Widow Capet**. Dim, dim, as if in disastrous eclipse; like the pale kingdoms of **Dis**! Plutonic Judges, Plutonic Tinville; encircled, nine times, with **Styx** and **Lethe**, with Fire-**Phlegethon** and **Cocytus** named of Lamentation! The very witnesses summoned are like Ghosts: exculpatory, inculpatory, they themselves are all hovering over death and doom; they are known, in our imagination, as the prey of the Guillotine. Tall *ci-devant* **Count d'Estaing**, anxious to show himself Patriot, cannot escape; nor **Bailly**, who, when asked If he knows the Accused, answers with a reverent inclination towards her, 'Ah, yes, I know Madame.' Ex-Patriots are here, sharply dealt with, as **Procureur Manuel**; Ex-Ministers, shorn of their splendour. We have cold Aristocratic impassivity, faithful to itself even in **Tartarus**; rabid stupidity, of Patriot Corporals, Patriot Washerwomen, who have much to say of Plots, Treasons, August Tenth, old Insurrection of Women. For all now has become a crime, in her who has *lost*.

Marie Antoinette, in this her utter abandonment, and hour of extreme need, is not wanting to herself, the imperial woman. Her look they say, as that hideous Indictment was reading, continued calm; 'she was sometimes observed moving her fingers, as when one plays on the Piano.' You discern, not without interest, across that dim Revolutionary Bulletin itself, how she bears herself queenlike. Her answers are prompt, clear, often of **Laconic** brevity; resolution, which has grown contemptuous without ceasing to be dignified, veils itself in calm words. 'You persist, then, in denial?' — 'My plan is not denial: it is the truth I have said, and I persist in that.' Scandalous **Hébert** has borne his testimony as to many things: as to one thing, concerning Marie Antoinette and her little Son,—wherewith Human Speech had better not further be soiled. She has answered Hébert; a Juryman begs to observe that she has not answered as to *this*. 'I have not answered,' she exclaims with noble emotion, 'because Nature refuses to answer such a charge brought against a Mother. I appeal to all the Mothers that are here.' **Robespierre**, when he heard of it, broke out into something almost like swearing at the brutish blockheadism of this Hébert; on whose foul head his foul lie has recoiled. At four o'clock on Wednesday morning, after two days and two nights of interrogating, jury-charging, and other darkening of counsel, the result comes out: Sentence of Death. 'Have you anything to say?' The Accused shook her head, without speech. Night's candles are burning out; and with her too Time is finishing, and it will be Eternity and Day. This Hall of Tinville's is dark, ill-lighted except where she stands. Silently she withdraws from it, to die.

Two Processions, or Royal Progresses, three-and-twenty years apart, have often struck us with a strange feeling of contrast. The first is of a beautiful Archduchess and Dauphiness, quitting **her Mother's City**, at the age of Fifteen; towards hopes such as no other Daughter of Eve then had: 'On the morrow,' says Weber an eye-witness, 'the Dauphiness left Vienna. The whole city crowded out; at first with a sorrow which was silent. She appeared: you saw her sunk back into her carriage; her face bathed in tears; hiding her eyes now with her handkerchief, now with her hands; several times putting out her head to see yet again this Palace of her Fathers, whither she was to return no more. She motioned her regret, her gratitude to the good Nation, which was crowding here to bid her farewell. Then arose not only tears; but piercing cries, on all sides. Men and women alike abandoned themselves to such expression of their sorrow. It was an audible sound of wail, in the streets and avenues of Vienna. The last Courier that followed her disappeared, and the crowd melted away.'

The young imperial Maiden of Fifteen has now become a worn discrowned Widow of Thirty-eight; grey before her time; this is the last Procession; 'Few minutes after the Trial ended, the drums were beating to arms in all Sections; at sunrise the armed force was on foot, cannons getting placed at the extremities of the Bridges, in the Squares, Crossways, all along from the Palais de Justice to the **Place de la Révolution**. By ten o'clock, numerous patrols were circulating in the Streets; thirty thousand foot and horse drawn up under arms. At eleven, Marie Antoinette was brought out. She had on an undress of *piqué blanc*. She was led to the place of execution, in the same manner as an ordinary criminal; bound, on a Cart; accompanied by a Constitutional Priest in Lay dress; escorted by numerous detachments of infantry and cavalry. These, and the double row of troops all along her road, she appeared to regard with indifference. On her countenance there was visible neither abashment nor pride. To the cries of *Vive la République* and *Down with Tyranny*, which attended her all the way, she seemed to pay no heed. She spoke little to her Confessor. The **tricolour Streamers** on the housetops occupied her attention, in the **Streets du Roule and Saint-Honoré**; she also noticed the **Inscriptions** on the house-fronts. On reaching the Place de la Révolution, her looks turned towards the *Jardin National*, whilom **Tuileries**; her face at that moment gave signs of lively emotion. She mounted the Scaffold with courage enough; at a quarter past Twelve, her head fell; the Executioner showed it to the people, amid universal long-continued cries of *Vive la République*.

Notes

This is a selection from *The French Revolution* which gives a most graphic account of that great historical drama, with its multitude of magnificent figures and many equally admirable larger scenes as the march to

Versailles, the storming of the Bastille, and the flight to Varennes. This episode of the trial of the French queen and her last procession to the place of execution is one that stands out in the reader's memory.

Marie Antoinette (1755—1793), daughter of Emperor Francis I and Maria Theresia of Hungary, and wife of Louis XVI of France. She was guillotined in 1793, a few months after the execution of her husband.

Palais de Justice, Court of Justice.

Fouquier-Tinville, Antoine Quentin (1746—1795), a French revolutionary. He was public prosecutor to the Revolutionary Tribunal of Paris from March 1793 to July 1794.

Widow Capet, i.e. Marie Antoinette. Capet was the name of the French dynasty founded by Hugo Capet in 987, which ruled until 1328, when it was succeeded by the House of Valois. Louis XVI was described as Louis Capet when tried before the Convention in 1793.

Dis, an underworld god, identical with the Greek Pluto.

Styx, Lethe, Phlegethon, Cocytus are all rivers encompassing or flowing in Hades, the kingdom of Pluto. Styx is the gloomy or hateful river, over which the shades of the departed were ferried. Lethe is the river of oblivion, of which the souls of the dead were supposed to drink, after they had been for a certain time confined in Tartarus. Phlegethon is the river whose waters were flames. Cocytus is the river of lamentation. Cf. Milton, *Paradise Lost,* ii, 575—581:

> 'four infernal rivers that disgorge
> Into the burning lake their baleful streams—
> Abhorred Styx, the flood of deadly hate;
> Sad Acheron of sorrow, black and deep;
> Cocytus named of lamentation loud
> Heard on the rueful stream; fierce Phlegethon

Whose waves of torrent fire inflame with rage.'

ci-devant, former.

Count d'Estaing, Charles Hector (1729—1794), French admiral. He became a 'patriot' at the time of the Revolution. On the trial of Marie Antoinette in 1793, he bore testimony in her favour. He was himself brought to trial and executed in April, 1794.

Bailly, Jean Sylvain (1736—1793), French astronomer and orator. He bined the revolutionary party, was chosen president of the Third Estate, but, like many other revolutionary leaders, was himself a victim of the guillotine in November, 1793.

Procureur Manuel, Louis Pierre (1751—1793), French writer and revolutionary. One of the leaders of the *émeutes* of June 10 and August 10, 1792, he was made procureur of the revolutionary Commune of Paris, soon lost public favour, and was executed a year later.

Tartarus, one of the regions of Hades where the most impious and guilty among mankind were supposed to be punished. It was surrounded by three impenetrable walls and the burning waters of the river Phlegethon.

Laconic, expressing much in few words, as did the ancient Spartans, who were inhabitants of Laconia.

Hébert, Jacques-Réne (1757—1794), French revolutionary and a member of the Commune; executed in 1794.

Robespierre, Isidore Maximilien De (1758—1794), one of the most prominent figures in the French Revolution, a leader of the extreme party. He was among the promoters of the Reign of Terror and finally exercised a kind of dictatorship, but was overthrown in July 1794, and executed.

her Mother's City, i.e. Vienna, where Marie Antoinette was born.

Place de la Révolution, name of a famous square in Paris.

Piqué blanc (French), a kind of white ribbed cotton fabric.

Vive la République (French), Long live the Republic.

tricolour Streamers, flags of the French Revolution, now the French national banner, blue, white, and red, in nearly vertical stripes.

Streets du Roule and Saint-Honoré, streets in Paris.

Inscriptions. The standard inscription was 'Republic One and Indivisible. Liberty, Equality, Fraternity, or Death!'

Tuileries, a royal palace in Paris, built by Catherine de Médicis, wife of Henry II, of France (1519—1559), on the site of *tuilerie,* or brickyard. It was changed to a National Garden (*Jardin National*) at the time of the Revolution; destroyed at the time of the Commune (1871).

【作品简介】

本文选自《法国革命史》，它对这一伟大的历史戏剧性事件做了最生动的描述，其中有许多重要人物和许多重大事件，如向凡尔赛宫进军、攻占巴士底狱、路易十六出逃事件。这篇选文描述的是审判法国王后以及她走向断头台的片段。卡莱尔的描述非常生动，给读者留下了深刻的记忆。

【作品解析】

Marie Antoinette：玛丽·安托瓦内特（1755—1793），匈牙利君主弗兰茨一世与玛丽亚·特蕾西娅的女儿，法国国王路易十六的妻子。1793 年，在丈夫被处决几个月之后，她也被送上了断头台。

Palais de Justice（法语）：司法宫。

Fouquier-Tinville：安托万·康坦·富基耶–坦维尔（1746—1795），法国革命者，1793 年 3 月至 1794 年 7 月，他担任巴黎革命法庭的检察官。

Widow Capet：寡妇卡佩，即玛丽·安托瓦内特。987 年，雨果·卡佩建立了法国卡佩王朝，该王朝的统治持续到 1328 年，后来被瓦罗亚王朝接替。路易十六在 1793 年公审之前，被称为路易·卡佩。

Dis：狄斯，冥界之神，等同于希腊神话中的冥王。

Styx，Lethe，Phlegethon，Cocytus：分别是愤怒之河、遗忘之河、地狱火河、悲哀之河，这些都是环绕或在冥府中流动的河流。愤怒之河是一条阴暗或者说充满仇恨的河流，在那里摆渡逝者的阴魂。遗忘之河是一条失去记忆的河流，逝者的灵魂在塔尔塔洛斯被囚禁了一段时间之后，就会饮用这条河中的水去忘却尘世。地狱火河是火焰之河，河里的水就是火焰。悲哀之河是悲伤的河流。参见弥尔顿《失乐园》，第二卷，第 575—581 行："这四条是地狱里邪恶的河流／将这罪恶的溪流，送进这燃烧的湖泊／可恨的愤怒之河，流淌着致命仇恨的洪水／悲伤的冥河，黑暗而又深邃／哀鸣的悲哀之河／在凄凉的溪流河上都听得到，那哀声恸哭／地狱火河，那奔腾的火焰，在怒火中燃烧。"

ci-devant：前者。

Count d'Estaing：查尔斯·赫克托，德斯坦伯爵（1729—1794），法国海军上将。革命时期，他变成了"爱国者"。1793 年，在对玛丽·安托瓦内特的公审中，他作了有利于她的证词。1794 年 4 月，他本人受到审判并被处决。

Bailly：让·西尔万·巴伊（1736—1793），法国天文学家和演说家。他与革命党结盟，被选为第三产业的领袖，但与许多其他革命领导人一样，他自己也于 1793 年 11 月被送上了断头台。

Procureur Manuel：路易·皮埃尔·曼努埃尔（1751—1793），法国作家和革命者。他是 1792 年 6 月 10 日和 8 月 10 日两次起义的领导人之一，被任命为巴黎革命公社的检察官，然而很快就失去了公众的青睐，并于一年后被处决。

Tartarus：塔尔塔洛斯，即地狱，人类中灵魂丑恶和有罪的人受到惩罚的地方。它被三堵难以穿透的墙壁和燃烧的地狱火河包围着。

Laconic：用很少的语言去表达，言简意赅，就像居住在拉科尼亚的古代斯巴达人一样。

Hébert：雅克-勒内·埃贝尔（1757—1794），法国革命家，巴黎公社成员，1794 年被处决。

Robespierre：马克西米利安·伊西多尔·德·罗伯斯比尔（1758—1794），法国大革命中最重要的人物之一，激进派的领导人。他是"恐怖统治"的主导者之一，最终实行了独裁统治，1794 年 7 月他的独裁专政被推翻，他也被处决。

her Mother's City：即维也纳，也是玛丽·安托瓦内特出生的地方。

Place de la Révolution：革命广场，巴黎一个著名的广场。

Piqué blanc（法语）：一种白色的罗纹棉织物。

Vive la République（法语）：共和国万岁。

tricolour Streamers：法国大革命的旗帜，即现在的法国国旗，由蓝、白、红三色垂直条纹组成。

Streets du Roule and Saint-Honoré：巴黎的杜鲁勒和圣奥诺雷街道。

Inscriptions：完整的标语是："共和国不可分割。自由，平等，博爱，要么死亡！"

Tuileries：杜伊勒里宫，巴黎的一座皇家宫殿，由法国国王亨利二世（1519—1559）之妻凯瑟琳·德·美第奇在杜伊勒里或者说是在砖厂遗址上建造的。法国革命时期，它被改建成了国家公园，1871 年巴黎公社成立时被摧毁。

【参考译文】

玛丽·安托瓦内特

1793 年 10 月 14 日星期一，在新的革命法庭上，一桩诉讼案正在司法宫临时法庭等待审判，诸如这类诉讼案连古老的石墙也从未见证过，那就是对玛丽·安托瓦内特的审判。这位曾经充满了荣耀的王后，如今已经丧失了以往的光环，被玷污，被污损，被遗弃。玛丽·安托瓦内特站在富基耶-坦维尔的被审判席上，为自己的生命做辩护。起诉书是前一晚送给她的。对于人类命运如此突如其来的变化，用什么样的语言形容才恰如其分呢？沉默，就足够了。

很少有人会见到如此富于悲剧性，如此令人毛骨悚然，而又如此具有深远影响的报刊，《革命特别法庭公报》在光秃秃的页面上刊登着"审判寡妇卡佩"的巨幅标题。日月无光，仿佛是在灾难性的日全食中，就像进入了那苍白的冥王国！冥国的法官，冥国的富基耶－坦维尔，被愤怒之河和遗忘之河、地狱火河和悲哀之河重重包围了九道圈。被传唤的证人就像是幽灵：有罪的在为自己开脱罪责，无罪的却无法为自己辩解，他们都在死亡和厄运中徘徊。在我们的想象中，他们都是断头台上的猎物。身材高大的德斯坦伯爵，急于向法官证明自己是爱国者，也无法逃脱厄运；在巴伊被问及是否认识被告人时，回答中带有一丝虔诚的恭敬："啊，是的，我认识夫人。"也同样没能逃脱厄运。前爱国人士在这里受到了严厉的处罚，就像前检察官曼努埃尔，前部长们，他们的显赫地位都被剥夺了。我们有无动于衷的冷漠贵族，即便是在地狱里，也依然会忠实于自己。还有那些狂热而愚蠢的爱国者下士（最低级士官）和洗衣女工，他们对阴谋、叛乱，以及对 8 月 10 日事件和曾经的妇女暴动有很多的情节要说。这些对玛丽·安托瓦内特这个失败者来说，都成了罪过。

玛丽·安托瓦内特，在这种彻底被抛弃和极度需要帮助的时刻，她并没有想到自己，这就是一个帝国女人。据报道说，在宣读那个可怕的起诉书的时候，她的表情依然很平静；"有时我们会看到她的手指在动，就像是在钢琴键盘上弹奏一样"。在那充满着阴森的革命公报上，你会颇有兴趣地发现，她是如何展现出自己那高贵的女王风范。她的回答迅速、清晰，通常简明扼要；她用沉着的言辞掩饰着自己，这种坚定从容充满了蔑视而不失尊严。"那么，你坚持否认到底吗？""我并没有否认！我所说的都是真相，我所坚持的，都是真相。"可耻的埃贝尔在许多事情上作了诽谤的证词，尤其是一件关于玛丽·安托瓦内特和她小儿子的事情——关于这一点，人类的语言最好不要再被玷污了。她驳斥了埃贝尔的说法。一名陪审员提醒她注意，还没有回答这一提问。"我还没有回答，"她带着高贵的口吻大声惊呼道，"因为人类的天性都会拒绝回答这种对一个母亲的指控！我向在座所有的母亲发出呼吁。"罗伯斯比尔一听到这件事就大发雷霆，似乎是在咒骂这个埃贝尔的粗俗愚蠢；他那肮脏的谎言，最后只能畏怯退缩到他那肮脏的头颅里。在星期三凌晨四点钟，经过两天两夜的审讯、陪审团的指控以及其他律师的庭外辩论，结果出来了：判决死刑。"你还有什么话要说的吗？"被告人摇了摇头，没有说话。夜晚的蜡烛正在燃尽；她的生命随着时间的流逝也正在接近尾声，这将是永恒的一天。整个坦维尔的大厅一片黑暗，只有她站立的地方才有一点点微弱的光亮。她默默地离去，走向死亡。

时隔二十三年的两次游行，或者说是皇室巡游，常常会给我们带来一种奇特情感上的对比。第一次是美丽的大公爵夫人和法国皇太子妃，玛丽·安托瓦内特在她十五岁的时候，便离开了她出生的城市维也纳，带着任何夏娃的女儿都没有的希望。"明天，"目击者韦伯说，"法国皇太子妃就要离开维也纳了。整个城市拥挤不堪，起初是带着一种寂静的悲怆。她出现了：你看她蜷缩在马车里，脸上满是泪水。她一会儿用她的手帕，一会儿又用她的双手遮住自己的眼睛。好几次她把头伸出窗外，再次看看她父亲的宫殿，她是再也回不去了。她用手势向正聚集在这里向她告别的善良的同胞们表示出了自己的遗憾和感激之情。见此情景，人们不禁声泪俱下，到处都是一片令人心碎的哭泣声，无论男女都沉浸在这悲伤之中。这种哭泣声在维也纳的大街小巷都可以听得到。直到跟随她的最后一位随从看不见了，人群才散开。"

当时只有十五岁的年轻皇室少女，现在已变成了三十八岁被削夺了王冠的寡妇。她比她实际的年龄更加衰老，这是她最后一次上街游行。审判结束后的几分钟，人们到处敲锣打鼓。当太阳冉冉升起时，武装部队已经守卫在从司法宫的临时法庭到革命广场的通道上，在桥梁的两端、广场和十字路口都放置了大炮。到了十点钟，街道上到处都是巡逻队，三万名步兵和骑兵被武装了起来。十一点钟，玛丽·安托瓦内特被带了出来。她身穿一条白色的罗纹长裙，像一个普通罪犯一样，被捆绑在囚车上；由一名穿着便装的宪政牧师陪同，在许多步兵和骑兵分队的看押下，她被带到了行刑地点。对于这些，以及一路上两旁守卫的双排军队，她似乎漠然得无动于衷。她脸上的表情既无羞愧也无傲慢。"共和国万岁"和"打倒暴政"的口号声，一路伴随着她，她似乎毫不在意。她几乎不和她的牧师说话。然而，在杜鲁勒街道和圣奥诺雷街道屋顶上的三色旗，引起了她的注意，同时，她还注意到了房屋正面的标语。在她到达革命广场时，她的目光转向了国家花园，以前的杜伊勒里宫，那一刻她的脸上流露出了轻松愉快的表情。她勇敢地登上了断头台。十二点十五分，她的首级掉落了下来。在持续不断的"共和国万岁"的欢呼声中，行刑者向人们展示了她的首级。

Shakespeare

We have no room to speak of Shakespeare's individual works; though perhaps there is much still waiting to be said on that head. Had we, for instance, all his plays reviewed as *Hamlet*, in *Wilhelm Meister*, is! A thing which might, one day, be done. **August Wilhelm Schlegel** has a remark on his Historical Plays, *Henry Fifth* and, the others, which is worth remembering. He calls them a kind of National Epic. **Marlborough**, you recollect, said, he knew no English History but what he had learned from Shakespeare. There are really, if we look to it, few as memorable Histories. The great salient points are admirably seized; all rounds itself off, into a kind of rhythmic coherence; it is, as Schlegel says, *epic*;—as indeed all delineation by a great thinker will be. There are right beautiful things in those Pieces, which indeed together form one beautiful thing. That **battle of Agincourt** strikes me as one of the most perfect things, in its sort, we anywhere have of Shakespeare's. The description of the two hosts: the worn-out, jaded English; the dread hour, big with destiny, when the battle shall begin; and then that deathless valour: '**Ye good yeomen**, whose limbs were made in England!' There is a noble Patriotism in it,—far other than the 'indifference' you sometimes hear ascribed to Shakespeare. A true English heart breathes, calm and strong, through the whole business; not boisterous, protrusive, all the better for that. There is a sound in it like the ring of steel. This man too had a right stroke in him, had it come to that!

But I will say, of Shakespeare's works generally, that we have no full impress of him there; even as full as we have of many men. His works are so many windows, through which we see a glimpse of the world that was in him. All his works seem, comparatively speaking, cursory, imperfect, written under cramping circumstances; giving only here and there a note of the full utterance of the man. Passages there are that come upon you like splendour out of Heaven; bursts of radiance, illuminating the very heart of the thing: you say, 'That is *true*; spoken once and forever; wheresoever and whensoever there is an open human soul, that will be recognised as true!' Such bursts, however, make us feel that the surrounding matter is not radiant; that it is, in part, temporary, conventional. Alas, Shakespeare had to write for the **Globe Playhouse**: his great soul had to crush itself, as it could, into that and no other mould. It was with him, then, as it is with us all. No man works save under conditions. The sculptor cannot set his own free Thought before us; but his Thought as he could translate it into the stone that was given, with the tools that were given. *Disjecta membra* are all that we find of any Poet, or of any man.

Whoever looks intelligently at this Shakespeare may recognize that he too was a **Prophet**, in his way; of an insight analogous to the Prophetic, though he took it up in another strain. Nature seemed to this man also divine; unspeakable, deep as **Tophet**, high as Heaven; 'We are such stuff as Dreams are made of!' **That scroll** in **Westminster Abbey**, which few read with understanding, is of the depth of any Seer. But the man sang; did not preach, except musically. We called **Dante the melodious Priest of Middle-Age Catholicism**. May we not call Shakespeare the still more melodious Priest of a *true* Catholicism, the 'Universal Church' of the Future and of all times? No narrow superstition, harsh asceticism, intolerance, fanatical fierceness or perversion: a Revelation, so far as it goes, that such a thousand fold hidden beauty and divineness dwells in all Nature; which let all men worship as they can! We may say without offence, that there rises a kind of universal Psalm out of this Shakespeare too; not unfit to make itself heard among the still more sacred Psalms. Not in disharmony with these if we understood them, but in harmony!—I cannot call this Shakespeare a 'sceptic,' as some do; his indifference to the creeds and theological quarrels of his time misleading them. No: neither unpatriotic, though he says little about his Patriotism; nor sceptic, though he says little about his Faith. Such 'indifference' was the fruit of his greatness withal: his whole heart was in his own grand sphere of worship (we may call it such); these other controversies, vitally important to other men, were not vital to him.

But call it worship, call it what you will, is it not a right glorious thing, and set of things, this that Shakespeare has brought us? For myself, I feel that there is actually a kind of sacredness in the fact of such a man being sent into this Earth. Is he not an eye to us all; a blessed heaven-sent Bringer of Light?—And, at bottom, was it not perhaps far better that this Shakespeare, everyway an unconscious man, was *conscious* of no Heavenly message? He did not feel, like

Mahomet, because he saw into those internal Splendours, that he specially was the 'Prophet of God' and was he not greater than Mahomet in that? Greater; and also, if we compute strictly, as we did in Dante's case, more successful...

Well: this is our poor **Warwickshire Peasant**, who rose to be Manager of a Playhouse, so that he could live without begging; whom the **Earl of Southampton** cast some kind glances on; whom **Sir Thomas Lucy**, many thanks to him, was for sending to the Treadmill! We did not account him a god, like **Odin**, while, he dwelt with us;— on which point there were much to be said. But I will say rather, or repeat: In spite of the sad state Hero-worship now lies in, consider what this Shakespeare has actually become among us. Which Englishman we ever made, in this land of ours, which million of Englishmen, would we not give-up rather than the Stratford Peasant? There is no regiment of highest Dignitaries that we would sell him for. He is the grandest thing we have yet done. For our honour among foreign nations, as an ornament to our English Household, what item is there that we would not surrender rather than him? Consider now, if they asked us, Will you give-up your Indian Empire or your Shakespeare, you English; have had any Indian Empire, or never have had any Shakespeare? Really it were a grave question. Official persons would answer doubtless in official language; but we, for our part too, should not we be forced to answer: Indian Empire, or no Indian Empire; we cannot do without Shakespeare! Indian Empire will go, at any rate, some day; but this Shakespeare does not go, he lasts forever with us; we cannot give-up our Shakespeare!

Nay, apart from spiritualities; and considering him merely as a real, marketable, tangibly-useful possession. England, before long, this Island of ours, will hold but a small fraction of the English: in America, in **New Holland**, east and west to the very **Antipodes**, there will be a **Saxondom** covering great spaces of the Globe. And now, what is it that can keep all these together into virtually one Nation, so that they do not fall-out and fight, but live at peace, in brotherlike intercourse, helping one another? This is justly regarded as the greatest practical problem, the thing all manner of sovereignties and governments are here to accomplish: what is it that will accomplish this? Acts of Parliament, administrative prime-ministers cannot. America is parted from us, so far as Parliament could part it. Call it not fantastic, for there is much reality in it: Here, I say, is an English King, whom no time or chance, Parliament or combination of Parliaments, can dethrone! This King Shakespeare, does not he shine, in crowned sovereignty, over us all, as the noblest, gentlest, yet strongest of rallying-signs; *in*destructible; really more valuable in that point of view than any other means or appliance whatsoever? We can fancy him as radiant aloft over all the Nations of Englishmen, a thousand years hence. From **Paramatta**, from New York, wheresoever, under what sort of Parish-Constable soever, English men and women are, they will say to one another: 'Yes, this Shakespeare is ours; we produced him, we speak and think by him; we are of one blood and kind with him.' The most common-sense politician, too, if he pleases, may think of that.

Yes, truly, it is a great thing for a Nation that it get an articulate voice; that it produce a man who will speak-forth melodiously what the heart of it means! Italy, for example, poor Italy lies dismembered, scattered asunder, not appearing in any protocol or treaty as a unity at all; yet the noble Italy is actually *one*: Italy produced its Dante; Italy can speak! The Czar of all the Russias, he is strong with so many bayonets, Cossacks and cannons; and does a great feat in keeping such a tract of Earth politically together; but he cannot yet speak. Something great in him, but it is a dumb greatness. He has had no voice of genius, to be heard of all men and times. He must learn to speak. He is a great dumb monster hitherto. His cannons and Cossacks will all have rusted into nonentity, while that Dante's voice is still audible. The Nation that has a Dante is bound together as no dumb Russia can be.—We must here end what we had to say of the *Hero-Poet*.

Notes

This is the last part of Lecture III, 'The Hero as Poet: Dante; Shakespeare' in *Heroes and Hero-worship*. Here in Carlyle, the movement for the coronation of Shakespeare as King of English poets, first started by the romantic critics, reached its culmination.

Wilhelm Meister, i.e. *Wilhelm Meisters Lehrjahre*, a novel by Goethe. For the criticism of *Hamlet*, see the *Lehrjahre*, bk, iv, chpt. iii to bk. v, chap. xii.

August Wilhelm Schlegel (1767—1845), a German Romanticist, chiefly known in England for his translation into the German language of the plays of Shakespeare. In Schlegel's *Lectures on Dramatic Literature*, he wrote: 'It is, as it were, a historical heroic poem in the dramatic form... of which the separate plays constitute the rhapsodies.'

Marlborough, John Churchill, 1st Duke of Marlborough (1650—1722), a great English general. 'In a discussion with Burnet upon some historical point, he displayed so incorrect a conception of the subject, that the Bishop asked him the source of his information. He replied that it was from Shakespeare's plays that he learnt all he knew of English history.' —Wolseley, *Life of Marlborough*, Vol.I, p. 33.

battle of Agincourt, fought at Agincourt, a village in the north of France where, on 25 Oct. 1415, Henry V of England defeated a superior force of the French. Schlegel commends specially this part of *Henry V* in which Shakespeare introduces this great historical battle.

'Ye good yeomen,' etc. From *Henry V*, Act III, scene i; part of the king's speech at Harfleur, not at Agincourt.

Globe Playhouse, the famous theater in Southwark, London, erected in 1598; Shakespeare was once its manager and most of his important plays were acted there.

Disjecta membra (Latin), scattered parts; fragments.

Prophet. In his previous lecture, Carlyle has discoursed on 'The Hero as Prophet. Mahomet: Islam.'

Tophet, hell.

That scroll, in Westminster Abbey, a reference to Shakespeare's statue by Kent in Westminster Abbey. In his hand is a roll with the passage from *Tempest*, Act IV, scene i, beginning 'The cloudclapped towers,' etc. and containing the following famous lines:

'We are such stuff
As dreams are made on, and our little life
Is rounded with a sleep.'

Dante the melodious Priest of Middle-Age Catholicism. In the same lecture, Carlyle has said previously, 'Dante, the Italian man, was sent into our world to embody musically the Religion of the Middle Ages, the Religion of our Modern Europe, its Inner Life.'

Warwickshire Peasant. Shakespeare's father was a husbandman (also variously described as a yeoman, a glover, a butcher, and a wool-dealer) and his mother, daughter of a well-to-do farmer. The village Stratford-on-Avon where Shakespeare was born is in Warwickshire.

Earl of Southampton, Henry Wriothesley (1573—1624), was one of Shakespeare's patrons, to whom Shakespeare dedicated his two poems *Venus and Adonis* (1593) and *Rape of Lucrece* (1594).

Sir Thomas Lucy, a Warwickshire squire. Shakespeare left Stratford about 1585 to avoid, it has been suggested, prosecution for poaching at Charlecote, the property of Sir Thomas Lucy. '*Sending to the Treadmill*' is a humorous modernization of whatever was the Elizabethan punishment for poaching.

Odin, the supreme god and creator in Norse mythology. See Lecture I, 'The Hero as Divinity. Odin. Paganism: Scandinavian Mythology' in *Heroes and Hero-worship*.

New Holland, name given to Australia by the Dutch navigator, Tasman, in 1644.

Antipodes, the regions or country of those who live on the diametrically opposite side of the globe.

Saxondom, kingdom of the Anglo-Saxons; 'the Nations of Englishmen.'

Paramatta, a town in New South Wales.

【作品简介】

本篇是《英雄与英雄崇拜》第三篇演讲中的最后一部分"诗人英雄：但丁；莎士比亚"。在卡莱尔看来，最初由浪漫主义评论家发起的加冕莎士比亚为英国诗人之王的运动目前已达到了高潮。

【作品解析】

Wilhelm Meister：即歌德的小说《威廉·迈斯特的学习年代》。关于对《哈姆雷特》的评论，请参阅该书的第四卷第三章至第五卷第十二章。

August Wilhelm Schlegel：奥古斯特·威廉·施莱格尔（1767—1845），德国浪漫主义作家，在英国他主要以翻译德文版的莎士比亚戏剧而著称。在施莱格尔的《戏剧艺术和文学讲稿》中，他写道："事实上，这是一部戏剧形式的历史英雄诗……以各个单独的剧本构成了这首狂想曲。"

Marlborough：约翰·丘吉尔，第一代马尔伯勒公爵（1650—1722），一位伟大的英国将军。"在与伯内特讨论某些历史问题时，他对这些问题的理解有许多是错误的，于是主教向他询问了信息来源。他回答道，他对英国历史所有的了解完全来源于莎士比亚的戏剧。"参见沃尔斯利《马尔伯勒公爵约翰·丘吉尔传记》，第一卷，第 33 页。

battle of Agincourt：阿金库尔战役，发生在法国北部一个叫阿金库尔的村庄，1415 年 10 月 25 日，英格兰国王亨利五世在那里击败了法国一支精锐部队。莎士比亚在戏剧《亨利五世》中描述了这场伟大的历史战役，施莱格尔对这一部分尤为赞赏。

"Ye good yeomen,"etc.：此句出自《亨利五世》第三幕第一场；其中国王演讲的那部分是在阿夫勒尔，而不是在阿金库尔。

Globe Playhouse：环球剧院，伦敦南华克著名的剧院，建于 1598 年；莎士比亚曾经是剧院的经理，他的大部分重要戏剧都在那里演出。

Disjecta membra（拉丁语）：分散的部件，片段。

Prophet：在卡莱尔上一次的演讲中，谈到了关于"先知的英雄；穆罕默德：伊斯兰教"。

Tophet：地狱。

That scroll, in Westminster Abbey：由肯特设计的位于西敏寺的莎士比亚雕像，他手里拿着一卷轴书，上面刻着《暴风雨》第四幕第一场的段落，以"云雾萦绕的塔楼"作为开场白，其中包含了以下几句著名的台词："我们就是这样的人，是由梦幻而铸成的；我们微小的生命，缭绕着酣睡的梦幻。"

Dante the melodious Priest of Middle-Age Catholicism：在同一次演讲中，卡莱尔曾经说过："意大利人但丁，来到我们的世界，以音乐的方式体现了中世纪的宗教，现代欧洲的宗教，以及它内在的精神生活。"

Warwickshire Peasant：莎士比亚的父亲是个农夫（也有人说是自耕农、手套商、屠夫，或者是个羊毛经销商），而他的母亲则是个富裕农庄主的女儿。莎士比亚出生在位于沃里克郡埃文河畔的斯特拉特福镇。

Earl of Southampton：亨利·里奥思利（1573—1624），南安普敦伯爵三世，是莎士比亚的赞助人之一，莎士比亚曾为他献上两首诗《维纳斯和阿多尼斯》（1593）与《鲁克丽丝受辱记》（1594）。

Sir Thomas Lucy：托马斯·露西爵士，沃里克郡的乡绅。据说，莎士比亚大约在1585年离开了斯特拉特福镇，是为了避免因在查莱克特偷猎而被起诉，查莱克特是托马斯·露西爵士的私人领地。"送去踏板车"这是一种现代幽默，是伊丽莎白时期对偷猎者的惩罚。

Odin：奥丁神，北欧神话中至高无上的神灵和创造者。参见《英雄与英雄崇拜》第一讲"神明英雄奥丁异教：斯堪的纳维亚神话"。

New Holland：新荷兰，1644年荷兰航海家塔斯曼给澳大利亚起的名字。

Antipodes：居住在地球另一侧，截然相反的地区或国家。

Saxondom：盎格鲁-撒克逊人的王国；"英国人的国度"。

Paramatta：帕拉马塔，澳洲新南威尔士的一个城镇。

【参考译文】

莎士比亚

由于篇幅所限，我们不能在这里一一讨论莎士比亚的个人作品；虽然有许多有关莎士比亚的话要说。比如说，我们是否能像《威廉·迈斯特的学习年代》中评论《哈姆雷特》那样，去评论莎士比亚的所有戏剧呢？是的！我们总有一天会这样做的。德国诗人奥古斯特·威廉·施莱格尔曾对莎士比亚的历史剧《亨利五世》发表过精辟的评论，值得我们铭记。他把莎士比亚的历史剧称为民族史诗。也许，你还记得马尔伯勒曾经说过，他不懂英国历史，都是从莎士比亚那里学到的。然而，如果我们仔细观察，就会发现除了在莎士比亚的作品里，几乎很少有更加令人难以忘怀的历史事件了。作者成功捕捉到了突出的历史事件，使之自成体系，转而创作出了一种有节奏的连贯性的情节，这就是施莱格尔所说的史诗；——事实上，伟大的思想家所想要描述的一切确实就像是史诗一般。历史剧中的每个片段，都有美丽的人物和事件，这样就构成了一件完美的作品。阿金库尔战役深深打动了我，在某种程度上，它是莎士比亚最完美的作品之一。在剧中他对两支军队的描述：衣衫褴褛、疲惫不堪的英国士兵，在战斗前夕那可怕的时刻，充满了宿命感；然后是无所畏惧的豪言壮语："好样的壮士们，你们是英格兰打造出来的！"这里蕴藏着一种高贵的爱国主义精神，与你有时所听说的莎士比亚的"冷漠"相差甚远。这是一颗真正英国人的心在跳动，既沉着冷静又坚不可摧，贯穿在他的整个事业之中；不喧哗，也不张扬，这样反而显得更加伟大。这里蕴藏着一种声音，就像钢环发出的声音，铿锵有力。如果莎士比亚在场的话，那么在他的内心深处，同样也会发出如此强烈的共鸣！

但我想要说的是，一般在莎士比亚的作品里，我们对这位作者几乎没有完整的印象，即使我们对许多人物有充分的了解。他的作品犹如许许多多的窗口，透过这些窗口，我们可以窥见他那一点点的内心世界。相对而言，他所有的作品似乎都是草率、不完美的，是在有限的环境中创作的；只是偶尔零散地记录下了这个剧中人物完整的对话。他的有些著作就好像是来自天堂的荣光，光芒四射，照亮事物的本质。你会说："这是真实的，一言既出，即成永恒；无论何时何地，一旦有了一个开放的人类灵魂，那将都是真真切切的！"然而，这突如其来的光芒，使我们周围的一切失去了光泽；在某种程度上是暂时的，墨守成规的。唉，遗憾的是莎士比亚不得不为环球剧院写作，他伟大的灵魂不得不尽其所能地强迫自己这样做，去适应当时的环境。除此之外，别无选择。这就是那时莎士比亚的处境，就像我们所有人一样。人们都是在特定的条件下工作的。雕塑家不能在我们面前自由地表达自己的思想，但他却可以使用现有的工具，把他的思想体现在石头上并加以塑造。对于诗人或者任何人，我们只有通过他们的只言片语，才能读到他们的思想片段。

凡是研究过莎士比亚的人，也许会意识到莎士比亚是一个以他自己的方式存在的先知，他具有一种类似先知的洞察力；虽然，他采用了另外一种文风。对他而言，大自然也是神圣的，无法用言语来表达，深邃如地狱，高耸如天堂："我们是梦幻的化身！"在西敏寺的那轴书卷，汇集了所有先知深奥的智慧，很少有人能够读得懂它。然而，这个人只会唱圣歌，除了音乐之外并不会布道。这个人叫但丁，我们把他称为中世纪天主教富于音乐美感的牧师，难道我们就不可以把莎士比亚称为真正天主教的未来和所有时代"普世教会"中更加富于音乐美感的牧师吗？这里没有狭隘的迷信，没有严酷的禁欲主义，没有不容异议，也没有狂热的偏激和刚愎自用。就目前而言，这是一个启示，在自然界中蕴藏着千千万万个美丽和神圣，让我们所有人都尽情地崇拜！我们可以不失公允地说，莎士比亚创造出了一种普世的诗篇，这些诗篇并非不适合放在更加神圣的诗篇中倾听。如果我们能够理解这些普世的诗篇，就不会感觉与这些诗篇不和谐，而是非常地和谐！——我不能像有些人那样，把莎士比亚称作"怀疑论者"，莎士比亚对那个时代的教义和对神学的争论，表现出来的漠不关心的态度误导了人们。事实并非如此：莎士比亚并非不爱国，尽管他很少提到他的爱国主义。他也不是怀疑主义者，尽管他很少提及他的信仰。他的这种"冷漠"正是他的伟大之处：他的整个心灵都沉浸在他自己崇拜的王国之中，我们姑且可以这么说。这些对他的争论，对于其他人来说是至关重要的；而对他来说，根本无关紧要。

然而，我们对莎士比亚给我们带来的作品加以崇拜，或者随便你怎么称呼它，这难道不是一件荣耀的事吗？对我而言，这样一个人能在这个大地上生活，其本身就具有神圣的意义。难道他不是我们众人的眼睛，是上天恩赐的光明使者吗？——说到底，这位莎士比亚无论从哪方面说，都是一个无意识的人，一个意识不到上天启示的人，这样不是更好吗？莎士比亚不觉得自己像穆罕默德那样，因为他看透了那些内在的辉煌，他就是"上帝的先知"，就这点而论他难道不比穆罕默德更加伟大吗？确实更加伟大；而且，如果按照我们严格的推理，就像我们对待但丁的事例那样，莎士比亚应当更加成功……

嗯：莎士比亚是我们沃里克郡穷苦的农民，由于受到南安普敦伯爵的青睐，升任为剧场的经理；这样他就可以不用以乞讨为生了。多亏了托马斯·露西爵士，因为他要把莎士比亚送去踏板车！莎士比亚和我们住在一起的时候，我们并没有把他当作像奥丁一样的神；——关于这一点有许多话可说。但我想要说或者重申的是：尽管现在英雄崇拜在我们国家的地位令人遗憾，但是可以想想这位莎士比亚在我们中间到底已经变成了什么样。除了这位斯特拉特福镇的农民，我们这片土地还产生过什么英国人？我们宁肯失去成千上万个普通英国人，也不愿失去这位斯特拉特福镇的农民。我们不会用他来交换任何最高权力，他是历年来我们所造就过的最伟大的人物。他为我们在国外赢得了荣誉，成为为我们英国大家庭增光添彩的人物，我们什么都可以放弃，唯有莎士比亚不可舍弃。试想一下，如果有人问我们，在印度帝国和莎士比亚之间，你们英国人会放弃哪一个？是愿意曾经拥有过印度帝国，还是愿意从来没有过这位莎士比亚？这的确是个难以回答的问题。官方人士无疑会用官方语言来回答；但对于我们而言，我们不应该被迫回答这一问题。有没有印度帝国，我们并不在乎，但我们不能没有莎士比亚！印度帝国终有一天会失去，然而莎士比亚却不会，他永远和我们在一起；我们不能放弃我们的莎士比亚！

不，除了精神层面之外，应该把莎士比亚看作一个真实的、有市场的、切实有用的财产。在不久的将来，英格兰，我们这个岛屿将只能容纳一小部分的英国人；而在美国，在新荷兰，在两极之间，从东方到西方，撒克逊人将会覆盖这地球上的广大地区。现在怎样才能将所有的这些撒克逊人凝聚在一起，形成一个民族，这样他们彼此之间就不会再相互争斗，而是和平相处，像兄弟般交往，互相帮助？这也是被人们公认为最大的实际问题。所有的主权国家和政府都在为之而奋斗。怎样才能实现呢？议会法案和政府首相皆不可能实现。就议会所能做的而言就是分离，美国已经与我们分道扬镳了。要解决这个问题也并非异想天开，因为这里面有不少实实在在的可能。这里，我是说，有这样一位英国国王，无论是在议会或者是在联合议会，无论何时，都不会有任何机会可以去罢免他！这位"国王"就是莎士比亚，难道他不是以至高无上的权威照耀着我们所有人吗？作为最高贵，最温文尔雅，然而也是最强大、坚不可摧的团结象征；在这点上，难道不比任何其他的手段和兵器更具有价值吗？我们可以想象一千年之后，莎士比亚仍然会在所有英国人的国度上空闪烁着光芒。从帕拉马塔到纽约，无论在什么地方，无论在什么地区管辖下，英国的男绅女士，他们都会奔走相告："是的，莎士比亚是我们英国人，我们造就了他，我们说话和思考的方式都是来源于他，我们与他是同一种族，血脉相承。"凡是具有常识的政治家，如果他愿意，可能也会这样想。

是的，的确，对于一个国家而言，能获得一个清晰的声音，这是一件伟大的事情；它造就了一位会优美地表达这个国家心声的人！例如，可怜的意大利，处在四分五裂的状态之中，没有任何一份协议或条约能够显示出它是作为一个统一的整体。然而，高贵的意大利实际上就是一个整体，意大利创造出了但丁，意大利可以为自己说话！俄罗斯沙皇，纵然拥有大量坚利的刺刀、哥萨克骑兵和大炮，确实很强大；并且他能在政治上把地球上一大片的土地统一在一起，这是一项伟大的壮举；然而，他现在却没有说话的能力。他的确伟大，但却是一种无声的伟大。他不具备语言的天才，这个时代和所有的人听不到他的心声。他必须学会说话，到目前为止，他仍然是一个无声的怪物。他的大炮将会生锈，哥萨克骑兵也会变得无足轻重，而但丁的声音依然可以被清晰地听到。拥有但丁的民族团结在了一起，这是无声的俄罗斯无法实现的。——让我们就此结束对英雄诗人的评论吧！

JOHN RUSKIN (1819—1900)

John Ruskin (1819—1900), the son of a wealthy wine merchant, was born in London. He was educated privately and at Oxford where he took his degree in 1840. As a result of his interest in the painter Turner (1775—1851), he produced a series of studies on *Modern Painters* (1843—1860) which, together with the *Seven Lamps of Architecture* (1849) arid the *Stones of Venice* (1851—1853), represents his most notable writings on art. In these works, Ruskin expounded his theory that a nation's art is the sole index of its moral and social conditions, and that great art is impossible unless it is founded on national greatness. In his later life, Ruskin turned from an art critic to a social reformer. He spent considerable time and energy in attempting to improve the living environments of the English working classes and gave a large part of his fortune to charitable objects. His later works such as *Sesame and LiLies* (1865), *The Crown of Wild Olive* (1866), and *Fors Clavigera* (1871) are chiefly concerned with labour and economic problems. In his old age, he was also for many years professor of art at Oxford and gave in his lectures great impetus to the Pre-raphaelite movement in poetry and painting.

Like Carlyle, Ruskin was one of the 'major prophets' of the Victorian age. In his interpretation of nature, he re-awakened his countrymen to the glories of what they were in danger of losing in the machine age. He directed with much moral ardour a campaign for reformation against the ugliness of the modern industrial world, the lack of beauty and harmony in life. In both his works on art and political economy, he revealed a fine emotional quality, a marvellous power of expression, and a superb style. The rich melodiousness with which he wrote placed him among the prose masters of his time.

【作者简介】

约翰·罗斯金（1819—1900），出生于伦敦，他是一个富有的葡萄酒商人的儿子。他接受私立教育，并于 1840 年获得了牛津大学的学位。由于他对画家特纳（1775—1851）的兴趣，他在《现代画家》（1843—1860）一书中进行了一系列的研究，这些绘画研究与他的《建筑的七盏明灯》（1849）和《威尼斯之石》（1851—1853）代表了他在艺术领域里最有建树的著作。在这些作品中，罗斯金阐述了他的理论，即一个国家的艺术是其道德和社会状况的唯一索引，伟大的艺术建立在国家强大的基础上，否则是不可能的。在他晚年的生活中，罗斯金从一个艺术评论家转变成了社会改革者。他花费了大量的时间和精力试图改善英国工人阶级的生活环境，并把他的大部分个人财产捐赠给了慈善机构。他的后期作品如《芝麻与百合》（1865）、《野橄榄花冠》（1866）和《劳动者的力量》（1871），主要涉及的是劳动和经济问题。在他晚年的时候，曾担任牛津大学艺术教授多年，并通过他的讲座对拉斐尔前派诗歌和绘画运动起到了巨大的推动作用。

　　和卡莱尔一样，罗斯金是维多利亚时代的"主要先知"之一。在对大自然的诠释中，他再次唤醒了他的同胞们，让他们重新意识到他们的荣耀很可能会在机器时代里丧失。他以"极大的道德热情"发起了一场改革运动，反对世界现代工业的丑陋，反对生活中缺乏美感与和谐。在他的艺术和政治经济学的作品中，体现出了完美的情感品质、非凡的表达能力和高超的文风。他创作的作品富有优美的韵律，使他跻身于他那个时代散文大师的行列之中。

The Earth-Veil

'To dress it and to keep it.'

That, then, was to be our work. Alas! what work have we set ourselves upon instead! How have we ravaged the garden instead of kept it—feeding our war-horses with its flowers, and splintering its trees into spear-shafts!

'And at the East a flaming sword.'

Is its flame quenchless? and are those gates that keep the way indeed passable no more? or is it not rather that we no more desire to enter? For what can we conceive of that first Eden which we might not yet win back, if we chose? It was a place full of flowers, we say. Well: the flowers are always striving to grow wherever we suffer them; and the fairer, the closer. There may, indeed, have been a Fall of Flowers, as a **Fall of Man**; but assuredly creatures such as we are can now fancy nothing lovelier than roses and lilies, which would grow for us side by side, leaf overlapping leaf, till the Earth was white and red with them, if we cared to have it so. And Paradise was full of pleasant shades and fruitful avenues. Well: what hinders us from covering as much of the world as we like with pleasant shade, and pure blossom, and goodly fruit? Who forbids its valleys to be covered over with corn till they laugh and sing? Who prevents its dark forests, ghostly and uninhabitable, from being changed into infinite orchards, wreathing the hills with frail-floreted snow, far away to the half-lighted horizon of April, and flushing the face of all the autumnal earth with glow of clustered food? But Paradise was a place of peace, we say, and all the animals were gentle servants to us. Well: the world would yet be a place of peace if we were all peacemakers, and gentle service should we have of its creatures if we gave them gentle mastery. But so long as we make sport of slaying bird and beast, so long as we choose to contend rather with our fellows than with our faults, and make battlefield of our meadows instead of pasture—so long, truly, the Flaming Sword will still turn every way, and the gates of Eden remain barred close enough, till we have sheathed the sharper flame of our own passions, and broken down the closer gates of our own hearts.

I have been led to see and feel this more and more, as I consider the service which the flowers and trees, which man was at first appointed to keep, were intended to render to him in return for his care; and the services they still render to him, as far as he allows their influence, or fulfils his own task towards them. For what infinite wonderfulness there is in this vegetation, considered, as indeed it is, as the means by which the earth becomes the companion of man— his friend and his teacher! In the conditions which we have traced in its rocks, there could only be seen preparation for his existence;— the characters which enable him to live on it safely, and to work with it easily—in all these it has been inanimate and passive; but vegetation is to it as an imperfect soul, given to meet the soul of man. The earth in its depths must remain dead and cold, incapable except of slow crystalline change; but at its surface, which human beings look upon and deal with, it ministers to them through a veil of strange intermediate being; which breathes but has no voice; moves, but cannot leave its appointed place; passes through life without consciousness, to death without bitterness; wears the beauty of youth, without its passion; and declines to the weakness of age, without its regret.

And in this mystery of intermediate being, entirely subordinate to us, with which we can deal as we choose, having just the greater power as we have the less responsibility for our treatment of the unsuffering creature, most of the pleasures which we need from the external world are gathered, and most of the lessons we need are written, all kinds of precious grace and teaching being united in this link between the Earth and Man; wonderful in universal adaptation to his need, desire, and discipline; God's daily preparation of the earth for him, with beautiful means of life. First, a carpet to make it soft for him; then, a coloured fantasy of embroidery thereon; then, tall spreading of foliage to shade him from sun heat, and shade also the fallen rain, that it may not dry quickly back into the clouds, but stay to nourish the springs among the moss. Stout wood to bear this leafage: easily to be cut, yet tough and light, to make houses for him, or instruments (lance-shaft, or plough-handle, according to his temper); useless, it had been, if harder; useless, if less fibrous; useless, if less elastic. Winter comes, and the shade of leafage falls away, to let the sun warm the earth; the strong boughs remain, breaking the strength of winter winds. The seeds which are to prolong the race, innumerable according to the need, are made beautiful and palatable, varied into infinitude of appeal to the fancy of man, or provision for his service: cold juice, or glowing spice, or balm, or incense, softening oil, preserving resin, medicine of **styptic**, **febrifuge**, or lulling charm: and all these presented in forms of endless change. Fragility or force, softness and strength, in all degrees and aspects; unerring uprightness as of temple pillars, or unguided wandering of feeble tendrils on the ground; mighty resistances of rigid arm and limb to the storms of ages, or wavings to and fro with faintest pulse of summer streamlet. Roots cleaving the strength of rock, or binding the transience of the sand; crests basking in sunshine of the desert, or hiding by dripping spring and lightless cave; foliage far tossing in entangled fields beneath every wave of ocean—clothing, with variegated, everlasting films, the peaks of the trackless mountains, or ministering at cottage doors to every gentlest passion and simplest joy of humanity.

Being thus prepared for us in all ways, and made beautiful, and good for food, and for building, and for instruments in our hands, this race of plants, deserving boundless affection and admiration from us, become, in proportion to their obtaining it, a nearly perfect test of our being in right temper of mind and way of life; so that no one can be far wrong in either who loves the trees enough, and every one is assuredly wrong in both who does not love them, if his life has brought them in his way. It is clearly possible to do without them, for the great companionship of the sea and sky are all that sailors need; and many a noble heart has been taught the best it had to learn between dark stone walls. Still if human life be cast among trees at all, the love borne to them is a sure test of its purity.

And it is a sorrowful proof of the mistaken ways of the world that the 'country,' in the simple sense of a place of fields and trees, has hitherto been the source of reproach to its inhabitants, and that the words 'countryman, rustic, clown, paysan, villager,' still signify a rude and untaught person, as opposed to the words 'townsman' and 'citizen.' We accept this usage of words, or the evil which it signifies, somewhat too quietly; as if it were quite necessary and natural that country-people should be rude, and townspeople gentle. Whereas I believe that the result of each mode of life may, in some stages of the world's progress, be the exact reverse; and that another use of words may be forced upon us by a new aspect of facts, so that we may find ourselves saying: 'Such and such a person is very gentle and kind—he is quite rustic; and such and such another person is very rude and ill-taught—he is quite urbane.'

At all events, cities have hitherto gained the better part of their good report through our evil ways of going on in the world generally; chiefly and eminently through our bad habit of fighting with each other. No field, in the Middle Ages, being safe from devastation, and every country lane yielding easier passage, to the marauders, peacefully-minded men necessarily congregated in cities, and walled themselves in, making as few cross-country roads as possible; while the man who sowed and reaped the harvests of Europe were only the servants or slaves of the barons. The disdain of all agricultural pursuits by the nobility, and of all plain facts by the monks kept educated Europe in a state of mind over which natural phenomena could have no power; body and intellect being lost in the practice of war without purpose, and the meditation of words without meaning.

Men learned the dexterity with sword and syllogism, which they mistook for education, within cloister and tiltyard; and looked on all the broad space of the world of God mainly as a place for exercise of horses, or for growth of food.

There is a beautiful type of this neglect of the perfectness of the Earth's beauty, by reason of the passions of men, in that picture of **Paul Uccello**'s of the battle of Sant'Egidio, in which the armies meet on a country road beside a hedge of wild roses; the tender red flowers tossing above the helmets, and glowing beneath the lowered lances. For in like manner the whole of Nature only shone hitherto for man between the tossing of helmet-crests; and sometimes I cannot but think of the trees of the earth as capable of a kind of sorrow, in that imperfect life of theirs, as they opened their innocent leaves in the warm springtime, in vain for men; and all along the dells of England her beeches cast their dappled shade only where the outlaw drew his bow, and the king rode his careless chase; and by the sweet French rivers their long ranks of poplar waved in the twilight, only to show the flames of burning cities on the horizon, through the tracery of their stems; amidst the fair **defiles** of **the Apennines**, the twisted olive-trunks hid the ambushes of treachery; and on their valley meadows, day by day, the lilies which were white at the dawn were washed with crimson at sunset.

Notes

'The East Veil,' taken from *Modern Painters*, is one of the modern protests against men's defilement of nature.

'To dress it and to keep it.' When God has created man out of the dust of the ground and planted a garden in Eden, he 'took the man and put him into the garden of Eden to dress it and to keep it.' (*Genesis*, ii, 7—15.)

'And at the East a flaming sword.' When Adam had taken the forbidden fruit, God sent him forth from the garden of Eden. 'And he placed at the east of the garden of Eden Cherubims, and a flaming sword which turned every way, to keep the way of the tree of life.' (*Genesis*, iii, 24.)

Fall of Man, the change by which the race passed from a state of innocence (Eden) to a sinful condition when Adam and Eve disobeyed the divine command.

styptic, substance that checks bleeding.

febrifuge, medicine to reduce fever.

Paul Uccello (1397—1475), Florentine painter. His battlepieces are particularly remarkable for the representation of the picturesque armour and costumes of his time.

Defiles, narrow passes or gorges.

the Apennines, a mountain chain in central Italy.

【作品简介】

本文选自《现代画家》，是作者用来抗议人类对大自然的亵渎的。

【作品解析】

"To dress it and to keep it.": 当上帝用尘土创造人类的时候，在伊甸园中种植了一个花园，他"把创造出来的人带到了伊甸园里，是为了让他们装扮和保护好伊甸园"（见《创世记》，第二卷）。

"And at the East a flaming sword."：当亚当偷吃了禁果，上帝就把他从伊甸园里赶了出来。"上帝又在伊甸园的东边安放了基路伯（有翅膀的智天使）和一把燃烧着的并能向四面八方转动的火焰剑，是为了守护通往生命之树的道路。"（见《创世记》，第三卷）

Fall of Man：指当亚当和夏娃违背了神的命令时，人类就从纯洁无罪的状态（伊甸园）堕落为邪恶有罪的状态。

Styptic：止血药。

Febrifuge：解热药，退烧药。

Paul Uccello：保罗·乌切罗（1397—1475），佛罗伦萨画家。他的战争题材作品尤其引人注目，因为他生动地再现了他那个时代美丽如画的盔甲和服装。

Defiles：狭窄的通道或者峡谷。

the Apennines：亚平宁山脉，意大利中部的一个山脉。

【参考译文】

大地面纱

"把伊甸园装扮起来，并将它保护好。"

这就是我们的工作。天哪！而我们却做了些什么呢！我们在蹂躏伊甸园，并没能把它保护好；——我们用它的鲜花喂养了我们的战马，用它的树木做成了长矛杆！

"在东方，有一把燃烧着的利剑。"

这燃烧的火焰不可熄灭吗？难道伊甸园的大门真的再也不可以通行了吗？或许，我们不再渴望迈进这扇大门了吗？如果可以让我们选择的话，我们能想象得到那个我们再也回不去的原始的伊甸园会是什么样的呢？我们会说，那是一个鲜花盛开的地方。嗯，不管我们怎样糟蹋它们，鲜花总是在努力地生长，而且愈发美丽漂亮，愈发茂盛稠密，一片连着一片。的确，也许曾经有过鲜花的凋谢，就像人的衰落一样。然而，我们可以确定的是，芸芸众生中没有比玫瑰花和百合花更加可爱的了。只要我们好好照料，玫瑰花和百合花就会生长在我们身边，叶子重叠着叶子，一直绽放下去，直到大地铺满了红色和白色的鲜花。伊甸园里到处是宜人的树荫和硕果累累的大道。好吧，那又是什么在阻碍着我们用宜人的树荫、纯洁的鲜花和丰硕的果实尽可能地去装饰我们所喜欢的世界呢？那么，又是谁在禁止山谷里长满谷子，直到它们不再拥有欢声笑语和歌声？究竟又是谁在阻止我们把幽灵般无人居住的阴暗森林改变成广袤无垠的果园？又再让那轻盈飘落的雪花覆盖着环抱的群山，远离那四月半明半暗的地平线？又是谁在阻碍着用丰硕的果实装扮整个秋天，使整个大地焕发出五彩斑斓的不一样的光彩呢？我们说，伊甸园是一个和平的地方，所有的动植物都是我们温顺的仆人。嗯，好吧，如果我们人人都是和平的使者，那么世界就是一个和平的地方。现实生活中，只要我们能够温和地对待这些生灵，那么它们也会忠诚、友善地对待我们。但是，只要我们把杀戮飞鸟和走兽作为一项运动取乐；只要我们选择与我们的同胞抗争，而从不去反思我们自己的过错；只要我们把草原变成战场而不是变成牧场——只要这些都是真实的发生，那就再见吧！燃烧的利剑将会向四面八方不停地旋转，伊甸园的栅栏大门也依然会紧紧地关闭着，除非我们收敛起那燃烧着的激情的烈火，敞开自己内心深处紧闭的大门。

每当我思考人和草木的互惠关系，就加深了我对这一点的领悟：人类最初是被派来照料这些花草树木的，而这些草木也须服务于人类以回报照料之恩；只要人类允许它们的影响存在，或者说履行自己对它们的义务，草木就会继续为人类提供服务。地球的一层植被是何等神奇！实际上也确实如此，有了这层植被，地球才成为人类的伴侣——人类的良师益友。我们在地球岩石中追踪到的各种状态中，只能看到它在为人类的生存做准备——这些特征能够使人类在地球上安全地生活，轻松地劳作——在所有的这些方面，地球都是无生命、处于被动状态的；但对地球来说，植被就是它的一个不够完美的灵魂，被赋予了与人类的灵魂相遇的机会。在地球的深处一定是无生命、寒冷的状态，除了缓慢的结晶变化之外，没有任何的活动迹象；然而，在人们所看到的并与之打交道的地球表层，地球是通过薄薄一层神奇的中介物向他们提供服务的；它呼吸，却没有声音；它可转动，却不能离开指定的位置；它终其一生没有意识；走向死亡却无痛苦；带着青春的美丽，却没有青春的激情；年老枯萎时，也没有枯萎的遗憾。

这个神奇的中介物，对我们唯命是从，我们可以随心所欲地任意处置。我们之所以拥有更大的权力，是因为我们对待这些未曾受过苦难的生物，只需要承担较轻的责任。人类需要从外部世界去搜集更多的快乐，需要记录下更多应该吸取的经验教训，这些各种各样珍贵的恩典和谆谆教导结合在一起，就形成了一条大地与人类之间紧密相连的纽带；大地在普遍适应人类的需求、欲望以及行为规则方面有着奇妙的能力；这些都是上帝赐予人类美好的生活方式以及生存的空间。上帝首先是铺上了一层“地毯”使之柔软；然后绣了一幅五彩缤纷的彩画；接着再种植高高的、枝叶茂密的参天大树为人类遮阴纳凉，使人类免受日晒，也可以免受雨淋；这样避免水分很快蒸发到云层中使得地面干裂，而是将雨水作为滋润的泉水留在了苔藓中。质地坚硬的树木，可以长出树叶，容易修剪；树枝既坚硬又轻巧，可以用来建造房屋，或者根据不同的特质和需求做成劳动器具，可以用作矛杆，也可以用作犁柄。然而，如果木质过硬，缺乏纤维，缺乏弹性，那就没有什么多大的用处了。到了冬天，遮阴的绿叶脱落了，留下了挺拔粗壮的树枝，温暖的阳光普照着大地，光影斑驳，竭力阻挡冬日里寒冷的强风。延续生命的种子，在各种需求下，被制成美味可口、变化无穷、引人入胜的产品，并为人类的需求提供了各种服务：冷果汁、赤红的香料、香脂、檀香、软化油、防腐树脂、止血药、退烧药、安眠药，所有的这些都是以无穷无尽的变化形式呈现在人们眼前的。脆弱与强大，柔软与坚硬，以各种不同程度的对比呈现在各个方面：如像庙宇里的梁柱一样总是那么挺拔，或是像地面上的缠藤漫无目的地蔓延；坚硬的树枝和枝干竭力抵御岁月的风暴，或是在夏日里随着那潺潺的溪流摇曳；树根有劈裂岩石的力量，或是束缚住瞬间而过的流沙；树冠在沙漠沐浴着阳光，或是躲藏在泉水滴落暗淡无光的岩洞里；树叶在海洋的每一个浪花中缠绵地漂荡着——色彩斑斓、经久不衰的薄薄云彩给荒无人迹的山峰披上了一件衣裳，或是在村舍小屋门前，感受着人类最温柔的情感和最淳朴的快乐。

就是这样，植物为我们做好了一切准备，使我们的世界变得美丽，有益于食物，有益于建筑，有益于我们手中的工具，值得我们无限喜爱和钦佩。植物为人类所付出的与其相应所获得回报的比例，成为对于我们人类的心态是否正确和生活方式是否良好的一个近乎完美的考验。这样，我们每个人是否对树木有足够的爱或者根本不爱，对与错都可以比较准确地检测出来。当然，有些人在生活中不需要树木也是很有可能的。对于水手们来说，只要有海洋和蔚蓝色的天空陪伴就足够了。而许多高尚的心灵，是在黑暗的路径和石墙之间被培养出来的。尽管如此，如果人类的生活被投放在丛林之中，对树木的爱无疑是对心灵纯洁的真正考验。人们认为"乡村"，简单地说，不过就是有田野和树木的地方，一直以来都是造成当地居民遭受责难的根源；"乡下人、农夫、乡巴佬、农民、村民"则与"城镇居民"和"市民"的词义截然相反，这些词语都含有粗鲁无礼和没有教养的意思。这是一种被世俗误解的可悲的验证。我们接受这些词语的用法，或者说，接受它们所表达的恶意，有点太过于心安理得了，平静得像无事人一样；好像乡下人就注定是粗鲁没有教养的，而城里人则是有礼貌有教养的。然而我相信，在世界历史发展的某些阶段，每一种生活模式都有可能出现正好完全相反的结果：也许事实迫使我们使用另一套词语，我们会说："某某人温柔善良，举止彬彬有礼，他是乡下人；某某人非常粗鲁没有教养，他是城里人。"

不管怎样，迄今为止，大部分城市都是通过我们以往在世界上的邪恶行径，主要是通过我们以往互相争斗的坏习惯，来获取对它们好的报道。中世纪的田野，没有一块可以免受战争的烽火，不受破坏；每一条乡间小道对掠夺者来说，都是敛财的轻易通道；爱好和平的人们必然会聚集在城市里，用城墙把自己围起来，尽可能减少穿越乡间的小道；而那些在欧洲乡间播种和收割庄稼的人，他们只是爵爷们的仆人和奴隶。贵族们对一切农活的藐视，修道士对所有明显的现实不屑一顾，使受过教育的欧洲人一直处于连自然现象也无能为力的一种心理状态。因此，在毫无目的的战争中，人们失去了身躯；在毫无意义的语言冥想中，失去了才智。人们在修道院和骑士的比武场里，研习三段论和剑法，误以为那就是教育。他们把上帝创造的广阔世界看作是练马场，或者是种植食物的地方。

人类由于自己的激情，从而忽略了一种美丽，那就是地球的完美无缺。意大利画家保罗·乌切罗的画作《圣罗马诺之战》，就是一个典型的例子。在这幅画中，两支军队在乡间的小路上相遇了，路边的篱笆长满了野玫瑰，娇嫩鲜红的花朵在头盔上方摇曳，低垂的长矛在闪闪发光。迄今为止，整个自然界都是以同样的方式照耀着人类，只有在头盔顶饰的摇曳之间，人们才能看到闪耀着的光芒。有时我们不得不想到，大地上的树木在它们那并不完美的生命中也许会感受到某种哀伤，就像它们在温暖的春天张开天真的叶子，然而这对于人类来说却是徒劳的；沿着英格兰的山谷，山毛榉树只有在亡命之徒拉弓射箭的地方才会投下斑驳的树影，而国王则骑着马漫不经心地追逐着猎物。在甜美的法兰西河畔，白杨树像排着长长的队伍，在暮色中摇曳，也只是为了透过树茎中像窗棂一样的图案，向我们呈现地平线上宛若燃烧着火焰的城市。在亚平宁山脉荆棘遍布的小道上，弯曲的橄榄树干中隐藏着背叛和伏击；在山谷的草原上，黎明时洁白的百合花被落日映衬得绯红。日复一日，周而复始。

Alpine Skies: Sunrise to Sunset

Stand upon the peak of some isolated mountain at daybreak, when the night mists first rise from off the plains, and watch their white and lake-like fields, as they float in level bays and winding gulfs about the islanded summits of the lower hills, untouched yet by more than dawn, colder and more quiet than a windless sea under the moon of midnight; watch when the first sunbeam is sent upon the silver channels, how the foam of their undulating surface parts and passes away, and down under their depths the glittering city and green pasture lie like **Atlantis**, between the white paths of winding rivers; the flakes of light falling every moment faster and broader among the starry spires, as the wreathed surges break and vanish above them, and the confused crests and ridges of the dark hills shorten their gray shadows upon the plain... Wait a little longer, and you shall see those scattered mists rallying in the ravines, and floating up towards you, along the winding valleys, till they crouch in quiet masses, iridescent with the morning light, upon the broad breasts of the higher hills, whose leagues of massy undulation will melt back and back into that robe of material light, until they fade away, lost in its lustre, to appear again above, in the serene heaven, like a wild, bright, impossible dream, foundationless and inaccessible, their very bases vanishing in the unsubstantial and mocking blue of the deep lake below... Wait yet a little longer, and you shall see those mists gather themselves into white towers, and stand like fortresses along the promontories, massy and motionless, only piled with every instant higher and higher into the sky, and casting longer shadows athwart the rocks; and out of the pale blue of the horizon you will see forming and advancing a troop of narrow, dark, pointed vapours, which will cover the sky, inch by inch, with their gray network, and take the light off the landscape with an eclipse which will stop the singing of the birds and the motion of the leaves, together; and then you will see horizontal bars of black shadow forming under them, and lurid wreaths create themselves, you know not how, along the shoulders of the hills; you never see them form, but when you look back to a place which was clear an instant ago, there is a cloud on it, hanging by the precipices, as a hawk pauses over his prey... And then you will hear the sudden rush of the awakened wind, and you will see those watchtowers of vapour swept away from their foundations, and waving curtains of opaque rain let down to the valleys, swinging from the burdened clouds in black bending fringes, or pacing in pale columns along the lake level, grazing its surface into foam as they go. And then, as the sun sinks, you shall see the storm drift for an instant from off the hills; leaving their broad sides smoking, and loaded yet with snow-white, torn, steam-like rags of capricious vapour, now gone, now gathered again, while the smouldering sun, seething not far away, but burning like a redhot ball beside you, and as if you could reach it, plunges through the rushing wind and rolling cloud with headlong fall, as if it meant to rise no more, dyeing all the air about it with blood... And then you shall hear the fainting tempest die in the hollow of the night, and you shall see a green halo kindling on the summit of the eastern hills, brighter—brighter yet, till the large white circle of the slow moon is lifted up among the barred clouds, step by step, line by line; star after star she quenches with her kindling light, setting in their stead an army of pale, penetrable, fleecy wreaths in the heaven, to give light upon the earth, which move together, hand in hand, company by company, troop by troop, so measured in their unity of motion, that the whole heaven seems to roll with them, and the earth to reel under them... And then wait yet for one hour until the east again becomes purple, and the heaving mountains, rolling against it in darkness, like waves of a wild sea, are drowned one by one in the glory of its burning; watch the white glaciers blaze in their winding paths about the mountains, like mighty serpents with scales of fire: watch the columnar peaks of solitary snow, kindling downwards, chasm by chasm, each in itself a new morning; their long avalanches cast down in keen streams brighter than the lightning, sending each his tribute of driven snow, like altar-smoke, up to the heaven; the rose-light of their silent domes flushing that heaven about them and above them, piercing with purer light through its purple lines of lifted cloud, casting a new glory on every wreath as it passes by, until the whole heaven, one scarlet canopy, is interwoven with a roof of waving flame, and tossing, vault beyond vault, as with the drifted wings of many companies of angels; and then, when you can look no more for gladness, and when you are bowed down with fear and love of the **Maker and Doer** of this, tell me **who has best delivered this His message** unto men!

<u>Notes</u>

This is a selection from *Modern Painters*, chapter 4 'Of Truth of Clouds,' (Part II, section 3, of entire work). It shows Ruskin as a master of the descriptive essay. In the representations of natural beauty, such as sunrise and sunset, the sky, the cloud, and the ocean, he is seldom surpassed by other English writers.

Atlantis, a mythical city lost beneath the waves of the Atlantic.

Maker and Doer, i.e. God.

who has best delivered this His message. In this section of the *Modern Painters*, Ruskin is arguing that Turner, more than other artists with whom he is compared, has been true in his representations of nature. So obviously, according to Ruskin, the answer is: It is Turner who has best delivered God's message.

【作品简介】

本文选自《现代画家》第四节《云的真相》(整个作品中的第二部分，第三章)。它充分表明了罗斯金是位叙事性的散文大师。在描绘诸如日出、日落、天空、云彩和海洋等自然美景的表现形式上，他很少被其他英国作家所超越。

【作品解析】

Atlantis：亚特兰蒂斯，一座在大西洋中消失的神秘城市。

Maker and Doer：即上帝。

who has best delivered this His message：在《现代画家》的这一部分中，罗斯金认为，特纳比其他艺术家更加能够真实地表现自然。所以，显而易见，根据罗斯金的说法，这个问题的答案是：特纳最能传达上帝的信息。

【参考译文】

阿尔卑斯山的天空：从日出到日落

拂晓十分，当夜幕下的云雾刚从平原上腾起，你站在某座孤山之峰，可以看到平原上白色的犹如湖泊般的田野，仿佛它们漂浮在平坦的海湾上，或蜿蜒曲折地环绕在那些形同岛屿的低谷山峦之巅。此时尚未得到黎明曙光的恩典，比在午夜月光下无风的大海更加宁静也更加寒冷。当第一缕阳光洒落在银色的海峡上，我们可以看到在水面上起伏的云雾，犹如浪花般白色的泡沫被驱散开来，渐渐地消失了。在云雾的深处，闪烁着荧光般的城市和绿色的牧场，就像亚特兰蒂斯一样，坐落在蜿蜒曲折的河流和白色小径之间。此时，在繁星密布的山峰之间，一缕缕银光瞬间急速地洒落下来，变得愈来愈快，面积也愈来愈大，就像汹涌澎湃的海浪扑打而过，最后消失在山峦之间。模糊不清的山峰和山脊也渐渐地退去了它们在地平线上灰色的阴影……又过了一会儿，你就会看到那些散落在山谷中薄薄的云雾，慢慢地聚集在了一起，沿着蜿蜒的山谷向你飘来，直到它们静静地蜷缩成一团，在晨曦的照耀下熠熠生辉。在高大宽阔的山峦之巅，那连绵起伏的一团一团云雾在不断地融化，又重新回归到了它们原有的本色之中，直到云雾的光泽渐渐消失。当云雾再次出现在平静清澈的天空中时，它们就像是自然生长的、明亮的、不可能实现的梦想；它没有根基，也无法接近，很快就消失在下方深邃的湖水那虚无缥缈的蓝色之中……又过一会儿，你就会看到那些薄薄的雾气聚集成了白色的塔楼，就像堡垒矗立在海角上一样，庞大而一动不动，只是不断地在空中堆积，愈堆愈高，在岩石上投下了越来越长的阴影。在淡蓝色的地平线上，你会看到一堆又窄、又暗、又尖的雾气正在聚集成群，并缓慢地向前推进，它们一点一点地用灰色的网遮盖住了天空，使天空变得昏暗，最后吞食了太阳，把阳光从大地上掠走；此时，鸟儿停止了歌唱，树叶也停止了摇摆；然后你会看到在天空下，形成了黑色横条阴影地带，同时沿着山岳之肩，呈现出一个色彩艳丽的环状云雾，你都不知道它们是怎样形成的；你永远看不到它们的形状，当你回过头去看，一瞬间，之前还是清澈晴朗的地方，现在上面已有了一片乌云，悬挂在悬崖边，就像一只鹰停靠在猎物的身上……然后，你会听到，像是从睡梦中被惊醒的呼啸的狂风；此时你会看到，那些由云彩堆积起来的蒸气塔楼从底部被吹散了，天空中晃动着的不透明的雨帘飘落到了山谷；黑色弯曲流苏状的雨帘从沉重的云层中纵身跃下，或沿着湖面以白皙的雨柱形式踱步，掠过湖面溅起了朵朵水花。然后，随着太阳落山，你会看到暴风骤雨瞬间就飘离了群山；在那宽阔的山坡上留下了缭绕的烟雾，弥漫着雪白的、破碎的、像蒸气一样变化无常散落的云雾，时而消失，时而又聚集在了一起；炙热的太阳在不远处翻腾，犹如一个灼热的火球在你身旁燃烧着，好似触手可及，当它穿过呼啸的狂风并俯冲而下一头栽进滚滚的云层，仿佛它不想再次升起，它把四周的天空染得通红……然后，你将会听到夜空中，暴风雨的声音愈来愈小，最后消失在夜幕之下。慢慢地你将会看到一圈绿色的光晕悬挂在东方的山顶上，越来越明亮——直到那轮硕大而洁白的圆月从被阻挡的云层中一步一步缓缓地升起；她用她那炽烈的光芒熄灭了一颗又一颗的星星，取而代之的是在天空中，呈现了一大群苍白的、可以穿透的、棉絮状的云朵，它们照亮了大地，手拉手，结伴而行，成群结队，步调缓慢而一致，以至于整个天空似乎都在跟着它们一起滚动，在天空之下的大地也随之滚动了起来……再过一个小时，直到东方再次变成紫色，起伏的群山就像在黑暗中急速地翻滚着的狂野的海浪一样，在燃烧的霞光中一座接着一座地被淹没了。你看那白色的冰河，像是在蜿蜒曲折的山间小路上闪烁着，犹如一条带有火鳞的巨蟒；你再看那孤零零的柱状雪山之峰，雪崩向下引爆，形成了一道道的断层，每一道断层都是一个崭新的早晨；接踵而来的雪崩，倾泻而下，比闪电还明亮，把每一片飞雪当作了祭品，就像祭坛上的云烟一样，送上了九霄云外的天国；寂静穹顶上的玫瑰色的光，照耀着四周的天空，把天空映得通红，它用那更纯净的亮光穿透紫色的云层，当每一个云环经过的时候，都会投下新的光辉，直到整个天空变成一个猩红色的天棚，与摇曳着的火焰交织在了一起，翻腾着，越过穹隆，宛如许许多多天使的翅膀在飞舞。这时，当你不再寻找快乐，当你对上帝产生了爱与敬畏，并拜倒在他的脚下时，请告诉我，谁才能把上帝的启示更好地传递给人类！

A Child's May-Day Party

Though I am no poet, I have dreams sometimes:—I dreamed I was at a child's May-day party, in which every means of entertainment had been provided for them, by a wise and kind host. It was in a stately house, with beautiful gardens attached to it; and the children had been set free in the rooms and gardens, with no care whatever but how to pass their afternoon rejoicingly. They did not, indeed, know much about what was to happen next day; and some of them, I thought, were a little frightened, because there was a chance of their being sent to a new school where there were examinations; but they kept the thoughts of that out of their heads as well as they could, and resolved to enjoy themselves. The house, I said, was in a beautiful garden, and in the garden were all kinds of flowers; sweet, grassy banks for rest; and smooth lawns for play; and pleasant streams and woods; and rocky places for climbing. And the children were happy for a little while, but presently they separated themselves into parties; and then each party declared it would have a piece of the garden for its own, and that none of the others should have anything to do with that piece. Next, they quarrelled violently which pieces they would have; and at last the boys took up the thing, as boys should do, 'practically,' and fought in the flower beds till there was hardly a flower left standing; then they trampled down each other's bits of the garden out of spite; and the girls cried till they could cry no more; and so they all lay down at last breathless in the ruin, and waited for the time when they were to be taken home in the evening.

Meanwhile, the children in the house had been making themselves happy also in their manner. For them, there had been provided every kind of indoor pleasure: there was music for them to dance to; and the library was open, with all manner of amusing books; and there was a museum full of the most curious shells, and animals, and birds; and there was a workshop, with **lathes** and carpenters' tools, for the ingenious boys; and there were pretty fantastic dresses, for the girls to dress in; and there were microscopes, and kaleidoscopes; and whatever toys a child could fancy; and a table, in the dining-room, loaded with everything nice to eat.

But, in the midst of all this, it struck two or three of the more 'practical' children, that they would like some of the brassheaded nails that studded the chairs; and so they set to work to pull them out. Presently, the others, who were reading, or looking at shells, took a fancy to do the like; and, in a little while, all the children, nearly, were spraining their fingers, in pulling out brassheaded nails. With all that they could pull out, they were not satisfied; and then, everybody wanted some of somebody else's. And at last, the really practical and sensible ones declared, that nothing was of any real consequence, that afternoon, except to get plenty of brassheaded nails; and that the books, and the cakes, and the microscopes were of no use at all in themselves, but only, if they could be exchanged for nail heads. And at last they began to fight for nail heads, as the others fought for the bits of garden. Only here and there, a despised one shrank away into a corner, and tried to get a little quiet with a book, in the midst of the noise; but all the practical ones thought of nothing else but counting nail heads all the afternoon—even though they knew they would not be allowed to carry so much as one brass knob away with them. But no—it was— 'who has most nails? I have a hundred, and you have fifty; or I have a thousand, and you have two. I must have as many as you before I leave the house, or I cannot possibly go home in peace.' At last, they made so much noise that I awoke, and thought to myself, 'What a false dream that is, of *children*!' **The child is the father of the man**; and wiser. Children never do such foolish things. Only men do.

Notes

This is a selection from Ruskin's lecture 'The Mystery of Life and Its Arts,' delivered in Dublin, May 13, 1868 and later appended to a revised edition of *Sesame and Lilies* in 1871. Ruskin explained the meaning of this dream as follows: 'I have sometimes been asked what this means. I intended it to set forth the wisdom of men in war contending for kingdoms, and what follows to set forth their wisdom in peace, contending for wealth.'

lathes, machines for holding articles of wood, metal, etc. and turning them rapidly against a tool used to shape them.

The Child is the father of the man. Cf. Wordsworth's poem 'My heart leaps up when I behold,' line 7: 'The Child is father of the Man.'

【作品简介】

本文选自罗斯金 1868 年 5 月 13 日在都柏林发表的演讲《人生的奥秘及其技艺》。后来，此文于 1871 年被收录在《芝麻与百合》的修订版中。罗斯金在解释这场梦的含义时说："人们常常会问我，写的这个梦意味着什么？我的本意是想借用这个梦来阐述在战争年代，人们用智慧为国而战；在随之而来的和平时代，人们的智慧却用在了为争夺财富而战上。"

【作品解析】

lathes：车床，一种通过快速旋转来加工金属、木料等其他原材料的切削机器。

The Child is the father of the man：参见华兹华斯的诗《我心雀跃》第七行："孩子是成年人的父亲。"

【参考译文】

儿童五朔节聚会

我不是诗人，然而我时常也会做梦——我梦见自己参加了一个孩子们的五朔节聚会。在这个聚会上，有个聪明善良的主人，为孩子们提供了各种各样的娱乐活动。聚会是在一个装饰华丽、大气的房子里举行的，房子外面有一个美丽的花园。孩子们在房子和花园之间无拘无束地玩耍，除了计划如何愉快地度过他们的下午时光之外，不需要关心其他任何事情。他们确实不知道第二天将会发生什么事情。我想，其中有些孩子会有点害怕，他们可能会担心被送进一所新的学校，并要求参加入学考试。然而，他们尽可能不去想这些事情，决定先痛痛快快地玩上一场。正如我上面所说的，房子是坐落在一个漂亮的花园里，里面种植着各种各样的鲜花，那里有片芬芳的、长满青草的河岸，孩子们可以休息；有块精心修整过的草坪，孩子们可以玩耍；还有怡人的小溪和树林，以及供孩子们攀登的岩石。孩子们开心地玩了一会儿，很快就把他们自己分成了不同的小组，然后，每一个小组宣布了他们自己将拥有的一小块花园，而那块花园其他的小组不可侵犯。接下来，他们就为自己想要独占的那块地方激烈地争吵了起来。最后，男孩们就像人们想象中男孩应该的那样，"实实在在地"操起了家伙，在花丛中搏斗了起来，直到五颜六色的鲜花几乎全被他们压倒了；然后，他们出于怨恨，还相互狠狠地践踏了对方占有的一小块地里的鲜花；女孩子们哭了，一直哭到她们筋疲力尽哭不出声来；最终，他们所有的人都躺在这片被践踏的花丛中，喘不过气来，等待他们的家长晚上接他们回家。

与此同时，房间里的孩子们也在用他们自己的方式尽情地享受着快乐。那里，为他们提供了各种室内娱乐：有音乐可以供孩子们跟着跳舞；有一个开放的图书馆，里面有各种各样有趣的书籍；有一个博物馆，里面陈列着奇光异彩的贝壳，以及珍稀动物和鸟类的标本；那里还有一个作坊，里面有车床和木匠用的工具，专门为聪明的男孩们所准备；还有漂亮的奇装异服，供女孩子们穿戴；有一些显微镜和万花筒，以及孩子们喜欢的各种玩具；在餐厅里还放了一张桌子，上面放满了美味可口的食品。

然而，在所有的孩子们中间，有两三个比较"务实"的孩子，他们被镶嵌在椅子上的黄铜钉吸引，决心想办法把这些钉子拔出来。于是，他们开始努力地去拔黄铜钉。不一会儿，那些正在阅读、正在欣赏贝壳的孩子，也都喜欢上了这样的玩法。又过了一会儿，所有的孩子几乎都伸出手指，模仿着他们去拔黄铜钉。尽管每个孩子竭尽全力都拔出了几个黄铜钉，但他们并不满足，每个人都想要别人的黄铜钉。最后，那几个真正"务实"而又聪明的孩子声称：那天下午，除了得到大量的黄铜钉之外，其他任何活动都没有意义。书本、蛋糕和显微镜根本一点用处都没有，除非能将它们换成黄铜钉。于是乎，所有的孩子都在为黄铜钉你争我夺，就像花园里的孩子们为了占地而大打出手一样。只有那些与世无争的孩子，自己拿着一本书躲在角落里，试图在一片嘈杂声中求得一点宁静。那些"务实"的孩子，却满脑子的黄铜钉，整个下午都在计算自己的黄铜钉——尽管他们知道，他们连一个黄铜纽扣也不允许带出房间，一个也不能。然而，不——是的——他们还是在比"谁的黄铜钉最多？我有一百个，你只有五十个；或者说，我有一千个，你只有两个。在我离开这所房子之前，我必须和你一样多，否则，我不可能就这样回家的"。他们争吵的声音愈来愈大，最后他们把我吵醒了。心想："这真是一个多么可笑的梦啊，一个有关孩子的梦！"孩子是成年人的父亲，而且比成年人更加聪明。孩子们从不做这种傻事，只有成年人才会这样做。

ROBERT LOUIS STEVENSON
(1850—1894)

Robert Louis Stevenson (1850—1894), the son of an engineer, was born in Edinburgh and educated at the University there. After a brief attempt at the study of law, he took up writing as a profession. He was a consumptive. The dire need of finding a climate more kindly than that of Edinburgh and a certain gipsy quality in his temperament drove him from one country to another. But he worked assiduously, producing stories, essays, and letters. 'I wonder if anyone had ever more energy upon so little strength,' he wrote in one of his letters. He died in Samoa, literally with pen in hand.

Stevenson's works include *Travels with a Donkey in the Cévennes* (1879), *Virginibus Puerisque* (1881), *The New Arabian Nights* (1882), *Treasure Island*

(1883), *Dr. Jekyll and Mr. Hyde* (1886), and *Kidnapped* (1886). He is now chiefly remembered as a successor of Scott in the province of romantic fiction, and the *Treasure Island* has gained him international popularity. Besides, he was also the author of some most delightful essays and poems. As an essayist, he was a disciple of Hazlitt, to whom he 'played the sedulous ape.'

【作者简介】

罗伯特·路易斯·斯蒂文森（1850—1894）是一位工程师的儿子，出生于爱丁堡，并在那里的大学接受教育。在短暂地尝试了法律研究之后，他决定以写作为职业。他是肺结核病患者，迫切需要寻找一个比爱丁堡的气候更加温和的地方；而他性格中某种吉卜赛人的特质，驱使他从一个国家走到另一个国家。他孜孜不倦地勤奋工作，不停地创作小说、散文和书信。他在一封信中写道："我想知道是否有人能在如此手无缚鸡之力的情况下，还能如此精力充沛。"斯蒂文森在萨摩亚去世时，手里依然握着笔。

斯蒂文森的著作包括《骑驴漫游记》（1879）、《维琴伯斯·普鲁斯克集》（1881）、《新天方夜谭》（1882）、《金银岛》（1883）、《化身博士》（1886）和《绑架》（1886）。人们现在主要把他作为在浪漫主义小说领域里司各特的继承人而铭记。《金银岛》这部作品使他在国际上享有盛名，赢得了声望。除此之外，他还写了一些令人愉悦的散文和诗歌。作为一名散文家，他是赫兹里特的门徒，他孜孜不倦地扮演着"猴子学样"的角色。

Walking Tours

It must not be imagined that a walking tour, as some would have us fancy, is merely a better or worse way of seeing the country. There are many ways of seeing landscape quite as good; and none more vivid, in spite of canting **dilettantes**, than from a railway train. But landscape on a walking tour is quite accessory. He who is indeed of the brotherhood does not voyage in quest of the picturesque, but of certain jolly humours—of the hope and spirit with which the march begins at morning, and the peace and spiritual repletion of the evening's rest. He cannot tell whether he puts his knapsack on, or takes it off, with more delight. The excitement of the departure puts him in key for that of the arrival. Whatever he does is not only a reward in itself, but will be further rewarded in the sequel; and so pleasure leads on to pleasure in an endless chain. It is this that so few can understand; they will either be always lounging or always at five miles an hour; they do not play off the one against the other, prepare all day for the evening, and all evening for the next day. And, above all, it is here that your overwalker fails of comprehension. His heart rises against those who drink their **curacoa** in liquor glasses, when he himself can swill it in a **brown john**. He will not believe that the flavour is more delicate in the smaller dose. He will not believe that to walk this unconscionable distance is merely to stupefy and brutalize himself, and come to his inn, at night, with a sort of frost on his **five wits**, and a starless night of darkness in his sprit. Not for him the mild luminous evening of the temperate walker! He has nothing left of man but a physical need for bedtime and a **double nightcap**; and even his pipe, if he be a smoker, will be savourless and disenchanted. It is the fate of such an one to take twice as much trouble as is needed to obtain happiness, and miss the happiness in the end; he is the man of the proverb, in short, who goes further and fares worse.

Now, to be properly enjoyed, a walking tour should be gone upon alone. If you go in a company, or even in pairs, it is no longer a walking tour in anything but name; it is something else and more in the nature of a picnic. A walking tour should be gone upon alone, because freedom is of the essence; because you should be able to stop and go on, and follow this way or that, as the freak takes you; and because you must have your own pace, and neither trot alongside a champion walker, nor mince in time with a girl. And then you must be open to all impressions and let your thoughts take colour from what you see. You should be as a pipe for any wind to play upon. '**I cannot see the wit**,' says Hazlitt, '**of walking and talking** at the same time. When I am in the country, I wish to vegetate like the country,' which is the gist of all that can be said upon the matter. There should be no cackle of voices at your elbow, to jar on the meditative silence of the morning. And so long as a man is reasoning he cannot surrender himself to that fine intoxication that comes of much motion in the open air, that begins in a sort of dazzle and sluggishness of the brain, and ends in a peace that passes comprehension.

During the first day or so of any tour there are moments of bitterness, when the traveller feels more than coldly towards his knapsack, when he is half in a mind to throw it bodily over the hedge and, like **Christian** on a similar occasion, 'give three leaps and go on singing.' And yet it soon acquires a property of easiness. It becomes magnetic; the spirit of the journey enters into it. And no sooner have you passed the straps over your shoulder than the lees of sleep are cleared from you, you pull yourself together with a shake, and fall at once into your stride. And surely, of all possible moods, this, in which a man takes the road, is the best. Of course, if he *will* keep thinking of his anxieties, if he *will* open the merchant **Abudah's chest** and walk arm in arm with the hag—why, wherever he is, and whether he walk fast or slow, the chances are that he will not be happy. And so much the more shame to himself! There are perhaps thirty men setting forth at that same hour, and I would lay a large wager there is not another dull face among the thirty. It would be a fine thing to follow, in a **coat of darkness**, one after another of these wayfarers, some summer morning, for the first few miles upon the road. This one, who walks fast, with a keen look in his eyes, is all concentrated in his own mind; he is up at his loom, weaving and weaving, to set the landscape to words. This one peers about, as he goes, among he grasses; he waits by the canal to watch the dragon-flies; he leans on the gate of the pasture, and cannot look enough upon the complacent kine. And here comes another talking, laughing, and gesticulating to himself. His face changes from time to time, as indignation flashes from his eyes or anger clouds his forehead. He is composing articles, delivering orations, and conducting the most impassioned interviews, by the way. A little farther on, and it is as like as not he will begin to sing. And well for him, supposing him to be no great master in that art, if he stumbles across no stolid peasant at a corner; for on such an occasion, I scarcely know which is the more troubled, or whether it is worse to suffer the confusion of your troubadour or the unfeigned alarm of your clown. A sedentary population, accustomed, besides, to the strange mechanical bearing of the common tramp, can in no wise explain to itself the gaiety of these passers-by. I knew one man who was arrested as a runaway lunatic, because, although a full-grown person with a red beard, he skipped as he went like a child. And you would be astonished if I were to tell you all the grave and learned heads who have confessed to me that, when on walking tours, they sang—and sang very ill—and had **a pair of red ears** when, as described above, the inauspicious peasant plumped into their arms from round a corner. And here, lest you should think I am exaggerating, is Hazlitt's own confession, from his essay *On Going a Journey*, which is so good that there should be a tax levied on all who have not read it:

> *'Give me the clear blue sky over my head,' says he, 'and the green turf beneath my feet, a winding road before me, and a three hours' march to—dinner—and then to thinking! It is hard if I cannot start some game on these lone heaths. I laugh, I run, I leap, I sing for joy.'*

Bravo! After that adventure of my friend with the policeman, you would not have cared, would you, to publish that in the first person? But we have no bravery nowadays, and, even in books, must all pretend to be as dull and foolish as our neighbours. It was not so with Hazlitt. And notice how learned he is (as, indeed, throughout the essay) in the theory of walking tours. He is none of your athletic men in purple stockings, who walk their fifty miles a day: three hours' march is his ideal. And then he must have a winding road, the epicure!

Yet there is one thing I object to in these words of his, one thing in the great master's practice that seems to me not wholly wise. I do not approve of that leaping and running. Both of these hurry the respiration; they both shake up the brain out of its glorious open-air confusion; and they both break the pace. Uneven walking is not so agreeable to the body, and it distracts and irritates the mind. Whereas, when once you have fallen into an equable stride, it requires no conscious thought from you to keep it up and yet it prevents you from thinking earnestly of anything else. Like knitting, like the work of a copying clerk, it gradually neutralizes and sets to sleep the serious activity of the mind. We can think of this or that, lightly and laughingly, as a child thinks, or as we think in a morning dose; we can make puns or puzzle out acrostics, and trifle in a thousand ways with words and rhymes; but when it comes to honest work, when we come to gather ourselves together for an effort, we may sound the trumpet as loud and long as we please; the great barons of the mind will not rally to the standard, but sit, each one, at home, warming his hands over his own fire and brooding on his own private thought!

In the course of a day's walk, you see, there is much variance in the mood. From the exhilaration of the start, to the happy phlegm

of the arrival, the change is certainly great. As the day goes on, the
traveller moves from the one extreme towards the other. He becomes
more and more incorporated with the material landscape, and the
open-air drunkenness grows upon him with great strides, until he
posts along the road, and sees everything about him, as in a cheerful
dream. The first is certainly brighter, but the second stage is the more
peaceful. A man does not make so many articles towards the end, nor
does he laugh aloud; but the purely animal pleasures, the sense of
physical well-being, the delight of every inhalation, of every time the
muscles tighten down the thigh, console him for the absence of the
others, and bring him to his destination still content.

Nor must I forget to say a word on bivouacs. You come to a
milestone on a hill, or some place where deep ways meet under
trees; and off goes the knapsack, and down you sit to smoke a pipe
in the shade. You sink into yourself, and the birds come round and
look at you, and your smoke dissipates upon the afternoon under
the blue dome of heaven; and the sun lies warm upon your feet, and
the cool air visits your neck and turns aside your open shirt. If you
are not happy, you must have an evil conscience, you may dally as
long as you like by the roadside. It is almost as if the millennium
were arrived, when we shall throw our clocks and watches over the
housetops, and remember time and seasons no more. Not to keep
hours for a lifetime is, I was going to say, to live forever. You have
no idea, unless you have tried it, how endlessly long is a summer's
day, that you measure out only by hunger, and bring to an end only
when you are drowsy. I know a village where there are hardly any
clocks, where no one knows more of the days of the week than by a

sort of instinct for the *fête* on Sundays, and where only one person can tell you the day of the month, and she is generally wrong; and if people were aware how slow Time journeyed in that village, and what armfuls of spare hours he gives, over and above the bargain, to its wise inhabitants, I believe there would be a stampede out of London, Liverpool, Paris, and a variety of large towns, where the clocks lose their heads, and shake the hours out each one faster than the other, as though they were all in a wager. And all these foolish pilgrims would each bring his own misery along with him, in a watch-pocket! It is to be noticed, there were no clocks and watches in the much-vaunted days before the flood. It follows, of course, there were no appointments, and punctuality was not yet thought upon. 'Though ye take from a covetous man all his treasure,' says Milton, 'he has yet one jewel left; ye cannot deprive him of his covetousness.' And so I would say of a modern man of business, you may do what you will for him, put him in Eden, give him the elixir of life—he has still a flaw at heart, he still has his business habits. Now, there is no time when business habits are more mitigated than on a walking tour. And so during these halts, as I say, you will fell almost free.

But it is at night, and after dinner, that the best hour comes. There are no such pipes to be smoked as those that follow a good day's march; the flavour of the tobacco is a thing to be remembered, it is so dry and aromatic, so full and so fine. If you wind up the evening with grog, you will own there was never such grog; at every sip a jocund tranquillity spreads about your limbs, and sits easily in your heart. If you read a book—and you will never do so save by fits and starts—you find the language strangely racy and harmonious;

words take a new meaning; single sentences possess the ear for half an hour together; and the writer endears himself to you, at every page, by the nicest coincidence of sentiment. It seems as if it were a book you had written yourself in a dream. To all we have read on such occasions we look back with special favour. '**It was on the tenth of April, 1798,**' says Hazlitt, with amorous precision, 'that I sat down to a volume of **the new *Héloise*** at the Inn at **Llangollen**, over a bottle of sherry and a cold chicken.' I should wish to quote more, for though we are mighty fine fellows nowadays, we cannot write like Hazlitt. And, talking of that, a volume of Hazlitt's essays would be a capital pocket-book on such a journey; so would a volume of **Heine's songs**; and for *Tristram Shandy* I can pledge a fair experience.

If the evening be fine and warm, there is nothing better in life than to lounge before the inn door in the sunset, or lean over the parapet of the bridge, to watch the weeds and the quick fishes. It is then, if ever, that you taste joviality to the full significance of that audacious word. Your muscles are so agreeably slack, you feel so clean and so strong and so idle, that whether you move or sit still, whatever you do is done with pride and a kingly sort of pleasure. You fall in talk with anyone, wise or foolish, drunk or sober. And it seems as if a hot walk purged you, more than of anything else, of all narrowness and pride, and left curiosity to play its part freely, as in a child or a man of science. You lay aside all your own hobbies, to watch provincial humours develop themselves before you, now as a laughable farce, and now grave and beautiful like an old tale.

Or perhaps you are left to your own company for the night, and surly weather imprisons you by the fire. You may remember how **Burns**, numbering past pleasures, dwells upon the hours when he has been '**happy thinking**.' It is a phrase that may well perplex a poor modern girt about on every side by clocks and chimes, and haunted, even at night, by flaming dial-plates. For we are all so busy, and have so many far—off projects to realize, and castles in the fire to turn into solid, habitable mansions on a gravel soil, that we can find no time for pleasure trips into the Land of Thought and among the Hills of Vanity. Changed times, indeed, when we must sit all night, beside the fire, with folded hands; and a changed world for most of us, when we find we can pass the hours without discontent, and be happy thinking. We are in such haste to be doing, to be writing, to be **gathering gear**, to make our voice audible a moment in the derisive silence of eternity, that we forget that one thing, of which these are but the parts—namely to live. We fall in love, we drink hard, we run to and fro upon the earth like frightened sheep. And now you are to ask yourself if, when all is done, you would not have been better to sit by the fire at home, and be happy thinking. To sit still and contemplate—to remember the faces of women without desire, to be pleased by the great deeds of men without envy, to be everything and everywhere in sympathy, and yet content to remain where and what you are—is not this to know both wisdom and virtue, and to dwell with happiness? After all, it is not they who carry flags, but they who look upon it from a private chamber, who have the fun of the procession. And once you are at that, you are in the very humour of all social heresy. It is no time for shuffling, or for big empty words. If you ask yourself what you mean by fame, riches, or learning, the answer is far to seek; and you go back into that kingdom of light imaginations, which seem so vain in the eyes of **Philistines** perspiring after wealth, and so momentous to those who are stricken with the disproportions of the world, and, in the face of the gigantic stars, cannot stop to split differences between two degrees of the infinitesimally small, such as a tobacco pipe or the Roman Empire, a million of money or a fiddlestick's end.

You lean from the window, your last pipe reeking whitely into the darkness, your body full of delicious pains, your mind enthroned **in the seventh circle of content**; when suddenly the mood changes, the weather-cock goes about, and you ask yourself one question more: whether, for the interval, you have been the wisest philosopher or the **most egregious of donkeys**? Human experience is not yet able to reply; but at least you had a fine moment, and looked down all the kingdoms of the earth. And whether it was wise or foolish, tomorrow's travel will carry you, body and mind, into some different parish of the infinite.

Notes

'Walking Tours,' from *Virginibus Puerisque*, is a good illustration and reminds us of Hazlitt's essay 'On Going a Journey,' the two of which should be read together as companion pieces on the art and pleasures of travelling.

dilettantes, properly lovers of the fine arts; here used of those extremists whose love of beauty prejudiced them against railways.

curacoa, liqueur of spirits flavoured with peel of bitter oranges.

brown john, an earthen jug. A 'brown george' is a large earthenware vessel; it is mentioned in *Tom Brown* as used for washing up tea-things. A 'demi-john' is a large bottle of glass or earthenware holding from 3 to 10 gallons. Stevenson seems to have combined the two terms.

five wits, the senses or the mind (archaic).

double nightcap, doubly strong alcoholic drink taken before going to bed.

'I cannot see the wit of walking and talking,' etc. From Hazlitt, 'On Going a Journey.' This is only one of many indications of Stevenson's debt to Hazlitt.

Christian, the hero of Bunyan's *Pilgrim's Progress*, where the load fell off Christian's backs.

Abudah's chest, referring to an oriental tale of an evil hag, who took up her residence in a merchant's chest. Abudah was haunted every night by an old hag from whom he only got free by learning to fear God and keep His commandments.

coat of darkness, like that worn by Jack the Giant Killer, rendering him invisible.

a pair of red ears, i.e. from blushing with shame at being caught.

'Though ye take from a covetous man,' etc. From Milton's *Areopagitica* (1644).

'It was on the tenth of April, 1798,' etc. From Hazlitt, 'On Going a Journey.'

the new Héloise, i.e. *La Nouvelle Héloise,* Rousseau's famous romance (1761).

Llangollen, a town in northern Wales.

Heine's songs. Heinrich Heine (1797—1856) was a German poet and miscellaneous writer, especially remarkable for his short lyrics.

Tristram Shandy, a novel by Laurence Sterne (1713—1768). Owing to its amazing discursiveness, it may be begun, or ended, at any point.

Burns, Robert (1759—1796), Scottish poet.

'*happy thinking*.' From Burns' poem 'The Rigs of Barley.'

gathering gear, getting material wealth together, laying up 'treasures on earth.'

Philistines, a term used by Matthew Arnold to designate the middle classes as being ignorant, narrow-minded, and deficient in general ideas.

in the seventh circle of content, in the greatest happiness of satisfaction. (Cf. the expression 'in the seventh Heaven.')

most egregious of donkeys, the grossest fool.

【作品简介】

《徒步旅行》选自《维琴伯斯·普鲁斯克集》，这是斯蒂文森模仿赫兹里特的一个很好的例证，它让我们想起了赫兹里特的散文《论旅行》，这两篇散文应该作为旅行的艺术和旅行的乐趣的姐妹篇一起阅读。

【作品解析】

dilettantes：真正的美术爱好者；这里是指那些极端主义者，他们对美好的东西极度的追求和热爱，使他们对火车旅行产生了偏见。

curacoa：库拉索酒，用苦橘子皮调制的烈酒。

brown john：一个用陶土制作的水罐。"brown george"指的是一个大的陶器，在《汤姆·布朗的求学时代》一书中提到人们用它来洗茶具。"demi-john"是一个可装 3 到 10 加仑溶液的大型玻璃器皿或陶器。斯蒂文森似乎把这两个词结合在了一起。

five wits：感知或智慧（古义）。

double nightcap：睡前饮用含有双倍酒精浓度的烈性酒。

"I cannot see the wit of walking and talking," etc.："我看不出边走边说妙在何处……"出自赫兹里特的《论旅行》，这只是斯蒂文森得益于赫兹里特作品的众多例子之一。

Christian：约翰·班扬在《天路历程》中描写的男主人公，最终到达天国圣城，在那里他从背上卸掉了重负。

Abudah's chest：指的是东方传说中的一个邪恶的女巫居住在一个商人的大木箱里。商人阿布达每天晚上都会被这个老巫婆缠住，他只有在学会敬畏上帝，遵守上帝的戒律之后，才能从女巫那里解脱得到自由。

coat of darkness：深色的外衣，就像那个巨人杀手杰克穿的，让别人看不见。

a pair of red ears：因为被碰撞而羞愧得面红耳赤。

"Though ye take from a covetous man," etc.：此句摘自弥尔顿的《论出版自由》（1644）。

"It was on the tenth of April, 1798," etc.：此句出自赫兹里特的《论旅行》。

the new *Héloise*：即 *La Nouvelle Héloise*，卢梭的著名浪漫小说《新爱洛伊丝》，作于 1761 年。

Llangollen：兰戈伦，威尔士北部的一个小镇。

Heine's songs：海因里希·海涅（1797—1856），德国诗人和杂文作家，尤其以短小的抒情诗而著称。

Tristram Shandy：劳伦斯·斯特恩（1713—1768）的小说《项狄传》。这篇小说惊人地散漫，可以在任何时候开始，也可以在任何时候结束。

Burns：罗伯特·彭斯（1759—1796），苏格兰诗人。

'happy thinking'：出自彭斯的诗歌《大麦之垄》。

gathering gear：聚敛物质财富，积攒"人间宝藏"。

Philistines：该词被马修·阿诺德用来形容中产阶级的无知、心胸狭隘、缺乏总体思维观念。

in the seventh circle of content：在最大的幸福中得到了满足。参考短语"in the seventh Heaven"。

most egregious of donkeys：最粗俗的傻瓜。

【参考译文】

徒步旅行

徒步旅行，绝不是像人们所想象的那样，仅仅是游览这个国家的一种更好的或者说更糟糕的方式。其实，有很多种观赏风景的方式都是相当不错的，再也没有比从火车上观看风景更加生动的了，尽管有一些业余爱好者并不这么认为。其实，在徒步旅行中观赏风景只是附带而已。对于真正有兄弟情怀的人来说，不是为了追求风景如画的感觉而远行，而是为了追求某种欢乐的心情或者说是某种感觉——在清晨即将开始行走时的那种兴奋与希望，以及到了夜晚安息时的宁静与精神上的满足。背上背包，还是放下背包，哪一种情景更加快乐？他自己也很难说得清楚。出发时的兴奋，对他抵达目的地时的快乐至关重要。无论他做了什么，不仅其本身是一种回报，而且接下来还会得到进一步的回报。因此，快乐将会在快乐的锁链中引发一系列无穷无尽新的快乐，然而很少有人能够理解这一点。他们要么是懒洋洋地待着不动，要么就是以每小时五英里的速度竞走。他们不会在两者之间做折中，而是整天忙着为晚上的宿营做准备，整个晚上又是在为第二天的行走做准备。而且更重要的是，正是这种在路途上的奔波，导致他们丧失了对徒步旅行的感悟。当他用陶土水罐大口痛饮时，极为反感那些用小酒杯饮用库拉索酒的人。他不会相信，只有小口品酒，才会感受到酒的香味更为浓郁，味道甘醇，口感细腻；他也不会相信，路途上的奔波会使他变得思维不清晰，丧失理智而变得粗暴。夜晚，到了客栈，他的神志已经恍惚麻木了，在他的精神世界里，那就是一片黑暗的无星之夜。他无法领略璀璨星空下闲庭信步的情趣。他除了生理上需要睡觉和在睡前饮下含有高浓度酒精的烈性酒之外，不会还有什么别的需求，即使他是个烟鬼，此时烟也变得索然无味，他对烟斗也失去了兴趣。这种人为了获得幸福需要付出双倍的努力，而最终仍然会错过幸福。简而言之，他就是谚语中所说的人物，走得越远，境遇越发糟糕。

现在，只有独自徒步旅行的人，才能充分享受到其中的乐趣。如果有人相伴，或者是成群结队而去，那么徒步旅行除了徒有其名，已经不再具有徒步旅行的意义了，而更像是另外一种具有野餐性质的郊游。徒步旅行应当独自行走，自由是最关键的本质。因为你可以按照你自己的方式和兴趣，沿着这条路或那条路，停下休息或者继续前行；因为你必须要按照你自己的步伐行走，既不用像争夺冠军那样竞走，也不用像女孩子走路那样磨磨蹭蹭。你必须要对你自己的感觉敞开心扉，让你的思想捕捉你所见的那五颜六色的景象。你应该像管风琴的音管，可以任风随意吹奏。赫兹里特曾经说过："我看不出边走边说妙在何处。当我在乡村行走时，我就希望自己能像乡村的植物一样静静的无声无息。"这就是以上关于徒步旅行的全部要点。清晨，你的身边不应该有咯咯的声音，来打扰清晨冥想中的寂静。只要人们还在理性地思考，就不能让自己陶醉在来自户外的美景之中；这种陶醉，起初会让人的大脑进入一种眩晕和迟钝的状态，最终会超越感悟，让内心深处达到一种宁静的状态。

在任何一次旅行中的第一和第二天，总是会有一些苦闷的片刻。当旅行者对他的背包感到非常冷漠，几乎就要把背包扔到树篱上时，他就像基督徒在类似的场合所做的一样，"先跳三下，然后再继续歌唱"；不过你很快就会感觉轻松起来。徒步旅行变得有吸引力了，徒步旅行的精神也就灌注在了其中。你刚把背包带在肩上背起，睡意就烟消云散了，你抖了抖，振作了起来，立刻迈开了你的步伐。当然，在所有可能的情绪当中，一个人徒步行走时的心情是最好的。当然，如果他总是苦思冥想、忧心忡忡，如果他总想着打开商人阿布达的箱子并与女巫手挽手而行——嗨，无论他在哪里，无论他走得快还是慢，他都不可能会快乐，这只会给他自己带来更多的羞愧！如果大约有三十个人在同一时间出发，我敢打赌，在这三十个人中间，绝不会再有一张反应迟钝的面孔。夏日的凌晨，在一片黑暗中，在最初几英里的路上，徒步旅行者一个跟着一个，这是一件不错的事情。这个人走得很快，眼神敏锐，全神贯注于自己的思想；他独出机杼，斟字酌句如同织梭，把风景编织成了文字。这个人一边走，一边在草丛中四处张望；他在运河边等着观看蜻蜓；他倚靠在牧场的门旁，看着踌躇满志的母牛，永远也看不够。又来了一位自言自语、边说边笑、对着自己做着手势的人。他的面部表情时不时地在变化，愤怒在他的眼中闪现，或者说愤怒笼罩了他的额头。顺便说一下，他正在撰写文章，准备发表演说，并进行最热烈的采访。再往前一点，他似乎就要开始吟唱了。假设他不是这门艺术的大师，如果他在某个角落无意间碰撞到了一个表情并不木讷的农民，这对他来说很好。在这种场合，我几乎不知道哪一种情况会更加麻烦，不知道是那位吟游诗人的困惑糟糕呢，还是那个乡下粗人真切的惊悚更为糟糕。除此之外，久居室内不外出的芸芸众生，见惯了普通流浪汉那种奇特机械式的姿势，更无法理解这些过往行人的欢乐。我认识一个男子，他曾被当作逃跑的精神病患者遭到了逮捕，因为他虽然是长着红胡子的成年人，但他在行走时却像个孩子一样蹦蹦跳跳。要是我告诉你们，那些严肃而博学的学者向我承认，他们在徒步旅行时都会歌唱——而且唱得难以入耳——就像我上面所描述的那样，当那个倒霉的农民从某个角落里和他们撞个满怀时，都会羞愧得面红耳赤，你一定会感到惊讶的。然而，为了免得你以为我在夸大其词，这里引用赫兹里特在《论旅行》一文中的一段自白。这篇文章写得太好了，应该向所有没读过的人征税：

　　"上帝赐予我头上一片清澈的蓝天，"他说，"还有我脚下绿色的草地，在我眼前是蜿蜒曲折的小路，还有三个小时的步行——然后晚餐——接着是思考！如果我在这孤独寂寞的荒野上，不能开始去做一些游戏，那简直太难了。我笑着，我奔跑着，我跳跃着，我高兴地唱着歌。"

太棒了！在我朋友和警察那次冒险经历之后，你不会介意我以第一人称发表那篇有关他们的文章，对吧？但是，我们现在还没有这种勇气，即便是在书中，我们也必须假装像我们的邻居那样迟钝和无知。赫兹里特却不同。请注意，他在徒步旅行理论方面是何等博学（事实上，都贯穿在了他的整篇文章中）。他不是你们那种穿着紫色长筒袜的运动健将，每天行走五十英里；三个小时的行程是他的理想。而且他必须要有一条蜿蜒曲折的小道，才会心满意足。他是一位在徒步旅行中真正的享乐主义者！

然而在他的这些话语中，有一点我不赞同；在我看来这一点在大师的实践中并不是完全明智的。我不赞成他那种跳跃和奔跑。这两项都会使人呼吸急促；它们都会把大脑从户外那种宜人的混沌状态中震醒，并打破原有的行走节奏。并且，不均匀的行走速度对身体来说并不舒适，而且它会分散注意力并刺激大脑。反之，一旦你步伐平稳均匀，就不需要你通过有意识地思考来保持一定的行走速度，但它会阻止你认真思考其他的任何事情。就像编织或抄写工作一样，不知不觉让大脑逐渐地松弛下来，让大脑进入睡眠状态，放下了严肃的思维活动。我们可以像孩子那样去想象，或者像在早晨我们认为的那样，轻松并愉快地想想这个或想想那个；我们还可以在离合诗里，找出双关语或者谜语，并用词语和声韵的千变万化来做文字游戏。然而，当谈到认真工作时，我们就会全身心投入，只要我们高兴，我们就可以随心所欲把号角吹奏得响亮而悠长；而这些伟大的思想家往往不会为道德真理呐喊，而是各自坐在家里，用火炉温暖着双手，沉溺于一己私念之中！

在一天的行走过程中，你会发现人有太多的情绪变化。从开始行走时的兴奋到抵达目的地的愉悦，在这中间当然会有相当大的变化。随着时间的流逝，徒步旅行者的心情从一个极端走向了另一个极端。他愈来愈融入大自然的景色之中，辽阔的大地让他陶醉，这种陶醉在他的身上快速地滋长，以至于使他停不下来脚步，这时环顾四周，就像是在一场愉快的梦境之中。徒步旅行的第一个阶段无疑是比较阳光的，第二个阶段则趋于平淡。所以徒步旅行到了快结束时，他不会写太多的文章，也不会开怀大笑。然而，纯粹是动物本能简单的快乐，身体健康的感觉，每一次呼吸空气的喜悦，每一次大腿绷紧肌肉时的感受，即使没有他人在场给予安慰，在他到达目的地时，他仍然会感到心满意足。

我也不能忘记说说露营时的话题。当你在一座小山上来到了一个路标处，或者是在树下与幽深小径交会的某个地方，你解开了背包，坐在树荫下抽着烟斗。你陷入了沉思，鸟儿围拢了过来，看着你。午后你抽着烟斗，烟雾在蓝色的天穹下渐渐地消散了，阳光温暖地洒在你的脚上，凉爽的空气抚摸着你的脖子，掀起你那敞开的衬衫。如果此时你感觉不到快乐，那么你的心底一定暗藏着邪恶。只要你喜欢，在路边你想待多久就可以待多久。就好像千禧年已经来临，我们将钟表扔到屋顶上，不需要再记住时间和季节。我想说的是，一辈子都不要去守着时间，而是永远这样活着。除非你亲身经历过，否则你不可能体会到夏日的漫长，你只能用饥饿来衡量，只有当你昏昏欲睡的时候，才知道这一天算是结束了。我知道有一个村庄，那里几乎没有一块钟表。在那里，人们除了出于在星期天举行庆典的一种本能之外，没人知道一周中其他的日子，也没有一个人能告诉你某个日子是这一个月中的某一天；如果有人告诉你，那她通常还都是错的。如果人们知道那个村庄里的时间过得有多慢，聪慧明智的居民被赐予了多少空闲的时间，我相信人们会从伦敦、利物浦、巴黎，以及各大城市蜂拥而至。因为在这些大城市里，钟表都失去了理智，时针走动得一个比一个快，就好像它们争着下赌注一样。所有前来的这些愚蠢的朝圣者，都会把自己的苦难统统放进装有钟表的口袋里！值得注意的是，在洪水来临之前（《圣经·创世记》中的挪亚方舟的故事）那些大肆吹嘘的日子里，是没有钟表的。当然随之而来也就没有预约，也就不需要考虑准时了。"尽管你从一个贪婪的人那里夺走了他所有的财富，"弥尔顿说，"他还剩下了一颗宝石；那就是你剥夺不了他的贪婪。"所以我想说，一个现代的商人，你可以为他做任何事，把他放进伊甸园里，给他生命的灵丹妙药——实际上，他内心依然有缺陷，他仍然有他自己的商业习惯。现在看来，不会有比在徒步旅行的这段时间更能缓解心情、改善商业习惯的时候了。所以在歇业期间，就像我所说的，你几乎感觉到了自由，不再受时间的任何约束。

晚饭之后，天还亮着，这才是最美好的时刻。随着一天愉快的徒步旅行结束之后，没有什么比抽上一斗烟更加陶情适性的了；烟草的味道令人回味无穷，它竟是如此干燥而又飘着芳香，如此饱满而又纯正细腻。如果你以格洛格烈酒来结束这个夜晚，你会感受到这种酒从未有过的醇正；当你每啜一口，宁静中的快乐就会蔓延到你的四肢，很容易让你心情舒畅。如果你在阅读一本书——除非心血来潮随意翻阅，你永远不会像现在这样——你会发现这本书的语言异常生动和谐，词语被赋予了新的含义；简单的一句话就可以在你耳畔徘徊半个小时；在每一页上作者都是以最美妙的一种恰如其分的情感来吸引你，博得你的喜爱。好像是你在梦中写给自己的一本书。我们在这种场合所阅读的一切，回想起来都具有一种特殊的情怀。"那是 1798 年 4 月 10 日，"赫兹里特富有情感而又精确地描述道，"我坐在兰戈伦旅馆里，喝着一瓶雪利酒，吃着一只冷鸡，看了一卷《新爱洛伊丝》。"我想引用更多的原文，虽然我们现在是同辈中非常优秀的人士，但我们仍然不能像赫兹里特那样去写作。谈到这里，赫兹里特的散文集在这类旅行中会是一本极好的便于携带的袖珍读物；海涅的一卷诗歌也是如此；对于劳伦斯·斯特恩的作品《项狄传》，我可以保证，读起来也会有同样的感受。

如果傍晚晴朗而温暖，生活中没有什么比日落时分在客栈门前休闲散步，或者俯身倚靠在小桥的栏杆上观赏水草和水中敏捷的鱼儿更惬意的了。只有这样，你才能充分体会到"快乐"这个词语的全部意义。你的肌肉放松得令你愉悦，你感觉自己是那么清新，那么强壮，却又是那么闲散，以至于无论你是走动还是静坐，你所做的一切都带着骄傲和王者般的愉悦。你愿意和任何人交谈，无论是聪明的还是愚蠢的，喝醉的还是清醒的。似乎是一场热了身的徒步行走，比其他任何事情都更加能消除你内心的狭隘和自傲自负的心理，只留下了好奇心，任其自由发挥作用，就像是在一个孩子或者在一个科学家的身上所见到的那样。你把你所有的个人爱好都搁置到了一边，观看在你面前展现出来的有趣的乡土风情，时而像是一出荒唐可笑的闹剧，时而却又像是一个古老的故事，显得庄严而美丽。

或许，你在无人陪伴之下独自一人过夜，而且恶劣的天气把你禁锢在了火炉的旁边。你也许还记得，罗伯特·彭斯是怎样把自己沉浸在过去"快乐思考"的时光之中的。"快乐思考"这个短语有可能会让可怜的现代人感到困扰，他们在每一个角落都会被时钟和钟声包围着，即便是在寂静的夜晚，也会被那闪亮的钟表盘所缠绕。我们整天忙忙碌碌，有许多遥远的计划需要实现，我们要在沙砾地上把在大火中烧毁的城堡变成坚固的可居住的宅邸；那么，我们确实就找不出时间去思想之地和虚荣之谷进行愉快的旅行。的确，时代变了，当我们不得不整个夜晚坐在火炉旁，两手抱在一起无所事事；当我们发现，我们可以毫无怨言地度过时光，并快乐地思考着，对于我们大多数人来说，这个世界变了。我们急于实施各种计划，急于写作，急于聚敛物质财富，急于让我们的声音在永恒的充满嘲笑的寂静中响起片刻；而这些只是其中的一部分，以至于我们忘却了一件事——那就是生活。我们坠入爱河，我们喝得酩酊大醉，我们就像受惊的绵羊一样在地球上来回地奔跑。现在，你要扪心自问，如果这一切都结束了，你是否还会认为原本坐在家里的火炉旁，快乐思考，这是你更好的选择？静静地坐在那里，一动不动，静静地冥想——回忆起那些女人的面孔而不带有任何欲望，对人们做出的伟大业绩感到高兴而无嫉妒之心；并且在做任何事情和在任何地方都带有同情心，满足于现状——这难道不是一种懂得与幸福并存的智慧和美德吗？毕竟，不是高举旗帜的人，而是从私人房间向外张望的人，享受着游行的乐趣。一旦你做到了这一点，你就会被说成是和各种社会异端邪说沆瀣一气。我们没有时间去梳理，也没有时间去说大话空话。如果你扪心自问，什么是所谓的名望、财富或者学问，答案很难找到；当你追溯到那个充满光明的想象王国，这些在那些为了追逐财富而汗流浃背的市侩的眼里，似乎都是徒劳和无望的；但对于那些饱受人世间不公平待遇的人来说，这些却又是如此重要。当面对巨大的星球，和无穷小到几乎微乎其微的物种，不可能停下来去将这两者之间的极度差异区分开来，这就如同烟斗和罗马帝国，一百万金钱和一把小提琴的弓尾。

你依偎在窗边，烟斗里最后一缕浓烈的白色烟雾飘进了黑色的夜幕之中。你的身体充满了美妙酸痛的感觉，你的思想升华到了极乐世界，在最大的幸福中得到了满足。当情绪突然发生改变，风向标也随风旋转时，你再问问你自己这样一个问题，在这段时间里，你是最聪明的哲学家还是最愚蠢的傻瓜？人类的经验无法回答。但至少你有过这么一个美好的时光，俯瞰了地球上所有的王国。无论是明智还是愚蠢，明天的旅行都会将你的身心带进那广阔无垠的大地。

图书在版编目（CIP）数据

英国散文精选：英汉对照／范存忠，柳无忌编注；
范家宁，王英译 . —南京：译林出版社，2023.12
ISBN 978-7-5447-9061-1

Ⅰ.①英… Ⅱ.①范…②柳…③范…④王… Ⅲ.
①英语－汉语－对照读物②散文集－英国－近代 Ⅳ.
①H319.4：I

中国版本图书馆 CIP 数据核字（2022）第 020399 号

英国散文精选 范存忠 柳无忌／编注 范家宁 王英／译

责任编辑 刘 池
装帧设计 陈 悦
校 对 戴小娥 王 敏
责任印制 颜 亮

出版发行 译林出版社
地 址 南京市湖南路 1 号 A 楼
邮 箱 yilin@yilin.com
网 址 www.yilin.com
市场热线 025-86633278
排 版 南京展望文化发展有限公司
印 刷 苏州工业园区美柯乐制版印务有限责任公司
开 本 880毫米 ×1240毫米 1/32
印 张 12.625
插 页 4
版 次 2023 年 12 月第 1 版
印 次 2023 年 12 月第 1 次印刷
书 号 ISBN 978-7-5447-9061-1
定 价 78.00 元